Mary Wollstonecraft and Mary Shelley

Writing Lives

Edited by Helen M. Buss,

D. L. Macdonald, and

Anne McWhir

Wilfrid Laurier University Press

WLU

This book has been published with the help of a grant from the Humanities and Social Sciences Federation of Canada, using funds provided by the Social Sciences and Humanities Research Council of Canada. We acknowledge the financial support of the Government of Canada through the Book Publishing Industry Development Program for our publishing activities.

National Library of Canada Cataloguing in Publication Data

Main entry under title:
  Mary Wollstonecraft and Mary Shelley : writing lives

Includes bibliographical references and index.
ISBN 0-88920-364-4 (pbk.)

1. Wollstonecraft, Mary, 1759-1797—Criticism and interpretation.
2. Shelley, Mary Wollstonecraft, 1797-1851—Criticism and interpretation.
I. Buss, Helen M. (Helen Margaret).   II. Macdonald, David Lorne, 1955-   .
III. McWhir, Anne Ruth, 1947-   .

PR5841.W8Z755 2001   828'.609   C2001-930468-4

© 2001 Wilfrid Laurier University Press
Waterloo, Ontario, Canada   N2L 3C5

Cover design by Leslie Macredie. Cover painting: *Horse Attacked by a Lion,* 1769, by George Stubbs. Reproduced courtesy of the Tate Gallery, London/Art Resource, New York.

Printed in Canada

Mary Wollstonecraft and Mary Shelley

Writing Lives

Table of Contents

Acknowledgements

The editors would like to thank the Calgary Institute for the Humanities, especially Jane Kelley (past Director), Rosemary Ommer (Director), Cindy Atkinson, and most especially Gerry Dyer, whose hard work and endless patience made this book possible. Marlo Edwards and Mical Moser also gave invaluable assistance.

The first production of Rose Scollard's *Caves of Fancy* featured Anne-Marie Herberts as Mary Shelley, Iam Coulter as Claire Clairmont, Vicki Stroich as Fanny Imlay, and Curt McKinstry as the Creature; it was directed by Brian Smith and designed by Gavin Semple. We are grateful to these artists for helping Rose to realize her vision.

For their generous financial support, we are grateful to the Social Sciences and Humanities Research Council of Canada; to the University of Calgary for a Conference Grant, Special Projects Grant, and Visiting Scholars Award; to the Markin-Flanagan Distinguished Writers Programme; to the Faculties of Communication and Culture, Education, Fine Arts, Graduate Studies, Humanities, Social Sciences, and Social Work; to the Departments of Drama; English; French, Italian, and Spanish; Germanic, Slavic, and East Asian Studies; Greek and Roman Studies; History; Philosophy; Political Science; and Religious Studies; and to the Eighteenth-Century Studies Group.

We are grateful to Broadview Press, for permission to quote from *The Vindications* by Mary Wollstonecraft, edited by D.L. Macdonald and Kathleen Scherf (1997); to Johns Hopkins University Press, for permission to quote from *The Journals of Mary Shelley*, edited by Paula R. Feldman and Diana Scott-Kilvert (1995) and *The Letters of Mary Wollstonecraft Shelley*, edited by Betty T. Bennett (1980-88); to Oxford University Press, for permission to quote from *The Wrongs of Woman; or, Maria* by Mary Wollstonecraft, edited by Gary Kelly (1980); to Penguin Books, for permission to quote from *Letters Written during a Short Residence in Sweden, Norway, and Denmark* by Mary Wollstonecraft and *Memoirs of the Author of* A Vindication of the Rights of Woman by William Godwin, edited by Richard Holmes (1987); and to Pickering and Chatto, for permission to quote from *Frankenstein; or, The Modern Prometheus* by Mary Shelley, edited by Nora Crook; *The Last Man* by Mary Shelley, edited by Jane Blumberg with Nora Crook; *Lodore* by Mary Shelley, edited by Fiona Stafford; and *Rambles in Germany and Italy* by Mary Shelley, edited by Jeanne Moskal; all in *The Novels and Selected Works of Mary Shelley*, edited by Nora Crook.

Abbreviations

 Unless otherwise indicated, the essays in this volume refer to the following editions of primary texts:

CC   Claire Clairmont et al., *The Clairmont Correspondence*, ed. Marion Kingston Stocking. 2 vols.

CLMW   *Collected Letters of Mary Wollstonecraft*, ed. Ralph M. Wardle

FMP   Mary Shelley, *Frankenstein; or, The Modern Prometheus*, ed. Nora Crook

JCC   Claire Clairmont, *The Journals of Claire Clairmont*, ed. Marion Kingston Stocking

JMS   *The Journals of Mary Shelley*, ed. Paula R. Feldman and Diana Scott-Kilvert. 2 vols., 1987; rpt. 1 vol., 1995

L   Mary Shelley, *Lodore*, ed. Fiona Stafford

LM   Mary Shelley, *The Last Man*, ed. Jane Blumberg with Nora Crook

LMWS   *The Letters of Mary Wollstonecraft Shelley*, ed. Betty T. Bennett. 3 vols.

LPBS   *The Letters of Percy Bysshe Shelley,* ed. Frederick L. Jones. 2 vols.

LWSR   Mary Wollstonecraft, *Letters Written during a Short Residence in Sweden, Norway, and Denmark,* ed. Richard Holmes

MAV   William Godwin, *Memoirs of the Author of* A Vindication of the Rights of Woman, 1798; ed. Richard Holmes, 1987

NSW   *The Novels and Selected Works of Mary Shelley,* gen. ed. Nora Crook with Pamela Clemit. 8 vols.

OED   *The Oxford English Dictionary,* 2nd ed.

PJ   William Godwin, *Enquiry Concerning Political Justice.* 2 vols.

RGI   Mary Shelley, *Rambles in Germany and Italy,* ed. Jeanne Moskal

SPP   *Shelley's Poetry and Prose,* ed. Donald H. Reiman and Sharon B. Powers

TED   Mary Wollstonecraft, *Thoughts on the Education of Daughters,* ed. Gina Luria

VRM   Mary Wollstonecraft, *A Vindication of the Rights of Men,* ed. D. L. Macdonald and Kathleen Scherf

VRW   Mary Wollstonecraft, *A Vindication of the Rights of Woman,* ed. D. L. Macdonald and Kathleen Scherf

WWM   Mary Wollstonecraft, *The Wrongs of Woman; or, Maria,* ed. Gary Kelly

Introduction

"It is not singular that, as the daughter of two persons of distinguished literary celebrity, I should very early in life have thought of writing" (*FMP* 176): so Mary Shelley put it, with characteristic modesty. Anne K. Mellor, more boldly, has described Shelley as "the fruit of the most radical literary marriage of eighteenth-century England" (*Mary Shelley* 1). Her parents were William Godwin, philosopher and novelist, and Mary Wollstonecraft, educator, novelist, critic, philosopher, and travel writer. Yet Shelley's illustrious birth in 1797 was almost immediately overshadowed by a double disaster: Wollstonecraft's death, ten days after the delivery; and the hostile public reaction to Godwin's *Memoirs of the Author of* A Vindication of the Rights of Woman, published the following year. Moreover, Shelley came to maturity in a historical moment of post-revolutionary despair very different from the moment of revolutionary optimism that had inspired her parents' most famous works.

The events of Wollstonecraft's and Shelley's lives are recorded in such modern studies as Claire Tomalin's *The Life and Death of Mary Wollstonecraft* (1974), William St Clair's *The Godwins and the*

Shelleys: The Biography of a Family (1989), and Emily Sunstein's *Mary Shelley: Romance and Reality* (1989), as well as in studies of Godwin, Percy Bysshe Shelley, and other members of the Shelley circle. In addition, Wollstonecraft's letters (edited by Ralph M. Wardle, 1979) and Shelley's letters (edited by Betty T. Bennett, 1980-88) and journals (edited by Paula Feldman and Diana Scott-Kilvert, 1987) allow the modern reader ready access to material not published during the writers' lifetimes.

Mary Wollstonecraft was born in 1759, eldest daughter in a family plagued by alcoholism, violence, and frequent dislocation. Following her mother's death, and after having helped one of her sisters to escape from an unhappy marriage, Wollstonecraft, together with her sisters and her close friend Fanny Blood, established a girls' school at Newington Green. Wollstonecraft's romantic friendship with Fanny ended with Fanny's death in Lisbon in 1785; in her novella *Mary, A Fiction*, published in 1788, Wollstonecraft recounts the experience of travelling to Portugal only to lose her friend. Forced to earn her own living, Wollstonecraft worked as a governess for the Kingsborough family in Ireland and subsequently (and more happily) as a translator and reviewer for the radical publisher Joseph Johnson.

In December 1792, Wollstonecraft went to France, where, at the height of the Terror, she fell in love with an American writer and entrepreneur, Gilbert Imlay, and, in 1794, gave birth to their daughter, Fanny. In order to promote Imlay's business interests (and to hold his wavering attention following his unfaithfulness and her first suicide attempt), she travelled to Scandinavia with her small daughter in 1795, recording her impressions in her *Letters Written during a Short Residence in Sweden, Norway, and Denmark* (1796). Back in London, she attempted suicide for the second time. Some time later, while working on her second novel, *The Wrongs of Woman; or, Maria* (posthumously published in 1798), she began the relationship with William Godwin recorded in his *Memoirs*; the last months of her life were a period of great personal happiness and literary productivity. In addition to her autobiographical novels and the intensely personal *Letters from Norway*, Wollstonecraft left an abundant textual legacy for her daughter: *Thoughts on the Education of Daughters* (1787), *Original Stories* (a children's book, 1788), *The Female Reader* (an educational anthology, 1789), *An Historical and Moral View of the French Revolution* (1794), and two political treatises: *A Vindication of the Rights of Men* (1790), and *A Vindication of the Rights of Woman* (1792). Godwin published his own *Memoirs* and Wollstonecraft's *Posthumous Works*, including some personal letters to Imlay, in 1798.

This legacy is suffused with Wollstonecraft's longing for a daughter—especially for a daughter she could educate—but also with maternal anxiety over the possible consequences of such an education. In her first book, written when she already had some experience of education but seven years before she would bear a daughter, this longing is a physical pang: "The suckling of a child also excites the warmest glow of tenderness—Its dependant, helpless state produces an affection, which may properly be termed maternal. I have even felt it, when I have seen a mother perform that office" (*TED* 4). In her most successful work, addressed to her lover from the wilds of Scandinavia, she explains her plans for educating their daughter, Fanny Imlay:

> With trembling hand I shall cultivate sensibility, and cherish delicacy of sentiment, lest, whilst I lend fresh blushes to the rose, I sharpen the thorns that will wound the breast I would fain guard—I dread to unfold her mind, lest it should render her unfit for the world she is to inhabit. Hapless woman! what a fate is thine! (*LWSR* 97)

In her last book (written while she was pregnant with the child whom she thought of as William but who would turn out to be Mary Shelley), she imagines a mother writing her memoirs for the benefit of the daughter she fears she has lost forever:

> From my narrative, my dear girl, you may gather the instruction, the counsel, which is meant rather to exercise than influence your mind.—Death may snatch me from you, before you can weigh my advice, or enter into my reasoning: I would then, with fond anxiety, lead you very early in life to form your grand principle of action. (*WWM* 124)

As Charles E. Robinson, Lisa Vargo, Jeanne Moskal, and Rose Scollard show in their contributions to this volume, Wollstonecraft's longing for her daughter is fully matched by Shelley's longing for the mother whom death had snatched from her, and for the education that lost mother might be able to offer her. (See especially Robinson's essay for a detailed account of when Shelley read her mother's works.)

Godwin's account of Mary Wollstonecraft's life, written in the shadow of her death, moves inexorably toward "the last fatal scene" (*MAV* 265), which is also the scene of Mary Shelley's birth. On 30 August 1797, Wollstonecraft gave birth to her second child, contracted puerperal fever following extraction of the retained placenta, and died "on Sunday morning, September the tenth . . . at twenty minutes before eight" (271). In addition to Godwin himself and their new baby, Wollstonecraft left her three-year-old daughter, Fanny Imlay.

Remembering Wollstonecraft's life and death, in his *Memoirs* her husband begins the writing of other lives as well. Attempting to honour Wollstonecraft's memory, he also undertakes (as Helen Buss shows in this volume) to justify himself. His book demonstrates some of the complexities of life writing that are explored in the present volume: its elusive subject, its paradoxical intent, and its historically contingent relation with its readers.

Far from honouring Wollstonecraft, as Godwin had intended, his *Memoirs*, published in 1798, had the effect of fuelling condemnation of Wollstonecraft's life, writings, and influence. The index to the *Anti-Jacobin*, which cross-lists "Mary Wollstonecraft" and "prostitution," is perhaps the most sensational insult to Wollstonecraft's memory; but it is entirely consistent with contemporary attitudes toward women's sexuality, employments, and social roles. In her writings and in her life (as in Godwin's account of her life), Wollstonecraft challenged the limitations and distortions imposed by these attitudes; she was therefore vilified for the very qualities her husband wished to praise. Reading her life and work involves context as well as text. "Lives" as both lived experience and literary production are inseparable from "works," a word that similarly includes both the process of production and the finished product, whether authorized, edited, distorted, or adapted.

Both the feminist works and the lifestyle for which Wollstonecraft was condemned, and the damaged reputation that resulted, were part of her daughter's inheritance. That daughter, named Mary Wollstonecraft Godwin like her mother, grew up under the gaze of John Opie's portrait of Wollstonecraft, in an atmosphere that included continued insults to her mother's reputation as well as the painful reconstitution of a family, in a household that included her half-sister, Fanny Imlay, and later Godwin's second wife, Mary Jane Clairmont, and her children, Mary Jane (later Claire) and Charles, and, in 1801, William Godwin Jr. In 1812, Mary Godwin met the poet Percy Bysshe Shelley, an admirer of her father's work who had been expelled from Oxford for atheism and who had married without his titled family's approval. On 26 June 1814, on a visit to her mother's grave in St Pancras churchyard, she told him that she loved him. They eloped to the Continent, taking along Mary's stepsister, Claire Clairmont. Returning to England, Percy Shelley eluded his creditors and Mary gave birth to their first child, a daughter who died at two weeks of age. In 1816, following the birth of their son William, Mary and Percy went to Switzerland with Claire, who was pregnant with Lord Byron's child. During this eventful year, Mary began writing *Frankenstein*, and both her half-sister, Fanny, and

Percy's wife, Harriet, committed suicide. Percy Bysshe Shelley and Mary Wollstonecraft Godwin were married on 30 December 1816.

The deaths of two more children—Clara (1818) and William (1819)—and the birth of a second son, Percy Florence (1819), were followed in July 1822 by Percy Bysshe Shelley's death by drowning off the coast of Italy. In eight short years, Mary Shelley had given birth to four children, suffered the deaths of three of them, written *Frankenstein*, and survived an often unhappy marriage. Unlike her mother, she would be given a span of life in which to make a reputation less defined by scandal. In 1823, at the age of twenty-six, she returned to England with her only remaining child, Percy Florence, and put her energy into writing, publishing, and negotiating with the Shelley family in her son's interests. Prohibited by her father-in-law, Sir Timothy Shelley, from writing a life of Percy Bysshe Shelley (and thus prevented from doing for her husband some version of what Godwin had done for Wollstonecraft), she turned other forms of writing and editing into vehicles for life writing, much as her mother had found ways to represent the conditions of her own life in her philosophical and literary texts. In addition to *Frankenstein* (1818, second edition 1823, revised edition 1831) and her novella, *Matilda* (unpublished during her lifetime), she wrote five other novels—*Valperga* (1823), *The Last Man* (1826), *The Fortunes of Perkin Warbeck* (1830), *Lodore* (1835), and *Falkner* (1837)—and various essays, reviews, short stories, travel books (*History of a Six Weeks' Tour*; *Rambles in Germany and Italy*), and biographical sketches (for Lardner's *Cabinet Cyclopaedia* in 1835, 1838, and 1839). She lived to see her son succeed to the Shelley estate and title, and died in 1851 of a brain tumour.

In bare summary, such a whirlwind of events—elopements, exiles, indefatigable writing and publishing, births, infidelities, deaths—may seem bewildering, even bleakly comical. How is one to do justice to their human meaning? That, in brief, is the question this volume tries to answer. It examines intersecting lives and intersecting texts. Most centrally, it considers the relationship between Mary Wollstonecraft and Mary Shelley. Recognizing Godwin's contribution to forming both the mother's memory and the daughter's mind, it also considers familial intersections—what William St Clair has described as "the biography of a family"—and, more generally, intellectual and cultural contexts beyond the immediate Wollstonecraft and Shelley circles. It considers intersections of genre that challenge such conventional distinctions as those between the private and the public (Wollstonecraft's *Letters from Norway*, Shelley's travel writing), between autobiography and fiction (novels by both writers), and between personal experience and intellectual achievement. Through their awareness of intertextuality, essays in this volume serve to counter residual assumptions about the Romantic artist (including Percy Bysshe Shelley) as a solitary genius whose work transcends shared experience and common influence. Most significantly, perhaps, the volume serves to demonstrate as well as to make a case for the intersection of creative and intellectual work: not only do the contributions examine the coexistence of imagination with both scholarship and rational discourse in the works of Wollstonecraft and Shelley, they also display the generic mixture they celebrate. "Life writing" refers to a wide range of discursive practices. The term is not limited to traditionally defined genres such as memoir, biography, autobiography, letters, and personal essays: it also includes such fictive forms as autobiographical novels; essays and manifestoes informed by the operation of rational thought working through the felt inspiration of the writer; and the lyric voice of poetry and poetic prose in which poets construct their self-development in their work.

Rose Scollard's original play, *Caves of Fancy*, shows how scholarly research can transform the members of the Wollstonecraft and Shelley circles into dramatic characters whose words give new life to the familiar texts they echo; other contributions employ critical perspectives as diverse as Marxism (Gary Kelly), stylistics (D. L. Macdonald, Syndy Conger, Lawrence R. Kennard), psychoanalysis (Eleanor Ty, S. Leigh Matthews, Jeanne Moskal), intertextuality (Jeanne Perreault, Anne McWhir, Lisa Vargo), memoir theory (Helen M. Buss), bibliography (Charles E. Robinson, Betty T. Bennett), deconstruction (Judith Barbour), and standpoint theory (Anne K. Mellor). Drawing on this wide variety of methodologies and theoretical positions, the contributions to this volume suggest the richness and complexity of life writing, both as creative/scholarly practice and as the object of scholarly, critical, and theoretical investigation.

This diversity of approach is reflected in our contributors' usage of names and short titles, which we have accordingly chosen not to regularize. The choice of a short title is a critical judgment: Richard Holmes, for example, first suggested *A Short Residence* as a short title for *Letters Written during a Short Residence in Sweden, Norway, and Denmark*, not only because it helped to distinguish the book from the actual letters Wollstonecraft wrote from Scandinavia, but also because its "melancholy overtone" seemed to him characteristic of the book as a whole (58). To follow his example, as Syndy Conger does, is (at least implicitly) to endorse his judgment. To call the book *Letters from Norway*, as Eleanor Ty does (and as we do here), is to emphasize its generic status as an epistolary travel book (and also to imply a certain attitude toward literary history, since this is the title by which it was known in the Romantic period).

The vexed question of the names of the Shelleys also has critical implications. To call Percy Bysshe Shelley "Shelley," and Mary Wollstonecraft Shelley "Mary Shelley," as Jeanne Moskal does, is to imply a judgment about the personal and literary relations between them; to call the former "Percy" and the latter "Shelley," as Lisa Vargo does, is to imply a different but equally valid judgment. By choosing not to regularize the names and titles used by the various contributors, the editors intend to underscore the effect of naming on life writing and the diversity of approaches this volume represents. (It should always be obvious that *A Short Residence* and *Letters from Norway* are the same book, and that the Shelleys are two different people.)

Difference of viewpoint is important in other ways as well. Rose Scollard's *Caves of Fancy* provides a vivid image of the primal scene of Wollstonecraft's death, not from Godwin's perspective in the *Memoirs*, but as it might have been inhabited by Fanny Imlay's suicidal imagination in 1816. Just before her own death, Scollard's Fanny recalls the wailing of her newborn half-sister:

> I was there, wasn't I? The bed, the walls, the little green-winged fly
> that buzzed in the window. The fever that gripped her and the chill
> that rattled her bones. And I heard that rattle and I heard my father's
> collapsing breath, and the little baby in the next room crying. . . .

In Scollard's play, the scene of Wollstonecraft's death is not only a window to the irrecoverable past—the last act of a tragedy—but the beginning of another generation's story that overlaps and intersects with the past.

This work of demonstrating the relationship between a mother and a daughter, between two writing lives, and—more broadly—between two generations of writers, has been from the beginning a collaborative venture. A conference sponsored by the Calgary Institute for the Humanities and held at the University of Calgary in August 1997 to correspond with the bicentenary of Shelley's birth and Wollstonecraft's death brought together scholars, biographers, creative writers, and theorists to explore Wollstonecraft and Shelley's lives and work in the context of life writing as theory and practice. During the year before the conference, in conjunction with the Markin-Flanagan writer-in-residence program at the University of Calgary, Rose Scollard wrote her play, consulting with members of the English and Drama departments at the university and with the editors of this volume. Through an intensive series of workshops, the play's director, Brian Smith of the

Department of Drama, worked with Scollard and with a group of scholars, student actors, and production staff to bring the play to life. A public reading and two brief runs—the second during the conference—introduced Wollstonecraft and Shelley and their circles to audiences that might previously have known little about these writers. This experience of participating in life writing as scholarly project overlapping with imaginative re-creation helped to shape our understanding of the book we wanted to edit—a collaborative volume integrated by diverse creative and scholarly energies, a collection that would be cross-referential, representing a wide range of approaches and expertise.

Although neither Mary Wollstonecraft nor Mary Shelley ever wrote what we would call an autobiography or memoir, Wollstonecraft was the subject of Godwin's memoirs (discussed by Helen Buss); and Shelley began a memoir of Godwin (discussed by Judith Barbour), in addition to writing five volumes of biographies of eminent literary and scientific men of France, Italy, Portugal, and Spain. A number of contributors to this volume suggest possible reasons for their reticence about themselves: Ty and Matthews argue that the established autobiographical forms available to them had been developed primarily by men, for the purposes of masculine self-expression, and Kelly argues that Shelley's post-revolutionary moment was especially hostile to women's autobiography; Buss examines Godwin's conflicted attempt to write his wife's life; Barbour analyzes the psychic tensions that eventually led Shelley to abandon her life of Godwin; Vargo points out that Shelley's father-in-law prevented her from writing a memoir of her husband by threatening to cut off the allowance on which she and her son depended; Moskal argues that certain aspects of Shelley's past were too painful for her to write about them explicitly. Nevertheless, both mother and daughter were prolific life writers in the more inclusive sense described above, notably, in their letters (see Bennett's essay), travel writing (see Conger, Kennard, Ty, and Moskal), and fiction (see Matthews, Perreault, Robinson, McWhir, Vargo, and Mellor); Macdonald and Moskal suggest that even apparently impersonal forms such as political treatises and art criticism can be forms of self-representation. Bennett and Mellor, finally, argue in various ways that contemporary academic criticism of the two authors also has inevitably autobiographical elements.

In one of the most wide-ranging essays in the volume, Gary Kelly undertakes to historicize the autobiographical elements in Wollstonecraft's and Shelley's works, arguing that autobiography was the "dominant discursive mode of the Revolution debate." In Kelly's view, the autobiographical projects of mother and daughter are equally political, but with a crucial difference: writing during the Revolutionary period, Wollstonecraft always regards the self-creation and consciousness-raising that life writing makes possible as means to the end of revolutionary action; for Shelley, writing during the Romantic aftermath of the Revolutionary era, these means become ends in themselves—and thus, ironically, they serve the purposes of the modern liberal state, by helping to bring into being the "sovereign subject," which is its ideal consumer-citizen.

While observing that the "feminized" subject of sensibility and the emphasis on the individuality of the revolutionary subject allowed women such as Wollstonecraft and Shelley to enter ideological and literary discourse, Kelly also recognizes the difficulty for women— "inevitably dependent" within the discursive mode he describes—of assuming such positions. He consequently traces feminist trajectories in the life-writing projects of both Wollstonecraft and Shelley as cultural revisions of the nature and power of maternity and experiments in authorial positioning and narrative voice, including the development of a "prose lyricism" in confessional format.

This first-person voice is the subject of D. L. Macdonald's analysis of grammatical forms in *A Vindication of the Rights of Men* and *A Vindication of the Rights of Woman*. Wollstonecraft's use of the first-person pronoun, Macdonald argues, creates a persona who is not only a subject (rather than an object) but also an active (rather than a passive) subject. Macdonald distinguishes between those self-references that refer to the self in the past (the "person") and those that refer to "the subject of enunciation" (the "persona") and suggests that, by taking up contemporary autobiographical modes of a self-referencing persona, Wollstonecraft "lays claim to a greater degree of subjecthood and agency in the moment of writing than in the rest of her experience" as a female person. Whereas Kelly, in a cultural context, notes the different location of women in Revolutionary and Romantic ideology, Macdonald demonstrates that this difference occurs at the linguistic level of the stylistics of self-reference. As he observes, "When Wollstonecraft refers to herself as part of a group of intellectuals engaged in a common project, her subjecthood, agency, and mentality are enhanced; when she refers to herself as part of the female sex, they are diminished."

Macdonald ends by conceding that an author's use of the first-person pronoun can hardly be understood except in dialectical relation to her use of the second-person pronoun. Syndy McMillen Conger takes up this suggestion in a discussion of "The unnamed *you*" in Wollstonecraft's *Letters Written during a Short Residence in Sweden,*

Norway, and Denmark. The *I* of the *Letters from Norway* is a more embodied, more gendered being than that of the polemical works discussed by Macdonald; the *you*, by contrast, though mentioned in the first letter, is not clearly identified as Wollstonecraft's unworthy lover until surprisingly late in the book. This strategy makes possible a blurring of boundaries (between the textual and the extratextual, author and text, text and reader, reader and addressee/lover) that may account for the book's extraordinary (and well-attested) affective power. Such blurring shows that autobiographical discourse is built not only on self-referential strategies but also, perhaps most prominently in women's texts, on self-performance anchored in its connections to others. Both Conger and Macdonald quote Shelley's description of *I* as "this sensitive, imaginative, suffering, enthusiastic pronoun." Their analysis of first- and second-person pronouns asks readers of life writing to focus on the effect of self- and other-referential strategies on subject formation in autobiography.

While strategies for reading life writing are enhanced by linguistic analysis, examining the particulars of genre and genre blending can also be helpful. Lawrence R. Kennard concentrates on some of the most remarkable passages in the *Letters from Norway*, which he identifies as "poetic reveries." Modelled on Rousseau's *Reveries of the Solitary Walker*, Wollstonecraft's reveries form a "liminal, intermediate, and transitional" sub-genre that, "as a form of meditative life-writing, questions subjectivity." Lying on the boundary between poetry and prose, reveries allow Wollstonecraft to blur the boundaries between the faculties of understanding and sensation, thought and sensibility; between internal meditation and external observation, the self and the world; between process and product; and even between life and death. Most importantly, they combine qualities traditionally considered masculine and feminine, enabling Wollstonecraft to move "beyond gendered ideology" to the "egalitarian poetics" theorized both in her second *Vindication* and in her late essay "On Poetry" (1797).

Like Conger's essay, Eleanor Ty's psychoanalytic reading of *Letters from Norway* tries to account for the book's affective power, which is attributable, in Ty's view, to the desire that "impels and haunts the narrative." Like both Conger and Kennard, Ty sees the book's achievement as lying in its blurring of a boundary: the integration of Wollstonecraft's private and public selves, a task made all the harder by the virtual unnameability of feminine desire in the masculine life-writing tradition she inherited. Thus, she can give public expression to her private feelings of desire only obliquely: through fantasies of escape, imagery of ascension, and her responses to the landscapes, peoples, and cultures of Scandinavia. For Ty, Wollstonecraft's "desire is in excess of what is expressed by her language" because of the limits that symbolic representation sets, particularly in expressing "desire in domestic representation." (Conger, Kennard, and Ty also all return, from their varied perspectives, to the "culture of sensibility" analyzed by Kelly in the opening essay.)

S. Leigh Matthews maintains that the disjunction between what a woman needs to express and what symbolic language can express leads us to experience a "dual" voice in Wollstonecraft's unfinished, and posthumously published, second novel, *The Wrongs of Woman; or, Maria*. Like Conger, Matthews sees Wollstonecraft's late writings as articulating an emphatically embodied, and gendered, selfhood; like Ty, she sees them as concerned with bringing private experience into the public sphere, in defiance of the myth (most tellingly expressed, in our time, by Jacques Lacan) that women's experience cannot be represented in language without being subordinated to masculine values. Wollstonecraft achieves this expression through a double discourse: while her text represents, and so reinscribes, the subordination of women, at the same time it critiques this subordination. Within the diegesis, this critique is not successful: the male authority figures to whom Maria appeals dismiss her protest as evidence of her madness. However, modern, feminist readers have a responsibility to give Maria's story a more alert reading, a critical practice better suited than traditional practices to women's life writing. Reading intertextually between life, philosophical writings, and the novelistic text reveals *The Wrongs of Woman* as not only a novel, but the autobiographical expression of a writer who is a philosopher and a woman.

Jeanne Perreault's essay on *The Wrongs of Woman* brings Matthews's feminist analysis into dialogue with other progressive political approaches, testing Wollstonecraft's use of slavery as a metaphor for the subjugation of women by comparing her novel with Harriet Jacobs's autobiography, *Incidents in the Life of a Slave Girl* (1861). Without eliding the differences between the oppression of women and of slaves, Perreault explores the striking parallels—and the historical reasons for these parallels—between the two forms of oppression. For both women and slaves, resistance to oppression involves taking possession of the self, so that it is no longer the possession of another. In an argument reminiscent of Conger's and Matthews's emphasis on the importance of the embodied self, Perreault suggests that the site of this resistance is the body of the woman and of the slave.

Like Kelly, Perreault analyzes the "modern liberal subject," but she finds it incongruent with the "figures of female selfhood" advanced by feminist theorists, which stress intersubjectivity, community, and maternity, rather than autonomy, sovereignty, and rationality. Like Macdonald, she examines how Wollstonecraft and Jacobs articulate a self "who is an agent of action in the world," but she rejects a "polarity of subject/object and its hierarchical implications." Perreault's analysis of actual slave women and women enslaved by patriarchy asks us to consider that in the autobiographical expression of such subjects something more than "the abjected being" or the "sovereign subject" is present. Emphasizing the importance of the trope of "self-possession" in these two women's writings, she proposes an autobiographical subject that represents "the intersubjective, the maternal, the communitarian subject."

The Wrongs of Woman was edited by William Godwin, along with Wollstonecraft's other posthumous works, in an attempt to keep her revolutionary ideas alive in the reactionary climate of the late 1790s. Ironically, the *Memoirs of the Author of* A Vindication of the Rights of Woman, which Godwin published along with his edition, did much to discredit those ideas for the next fifty years. Helen M. Buss attributes this biographical misunderstanding to the conflicting roles forced on Godwin by the demands of the memoir format, and to his ambivalence about Wollstonecraft's achievement and her death. The memoir, like the reverie, is a cross-generic form; Godwin's attempt to negotiate the boundary between "private person and public ideology" (as Wollstonecraft herself had succeeded in doing in *Letters from Norway*) led Robert Southey to accuse him of stripping his dead wife naked. However, Buss does not argue that Godwin's text is less valuable as memoir because of the scandal that surrounded its publication. Rather, she argues that the "classic" memoir is not an impartial, objective genre, as biography claims to be, but that it depends on the partiality and the participatory role of its narrator for its strength as a form: its ability to portray authentically the multiple subject positions of the memoir writer. For Buss, Godwin's memoirs illustrate that "new approaches to writing lives are not accomplished by taking safe paths."

Certainly the young Mary Shelley did not take "safe paths" in writing *Frankenstein*, for, as Charles E. Robinson points out, the mother who became a pariah after her death is alive in the daughter's work. Critics such as Joyce Zonana have argued that *Frankenstein* is, in part, Shelley's attempt to keep her mother's ideas alive. Robinson backs up Zonana's critical insight with "the hard facts of the letters and journals" and his own work on the manuscript of *Frankenstein*, which show that

Mary Shelley's first recorded reading of *A Vindication of the Rights of Woman* (on 6-9 December 1816) coincided with her writing of the story of Safie, the most obvious allusion to Wollstonecraft, and the most overtly feminist passage, in the novel. The allusion may not, however, be entirely uncritical, for Safie, despite the Wollstonecraftian education given her by her mother, fails (like everybody else in the book) to recognize the essential humanity of the monster. The story of Safie may acknowledge the limits, as well as the power, of the "passion for reforming the world" that Shelley celebrated in her mother.

Robinson observes that "there is a book begging to be written on mother and daughter, a study of the ways that Mary Wollstonecraft and her literary texts play out in the lights and shadows of Mary Shelley's life and works." Robinson's essay, along with those that follow his in this volume, begins the work of reading and writing the daughter's life and works in relation to the mother's. But these essays also participate in another intergenerational project: connecting the lives of this mother and daughter helps us to read the connections between the lives of writing women who follow Wollstonecraft and Shelley.

Shelley was emphatically conscious of herself as "the daughter of *two* persons of distinguished literary celebrity" (*FMP* 176; our emphasis), and her writings respond to her father as often as to her mother. This is most obvious in her unfinished biography of her father, which, as Judith Barbour shows, was inhibited not only by the discouraging example of Godwin's *Memoirs* of Wollstonecraft but also by Shelley's mixed feelings about the roles women other than her mother played in her father's life. Barbour's account of Shelley's single most elaborate life-writing project details the strategies by which she attempted to contain those feelings, and her reasons for finally abandoning the project, pointing to the difficulties that await those who, like Godwin, attempt to become the biographers of their loved ones.

Anne McWhir considers *Frankenstein* and *The Last Man* as responses both to Shelley's mother's polemic and to the mythological writings of her father and husband. Godwin's *The Pantheon* censors the misogyny of his source, Hesiod; Percy Shelley's *Prometheus Unbound* idealizes it out of existence; but Mary Shelley draws on it to show how Victor Frankenstein's fear of women and of sexual reproduction disastrously deforms his scientific ambitions. McWhir explores not only the parallels but also the differences among the kinds of life that can be given by an artist, a scientist, and a parent; not only the complex interdependencies but also the conflicts between the ideal life of the work of art and the life of the breathing human body. In proposing that the "life writer" is the "bestow[er] of animation on lifeless matter," McWhir poses Mary Shelley as the progenitor of our own self-making in con-temporary times, the life writer who creates us, her "late-twentieth-cen-tury readers . . . [, as the] hideous progeny of those ideas about nature and art she popularized in her fiction." McWhir's analysis presents us with an important frame for the critical study of subjectivity in contem-porary life writing. If we are Mary Shelley's creatures, in that her images of creation and construction have become culturally dominant— and, by implication, if we are the creatures of Mary Wollstonecraft, as her feminist concerns have developed into contemporary preoccupa-tions—we must look to these works to understand contemporary sub-jectivity and the life-writing genres in which it is shaped.

Like S. Leigh Matthews, Lisa Vargo asks us to read a novel, in this case Shelley's *Lodore,* intertextually with the writer's life-long con-cerns. Although *Lodore* is often neglected or dismissed as a purely commercial "silver-fork" novel, Vargo shows that Shelley appropriates a popular fictional form in order to question contemporary assumptions about women. Proposing that Shelley was "a careful reader of her mother's writings," Vargo reads *Lodore* as an imagined conversation with Wollstonecraft, in which Shelley tries to repair the damage done by Godwin's *Memoirs* by concentrating on the details of her mother's ideas rather than her life. Like Robinson, Vargo sees Shelley as most interested in Wollstonecraft's ideas on education. Unlike Robinson, who suggests that "Mary Shelley felt unworthy or unlike her mother with respect to women's rights," and Kelly, who sees Shelley as essen-tially complicit in the establishment of the modern liberal subject, Vargo argues that Shelley is anxious not to "degenerate" from her mother's revolutionary example.

Vargo also proposes that *Lodore* enacts in its plot the "reunion of mother and daughter" that Shelley's careful reading of her mother's works makes possible. Vargo's argument, that traditional concepts of the absolute boundaries between novel and autobiography disadvan-tage novels such as *Lodore*, can be equally applied to a number of works by both Wollstonecraft and Shelley discussed in this volume. Vargo significantly points out that in referring to "the memory of the mother," Shelley is referring to a mother she has never known, thus to a fiction. The recuperation of that mother, then, through an act both fic-tive and biographical, illustrates that life writing accomplishes its goals by crossing generic boundaries. The critical reader of life writing must not feel limited by the designations that contain women's texts inside such narrow interpretive boundaries.

While Vargo is concerned with reading Shelley's novels for their autobiographical reference, Jeanne Moskal takes a similar approach to

Shelley's art criticism, showing how her last book, *Rambles in Germany and Italy* (1844), uses the apparently impersonal form of art criticism to work through the trauma of her deepest loss—not that of her husband, but of her children. Shelley was drawn to a statue of Niobe, the bereaved mother of classical myth, and especially to paintings of the Virgin Mary, the ideal mother of Christian myth. These paintings allowed Shelley to engage in a healing reliving of the roles of both mother and daughter, a process aided by the fact that both Shelley and Wollstonecraft had the same name as the Virgin. Shelley's "oddly lyrical, dreamy passages of art criticism" are comparable to the reveries Kennard analyzes in her mother's work. Like Kennard, Moskal is interested in the politics of reverie: through her analysis of the treatment of Catholic iconography in Shelley's reveries, she argues, like Vargo, that the daughter has not retreated from the radical politics of the mother.

In proposing her "analogy between dream-work and life writing," Moskal theorizes that autobiography, traditionally seen as revealing the self, may sometimes be concerned with "protect[ing] the self" from "unspeakable" memories. If, as in Mary Shelley's case, the past is full of "dispiriting realities" that involve guilt and despair over lost children and other tragedies, then the dream-work of art criticism can act as a "defence against full knowledge" while it allows the writer to dwell indirectly on the very traumas that are "unspeakable." Moskal's essay highlights once more the tasks of the reader as decoder of the unspeakable autobiographical materials inside the conventional discourse.

Like McWhir, Betty T. Bennett and Anne K. Mellor see *Frankenstein* as (in one way or another) an allegory of life writing; and all three incorporate life writing (in one way or another) into their criticism. Drawing on her experience as editor of Shelley's letters, Bennett suggests that letters are the "component parts" of a biography and describes the challenges they present to the editor, who has to bring them together, and to the biographer, who has to endue them with vital warmth. She stresses the importance (for Shelley herself as well as for the modern scholar) of maintaining the boundaries between the public and the private, the fictional and the factual. At the same time, she stresses that even the most rigorously scholarly biography inevitably has an imaginative component.

Mellor reads *Frankenstein* as an allegory of Shelley's life, and at the same time reflects on the experiences in her own life—her conflict with her father and her commitment to feminism—that have led her to read Shelley's work in this way. For a critic to acknowledge such influences is not "wilful 'subjectivity'" but a "strong objectivity" that recognizes the inevitably situated nature of all knowledge; thus, Mellor contests the more conventional notion of objectivity by including her own autocritography. While using feminist stand-point theory to evolve her own autocritical position, Mellor reminds theorists of life writing that biography is not necessarily the objective opposite of subjective autobiography. Since biographical writing is inflected by the subject positions of biographers, it may be that, as Mellor wryly observes, "Biographies are autobiographies that dare not speak their name." Mellor's advice to biographers, to practise a "dialogic" mode between self, object of study, and reader, is in the spirit of the critical practice of this volume.

Finally, Rose Scollard brings Shelley and her circle to life in a play that interweaves many of the themes and issues that run through the essays: issues of life writing, feminist revisionism, creative work as allegorical autobiography, and even textual scholarship. Scollard's play is densely intertextual, drawing on Wollstonecraft's and Shelley's writings and on those of their circles to evoke their lives and their work through their own words. Here the distinction between "life" and "work" is practically eliminated: "life" emerges from the texture of words, and Scollard shows how life writing is allied both to the creation of Frankenstein's monster and to the playwright/scholar's piecing together and enlivening of fragments.

The play focuses on the three sisters—Fanny Imlay, Claire Clairmont, and Mary Shelley—and dramatizes episodes in their lives from about 1814 (when Shelley and Percy eloped) until the 1830s. Yet it is far from being a linear account of events. At its centre is the Creature, brought to life through imagination—a shape changer who at various points (and sometimes simultaneously) plays the roles of Mary Wollstonecraft, Byron, Frankenstein's creature, Fanny Imlay's demon lover, Leigh Hunt, an actor playing the monster on the early-nineteenth-century stage, Prosper Mérimée (flirting with Shelley in Paris in 1828), and "Mrs Mason" (Margaret King, Lady Mount Cashell, one of Wollstonecraft's pupils in Ireland in 1786, whom the Shelleys met on the Continent in 1818 after she had left her husband to live with George William Tighe). The Creature functions as chorus, as critic, and as comic counterpoint to his own evocation of death, loss, and loneliness. Centrally, he comments on the difficulties and ironies of conjuring and writing life: "I was conceived as a beautiful creature, but somehow along the way I accumulated ugliness. I was meant to be an exemplary man. But the skin just couldn't be managed, and the eyes . . . I filled my maker with horror."

This evocation of Frankenstein's creature is one obvious metaphor for the scholar and playwright's work. As an allegory of its own process of coming to life, Scollard's play adopts another central metaphor from Mary Shelley's writing—that of the leaves on the floor of the Sibyl's Cave in *The Last Man*, fragments of prophecy that need to be pieced together and interpreted. Caves as inner space—womb, imagination, memory—recur in the play, most significantly in the womb-space of the opening scene and in the Gabinetto Fisico of Act Two, based on a place Shelley actually visited in Florence in January 1820 but overlaid in the play with the Sibyl's Cave, a "cabinet of wonders" that is also a Gothic space inhabited by the dead. Textual fragments flutter to the ground throughout the play, both literally and in the ways its language teases the reader's or audience's memory: letters, manuscript pages, and projected kaleidoscopic images are visual props as well as material for creative reconstruction. The play's final scene, in which Claire, Mary, and the sibylline figure of Fanny engage in the *sortes Virgilianae* (pointing to a random passage in Virgil and interpreting it as a prophecy), sums up the play's focus on what Scollard calls "reading the fragments."

The parts of this volume, we hope, provide an integrated and cohesive reading of fragments even while they consider life writing from many different perspectives. Unlike Frankenstein, who toiled in obsessive solitude to bring his creature to life, we have worked collaboratively as editors, writers, playwright, and scholars; unlike the author-editor in the Sibyl's Cave of *The Last Man*, we have worked with strong individual texts, contributions to a conversation rather than cryptic fragments. As reflection on and experiment in life writing, this volume as a whole exemplifies in some degree the intertextual, historically contingent, and still unfinished nature of its subject.

The Politics of Autobiography
in Mary Wollstonecraft
and Mary Shelley

Gary Kelly

Autobiography may be seen as socially and culturally recognized forms of writing the self, in separate works or in any style, form, genre, or discourse. Interest in autobiography has proliferated rapidly in the past few decades, partly in response to claims made for its educational, therapeutic, and emancipatory potential, especially for those marginalized in contemporary society and culture and the modern state (see Coleman; Franklin; Personal Narratives Group; S. Smith). What such studies and such claims assume, though not always openly, is that autobiography, like other genres and discourses, is inevitably political and historically particular. It is used to participate in, collude with, or resist the institutions, structures, and distribution of power at the time and in the place where the particular autobiography or autobiographical discourse is produced (Bruss). Even analyses of various studies of autobiography point out that definitions, histories, and criticism of autobiography are always political, in the sense that they serve some interest of their authors and address issues of the times in which they are written (Fleishman, Introduction; L. Marcus).

Note is on p. 30.

In particular, a recognizably "modern" kind of autobiography seems to have emerged in Britain and elsewhere in Western Europe some time between the late sixteenth and the late eighteenth centuries (Mascuch; Steussy), during the complex economic, social, cultural, and political transformations known as modernization. This kind of autobiography usually deals centrally with inner or subjective identity and experience, rather than with social and public identity and actions. The ideology of authentic individuality that was developed and promoted in such autobiography, and increasingly extended to such genres as the novel and poetry, was implicated in a series of powerful and broad revolutionary movements.[1]

The eighteenth-century Enlightenments—with their attack on customary, communal, and hierarchical forms of the economy, social structure, culture, and state—were part of such movements. The Enlightenments supported the related movement of economic, social, and institutional modernization based on capitalist individualism. Produced by and furthering these movements were the late-eighteenth-century and early-nineteenth-century political revolutions that emphasized the rights of individuals. Movements partly reacting against and partly developing these revolutions resulted, during the early and mid-nineteenth century, in the founding of modern liberal nation-states based on the idea of the sovereign subject. This sovereign subject, of autobiography and of the modern state, was usually male, white, and European; but successive groups have claimed inclusion in the modern liberal state, calling for appropriate reforms in society, culture, and state constitutions, and, through to the present day, they have used autobiography, in itself and in other genres, to make this claim.

In this essay I want to locate Mary Wollstonecraft and Mary Shelley in a critical and complexly articulated development in the history of the modern subject—or the subject of modernity, modernization, and especially the modern liberal state—and of the forms of autobiography that enabled it. This development followed a trajectory from the late-eighteenth-century culture of sensibility through its mobilization in the French Revolution and related movements to the sublation of sensibility and Revolution in what later became known as romanticism and the founding of the modern liberal state. First I'll sketch this complex articulation and then briefly examine the connected engagement of Wollstonecraft and Shelley in it. I'll conclude by reflecting on our current interest—in several senses—in that engagement.

The late-eighteenth-century culture of sensibility was both important and problematic in the formation of Wollstonecraft's identity, ideology, politics, and poetics. Sensibility was based on an ideology of authentic and socially transcendent subjectivity in opposition to customary and communal forms of identity and social and economic relations (Barker-Benfield; Mullan). Biography and autobiography were used increasingly, in themselves and as elements of other genres and discourses, in the literature of sensibility. As several essays in this volume note, the poetics of sensibility, especially as autobiography, were developed fully and broadly by Jean-Jacques Rousseau. He styled himself "Citizen of Geneva" in a deliberate allusion to that city-state's bourgeois, democratic, commercial civil society, in opposition to the society of contemporary court monarchies, with their aristocratic cosmopolitanism on the one hand and plebeian communalism and custom on the other. Woman and the feminine had long been associated with emotional and sympathetic subjectivity, and the "man of feeling" was a purposely feminized male subject countering the supposedly over-masculinized subjects of courtly upper classes and brutalized plebeians. Accordingly, sensibility provided an opportunity that some women writers, including Wollstonecraft and Shelley, exploited.

The broad political character and potential of autobiography (and biography) were revealed quickly by their deployment in the Revolutionary and counter-Revolutionary polemics of the 1790s. Mary Wollstonecraft contributed largely to this literature, and Mary Shelley later read much of it. Indeed, one could argue that the dominant discursive mode of the Revolution debate was autobiographical. The subjective if not the egotistical sublime—an element of the autobiographical—was used to validate any politics, in works ranging from Edmund Burke's anti-Revolutionary *Reflections on the Revolution in France* (1790), which virtually initiated the Revolution debate in Britain, to Helen Maria Williams's series of pro-Revolutionary *Letters from France* (1790-96), perhaps the leading eyewitness account of the Revolution for the British reading public. This rhetorical strategy was both used in polemical works as such, including those of Wollstonecraft, and also developed widely in the novel, poetry, and drama.

The place of women in this general mobilization of revolutionary subjectivity was problematic, as numerous women writers in Britain, from Mary Wollstonecraft to Germaine de Staël, pointed out. The role of women, and especially of Manon Roland, in the salons that managed the Girondin Revolution was made a political scandal by the Jacobins, who assigned revolutionary women the primarily biological and domestic roles of producing (male) citizens-to-be and dispensing "le lait républicain" to them. The Thermidorean reaction and the Directory period of the mid-1790s, with their apparent recrudescence of courtly decadence, "backstairs politics," and the courtly "mistress system," enabled counter-Revolutionaries to characterize the Revolution as the court system restaffed by an upstart bourgeoisie. Bonaparte's increasingly courtly, monarchic, and indeed imperial regime seemed to confirm this characterization. The pseudo-courtliness of the Directory and Bonapartist periods enabled loyalists in Britain to represent a restricted domesticity and the exclusion of women from the public political sphere as not only counter-revolutionary but patriotic. Paradoxically, then, both revolutionary and counter-revolutionary discourse excluded women from political subjectivity. Furthermore, many counter-revolutionary writers, including women, eschewed the autobiographical mode, remained suspicious of subjectivity, and relentlessly mocked pretensions to sensibility. To autobiographize, beyond certain limits, and especially for women, could be taken as a sign of what the magistrate in Wollstonecraft's *The Wrongs of Woman* calls, in response to the heroine's public and legal self-vindication, "French principles" (199).

Following the Revolution and its Napoleonic aftermath, the modern and modernizing subject had to be reconstructed to purge its association with revolutionary excess, including mob violence and militarism. The implicitly feminized subject of sensibility was rapidly developed in romantic culture as, on the one hand, the feminine subject constructing the domestic sphere as fount and foundation of community, nation, and empire, and, on the other hand, the feminized male subject of the public and political sphere, or civil society. This subject covertly subsumed major traits of the subject in and for civil society as posited by Enlightenment social philosophy, as "citizens of Geneva" — sympathetic, "sensible" (i.e., sentimental), and self-governed, and therefore pacific, sociable, and "liberal" in the sense of autonomous, self-validated, and free from the bonds of both aristocratic patronage and plebeian dependency. This was the subject of a modern state internalized in individual subjectivity, rather than the subject of the *ancien-régime* state based on external compulsion, or threat of compulsion, by main force. This is also, repeatedly, the protagonist of Mary Shelley's proto-liberal fiction. The question at large, again, was whether or not women, almost inevitably dependent in every class, could be such "liberal" subjects. To mask the revolutionary character of the liberal subject and the state constructed on it, the subject was represented in various ways: as constructed by and imbricated with sublime nature; as the construction of a specifically Christian, Western, and post-classical yet historic and even "traditional" culture, called "chivalry"; and as the subject sublimated by and from history — as the "end" of history.

Wollstonecraft and Shelley exemplify the feminine and feminist inflection of this historical trajectory, of this critical development in the politics of the modern subject and its autobiographical discourse. This was also an important moment in the effort to recover women, as subjects, from "masculine," destructive history for a future that would be better because it incorporated, at last, women and the feminine (Wake). For this was the moment of production of the liberal subject out of Revolutionary history and as the end of history that would otherwise, through violent revolution, end in the abyss of mass death, global war, and the fall of civilization. The period is full of apocalyptic imaginings, of which Wollstonecraft's pessimism in her *Letters from Scandinavia* and Shelley's in *Frankenstein* and *The Last Man* are only three examples, though salient ones because they seem to oppose apocalypse to exemplary autobiographical selfhood. For the autobiographical work of Wollstonecraft and Shelley was designed both to exemplify the capacity of women to be liberal subjects and to insist that the liberal state would be ill-founded if women were not so recognized. Nevertheless, there were important differences between the distinct moments of Wollstonecraft and Shelley in the articulated foundation of the liberal subject.

Wollstonecraft exemplifies the articulation of sentimental, Revolutionary, and incipiently post-Revolutionary discourse, and her daughter the articulation of the post-Revolutionary, romantic, and incipiently liberal. Wollstonecraft's self-appointed role was to exemplify, in her texts and in the life choices that supposedly grounded them, the (female) revolutionary subject. Shelley's role, as her mother's daughter, was specifically and in an exemplary way to subsume her mother's revolutionary feminism in a post-Revolutionary and romantic feminism that also countered masculine revolution as a manifestation of masculine history. Wollstonecraft was the more prominently autobiographical writer, first within the developing culture and poetics of sensibility and then within Revolutionary discourse, or the way in which politics were personally and self-referentially validated in the Revolution debate.

For example, Wollstonecraft's *Original Stories* (1788) may be read as a manual of education, especially for females, in the moral and subjective self-culture of sensibility as oppositional culture for the future state. Her reviews of books of all kinds are highly personal and return repeatedly to the paradoxes of sensibility as both personally and socially emancipatory yet also potentially degrading and oppressive for women. Her first novel, *Mary: A Fiction* (1788), is manifestly and purposefully autobiographical, showing that afflicted female sensibility is the result of internalizing social contradictions of class and gender. Her pro-Revolutionary polemic, *A Vindication of the Rights of Men* (1790), is a demonstration of autonomous self-possessed subjectivity for Revolutionary ideology. Her feminist polemic, *A Vindication of the Rights of Woman* (1792), extends that demonstration to the reconstruction of the Revolutionary state through education, and especially the education of women. Wollstonecraft began a vindication of the Revolution in the highly autobiographical style already developed successfully by Helen Maria Williams; but, no doubt aware of her predecessor's mastery of the field, she turned from the immediacy of autobiographical self-authorization to an Enlightenment model of the authoritative spectatorial "view" characteristic of "philosophical history," in her *Historical and Moral View . . . of the French Revolution* (1794). After this, her personal-political engagement with the Revolution itself was broken. The last book she published in her lifetime, *Letters Written during a Short Residence in Sweden, Norway, and Denmark* (1796), seems to be her most directly autobiographical work, reworking the well-established genre of sentimental travelogue—that is, a travelogue foregrounding the traveller and especially the traveller's subjective responses. Yet in this work Wollstonecraft constructs yet another autobiographizing political persona—the "female philosopher" as subject of the revolutionized state, a state that as yet exists only potentially in this subject and in others like her. In her final major work, left incomplete at her death, Wollstonecraft returned to the novel, a form already well exploited in the circle of her companion William Godwin for linking the personal and subjective with the public and political. *The Wrongs of Woman; or, Maria* (1798) is a characteristically English Jacobin novel in using the "confessional" mode to dramatize what we would nowadays call consciousness-raising.

It has been argued that Mary Shelley, too, was largely and centrally influenced by the "Godwinian novel" (Clemit). Yet, beyond what Mary Shelley may have written in youth for her father's and stepmother's Juvenile Library, and her travel books, her published works are less overtly autobiographical than her mother's. There are several reasons for this. During the aftermath of the Revolution, autobiographical-political discourse of the kind common in the Revolutionary decade was tainted by association with Revolutionary excess, including excess of self. This association of interrelated personal and political transgressiveness was reinforced by the career of the imperialist individualist, Napoleon. In the Revolutionary aftermath, such associations were applied with additional force to women because of the renewed emphasis on domestic ideology and the domestic identity and roles of women. Furthermore, after Percy Shelley's death, Mary Shelley was under her father-in-law's injunction to avoid publicizing his son's—and by extension her own—name. Nevertheless, as Anne K. Mellor (in *Mary Shelley*) and many other critics have pointed out in the past decade and more, autobiographical elements appear in all of her fiction, and elsewhere.

Versions of Mary Shelley, Percy Shelley, her parents, and members of their circles appear in the novels beginning with *Frankenstein*, especially in *The Last Man* and *Lodore*. In other novels, as recent editions have pointed out, autobiographical elements again appear, though again generalized to formulate (as protagonist and as agonistic) the subjectivity required for the not-yet-realized liberal state. The heroine of *Valperga* has been taken as a version of Shelley herself, as has Lady Katherine Gordon in the historical novel *Perkin Warbeck,* Ethel in *Lodore,* and Elizabeth Raby in *Falkner.* It is now widely assumed (though this has been challenged) that one story, "Mathilda," sent to Godwin from Italy where Shelley was then living, was left unpublished because Godwin considered it improperly autobiographical. It has been argued that even Mary Shelley's edition of her late husband's poems invoked autobiography, or personal knowledge and experience, to contextualize and thus mediate the reception of his avant-garde poetry (Wolfson). More generally, judgments and feelings that manifestly invoke autobiographical authority are scattered throughout the novels. It should be clear by now, however, that as in Wollstonecraft's *The Wrongs of Woman*, the autobiographical is used rhetorically, as part of a large political vision and social critique.

In their diverse exemplifications and textualizations of the politicized and female or feminized subject, Wollstonecraft and Shelley deploy, each in her own way, similar repertories of themes and formal devices derived and adapted from elements in the larger repertory of sentimental and romantic poetics. These themes and devices, and the presence of the "author" and the disclosures of autobiographical reference in the text, whether fictional or non-fictional, are used to construct what may be called the coterie or vanguard text. This is designed to represent and to promote a gradualist revolution through a small but proliferating intellectual, political, cultural, and even sexual coterie or vanguard. Here I can deal only briefly with themes and devices most closely associated with the autobiographical mode developed by Wollstonecraft and Shelley, and show how these devices exemplify the authors' politics of autobiography.

Among the major themes developed by Wollstonecraft and Shelley are several that figure prominently, though they are interpreted differently, in the essays gathered in this volume. For example, Wollstonecraft and Shelley both use maternity as an authorial validation and as a uniquely female knowledge. Wollstonecraft refashions maternity in the context of the late Revolution debate, for example in the *Letters* from Scandinavia and *The Wrongs of Woman,* to incorporate the character of what would otherwise be gendered masculine—that is, the character of "philosophy" as understood in her time: a form of social critique based on self-reflection. Shelley, in such works as *Frankenstein* and *The Last Man,* uses the maternal—or perhaps parental—to exemplify the unique knowledge derived by women from victimization by an illiberal society and state. These uses of maternity, especially as contrasted to the contradictions of paternity, form part of a wider deployment of female knowledges that, Shelley implies, must be incorporated in the middle-class cultural revolution if it is to succeed. It could be argued that Wollstonecraft similarly deploys themes of uniquely or predominantly female experience and knowledge as accepted in her time, including female sexuality, socialization and acculturation, devotional religion, marriage and property, social sympathy, and narration in everyday life and relationships.

Wollstonecraft and Shelley advance such themes by certain appropriate techniques of authorial self-positioning and textual structuring. These include, most prominently, the self-reflexive author-in-the-text, seen particularly in Wollstonecraft; the effusive or lyrical authorial or narrating voice, seen in both Wollstonecraft and Shelley; and the sympathetic or empathetic third-person narrator, seen particularly in Shelley. There is a movement from Wollstonecraft to Shelley in form and rhetorical use of narrative voice, from autobiographical "I" to third-person narrator. This movement indicates, as I have suggested earlier, a response to the changing valuation of the personal in the text, from the Revolutionary decade to the Revolutionary aftermath and romanticism, especially for women writers. Wollstonecraft's and Shelley's formal autobiographizing practice is complex and diverse and is elaborated through their use of expressivity and relating, setting, and plot.

The late-eighteenth- and early-nineteenth-century rhetoric of expressivity, as summarized in such texts (well known to Wollstonecraft) as Hugh Blair's *Lectures on Rhetoric and Belles-Lettres* (1783), was adapted from the classical rhetoric of ethos, basing persuasiveness on the known character of the speaker, as exhibited in his (uncommonly her) discourse. From at least the latter half of the eighteenth century, the rhetoric of expressivity comprised a set of devices to enable the textual construction of an exemplary subjectivity in several genres. In all the forms used by Wollstonecraft and Shelley, but especially in novels and travelogues, the dominant stylistic register is what could be called prose lyricism and the dominant form can be characterized as confessional. These were among the major modes of post-Revolutionary and of romantic self-representation for men and women writers, in various genres and discourses. In their novels, Wollstonecraft and Shelley use both first-person and third-person narration, modified so as to foreground subjectivity under duress as exemplary subjectivity. The relationship between protagonists' subjectivities is precisely that of relating, in the sense of narrating a life experience that exemplifies and validates a broad critique of the social, economic, and political order. This narrating shows how the order places exemplary subjects under duress and thus "proves" the inadequacy of that order to authentic subjectivity. This is why Wollstonecraft's and Shelley's texts are often elegiac in tone, or end on a plaintive and uncertain note. The elegiac and uncertain tone or closure does not primarily express loss, though there are implications in Shelley's early work of a general loss of the heroic impulse of the Revolutionary decade. Rather, the lament is for a future promised in Revolutionary action but not realized, or not yet realized. The implication is that the order is yet to be established that can accommodate, indeed nurture, the exemplary subjects of Wollstonecraft's and Shelley's novels and non-fiction prose works. This implication is revolutionary in that it constitutes a call to transformation in the real world of the readers. Third-person narrators, in this formal practice, are again model subjects of a state not yet brought into being, and call upon readers to assume a similar subject identity.

Yet the revolutionary order does exist, though as a revolutionary vanguard rather than a revolutionized state. In Wollstonecraft's case, the implied state is led, in such works as the *Vindication of the Rights of Woman* and *Letters* from Scandinavia, by a middle-class elite of both women and men. This vanguard resembles those that Wollstonecraft encountered in Britain in the mainly Dissenting, professional intellectuals of Joseph Johnson's "academy" and in the network of Scottish and English provincial Enlightenments, and, in France, in the Girondins and the mixed expatriate circles with whom she associated from 1792 to 1795. In Shelley's fiction and travels, the vanguard is composed, in past, present, or future, of characters resembling the coterie to which Shelley herself belonged until her husband's death and less directly and continuously thereafter. In the early 1820s, as is well known, this coterie identified strongly with the liberal revolts of southern Europe as the vanguard of an actual existing state soon to be realized. These differences between Wollstonecraft and Shelley mark, however, important differences and redirections between the revolutionary subjectivities they promoted. We can adumbrate these differences a little further by looking at Wollstonecraft's and Shelley's use of settings, or particular times and places in which the revolutionary subject may be located.

There are obvious differences between Wollstonecraft's and Shelley's use of temporal settings for the excursions of their authentic revolutionary subjects. These differences mark the two writers' different situations in the changing articulations of revolutionary and post-revolutionary subjectivity. Like other English Jacobin women writers of the 1790s, in fiction or non-fiction, Wollstonecraft uses settings from contemporary life, yet historicizes them, treating the contemporary with a critique similar to that applied to past eras of "unreason" by Enlightenment "philosophical history" and such post-Revolutionary historians as Sismondi. Whereas many male writers, such as Barthélemy, Volney, and Burke, employed overt historicism, treating revolution and the Revolution as historical objects, women writers of the 1790s, such as Wollstonecraft, Helen Maria Williams, and Mary Hays, treat the contemporary with a historicist critique that has relatively little to say directly about the past of the historiographers, almost all of whom were men. By contrast, Shelley, in her earlier novels at least, deploys history and historiography (including Sismondi) extensively, yet in reference to contemporary and highly topical political events and places, which could be categorized generally as scenes of the struggle between contemporary liberalism and restorationism in Western Europe. The important point, however, is that both Wollstonecraft and Shelley fuse the personal and historical, either historicizing the present or near-present experienced by the textual persona, by the use of names, allusions, and other devices (Wollstonecraft), or personalizing the historical (Shelley), by representing history from the experience of an autobiographical yet fictitious persona.

Wollstonecraft and Shelley not only represent the condition of the oppressed exemplary subject in appropriate historical circumstances resonant for the present, however. They also emplot transformation— revolutionary and potentially revolutionizing transformation. This plot is the form of what in Wollstonecraft's time was called the political romance. It is structured as an overtly politicized romance excursion— from "home" as the site of miseducation, into a world of relative and merely social value under a vitiated and vitiating economic, social, and political order, to a closure that is not a resolution but a recognition of certain central political truths. These truths are the subject's authenticity;

the otherness of the economic, social, and political order to that authenticity; and uncertainty as to a way forward from this conflict or impasse. The vitiated regime is not just that of patriarchy, for these critiques go beyond gender critique to a consideration of the systemic injustice and oppression of which patriarchy is but a part, though a central one—the obvious examples being Wollstonecraft's *The Wrongs of Woman* and Shelley's *Valperga*.

The political romance in itself produces not so much a solution to systemic injustice as a representation of it as experienced by the individual subject, or by a small coterie of subjects. This experience, necessarily temporal, grounds the exemplary subject as a particularly "raised" consciousness produced by the temporal; thus, contemporary life is seen as historicized. For Wollstonecraft and Shelley, oppression produces, at least in superior, revolutionary vanguard subjects such as Maria Venables or Euthanasia, the recognition of oppression as systemic and not an individual "fate" or fault. The sublated or "raised" consciousness is superior to those subjects, such as George Venables or Castruccio Castracani, who are merely immersed in the vitiated regimes and the ideology (as false consciousness) which those regimes engender and on which they depend. More positively, the "raised" consciousness such as Maria Venables or Euthanasia is also the subject poised for revolutionary action.

This position could become an end in itself, however. Here is another significant difference between Wollstonecraft and Shelley, and their respective moments and uses of the autobiographical. In Wollstonecraft's texts, despite the moments of self-abjection and uncertainty, there is a strong sense that revolutionary action grounded in raised consciousness is possible and necessary for the raised consciousness, though what that action might be remains momentarily unclear without further excursion into utopian representation. Shelley's protagonists, however, seem to disappear into nature or history, remaining a potential for revolutionary transformation within the text, or literary artifact. Literature, then in process of formation as a major institution for the liberal nation-state, becomes the true or final or only home of the revolutionized subject. In Shelley the raised consciousness is also still a claim to qualification for revolutionary life and leadership of a kind. That kind could be subsumed, however, in the avant-garde, widely represented and glamorized in modern culture as Bohemianism. In the literary and cultural (and operatic) Bohemia, the citizens subsume the best of all non-Bohemian classes, with a plebeian carnivalesque lifestyle, aristocratic "liberality" of morals and mores, and middle-class beauty of soul (inherited from the culture of sensibility).

Bohemia, or the space of counterculture within the hegemonic, is the utopian romantic space, a consolation for the apparent failure and withdrawal of a revolutionized global reality, or perhaps a semi-domesticated, semi-private space in the midst of a reformable but after all irredeemably vitiated public political sphere.

I conclude that whereas Wollstonecraft exploited the poetics of sensibility to form an autobiographical Revolutionary discourse in which women, too, could participate, Shelley refashioned Revolutionary autobiographical discourse, including her mother's, to construct the exemplary subject of the future liberal state. Ironically, the liberal state declined to accommodate women, along with other subaltern groups, until forced to do so much later. As the studies referred to at the beginning of this essay indicate, part of the motive for the revival of an emancipatory autobiographical discourse in the past few decades has been to advance the claims of women and other subaltern groups to full participation in the modern liberal state. Since the cataclysmic events of 1989, this (more accommodating) state has been proclaimed as the culmination or "end" of history (Fukuyama). As we examine the use of autobiography in the past, such claims should give us pause, or at least make us wary that in such an examination we are not reinforcing and reinscribing ourselves in a modern liberal state that may have irremediable contradictions, contradictions which should be subjected to our disciplinary practice and critique, and about which Wollstonecraft and Shelley may still have lessons to teach us.

Note

1   In this essay I capitalize "Revolution" and its derivatives when referring to the French Revolution and leave the word and its derivatives uncapitalized when referring to radically transformative events or movements in general or beyond France.

The Personal Pronoun as Political:
Stylistics of Self-Reference
in the Vindications

D. L. Macdonald

In a famous letter to William Roscoe, Wollstonecraft predicts that a portrait of her that he has commissioned "will [not] be a very striking likeness." To make up for it, she promises: "I will send you a more faithful sketch—a book that I am now writing, in which *I* myself . . . shall certainly appear, head and heart" (*CLMW* 202-03). This paper is an attempt to understand that promise in as literal a sense as possible. It is a study of the ways in which *I*, *myself*, and the other forms of the first-person pronoun, appear in *A Vindication of the Rights of Woman*, the book mentioned in her letter, and in its precursor, *A Vindication of the Rights of Men*. It is a study of self-reference; that is, of the ways in which Wollstonecraft uses those pronouns to refer to herself. By her *self*, I mean only the referent of her first-person pronouns, not some pre-existent metaphysical entity (cf. Lyons 14).

I am not the first critic to take an interest in this aspect of Wollstonecraft's style. In 1823, Mary Shelley argued that "this *I*, this sensitive, imaginative, suffering, enthusiastic pronoun, spreads an inexpressible charm over Mary Wollstonecraft's Letters from Norway" ("Giovanni Villani," *NSW* 2: 130-31).[1] In the vindications,[2] however,

Notes are on pp. 41-42.

works of a very different genre and purpose, the pronoun is deployed to very different effect.

I began by noting all the occurrences of the first-person pronoun in the two vindications,[3] and, for purposes of comparison, in selected passages from Richard Price's *A Discourse on the Love of our Country*, Edmund Burke's *Reflections on the Revolution in France*, and Catharine Macaulay's *Observations on the Reflections of the Right Hon. Edmund Burke* and *Letters on Education*.[4] I began with the impression that the first-person pronoun is unusually prominent in the vindications; that they are, in this sense, unusually personal. This impression turned out to be mistaken. In the first vindication, which is 23,996 words long, forms of the first-person pronoun occur 419 times, making up 1.75 percent of the word count. In the second, which is 85,590 words long, they occur 1,197 times, for 1.40 percent. These figures actually place the vindications at the lower end of a spectrum ranging from Macaulay (1.35 percent) to Price (3.22 percent).

In analyzing Wollstonecraft's self-references, it is useful to identify the selves they refer to: to distinguish between references to the persona(e) of the vindications and those to the person of Mary Wollstonecraft, whose experiences are one of the topics of the vindications. These are both textual constructs, and it might be argued that what I call the person is simply an aspect of the persona; I would certainly not argue that the references to the person offer greater access to Wollstonecraft's historical sensibility than those to the persona. Nevertheless, the two words do provide a simple way of distinguishing between Wollstonecraft's references to herself as the writer of the vindications and her other self-references. This distinction corresponds to the distinction between "the present instance of the discourse" (Benveniste 218)—that is, the moment of writing—and its historical context. Thus, it is usually, but not always, marked by verb tense: present for the persona (e.g., "I war not with an individual when I contend for the *rights of men*" [*VRM* 35]; "I call with the firm tone of humanity; for my arguments, Sir, are dictated by a disinterested spirit—I plead for my sex—not for myself" [*VRW* 101]; "I utter my sentiments with freedom" [*VRW* 102]); past for the person (e.g., "Returning once from a despotic country to a part of England well cultivated, but not very picturesque—with what delight did I not observe the poor man's garden!" [*VRM* 93]; "I once knew a weak woman of fashion" [*VRW* 156]; "I cannot recollect without indignation, the jokes and hoiden tricks, which knots of young women indulge themselves in, when in my youth accident threw me, an awkward rustic, in their way" [*VRW* 261]). Although the distinction is usually clear, it is never incontrovertible (does the *I* in the last quotation refer to the person or the persona?): it is a matter of interpretation. Stylistics is never independent of critical judgment (Toolan 14).

Having made this distinction, the first thing I noticed is that Wollstonecraft refers to her persona much more frequently than to her person. Of the 194 direct self-references—that is, occurrences of *I* and *me*—in the first vindication, only 17, or 8.76 percent, refer to the person; the other 177, or 91.24 percent, refer to the persona. In other words, she refers to her persona about ten times as often as to her person. The second vindication is less, but still, unbalanced: of its 761 occurrences of *I* and *me*, 125, or 16.43 percent, refer to the person, and 636, or 83.57 percent (five times as many), refer to the persona.

The second thing I noticed is that the persona and the person behave differently. When, for example, an author complains that women have been rendered "objects of pity" (*VRW* 111) or "insignificant objects of desire" (113), it seems interesting to ask how often she refers to herself as an object (*me*), and how often as a subject (*I*). Both her person and her persona display a marked preference for subjecthood over objecthood, but the persona's preference is more strongly marked.[5] In the first vindication, the person of Wollstonecraft is the object of a verb or preposition only 4 times; she is the subject of a clause 14 times, or 3.50 times as often: we might say that the "subjecthood ratio" of the person in the first vindication is 3.50. The persona is an object 13 times and a subject 163 times, for a subjecthood ratio of 12.54—3.58 times greater than the person's. In the second vindication, the person is an object 15 times and a subject 110, for a subjecthood ratio of 7.33; the persona is an object 53 times and a subject 583, for a subjecthood ratio of 11.00, 1.50 times greater than the person's—a less dramatic difference than in the first vindication, but still a substantial one.

When an author complains about "passive indolent women" (*VRW* 145) and expresses a hope that they will become "active citizen[s]" (284), it seems interesting to ask how often she refers to herself as passive and how often as active.[6] As Nancy M. Henley, Michelle Miller, and Jo Anne Beazley point out, the "passive voice may be used to deprive subordinates of their agency" (63), and Wollstonecraft herself is a member of the subordinate group with which the second vindication is primarily concerned. Not surprisingly, both her person and her persona prefer to be active; otherwise, the comparison between them is more complicated than in the case of subjecthood. In the first vindication, the person is the subject of only 14 clauses, all of them active, for what we might call an "agency ratio" of infinity—an anomaly for which

I am, frankly, unable to account: the numbers may simply be too small to form a coherent pattern.[7] The persona is the subject of 9 passive and 147 active clauses, for an agency ratio of 16.33. In the second vindication, the person is the subject of 8 passive and 98 active clauses, for an agency ratio of 12.25; the persona is the subject of 35 passive and 526 active clauses, for an agency ratio of 15.03, 1.23 times greater than the person's. In both vindications, many of the references to the persona are, strictly speaking, redundant: Wollstonecraft habitually says things like "I know . . ." (*VRM* 36), "I acknowledge . . ." (37), "I grant . . ." (38), "I maintain . . ." (*VRW* 132), "I assert . . ." (135), or "I say . . ." (138), instead of simply stating what it is that she knows, acknowledges, and so on. Such expressions add little to the argument, but they do much to enhance the persona's status as an active subject (as opposed to a passive, indolent one).

Table 1
Subjecthood and Agency Ratios

	Subjecthood	Agency
VRM (person)	3.50	Infinity
VRM (persona)	12.54	16.33
VRM (overall)	10.41	17.89
VRW (person)	7.33	12.25
VRW (persona)	11.00	15.03
VRW (overall)	10.19	14.49
Price	64.00	18.67
Burke	Infinity	27.00
Macaulay	18.00	22.00

Students sometimes express surprise at the contrast between the self-confident persona of the vindications and the sometimes rather desperate Wollstonecraft of the historical record (cf. Poovey 48). Our stylistic analysis, so far, suggests a similar contrast. The persona of the vindications has a consistently higher subjecthood ratio, and, at least in the second vindication, a higher agency ratio, than the person of Wollstonecraft as portrayed in the vindications. In other words, Wollstonecraft lays claim to a greater degree of subjecthood and agency in the moment of writing than in the rest of her experience. Even so, she may only be struggling towards a degree of subjecthood and agency that her contemporaries take for granted. In my comparison passages, Richard Price has an agency ratio of 18.67; Catharine Macaulay, of 22; and Edmund Burke, of 27—the last almost twice that of the persona of the second vindication. Macaulay has a subjecthood ratio of 18; Price, of 64; and Burke, who uses *I* 32 times and *me* not once in over 4,000 words, of infinity (see Table 1). Being the mouthpiece of established power evidently has its stylistic perquisites.

Moreover, Wollstonecraft's enhancement of her subjecthood and agency comes with a price. Mary Poovey, among other critics, has complained about the "immateriality" of Wollstonecraft's style (78), the "ideal, disembodied state" to which she seems to aspire (80). Poovey attributes these tendencies to Wollstonecraft's fear of feminine sexuality. A stylistic analysis both confirms that Poovey is right about Wollstonecraft's immateriality and suggests another reason for it, or at least puts it into a new perspective.

Drawing on the work of Michael Halliday and Margaret Berry, Deirdre Burton has outlined a model for analyzing the "transitivity" of a text (199). In such an analysis, the text is divided into *material processes*, *mental processes*, and *relational processes*, or copulas ("I am a woman," to take an example from Wollstonecraft [*VRW* 110]). Material processes are subdivided into *events* (e.g., "a thaw, whilst it nourishes the soil, spreads a temporary inundation" [*VRM* 38]) and *actions*; actions are further subdivided into the *intentional* (e.g., "I went to visit a little boy at a school" [*VRW* 306]) and the *superventional* (e.g., "I blush" [*VRM* 42]). Mental processes are subdivided into the *externalized* (e.g., "I beseech you" [*VRM* 35]) and the *internalized*; internalized mental processes are further subdivided into *perceptions* (e.g., "I perceive, from the whole tenor of your Reflections, that you have a mortal antipathy to reason" [*VRM* 38]), *reactions* (e.g., "I am astonished" [*VRM* 60]), and *cognitions* (e.g., "I have been led to confine the term romantic to one definition" [*VRM* 61]).

I analyzed the transitivity of all the processes in which the person or persona of Wollstonecraft was involved, as subject or object, agent or patient, in the two vindications. For the purpose of addressing Poovey's concerns, the most important distinction is that between material and mental processes.[8] In the first vindication, Wollstonecraft refers to herself as involved in 22 material and 170 mental processes, for what we might call a "mentality ratio," or, in Poovey's pejorative terms, an "immateriality ratio" of 7.73; in the second, she refers to herself as involved in 44 material and 717 mental processes, for a mentality ratio of 16.30. Such high mentality ratios clearly prove Poovey's point about Wollstonecraft's immateriality, and the much higher mentality ratio of the second vindication, where sexuality is at issue, may tend to confirm Poovey's point about sexuality.

Wollstonecraft's mentality ratios, however, are not particularly high by the standards of late-eighteenth-century political treatises. In my comparison passages, Price's mentality ratio is 12.20, midway between that of the first and second vindications; Burke's is 31, almost twice that of the second vindication; and Macaulay's is infinity (see Table 2).

Table 2
Mentality Ratios

VRM (person)	1.83
VRM (persona)	9.94
VRM (overall)	7.73
VRW (person)	5.53
VRW (persona)	24.48
VRW (overall)	16.30
Price	12.20
Burke	31.00
Macaulay	Infinity

Moreover, the mentality ratios of the vindications are partly a consequence of the dominance of the persona—which enables the enhancement of Wollstonecraft's subjecthood and agency. The person of Wollstonecraft, in the first vindication, is involved in 6 material and 11 mental processes, for a mentality ratio of only 1.83. This still, as Poovey might point out, indicates a distinct preference for mental processes; but the persona is involved in 6 material and 59 mental processes, for a mentality ratio of 9.94, more than five times higher than that of the person. In the second vindication, the person has a mentality ratio of 5.53; the persona, one of 24.48, more than four times higher (see Table 2).

A persona, after all, is basically a mental being; she can hardly take part in a material process, except in a metaphor (e.g., "I should not have meddled with these troubled waters" [*VRM* 37]), a metonymy (e.g., "I glow with indignation" [*VRM* 38] for "I am indignant"), or a counterfactual speculation (e.g., "I should instantly dismiss [Fordyce's sermons] from my pupil's [library], if I wished to strengthen her understanding . . . . I should not allow girls to peruse them, unless I designed to hunt every spark of nature out of their composition" [*VRW* 216-17]; that is, she might do these things if she were a governess, rather than a persona). Wollstonecraft uses these rhetorical tactics frequently enough to suggest a deliberate effort to materialize her persona. Almost the only material processes the persona can literally take part in, however, are reading (*VRW* 144) and writing (*VRW* 170)—if we consider these different from, and more material than, seeing and saying.[9]

The subdivisions in the transitivity model are also of some interest. In both vindications, both person and persona favour mental over material processes; but they favour different ones. The person favours perceptions: 9 of her 11 mental processes in the first vindication, and 45 of her 105 in the second, are perceptions—more than any other kind of process. The person of Wollstonecraft, as depicted in the vindications, is above all an observer (rather than, as one might have expected, a thinker). The persona, not surprisingly, favours externalized mental processes, or utterances: 59 of her 159 mental processes in the first vindication, and 297 of her 612 in the second, are externalized—again, more than any other kind of process. The externalization of mental processes, after all, might be said to be the métier of a persona, as the forgiveness of sins is said to be that of God.

Turning to Wollstonecraft's use of plural pronouns, the first thing I noticed was how much less often she uses them than singular ones— how much more often, to put it in positive terms, she refers to herself as an isolated individual than as part of a group. In the first vindication, she uses singular forms of the first-person pronoun 239 times and plural forms 180 times, for what we might call an "isolation ratio" or "alienation ratio" of 1.38. In the second, she uses singular forms 912 times and plural forms 285 times, for an alienation ratio of 3.20, more than twice as high as that of the first. Wollstonecraft's contemporaries, in my comparison passages, all have strikingly lower alienation ratios: Burke's is 1.00; Macaulay's is 0.78; and Price's, in the cozy confines of the Old Jewry chapel, is only 0.61—less than one-fifth that of the second vindication (see Table 3).

As in the case of the singular, we can ask about the referent of the first-person pronoun plural; and as in the case of the singular, the answer is a critical judgment, not an objective determination. Once in each vindication, Wollstonecraft seems to use a kind of editorial *we*, whose referent is presumably the persona ("The tithes are safe!—We will not say for ever" [*VRM* 70]; "we may instance the example of military men" [*VRW* 131]). Almost all the other occurrences of *we* and *us* include both person and persona in their referent; most of them include both Wollstonecraft and her readers. The largest identifiable group, in fact, includes everybody. Of the 104 occurrences of *we* and *us* in the first vindication, 63 (60.58 percent) refer to humanity in general (e.g., "a present impulse pushes us forward, and when we discover that the game did not deserve the chace, we find that we have gone over much ground, and not only gained many new ideas, but a habit of thinking. The exercise of our faculties is the great end, though not the goal we had in view when we started with such eagerness" [46]; "In what respect are we superior to the brute creation, if intellect is not allowed to be the guide of passion?" [63]; "What can make us reverence ourselves, but a reverence for that Being, of whom we are a faint image?" [73]). The smallest group, comprising 14 occurrences (13.46 percent), refers to the English ("It is a well-known fact, that when *we*, the people of England, have a son whom we scarcely know what to do with—*we* make a clergyman of him" [68]; "Have we half a dozen leaders of eminence in our House of Commons, or even in the fashionable world?" [82]; "it is time we broke loose from dependance—Time that Englishmen drew water from their own springs" [97]). The third identifiable group refers to readers of the *Reflections on the Revolution in France* ("Will Mr. Burke be at the trouble to inform us, how far we are to go back to discover the rights of men . . . ?" [39]; "you tell us that you have a heart of flesh" [58]; "We must, to carry your argument a little further, return to the Spartan regulations" [81]). This is the group that most emphatically includes Wollstonecraft's readers, whom she clearly imagines as reading Burke along with her. Logically, it is (in November 1790) a subset of the English; in fact, it is a larger group, comprising 25 occurrences (24.04 percent).

Since Wollstonecraft refers to herself as belonging to a socio-political group, the English, only 14 times, and as belonging to a universal category, humanity, 63 times, or 4.5 times as often, we might say that she has a "universalism ratio" of 4.5. This pronounced tendency toward universalist humanism is what we might have expected from a writer with such a pronounced preference for the mental over the material. A comparison of the mentality ratios of the two groups, moreover, is telling. "We humans" are involved in 43 mental and 20 material processes, for a mentality ratio of 2.15; "we the people of England" are involved in only 6 mental and 8 material processes, for a mentality ratio of only 0.75. In other words, when Wollstonecraft refers to herself as part of a social and political group, she refers to herself primarily in material terms; when she refers to herself as part of a universal category, she refers to herself primarily in mental terms. ("We readers of the *Reflections*" have an even higher mentality ratio, of 7.33: this is not surprising, since they are collectively engaged in the sustained intellectual work of understanding and refuting Edmund Burke.)

Table 3
Alienation and Universalism Ratios

	Alienation	Universalism
VRM	1.38	4.5
VRW	3.20	37.33/4.48
Price	0.61	1.63
Burke	1.00	0.31
Macaulay	0.78	Infinity

The first, higher universalism ratio is obtained by dividing references to "we humans" by those to "we English"; the second (strikingly similar to that of the first vindication) by dividing references to "we humans" by those to "we women."

Universalist humanism, however, had a somewhat different political valency in the pamphlet wars of the 1790s than it does in the academy of the 1990s. Richard Price, whose *Discourse on the Love of Our Country* is really devoted to the praise of "UNIVERSAL BENEVOLENCE" (qtd. in *VRW* 358), has a universalism ratio of 1.63. Burke, who rejects the abstract rights of men for the inherited rights of Englishmen (Arendt 299), has a universalism ratio of only 0.31 (it might be better to put this in positive terms and call it a patriotism ratio of 3.25).[10] Wollstonecraft's universalism reaffirms that of Price, in response to Burke's attack on it, and in defiance of the political developments that would eventually lead to war with France (see Table 3).

In the second vindication, the pattern is in some ways similar, and in some ways even more interesting. The 200 occurrences of *we* and *us* can, once again, be divided into three main groups. Humanity in general is referred to 112 times (56 percent). Only three refer to the English. Their place is taken by another socio-political group, women, with 25 occurrences (12.5 percent); this is the least inclusive of the three groups, since Wollstonecraft points out that some of her readers are "male readers" (173). Corresponding to the readers of the *Reflections* is a somewhat less well-defined group made up of Wollstonecraft and her readers going about their intellectual work, sometimes, in the course of it, reading Burke (e.g., "Why are we to love prejudices, merely because they are prejudices?" [241]), and sometimes Rousseau (e.g., "Is this the man, who, in his ardour for virtue, would banish all the soft arts of peace, and almost carry us back to Spartan discipline?" [133]). This group comprises 57 occurrences (28.5 percent); once again, this is the most emphatically inclusive of the three groups. The relative sizes of the three groups are strikingly similar to those in the first vindication.

Table 4
Mentality, Subjecthood, and Agency Ratios
in *A Vindication of the Rights of Woman*

	Mentality	Subjecthood	Agency
We Humans	4.52	2.39	6.73
We Readers	13.5	3.38	14.33
We Women	0.93	0.67	0.67

The mentality ratios also form a pattern like that in the first vindication: "we humans" have a mentality ratio of 4.52; Wollstonecraft and her readers, of 13.5; and "we women," of only 0.93. Once again, Wollstonecraft's mentality ratio is lowest when she refers to herself as part of a socio-political group. Unexpectedly, however, the subjecthood and agency ratios form the same pattern. "We humans" have a subjecthood ratio of 2.39; Wollstonecraft and her readers, of 3.38; "we women," of only 0.67. "We humans" have an agency ratio of 6.73; Wollstonecraft and her readers, of 14.33; "we women," of only 0.67 (see Table 4).

When Wollstonecraft refers to herself as part of a group of intellectuals engaged in a common project, her subjecthood, agency, and mentality are enhanced; when she refers to herself as part of the female sex, they are diminished. When Wollstonecraft refers to herself as part of the female sex, she—and they—are objects more often than subjects, patients more often than agents, material more often than mental beings. This collective female identity is different in all three respects from her singular self, whether person or persona. The high alienation ratio of the second vindication—the excess of singular over plural self-references—may be a measure of her preference for this singular self over that collective identity. The singular self (and especially the persona of the second vindication) has, I suggest, been constructed to overcome the collective identity (cf. A. E. Smith 560).

An analysis of a writer's use of pronouns may seem trivial. After all, Wollstonecraft described herself as "employed about things, not words!" (*VRW* 112), but she was employed about words too, as in her critique of "the language of men," which "robs the whole [female] sex of its dignity" (167-68). She knew that language shapes reality. It does not, of course, do so in isolation; and no linguistic element, such as the one I have isolated for study here, does so in isolation from the rest of the linguistic system. Since, as Emile Benveniste says, "Consciousness of self is only possible if it is experienced by contrast" (224), we cannot fully understand Wollstonecraft's use of the first-person pronoun except in dialectical relation to her use of the second.[11] Nevertheless, I believe that even a limited study like this can begin to show how Wollstonecraft used the language of the vindications to shape a new reality for herself—and a new self, "the first of a new genus," for that reality (*CLMW* 164). "It is in and through language," Benveniste says, "that man constitutes himself as a *subject*" (224). I say the same of woman.

Notes

1   I owe this reference to Charles E. Robinson.

2   In order to avoid tedious questions about the italicization of possessives and plurals, I use "vindication" as a common noun, a genre term like "novel" or "tragedy."

3   I restricted myself to cases where Wollstonecraft is writing *in propria persona*, ignoring quotations (real or imaginary): see Benveniste 218.

4   These are selected, not random, samples: they are passages that I happened to have available in electronic form. They are, however, fairly substantial: 6,084 words of Price (most of the *Discourse*), 4,312 words of Burke, and a total of 5,396 words of Macaulay. In any case, I use the comparisons only for illustration: my argument is based on my study of Wollstonecraft's own texts.

5   I follow John Lyons (11) in using *subjecthood* to correspond to the grammatical sense, and *subjectivity* to correspond to the philosophical sense, of *subject*. Wollstonecraft herself never (at least, in the vindications) uses *subject* in either sense, though she does use it in the political sense (e.g., *VRM* 41, 53, 93; *VRW* 122, 198, 226).

    Compare Paula A. Treichler's observation that Edna Pontellier, the doomed protagonist of Kate Chopin's *The Awakening*, "is often . . . a grammatical object" (240). Treichler also claims that "the novel's personal pronouns are revealing: one could argue that *The Awakening* charts Edna Pontellier's growing mastery of the first person singular" (239; cf. 246, 251, 254).

6   Treichler comments on "the ongoing syntactic interplay between active and passive voice which parallels, and not infrequently undermines, the overt narrative" of *The Awakening* (239).

7   My "agency ratio" is simply the inverse of the "Passive-to-Active Ratio" used by Henley, Miller, and Beazley (68). (I did not include copular verbs in my calculation of agency ratios.)

8   Wollstonecraft hardly ever refers to herself as involved in a relational process—not at all in the first vindication and only twice in the second. While she does frequently refer to herself as the subject of *to be*, the verb almost always turns out to describe a material or mental process (cf. Poynton 72).

9   Wollstonecraft certainly did plenty of both: between 1787 and 1792 she published nine books and reviewed (if Todd and Butler are right [7: 14-18]) more than four hundred. She had some reason to refer to herself as primarily a mental being.

10   In my sample passages from Macaulay, *we* and *us* refer to an author-and-reader group, like Wollstonecraft's third group, 16 times, and to humanity 6 times. They do not refer to the English as a group at all.

11   This dialectic is particularly interesting in the first vindication, where the referent of the second-person pronoun is always (all 393 times) Edmund Burke. In "Mary Wollstonecraft as *Vir Bonus*," Gary Kelly has discussed how the rhetoric of the first vindication is developed dialectically from that of the *Reflections*; a parallel analysis could be carried out at the stylistic level.

৵

The Power of the Unnamed *You* in Mary Wollstonecraft's *Letters Written during a Short Residence in Sweden, Norway, and Denmark*

Syndy McMillen Conger

The term "life writing," inclusively defined by Marlene Kadar as "texts that are written by an author who does not continuously write about someone else, and who also does not pretend to be absent from the . . . text himself/herself" ("Coming" 10), might have been invented to talk about the texts of Mary Wollstonecraft; for Wollstonecraft's "lifelong project," according to Catherine N. Parke, was "to get herself both more into and more out of her work, which is to say, to write both more and less personally" (105).[1] From the beginning of her literary life she wove fictions into her life and her life into her fictions.[2] Her last completed book, *Letters Written during a Short Residence in Sweden, Norway, and Denmark* (1796), can be seen as the final contribution to these lifelong projects of literary confession and self-fictionalization. It shares with her other works a haunting liminal quality:[3] whatever ostensible subject it pursues, it is also always constituting or revealing the authorial subject, gesturing from the textual threshold toward some shadowy but intensely personal emotional life beyond the text. This quality is often noticed but perceived as an interruption—as "sentimental . . . wanderings" (Nyström 34), "personal reverie" (Bohls 73), or "intrusive personal voice" (Ty, "Writing" 64)—when it might be

Notes are on pp. 51-53.

rately described as the pretext for writing that frequently itself
more interesting to writer and readers than the text.

William Godwin, her husband and biographer, believed the book
had the power to inspire "a man" to fall "in love with its author" (*MAV
[1987]* 249). Robert Southey testified to a slightly different evocative
power of Wollstonecraft in *A Short Residence*: "She has made me in
love with a cold climate, and frost and snow, with a northern moon-
light" (Wardle 255-57). Perhaps more remarkable than the book's
appeal to these two contemporaries, one her husband-to-be, the other a
long-time admirer, has been its continuing capacity to wrest compliments from unlikely sources. Even some of the often dour book reviewers of Wollstonecraft's day managed to offer *A Short Residence* special
praise for its "sensibility" or its keen observations (Todd, *Mary
Wollstonecraft* 1-25). It also elicited a rare instance of warm, public
praise from Wollstonecraft's usually circumspect and silent daughter,
Mary Shelley: "this *I*, this sensitive, imaginative, suffering, enthusiastic
pronoun, spreads an inexpressible charm over Mary Wollstonecraft's
Letters from Norway."[4] Later surprising admirers include a professor of
moral philosophy in nineteenth-century Edinburgh, who was inspired
by *A Short Residence* to write a poetical tribute to Wollstonecraft, and
a twentieth-century governor of Gothenburg (Göteborg) by the name
of Per Nyström, who was so astonished by Wollstonecraft's ability
to capture "as nobody before her had done" what he believed to be
the "distinctive character" of his people and their country—"harsh
beauty . . . realism in the midst of . . . rapture"[5]—that he felt compelled to track her journey in careful detail and to research "the question of why this enigmatic Englishwoman traveled alone to Sweden in
the summer of 1795" (35). He describes his own personal reward for
his painstaking work not in terms of knowledge acquired but in terms
of acquaintance gained: she was "one of the boldest and warmest personalities of the time" (4).

Clearly, *A Short Residence* has inspired generations of readers to
become Wollstonecraft sympathizers or sleuths. Not so easy to ascer-
tain is the cause of its special evocative power. Many books written at
the same time within the same literary context of the "culture of sensibility" (Barker-Benfield's term)—a culture whose primary aims were
the expression and evocation of feeling through language, elicited no
such response. In this essay, I offer an analysis of the passages in *A
Short Residence* that make innovative use of the pronoun *you*, based on
the premise that such usage contributes to the text's remarkable liminal
quality. This humble three-letter pronoun, coupled imaginatively by
Wollstonecraft with the one-letter *I*, draws the reader into, then beyond,

the text to empathize with and wonder about the inferred author of the text, thereby destabilizing any attempt to interpret the book in purely decontextualized, structural terms.

Since this analysis attempts to connect structural features and reader responses, its conclusions must remain speculative. The act of reading is never entirely dependent upon the variously described structural invitations of a text; instead it is always potentially anarchic: "Reading . . . needs structure, it respects structure; but reading *perverts* structure. . . . [R]eading is the site where structure is made hysterical" (Barthes, "On Reading" 36, 43). Reading is especially challenged and the structure is especially endangered when texts include the pronouns *I* and *you*. They are pronouns belonging to a special group of expressions linguists have termed "deictics" or "shifters," whose "referents can only be determined" by the non-linguistic context (Ducrot and Todorov 252). Emile Benveniste goes so far as to claim that deictics have "*no linguistic existence* except in the act of speaking" (emphasis mine) and otherwise "lack material reference."[6] When deictic pronouns are added to the volatile mix of text and reader, according to Barthes, the collapse of the text's integrity can be—at least for the moment—complete: "the pronoun, which is doubtless the most dizzying of the shifters, belongs structurally (I insist) to discourse; this is, one might say, its scandal" (Barthes, "To Write" 20).

A Short Residence plunges its readers immediately into the scandal of double pronominal uncertainties. Most readers of travelogues expect to find them written in the first person; but in the case of this book, readers learn in the prefatory Advertisement that its narrator is unusually self-preoccupied. "In writing these desultory letters," the narrative voice begins, "I found I could not avoid being continually the first person—'the little hero of each tale.'" The ensuing remarks insist that this decision was in the readers' best interest, guaranteeing them a book that "flows" and has better descriptions, and a narrator who is witty and interesting and perhaps even deserving of their affection. The Advertisement concludes with the narrator asserting the right to be an "egotist": "Whether I deserve to rank amongst this privileged number, my readers alone can judge—and I give them leave to shut the book, if they do not wish to become better acquainted with me" (62). This pervasive "heroic" and self-indulgent *I* of *A Short Residence* almost certainly evoked associations among Wollstonecraft's contemporaries with Laurence Sterne's Tristram Shandy or Parson Yorick and alerted them that they should seek elsewhere if they wanted a factual chronicle of a trip through Scandinavia. At the same time, however, it identified *A Short Residence* as a sentimental journey in the manner of

Sterne's *A Sentimental Journey through France and Italy* (1768), one that could offer them insight into the complexities of the human heart.

A Short Residence, to a much greater extent than Wollstonecraft's earlier publications, is told by a personalized, embodied and engendered voice,[7] an *I* who is unmistakably identifiable as a woman traveller, a mother, and a philosophically inclined cultural observer. This *I* often turns aside from her running account of travels, business, or vignettes of herself, her infant daughter, the northern landscape, or the manners or customs of the inhabitants, to address a *you*. Already in the first letter, readers meet, but then only fleetingly, this second person—a shadowy, unidentified *you* to be reckoned with:

> Eleven days of weariness on board a vessel not intended for the accommodation of passengers have so exhausted my spirits, to say nothing of the other causes, *with which you are already sufficiently acquainted*, that it is with some difficulty I adhere to my determination of giving you my observations, as I travel through new scenes. (63; emphasis added)

The *you* addressed in these lines is one whom readers cannot elide with themselves because this *you* has prior knowledge ("sufficient acquaintance") of both a melancholy narrator and sad circumstances that they are not privy to. They must conclude that this *you* refers to someone beyond the verbal limen of the text; and they can only hope that, eventually, this *you* will constitute itself within the text. The readers eventually surmise this *you* to be the speaker's closest estranged friend or lover, but *you* remains throughout the text, diametrically unlike the speaking *I*, mysteriously absent, disembodied, unidentified, and silent. It remains a disconcerting intrusion of the discourse of narrative context—in the form of an unspecified co-reader sitting, as it were, beside the actual reader—into the discourse of the literary text itself.

In the readers' minds, unidentified textual subjects like this stimulate questions that correspond to the text's virtual dimension, the realm where unexplained elements hover, pending their explanation (Rabinowitz 133). Key among those questions in this case are inevitably "who is this *you*?" and "what does this *you* have to do with the narrator's weariness of spirit?"; these questions will rivet the reader's attention on the few insignificant details to be learned about the *you* in the course of *A Short Residence*. In this instance, however, what Wollstonecraft's text does each time the *you* is mentioned is to withhold any other information of a conclusive kind about it. Instead, the text clusters subjective impressions or expressions around the mysterious *you*, finally driving the reader from the text to Wollstonecraft's life to seek answers to key questions. The evocation of the *you* takes a number of forms: direct address (*you, my friend*), inclusive address (*we*), and indirect address in the form of imperatives or intimation. No epistolary replies of the addressee are included in the text (Ty, "Writing" 64).

Sometimes the use of the *you* or *my friend* seems perfunctory—a mere technique to sum up one subject or announce another. "I am, *my friend*," the traveller notes summarily as she nears the end of letter three, "more and more convinced that a metropolis . . . is the best calculated for the improvement of the heart, as well as the understanding" (79). "*You know*," she heads a paragraph of interjected worry about her infant daughter in letter six, "that as a female I am particularly attached to her—I feel more than a mother's fondness and anxiety, when I reflect on the dependent and oppressed state of her sex" (97; emphasis added). A list of eventualities the mother most dreads follows: that her daughter "should be forced to sacrifice her heart to her principles, or principles to her heart"; that she should suffer if she is trained to be a woman of true sensibility; that, if her mind is trained, she will be "unfit for the world." The mother's final melodramatic words call attention to themselves: "Hapless woman! what a fate is thine!" (97). Obviously, even in cases like this in which the *you* is seemingly mentioned in passing, indeed is seemingly inundated by the sentiments around it, its presence can temporarily distract readers: they might comb the context for clues about that *you* even as they find that the *you* casts new light on the context. Discussions of where to live, worries about an infant daughter's future, might well be aimed at an absent lover, readers might infer, building up evidence about the *you*'s identity. They suggest as well that the lover—who does not seem to know the traveller's wishes or fears—is not very much in tune with the mother of his child.

At other times, the traveller gives a sustained notice to her addressee which can lodge the reader's attention in implied extratextual matters. The concluding paragraph of letter six is a good case in point, with a variety of evocations of *you*. It begins by stating a sentimental assumption about the operation of "strong impressions" on memory: "imagination renders even transient sensations permanent, by fondly retracing them" (99-100). What follows is an example freighted with mystifying allusions to shared experiences the readers cannot be privy to: "I cannot, without a thrill of delight, recollect . . . looks I have felt in every nerve which I shall never more meet." After a sentence recalling the sad death of her best friend in her youth, the traveller returns to her own opaque, largely private reveries: "Fate has separated me from another, the fire of whose eyes . . . still warms my breast. . . . And, smile not, if I add, that the rosy tint of morning reminds me of a suffusion, which will never more charm my senses, unless it reappears on the cheeks of my child." The letter ends abruptly but not without one more deictic intervention: "I cannot write any more at present. Tomorrow we will talk of Tønsberg" (100). The *we*—a collective deictic pronoun—functions as a linguistic attempt to unite the separated, clearly somewhat alienated, *I* and *you* into a pair. The sentence in which it appears is at once an end (an end of the lament the preceding letter has become) and a revolutionary beginning: an announcement of a new object; a seeming new, positive tone; and a proposed, if arbitrary, new oneness of *I* and *you*.

At this point, roughly one-quarter of the way through the book, surprising as it seems, not even the gender of the *you* could be established from the text alone with any certainty. Even letter seven, over one-third of the way through the volume, only confirms earlier hints that the author is inordinately fond of the *you*. A "God bless you!" explodes into the middle of its final paragraph, which describes, then ruminates on, some embalmed corpses the narrator has just seen and finds quite revolting. Her final sentence offers a justification for this desperate non sequitur, acknowledging the narrator's affection for the mysterious *you*: "Thinking of death makes us tenderly cling to our affections—with more than usual tenderness, *I therefore assure you that I am your's* [*sic*], wishing that the temporary death of absence may not endure longer than is absolutely necessary" (109; emphasis added).

Two pages later, the traveller's state of mind becomes clearer in an often-cited passage, although the reader's image of the unidentified *you* remains blurred; the traveller is in love (if the readers infer this from her allusion to Sterne's Maria in *Sentimental Journey*) with someone she has lost:

> *You* have sometimes wondered, my dear friend, at the extreme affection of my nature—But such is the temperature of my soul—It is not the vivacity of youth, the hey-day of existence. For years have I endeavoured to calm an impetuous tide—labouring to make my feelings take an orderly course.—It was striving against the stream.—I must love and admire with warmth, or I sink into sadness. Tokens of love which I have received have rapt me in elysium—purifying the heart they enchanted.—My bosom still glows.—Do not saucily ask, repeating Sterne's question, "Maria, is it still so warm!" Sufficiently, O my God! has it been chilled by sorrow and unkindness—still nature will prevail—and if I blush at recollecting past enjoyment, it is the rosy hue of pleasure heightened by modesty; for

the blush of modesty and shame are as distinct as the emotions by
which they are produced. (111; emphasis added)

The allusion to Sterne's *Sentimental Journey* in this impassioned passage allows the readers, for the first time in their reading of *A Short
Residence,* to envision a possible proximate relationship between the
narrator and the mysterious *you,* and to draw inferences based on that
envisioning. The "dear friend" or *you* becomes Sterne's sentimental
traveller Parson Yorick, at the moment in his travels when he seeks out
a poor, crazed young woman named Maria, who is mourning the
betrayal of a lover and the loss of a father in close succession. Yorick
knows from the outset that he cannot cure her madness but, once he
finds her, he does sit down beside her to offer her his tears and his
handkerchief. What seems apparent here is the value the narrator
places on feeling and its expression; she seems to acknowledge (for
the first time, if indirectly) that she has irrevocably lost her dear friend
and to admit that she would settle for nothing more or less than his
sympathy and his proximity. This is one of the narrator's moments of
greatest pain and keenest recognition; much poignancy emerges from
her self-presentation as Maria—bereaved, mad, yet still in love—and
her presentation of her friend as "saucily" unaware of the depth of suffering she feels.

Only in the second half of the book does the shadowy outline of a
male addressee begin to come into focus from the text surrounding
instances of the pronoun *you.* A rhetorical pattern is replicated around
each mention of that *you*: the mode shifts more persistently from
descriptive or expository to sentimental or satiric. The *you* is lassoed
into the text, then the text works to please it, to elicit pity from it, to
chastise it, but also, almost always, to woo it. The readers, in this case
invited to be voyeurs, can witness these shifts but cannot understand
them in the absence of solid information about the *you*:

> I have been laughing with these simple, worthy *folk,* to give *you* one
> of my half score Danish words, and letting as much of my heart
> flow out in sympathy as they can take. *Adieu!* I must trip up the
> rocks. The rain is over. *Let me* catch pleasure on the wing—I may
> be melancholy to-morrow. Now all my nerves keep time with the
> melody of nature. Ah! let me be happy whilst I can. (128; emphasis
> added, except on "*folk*")

> How I am altered by disappointment!—When going to Lisbon, the
> elasticity of my mind was sufficient to ward off weariness, and my
> imagination still could dip her brush in the rainbow of fancy, and
> sketch futurity in glowing colours. Now—but let me talk of some-

thing else—*will you go with me to the cascade?* (151; emphasis added)

. . . men entirely devoted to commerce never acquire, or lose, all taste and greatness of mind. An ostentatious display of wealth without elegance, and a greedy enjoyment of pleasure without sentiment, embrutes them till they term all virtue, of an heroic cast, romantic attempts at something above our nature. . . . But *you* will say that I am growing bitter, perhaps, personal. Ah! shall I whisper to *you—that you—yourself*, are strangely altered, since *you* have entered deeply into commerce—*more than you are aware of—never allowing yourself to reflect*, and *keeping your mind*, or rather passions in a continual state of agitation—*Nature has given you talents*, which lie dormant, or are wasted in ignoble pursuits. (191; emphasis added)

These passages together represent a sad succession—three stages in bereavement that the narrator visits and revisits in the course of the latter half of *A Short Residence*: separation anxiety, denial of the separation, and anger about it. Ironically, perhaps, only in the angriest passage in the book—the one unique for its polemical attack on the mysterious *you* as one of the self-indulgent, commercial tribe—does that *you* begin to emerge from the extratextual shadows to assume a more active and actual role, but one ("ignoble pursuits") capable only of alienating the readers. If readers were until this moment still suspending sympathy for the narrator pending more information, chances are this passage would enlist them onto her side.

Just as only readers with hearts of stone would not by now have perfect empathy with the narrator, so also only readers completely devoid of curiosity would not now have established for themselves that the unnamed, absent "you" in these pages is in all likelihood Gilbert Imlay, father of Wollstonecraft's first daughter and a shady American profiteer, running England's embargo against France for his own advantage. Like the sympathetic early reader Godwin, they at some point abandoned any consciousness of the text as literary text; instead their reading sprang the structure to imagine the discursive context of the text and respond affectively to some portion of it. They might also have noticed in the course of their extratextual biographical excavations that the *you* passages in *A Short Residence* motivated those excavations. Although Wollstonecraft had already demonstrated awareness of the power of pronouns in her polemical period,[8] the use of the deictics in *A Short Residence* nevertheless constituted a genuine breakthrough for her. They allowed her to write something that was both a travelogue and her travel story, and to address a reader that was at once an impersonal *everyone* and a very particular, personal *someone*. They allowed her to invite every reader into the scandalously intimate proximity she shares with that *someone*. Readers, both real historical and imagined critical, respond by speculating about or identifying with the writer in her relationship to the absent, silent, and mysterious addressee. In one of his best-known short stories, "A & P," John Updike's young working-class hero, upon hearing a swimsuit-clad young rich woman speak, is imaginatively able to slide down her voice into her living room even though he has never met her before; the deictics in *A Short Residence* function in a similar way. They successfully unite readers with an imagined extratextual writer who wants protection and an imagined mysterious extratextual *you* who refuses to give it; and imagining those extratextual others aligns readers with the writer in a particularly powerful and partisan way. These readers leave Wollstonecraft's travelogue with the conviction that art and life are interwoven, and that life writing and writing are, at least in the case of Wollstonecraft and her *A Short Residence*, one and the same.

Notes

My thanks to friend and colleague Joan Livingston-Webber, whose understanding of the linguistic subtleties of the language is matched only by her skill in making them clear and fascinating to others, for introducing me originally to the concept of *deixis* when I described to her the continuing magic Wollstonecraft's *A Short Residence* works on first-time readers.

1   For a rich collection of ideas on life writing in general, see Kadar's *Essays*.

2   This is one of the premises of Conger, *Mary Wollstonecraft*. See especially the preface (xxix-xlix) and Chapter 1, "Epistolary Revelations" (5-34).

3   I am much indebted to the members of the English 515 Age of Revolution class of the spring semester 1998; their desire to understand eighteenth-century life writers as thoroughly as possible inspired me to think again about ways of presenting Wollstonecraft's *A Short Residence*. Out of one evening's session came a general concurrence among us not only that there was a liminal quality about the text, but that there actually

seemed to be in this remarkable document a spectral *liminal self* operating on its own premises, agenda, ideas, and associations — sometimes in contradiction to the ideas espoused in the actual text.

4   Mary Shelley's comment is a passing one in "Giovanni Villani," an essay she wrote for *The Liberal* 4 (1823): 281-97. It is cited from *NSW* 2: 130-31.

5   Bohls's Chapter 5, "Mary Wollstonecraft's Anti-aesthetics," 140-69, also discovers realism in Wollstonecraft's feminist resistance.

6   "This sign is . . . linked to the *exercise* of language. . . . It . . . establishes the basis for individual discourse, in which each speaker takes over all the resources of language for his own behalf. . . . Thus the indicators *I* and *you* cannot exist as potentialities; they exist only insofar as they are actualized . . . [and] their role is to provide the instrument of conversion that one could call the conversion of language into discourse" (Benveniste 218, 220). Benveniste offers contingent definitions of *I* and *you*: *I* is "the individual who utters the present instance of discourse containing the linguistic instance *I*"; *you* is "the individual spoken to in the present instance of discourse containing the linguistic instance *you*" (218). Compare Charles Fillmore's *Santa Cruz Lectures on Deixis 1971*: "I said in the first lecture that one of my goals in these talks was to become clear about the ways in which the grammars of natural languages reflect what Rommetveit calls the 'deictic anchorage' of sentences — an understanding of the roles sentences can serve in social situations occurring in space and time. Frequently, as I tried to show in that lecture, a sentence can only be fully interpreted if we know something about the situation in which it has been used" (16).

7   For insightful descriptions of Wollstonecraft's persona, see Jeanne Moskal, "Picturesque," and Eleanor Ty, "Writing."

8   From the beginning of her writing career, Wollstonecraft relied upon the bold, first-person, direct address of readers. Her earlier narrative or expository *I*'s, however, remained disembodied, generic voices (the intelligent yet sentimental heroine, the angry social reformer, the magisterial pedagogue or editor), and the *you*'s she addressed in her early works were either nameless groups (teachers, pupils, kings, men, women) or named, usually prominent, individuals (M. Talleyrand, Jean-Jacques Rousseau, or Edmund Burke). Two existing studies of Wollstonecraft's pronoun usage in *A Vindication of the Rights of Woman* certain-

ly reveal on her part an early sophisticated consciousness of them and their power to guide reader response: see Janet Todd, "Language," and Amy Elizabeth Smith, "Roles."

Reveries of Reality:
Mary Wollstonecraft's
Poetics of Sensibility

Lawrence R. Kennard

In a well-known passage in the introduction to *A Vindication of the Rights of Woman*, Mary Wollstonecraft speaks out against the gendering of language. "I shall disdain to cull my phrases or polish my style," she announces; "I shall try to avoid that flowery diction which has slided [*sic*] from essays into novels." Renouncing the language of feminized politeness, she will "be employed about things, not words" (112). As we know, Wollstonecraft protests too much; she is indeed employed about words, as the rhetorical strategies of *The Rights of Woman* demonstrate.[1] But the statements about language are useful, because they show how, in writing a work that opposes one kind of gender ideology, she is aware that language is part of the problem; the writer who challenges a dominant ideology must, somehow, find literary forms that are appropriate to the task.

By examining her attempt to renegotiate the poetics of sensibility, I will focus on one way in which Wollstonecraft tries to find new forms. In doing this I will initially consider her late essay "On Poetry" (1797), setting it in the context of two prior works, *A Vindication of the Rights of Woman* (1792) and her epistolary travel journal, *Letters Written during a Short Residence in Sweden, Norway, and Denmark* (1796).

Notes are on pp. 67-68.

Through detailed examination of extracts from the Scandinavian *Letters,* I will show how Wollstonecraft, in the "poetical reverie," finds one solution to the problem of ideological form. The poetical reverie is a sub-genre that, set within a work of autobiography or life writing, mediates the relationship between self and world.

The essay "On Poetry, and Our Relish for the Beauties of Nature" recommends a shift in poetic practice. The shift has two key features: first, the new poetry must combine sensibility and understanding; second, it must undergo a primitivist linguistic turn, renouncing the artificiality of a poetic diction that imitates words and phrases rather than nature itself. Neither of these two features is really new; William Wordsworth's emphasis on both, in the Preface to *Lyrical Ballads* (1800), seems less like evidence of Wollstonecraft's influence on Wordsworth (although that is possible) than of the prevalence of these ideas at the time.[2] What is indeed new in Wollstonecraft's poetics is the egalitarian and feminist tenor of her remarks on education, which I discuss later.

After noting in her essay that "few people seem to contemplate nature with their own eyes" (7), Wollstonecraft proceeds to emphasize the key points that I have mentioned:

> Having frequently had occasion to make the same observation, I was led to endeavour, in one of my solitary rambles, to trace the cause, and likewise to enquire why the poetry written in the infancy of society, is most natural: which, strictly speaking (for *natural* is a very indefinite expression) is merely to say, that it is the transcript of immediate sensations, in all their native wildness and simplicity, when fancy, awakened by the sight of interesting objects, was most actively at work. At such moments, sensibility quickly furnishes similes, and the sublimated spirits combine images, which rising spontaneously, it is not necessary coldly to ransack the understanding or memory, till the laborious efforts of judgment exclude present sensations, and damp the fire of enthusiasm.
>
> The effusions of a vigorous mind, will ever tell us how far the understanding has been enlarged by thought, and stored with knowledge. The richness of the soil even appears on the surface; and the result of profound thinking, often mixing, with playful grace, in the reveries of the poet, smoothly incorporates with the ebullitions of animal spirits, when the finely fashioned nerve vibrates acutely with rapture, or when, relaxed by soft melancholy, a pleasing languor prompts the long-drawn sigh, and feeds the slowly falling tear. (7)

Against a poetry in which understanding follows—and in doing so largely excludes—sensation, Wollstonecraft wants one of immediate sensation and sensibility, a poetry in which sensibility incorporates prior thought spontaneously. Understanding is now to feed feeling, rather than the reverse. The metaphors of surface and depth suggest a topographical, conscious/unconscious, model of the mind, and the notion of "spirits" rising to combine images may seem to anticipate the Freudian concept of condensation. These notions probably derive, however, from eighteenth-century associationism, and are echoed by David Hartley's proposal in his *Observations on Man* (1749) that ideas and images "rise" to "hang together" and "coalesce" in dreams (385-86).[3] Reverie is the preferred mode of composition because of its associative or combining power. With this in mind we might note that the long sentence that concludes the extract is performative: it exemplifies, as if in reverie itself, the very combination or incorporation of thought and feeling that it recommends as it moves sequentially from metaphorical description of "profound thinking" to rhetorically charged allusion to the long-drawn sigh and "slowly falling tear" as accompaniments of emotion.

The poet, Wollstonecraft notes later, "gives us only an image of his mind, when he was . . . marking the impression which nature has made on his own heart." But, at the same time, in further subliminal condensation, "the idea of some departed friend . . . intrude[s] unawares into his thoughts." The result is "artlessly, yet poetically expressed"—and, Wollstonecraft adds, "who can avoid sympathizing?" (8). Sympathies of sensation, thought, and feeling are propagated outwards and carried over to the reader. The recommended partnership between understanding and sensibility echoes back to *The Rights of Woman*. There, Wollstonecraft had already praised Catharine Macaulay's educational writings, which combine judgment and understanding with "sympathy and benevolence." In Macaulay's style of writing, Wollstonecraft argues, "no sex appears, for it is like the sense it conveys, strong and clear." She continues:

> I will not call hers a masculine understanding, . . . but I contend that it was a sound one, and that her judgment, the matured fruit of profound thinking, was a proof that a woman can acquire judgment, in the full extent of the word. Possessing more penetration than sagacity, more understanding than fancy, she writes with sober energy and argumentative closeness; yet sympathy and benevolence give an interest to her sentiments, and that vital heat to arguments, which forces the reader to weigh them. (231)

Through her combination of stylistic elements which might conventionally be gendered masculine and feminine, Macaulay has, in other

words, found a form that moves beyond gendered ideology. By implication, Wollstonecraft can do the same. Indeed, as her varied rhetorical strategies suggest, she may already be doing so in *The Rights of
Woman*.[4]

In "On Poetry," Wollstonecraft turns specifically to language, presenting a "paradoxical" observation. In modern poetry, the understanding, using artificial language, has almost extinguished the essential
"blaze" of poetic sensibility; her poetics, however, would employ the
understanding for beneficial purposes, allowing it to direct sensibility
so as to "discriminate things" just as the "first observers of nature, the
true poets," had done (9). In making her linguistic turn, Wollstonecraft
favours an egalitarian poetics. The education received by upper- and
middle-class boys positively hinders attempts to find a discriminating
poetic language: "[b]oys who have received a classical education, load
their memory with words, and the correspondent ideas are perhaps
never distinctly comprehended" (9). The new poetics will, implicitly,
be available to all classes, and both genders. The argument, with its
particular reference to "things" (rather than words), echoes back to the
Introduction to *The Rights of Woman* and Wollstonecraft's intention,
discussed above, to be "employed about things, not words." In both
cases, Wollstonecraft wants to find a "natural" language that can take
her beyond, or through, the artifices and conventions, or fixed stereo-
types, of ideology.

Nature and *natural* are key terms in both "On Poetry" and *The
Rights of Woman*. "[N]atural is a very indefinite expression,"
Wollstonecraft notes in the former (7). For her, "natural" poetry is "the
transcript of immediate sensations"—the emphasis being on immediacy and fidelity. The transcript is not, we note, of "things" or "nature"
themselves, but of sensations. Mediating between the subject and the
external world, they may be as close as we can get to reality. In *The
Rights of Woman* Wollstonecraft also questions the nature of nature.
Highlighting the word through italic emphasis, she intimates that, in the
mystifying ideology of Rousseau and others, cultural or gendered
forms mask themselves as "natural" ones (155, 178, 223).

In "On Poetry," natural poetry is the product of "fancy." Generated
through "the reveries of the poet" (7), it is a dreamlike form that com-
municates itself as in a dream—if communication fails through the use
of unnatural language, then "the dream is over," Wollstonecraft says
(9). It might seem to be another paradox that dreams, so frequently a
metaphor for illusions, can give direct access to nature; but then, as
David Hartley emphasized earlier in his *Observations on Man* (387),
dreams are not experienced primarily as language, but as sensation.[5]

We can trace a changing metaphorics of dreams in *The Rights of Woman*. There, Wollstonecraft initially characterizes the illusions of ideology as dreams, reveries, or fancies. Linking reverie with sensibility, she finds that prejudices "give a sex to virtue, and confound simple truths with sensual reveries" (113). Later on, she castigates Rousseau's ideas as "reveries of fancy" (213), and notes that "reveries of the stupid novelists" distort the truth and promote sentimentality (330). Yet, if truth is distorted in dreams, dreams may also take us back to truth. This is indeed Wollstonecraft's own chiasmic path; her arguments in *The Rights of Woman*, she notes reflexively, may be termed "Utopian dreams" (147)—illusions possibly, but also visions of a truer, less ideologically infected reality.

How can the new poetics work in practice? How can the poet—or more properly, in this instance, the poetically inclined prose writer— combine the aims I have mentioned? How (to summarize these aims) can she use the language of dreams, "the transcript of immediate sensations," to unite thought and feeling, while also finding a form that will resist ideological appropriation? To attempt to answer these questions, I turn to Wollstonecraft's travel journal, *Letters Written during a Short Residence in Sweden, Norway, and Denmark*.

The poetic bearings of the letters from Scandinavia are self-acknowledged. In the sixteenth letter, Wollstonecraft reflects on her own meditations: "I forgot that the night stole on, whilst indulging affectionate reveries, the poetical fictions of sensibility" (154). Among the varied contents of the *Letters*—descriptions of towns and country-side, of people and their homes; social and economic facts; political observations; anecdotes and conversational reportage; and frequent references to her own situation, that of a single mother travelling abroad on business—we find the poetical reveries. They are not foregrounded or marked out by indentation, metrical regularity, or rhyme, nor by any of the other clear generic signals that, almost definitively, announce the onset of poetry. Rather, they are almost camouflaged through seamless inclusion within an apparently artless, desultory text. Often, the reveries are meditative night-thoughts or evening-thoughts. They embody the program of Wollstonecraft's essay by recording sensations, while reflecting internal thoughts or emotions. They are written, significantly, in a "poetic" prose that is modulated by heavy use of alliteration, assonance, and consonance. These latter features identify the poetical qualities of the meditations; they answer quite precisely to Roman Jakobson's well-known formalist definition of the poetic function, which "projects the principle of equivalence from the axis of selection onto the axis of combination" (27). They also duplicate what Northrop

Frye identifies as the particular form of the poetry of sensibility, its predilection for "assonances, alliterations, inter-rhymings and echolalia" (147). In Frye's account, these features result from an emphasis on compositional process rather than communicated product:

> In the composing of poetry, where rhyme is as important as reason, there is a primary stage in which words are linked by sound rather than sense. From the point of view of sense this stage is merely free or uncontrolled association, and in the way it operates it is very much like the dream. . . . Where the emphasis is on the communicated product, the qualities of consciousness take the lead. . . . Where the emphasis is on the original process, the qualities of subconscious association take the lead, and the poetry becomes hypnotically repetitive, oracular, incantatory, dreamlike and in the original sense of the word charming. (147-48)

Quite appropriately, Wollstonecraft's poetical reveries share some of these dreamlike linguistic properties, signalling a writing-in-process while also confirming their allegiance to the literature of sensibility.

But reverie also has a wider significance in the literature of the time. Foregrounded by writers such as Rousseau, it is a meditative discourse that, conceived in solitude, turns inward to the self. It is in reverie, Rousseau states in his late work, *The Reveries of the Solitary Walker*, that he may finally confront the mystery of self-identity, the problem of "[W]hat am I?" (1).[6] But the dichotomy of process and product that Frye highlights confounds any easy solution to the problem, since the self that is sought, a being or product, is also, necessarily, a becoming-self, a self-in-process, an existential self that denies essence. In short, the reverie is a sub-genre that, as a form of meditative life-writing, questions subjectivity. And a writing-in-process, to put it another way, may well point to, and help to shape, a writer-in-process.

Let me give some examples of the sub-genre, from the Scandinavian *Letters*. In the first letter, Wollstonecraft begins by contemplating external nature, and then turns inward:

> Nothing, in fact, can equal the beauty of the northern summer's evening and night; if night it may be called that only wants the glare of day, the full light, which frequently seems so impertinent; for I could write at midnight very well without a candle. I contemplated all nature at rest; the rocks, even grown darker in their appearance, looked as if they partook of the general repose, and reclined more heavily on their foundation.—What, I exclaimed, is this active principle which keeps me still awake?—Why fly my thoughts abroad

when every thing around me appears at home? My child was sleeping with equal calmness—innocent and sweet as the closing flowers.—Some recollections, attached to the idea of home, mingled
with reflections respecting the state of society I had been contemplating that evening, made a tear drop on the rosy cheek I had just
kissed; and emotions that trembled on the brink of extacy and agony
gave a poignancy to my sensations, which made me feel more alive
than usual.

What are these imperious sympathies? How frequently has melancholy and even mysanthropy taken possession of me, when the
world has disgusted me, and friends have proved unkind. I have then
considered myself as a particle broken off from the grand mass of
mankind;—I was alone, till some involuntary sympathetic emotion,
like the attraction of adhesion, made me feel that I was still a part of
a mighty whole, from which I could not sever myself. (69-70)

In the second paragraph Wollstonecraft questions the involuntary
nature of the emotional sympathies, as she calls them, expressed in the
first paragraph. But the writing is sympathetic in a second sense, in that
it conveys emotions in phonically sympathetic language, a language
that exploits associative or symphonic patterns of sound, poetically
projecting equivalence or resemblance along the narrative axis. The
resemblances are felt poetically, rather than being apprehended pro-
saically. Consider the sequence: "rocks," "repose," "reclined," "closing," "flowers," "recollections," "reflections"; we feel, or indirectly
grasp, as it were, the bond between the external world and the author,
as we ride the dreamlike train of resemblance—"And who can avoid
sympathizing"? In the essay "On Poetry" (presumably written shortly
after the Scandinavian *Letters*, judging by the dates of publication),
Wollstonecraft notes that in poetical reverie, recollections may blend
"unawares" with externally prompted sensations (8). Since the very
same conjuncture occurs in the quoted passage, it seems probable that
the experiences recorded in the *Letters* had a role in shaping the poetics of the essay and its insistence that poetry may "incorporate" or con-
dense sensation, thought, and feeling.

In a second passage, Wollstonecraft reflects upon reverie itself:

But I have rambled away again. I intended to have remarked to you
the effect produced by a grove of towering beech. The airy lightness
of their foliage admitting a degree of sunshine, which, giving a
transparency to the leaves, exhibited an appearance of freshness and
elegance that I had never before remarked, I thought of descriptions
of Italian scenery. But these evanescent graces seemed the effect of
enchantment; and I imperceptibly breathed softly, lest I should

> destroy what was real, yet looked so like the creation of fancy.
> Dryden's fable of the flower and the leaf was not a more poetical
> reverie. (*LWSR* 123)

In a passage that plays with sympathetic effect upon the letters *e* and *f*,
Wollstonecraft blends sensation and thought so that thought, almost
turning against itself, gives preference to sensation. Dryden's allegory
The Flower and the Leaf (1700) contrasts the flower, the emblem of
"loose Delights," unfavourably with the laurel leaf, the "Sign of Labour
crown'd" (Dryden 1664-65). The leaf "suffers no decay," while the
flower soon fades and dies. But now allegory turns to reverie itself, and
to its incorporation of the contrast between sensation and thought, or, in
Frye's scheme, process and product. Wollstonecraft prefers sensation
because it is "real," although it seems to be imaginary, a fleeting
enchantment of fancy. Does the lasting leaf of fully conscious, conceptual thought, then, suppress reality itself much as, in the essay "On
Poetry," the "laborious efforts of judgment" may work to "exclude present sensations" (7)? Once again we can see that Wollstonecraft in the
Letters anticipates her later essay, and that the notion that a poetry of
reverie might provide an effective means of discriminating reality both
develops from and informs the reveries of that book.

In the *Letters,* Wollstonecraft links observation and judgment as
she uses her sympathetic poetics to probe the social scale, playing on
the letters *c* and *p*:

> We glided along the meadows, and through the woods, with sun-
> beams playing around us; and though no castles adorned the
> prospects, a greater number of comfortable farms met my eyes, dur-
> ing this ride, than I have ever seen, in the same space, even in the
> most cultivated part of England. And the very appearance of the cot-
> tages of the labourers, sprinkled amidst them, excluded all those
> gloomy ideas inspired by the contemplation of poverty. (138)

Four pairs—"*c*astles" and "*p*rospects," the "*c*ultivated *p*art of England,"
the "*app*earance of the *c*ottages," and "the *c*ontemplation of *p*overty"—
form a sequence of resemblance that moves down the social scale. In
Scandinavian society there is a sympathy or social bonding between
classes, while in England, Wollstonecraft hints, the prospect of castles
clashes very unsympathetically with the contemplation of poverty. The
language of dreams questions social inequality through ironically foregrounding resemblance. I include this example both to stress how
Wollstonecraft can use her poetics for radical political comment and also
to show how, generically, the poetics spills out beyond the strict limits of
reverie (as meditative, reflexive, evening- or night-thoughts) itself.

In a further example, Wollstonecraft again combines, or moves between, external sensation and internally prompted thought:

> I have often mentioned the grandeur, but I feel myself unequal to the task of conveying an idea of the beauty and elegance of the scene when the spiral tops of the pines are loaded with ripening seed, and the sun gives a glow to their light green tinge, which is changing into purple, one tree more or less advanced, contrasting with another. The profusion with which nature has decked them, with pendant honours, prevents all surprise at seeing, in every crevice, some sapling struggling for existence. Vast masses of stone are thus encircled; and roots, torn up by the storms, become a shelter for a young generation. The pine and fir woods, left entirely to nature, display an endless variety; and the paths in the wood are not entangled with fallen leaves, which are only interesting whilst they are fluttering between life and death. The grey cobweb-like appearance of the aged pines is a much finer image of decay; the fibres whitening as they lose their moisture, imprisoned life seems to be stealing away. I cannot tell why—but death, under every form, appears to me like something getting free—to expand in I know not what element; nay I feel that this conscious being must be as unfettered, have the wings of thought, before it can be happy. (152)

The most striking poetical or linguistic feature of this frequently quoted passage is, surely, its sympathetic deployment of the letters *p* and *s*. Consider the sequence beginning with "the spiral tops of the pines" and running through "ripening seed," "purple," "profusion," "pendant," "prevents," "surprise," "sapling," "pine," "display," "paths" "appearance," and "pines" to the thought of "imprisoned life." Repeated alliteration and consonance help to blend, or smoothly incorporate, external observation with the internal meditation that it prompts and images. And, in further acts of antithetical incorporation, the passage fuses life and death, continuity and conclusion. The pines are living, yet in decay; they suggest life "stealing away" while, in sympathetic reversal, "death . . . appears to me like something getting free." "[I]mprisoned" harks back to "pines" phonetically, while it also encloses it anagrammatically as a form of life-in-death, or the external internalized, living openness as closure, the world as prison or (to stress the revolutionary context) Bastille. And while the pines are plainly trees, a plural noun, they also conceal—and reveal, as a subliminal afterthought or second intention—their other, verbal existence that yearns, or wastes away, and hints at the yearning, wasting subject.[7] But verb and noun suggest process and product, or Dryden's flower and leaf, in further intertextual sympathy. Then again, if "pines" has punning second thoughts, what of "spiral"? Ostensibly it might mean "spire-shaped." But not far below this we sense the presence of "coiled" or (etymologically) "breathing," so that the pines present an image that condenses living aspiration and dying expiration. And, to focus the investigation even more narrowly, we might consider the phonetic properties of the letters *s* and *p*. As sibilant and stop, do they not already suggest, on the one hand, the slippery continuity of process and, on the other hand, stasis, or the more precise and palpable outline of the object or product? As a result the *sp . . . ps* sequence in "spiral tops" not only imitates the reversed symmetry of the "spiral" profile of the pine-tops, but also intimates onomatopoeically (as stopped aspirate and aspirated stop) the very interpenetration of process and cessation, or life and death, that the larger passage converges upon.

I have included the somewhat detailed analysis of the last paragraph with two aims in mind. First, for those who need convincing, such an analysis demonstrates what ought to be obvious—that Wollstonecraft's poetical reveries are indeed poetical, in a rigorously technical as well as in a metaphorical sense. Second, her reveries may be characterized as highly condensed, in either the Freudian or the Hartleian sense. Moreover, the phonetic properties of the reveries are by no means mere poetic veneers on what are essentially prose compositions. Rather, as the last example may help to confirm, they function as full working parts of the reveries, assisting in the process of condensation that, ideally, incorporates sensation with feeling and thought in the manner recommended in the essay "On Poetry." (For a further demonstration of the way that alliteration and consonance act to ease the passage between thought and emotion, the reader might look back at the final sentence of the long extract from "On Poetry," and examine its reverie-like inclusion of consonantal play).

In its most typical form, the reverie, Wollstonecraft's renegotiated poetics of sensibility becomes liminal, intermediate, and transitional, a poetics of evening or dawn, halfway between the worlds of light and dark, outside and inside, reason and passion, things and processes, the material and the immaterial, conscious volition and unconscious association, poetry and prose. To this list I should add the key antithesis of subject and object. In moving, as they often do, between external observation and internal reflection, Wollstonecraft's poetical reveries also move between two aims that seem to be quite at odds with each other. As a mediating, subjective/objective discourse, the reverie might satisfy her aim, expressed in the essay "On Poetry," of discriminating "things"; at the same time, turning to the subject, it helps to discriminate the self, addressing Rousseau's "What am I?" Perhaps, indeed, the message is that we discriminate things through the self, and the self through external observation, so that the written world can never be totally isolated from the writing subject, and vice versa. Mitzi Myers urges us to consider the *Letters* as a whole:

> [m]oments of spiritual autobiography subside into objective travelogue with no transition—a method that implies I am this, but also simultaneously this. There are no separations . . . personal and social themes, rational assessments and emotional epiphanies, flow into one another joined by a use of an associationism quite subtle and sophisticated. ("Mary Wollstonecraft's *Letters*" 181)

In contemporary theoretical terms, the subjective/objective emphasis then parallels the shift from a narrower focus on "autobiography" to the broader scope of a "life writing" that blurs the conventional boundaries of genre.[8] As recent commentators have emphasized, blurred boundaries both reflect and help to constitute a self that is less autonomous and unified, and more relational and contextual, than the one that conventional autobiography usually projects.

Wollstonecraft's poetical reveries blur boundaries, I suggest, at three different levels. First, they blur the apparent autonomy of individual words through the sympathetic play of resemblance along the horizontal or sequential axis. In this way they become, transgressively, a poetic prose, a blend of two genres or kinds usually regarded as quite distinct. (Poetic prose is transgressively "unnatural," in that it violates what Clara Reeve, writing in 1785, had called "the barrier, which nature has placed, between poetry and prose" (2: 67): linguistic hybridity or miscegenation seems to offend against ancient, deep-rooted taboos).[9] Second, condensation blurs the shifts between different discursive or intentional modes (between description, meditation, and emotive expression, for example) within the reverie. These two features, verbal sympathy and condensation, combine to give Wollstonecraft's prose in the reveries a distinctive fluid power. Third, the transitions in Wollstonecraft's prose blur the edges of the sub-genre itself; what precisely defines the reverie, and where are its limits in the Scandinavian *Letters*? Let me be clear that I do not regard blurred boundaries as being synonymous with a narrative continuity that implies a self in "pure"—that is, smooth and integrated—development; that would, surely, be little different from the smooth unity of standard, traditional autobiography, and the seamless self-continuity that such narrative integrity must then imply. On the contrary, Wollstonecraft's blurred boundaries and discursive overlaps are generally, and pervasively, accompanied by a variety of abrupt shifts, gaps, and reversals in tone, mode, or sub-genre. Thus, Wollstonecraft can veer suddenly "from romantic flights in one sentence to coffee and milk in the next" (Myers, "Mary Wollstonecraft's *Letters*" 180-81), or from "the loveliest banks of wild flowers" to the smell of "putrifying herrings" within the same sentence (*LWSR* 87). Shifts in tone and topic between adjacent paragraphs are, as one might expect, frequently abrupt and sudden in the *Letters*. Such discontinuities are indeed allowed and encouraged by the very informal protocols governing Wollstonecraft's chosen generic vehicle, the epistolary travel journal.

The blurred edges of linguistic form register, and help to shape, a self-in-process that is also a discontinuous, heterogeneous self. A poetics of process, or discontinuous process, questions the reality of the fixed stereotype or inflexible abstraction, just as it questions the truth of a world that, relying on judgment rather than sensation, seems to be constructed in terms of exclusive binary oppositions (life versus death, poetry versus prose, subjective versus objective, woman versus man, and so on). Against such a hardened, stereotyped construction of reality, I argue that Wollstonecraft's poetics of sensibility, which is also a poetics of reverie, shapes a discontinuous reality-in-process, a reality centred on the momentary flux of being-in-the-world. I conclude that in reverie, a prose-poetical kind of life writing, Wollstonecraft finds an exemplary counter-ideological form. Twentieth-century theorists such as Louis Althusser emphasize that ideology helps to construct both social reality and the subject, while they also stress the key role that language plays in ideological interpellation.[10] Clearly, Wollstonecraft is aware of all three dimensions of ideology, and of the fact that they cannot really be separated. Her poetics of sensibility and her poetical reveries represent attempts to reconstruct both self and reality, or self/reality, in counter-ideological language. I can argue, then, that in the sub-genre of reverie, an informal form of life writing, Wollstonecraft resolves the problem of language that she had raised in the introduction to her second vindication. For Marlene Kadar, life writing moves "from Genre to Critical Practice." Surely this is true of Wollstonecraft's reveries, which offer a critique, not simply of generic conventions but also of ideological binarism and the stereotyped subject. Doubtless the subject is never beyond ideology. But if literary form helps to form the self, the reveries essay self-liberation, a "getting free" from all kinds of ideological incarceration.

———

Notes

1   For discussion of the gendered double-bind, or sense/sensibility trap, that Wollstonecraft alludes to, see Jacobus 27-34. For reference to Wollstonecraft's varied rhetorical and stylistic strategies in the second vindication see Kelly, *Revolutionary Feminism* 108-11.

2   The primitivist linguistic turn that Wollstonecraft recommends echoes the arguments of Hugh Blair's *Lectures on Rhetoric* (1785), which Wollstonecraft had read in 1787. See Blair 99 and *CLMW* 138. As W. J. B. Owen points out in his edition of William Wordsworth's Preface to *Lyrical Ballads* (193), Blair echoes many other eighteenth-century theorists. Owen traces Wordsworth's emphasis on the union of thought and feeling back to John Dennis's early-eighteenth-century writings (Wordsworth 164-65). S. T. Coleridge also claimed to have made the same emphasis in the 1790s (Coleridge, vol. 1, 25, 80). And Wollstonecraft herself repeatedly stresses in her second *Vindication* the importance of "enlarging" or "expanding" the heart through understanding (*VRW* 205, 258, 308, 336, 340).

Gary Kelly notes that "On Poetry" "anticipates the preface to *Lyrical Ballads*" (*Revolutionary Feminism* 203). The possibility that the essay may have influenced the preface is suggested by their common emphasis on poetic spontaneity, fidelity to nature, simple diction, and the combination of understanding and feeling.

3   The quoted passage from "On Poetry" should be compared both with Hartley on dreams (*Observations* 383-89) and with Wollstonecraft's own assent to the doctrines of associationism in the second vindication. There she explains how association, activated by "animal spirits, . . . the essence of genius," can work with great rapidity to "concentrate pictures" (*VRW* 244-45). "Animal spirits" also feature in Hartley's materialist associationism as a "glandular secretion, called nervous Fluid" (Hartley 18), and as "a very subtle active Fluid in the Brain," attributed to the doctrines of Boerhaave (20-21). The phrases quoted from Hartley, together with the examples that he gives, suggest that his notion of coalescence in dreams anticipates Freudian condensation. Both are combinatory modes that rely upon association.

4   See the reference to Gary Kelly's discussion of Wollstonecraft's rhetorical strategies in note 1, and see also Syndy Conger ("Sentimental Logic") on Wollstonecraft's "sentimental" prose.

5   "Dreams consist chiefly in visible Imagery," Hartley notes (387); he also stresses the realism of the dream experience, in

which we "suppose ourselves present, and actually seeing and hearing what passes" (384).

6   Looking to find, through solitary meditation, respite from the "torment" of society, Rousseau questions his own being in the late essays that make up the *Reveries of the Solitary Walker* (1776): "But I, detached from them [his tormentors] and from everything, what am I? That is what remains for me to seek" (1). That Wollstonecraft had at least some general familiarity with Rousseau's *Reveries* is suggested by her teasing William Godwin, in a letter written during their courtship in 1796, with the thought that she might "become again a Solitary Walker" (Godwin and Wollstonecraft 15). Like Wollstonecraft in her Scandinavian *Letters*, Rousseau tropes reverie as walking or wandering; the pedestrian topos is, of course, common in essayistic writing at the time.

7   Yearning is a form of desire, traditionally troped by dream. Hence this and other reveries support Eleanor Ty's arguments (in this volume) concerning desire in the Scandinavian *Letters*.

8   In Marlene Kadar's definition, "life writing comprises texts that are written by an author who does not continuously write about someone else, and who also does not pretend to be absent from the . . . text himself/herself" ("Coming" 10). Such texts frequently transgress antithetically constituted boundaries such as that between "fiction" and "non-fiction" or, as in Wollstonecraft's letters, that between the personal letter and a travel record intended for a wider public audience. The concept is discussed further in the articles by Kadar and Helen M. Buss in Kadar, ed., *Essays in Life Writing*. For contemporary representations of the (female) subject, see the seventh chapter of Anne K. Mellor's *Romanticism and Gender*.

9   Writing on *Fingal* in *The Progress of Romance*, Reeve's spokesperson Euphrasia observes that Macpherson's epic "is neither prose nor verse,—this sort of writing corrupts and spoils our language" (2: 67). Euphrasia, ever anxious to distinguish and categorize, also disapproves of "mixed characters" (1: 139).

10   See Althusser's classic essay "Ideology and Ideological State Apparatuses," and, for a wider view, Catherine Belsey's discussion of ideology, language, and the subject in *Critical Practice* (56-84).

რ

"The History of My Own Heart": Inscribing Self, Inscribing Desire in Wollstonecraft's *Letters from Norway*

Eleanor Ty

Letters Written during a Short Residence in Sweden, Norway, and Denmark (1796) signals a turning point in Mary Wollstonecraft's career. In this book, Wollstonecraft develops a voice and style different from those of her juvenile fiction and her polemical essays. More than she was able to do before, she integrates her public and private selves, writing a narrative that incorporates observations about the culture of Scandinavia, about its landscape, about nature, about the joys and pains she encounters during her journey, through the genre of a travel book in the form of letters. Mitzi Myers has remarked that the book is a "generic hybrid, a kind of subjective autobiography superimposed on a travelogue" ("Mary Wollstonecraft's *Letters*" 166). Gary Kelly notes that *Letters from Norway* "includes lyrical description, apostrophe, self-reflection, political disquisition, deictic expressions, anecdotes, autobiographical allusions, literary quotations, maxims and typographical devices of expressivity" (*Revolutionary Feminism* 178). In Syndy Conger's reading, *Letters from Norway* marks Wollstonecraft's "complete and newly self-conscious return to the ethics and aesthetics of sensibility" (*Mary Wollstonecraft* 147),

---

Notes are on pp. 83-84.

while for Elizabeth Bohls, this writing produces "alternative aesthetics" that "situate aesthetic pleasure in a practical, material matrix extending from the body and its sensations to political engagement" (141).[1] What most readers from the eighteenth century to the present seem to agree on is that despite its generic inconsistencies, *Letters from Norway* is a thoroughly delightful work, revealing a philosophical but sensitive and intense mind at work. As William Godwin puts it, "If ever there was a book calculated to make a man in love with its author, this appears to me to be the book. . . . Affliction had tempered her heart to a softness almost more than human; and the gentleness of her spirit seems precisely to accord with all the romance of unbounded attachment" (*MAV* 249).

This last statement, though written by a man who was clearly predisposed to the author and very much in love with her, nevertheless points to a crucial element of *Letters from Norway* that merits closer examination. What impels and haunts the narrative is woman's desire. Mary Favret argues that one should avoid reading *Letters from Norway* as belonging to "an intimate, sentimental and properly 'feminine' genre" because the published *Letters* "do not copy or even expand upon the private correspondence between Wollstonecraft and her lover, Gilbert Imlay. Rather, they deliberately rewrite and replace the love letters, transforming Wollstonecraft's emotional dependence and personal grief into a public confrontation with social corruption" (101). Nevertheless, I suggest that the enchantment of the book comes largely from its articulation of female desire and female subjectivity. Like Mary Hays's *Memoirs of Emma Courtney,* which was published in the same year and was also based on letters to a lover, Wollstonecraft's travelogue is a text inscribing the female self and her passions. Catherine Belsey points out that desire "is the location of the contradictory imperative that motivates the signifying body which is a human being in love. Desire is in excess of the organism; conversely, it is what remains unspoken in the utterance" (*Desire* 5).[2] Desire is difficult for any human animal to articulate, but I would argue, that given the socio-historical conditions of the late eighteenth century, desire was particularly difficult for a woman to express in a public genre. In *Letters from Norway*, it becomes the unnameable subject that is consciously banished by the reasoning observer, the mother, and the traveller. For Wollstonecraft, desire is more than mere sexual desire; it is a desire for all those "emotions that trembled on the brink of extacy and agony," those things that make her "feel more alive than usual" (*LWSR* 69).

Elsewhere I have discussed the ways in which Wollstonecraft's gendered subjectivity affected her ability to use without question the public discourse of travel narrative. I argued that her resistance to the symbolic order accounts for many of the ambiguous tendencies in *Letters from Norway* (see Ty, "Writing"). In this paper, I would like to focus on the work as a narrative of desire. In both Freud's and Lacan's psychoanalytic theories, desire and sexuality are linked to an original object that is lost. For Lacan, "desire is produced in the beyond of the demand" (*Ecrits* 265), and is distinguishable from need. As Catherine Belsey explains, "Desire is the effect of the lost needs: loss returns and presents itself as desire" (*Desire* 57). As another critic puts it, desire "is always in excess of its object, the object being only a partial representation of something beyond it, and thus implicated in a chain of deferrals and transferences" (Rajan, "Autonarration" 154). Thus, Wollstonecraft's desire is not solely for Gilbert Imlay, or for another lover. *Letters from Norway* reveals the complex ways in which female desire is channelled, presented, and represented. Belsey observes that "desire is also the location of resistances to the norms, proprieties and taxonomies of the cultural order. . . . Desire, even when it is profoundly conventional, is at the same time the location of a resistance to convention. It demonstrates that people want something more" (*Desire* 6-7).

Wollstonecraft's struggle to analyze her passion for an individual, in this case Gilbert Imlay, is an important element in the *Letters*, and the working out of her desire can be explained in part by Lacan's psychoanalytical theories of sexuality and signification. For Lacan, sexuality and desire are both "manifested by and hidden in language. . . . [His] account of sexuality relies on a distinction between need, demand, and desire" (Grosz 59). To briefly summarize the three terms, in Elizabeth Grosz's words, needs are "the requirements of brute survival: Nourishment, shelter, warmth, freedom of movement, a minimal community, and so on" (59). These basic elements are what the Swedish cottagers have, in Wollstonecraft's view. Demand "takes the form of the statement, 'I want . . .,' or the command 'Give me. . . .'" It is articulated in language, which necessarily "narrows down and specifies the amorphous need by tying it to a concrete object, thus particularizing it. It converts the need from a quasi-biological status to a linguistic, interpersonal, and social phenomenon" (Grosz 61). At the time that she was travelling, Wollstonecraft expressed the wish to be united with her lover. However, in Lacanian terms, this articulated demand, whether for food, attention, or undying love, is always addressed to an Other, and falls short of what one needs. As Grosz explains, "this is because the demand is really for something else, for the next thing the other can give, for the thing that will 'prove' the other's love. Demand requires the affirmation of an ego by the other to such a degree that only an imaginary union or identification with them, an identity they share, could bring satisfaction" (61). Thus, Imlay, even if he were present and faithful to Wollstonecraft, would never fully satisfy her, as he is merely an object that stands for something else. He is, for the moment, what she believes would bring her closer to "an imaginary union" with an Other. The third term, desire, like both need and demand, "is based on the absence or privation of its object. . . . In opposition to demand (and in accordance with need), desire is beyond conscious articulation, for it is barred or repressed from articulation" (64-65).

In the eighteenth century, as it is to a certain extent today, desire is linked to the sensual, to erotic impulses, while virtue, especially for women, means sexual chastity. The need to preserve a woman's virtue and to control desire resulted in countless formal and informal letters from parents, as well as conduct books, novels, and treatises, that extolled the virtues of innocence and modesty. *The Ladies Calling* of 1673 considered modesty "the most indispensible requisite of a woman; a thing so essential and natural to the sex, that the very least declination from it, is a proportional receding from Womanhood." It even proposed that "an impudent woman is lookt on as a kind of Monster; a thing diverted and distorted from its proper form" (Allestree 1: 14-15). A century later, Dr John Gregory similarly advised his daughters: "One of the chief beauties in a female character is that modest reserve, that retiring delicacy, which avoids the public eye, and is disconcerted even at the gaze of admiration" (26). In her *Vindication of the Rights of Woman* (1792), Wollstonecraft also struggled with this concept of modesty, but suggested a definition that was not "highly eroticized and gendered" (see Yeazell 8). For her, one should discriminate "purity of mind" from "simplicity of character." Wollstonecraft was one of the few writers to believe that in order "[t]o render chastity the virtue from which unsophisticated modesty will naturally flow, the attention should be called away from employments which only exercise the sensibility" (*VRW* 254). Instead, women should be encouraged to pursue intellectual interests.

However much Wollstonecraft wished to argue for a less sexualized application of modesty, she was aware that contemporary ideologies about woman were closer to Jean-Jacques Rousseau's view, with which she disagreed in *The Rights of Woman*, than to her own. Rousseau had argued that, even "if the timidity, *pudeur,* and *modestie* which are proper to them are social inventions, it is essential for society that women acquire these qualities; it is essential that they be cultivated in women, and any woman who disdains them offends good morals" (*Lettre à M. D'Alembert*, qtd. in Yeazell 30-31). I suggest that even when writing in a private genre, such as letters, Wollstonecraft was constrained by these ideologies and by the social construction of what Mary Poovey calls the "proper lady" (x).[3] In *Letters from Norway* Wollstonecraft hints at her own attempts to control her passion, or the "extreme affection" of her nature: "For years have I endeavoured to calm an impetuous tide—labouring to make my feelings take an orderly course" (111). Yet she believes that her feelings are not the "promiscuous amours" of the idle. She writes, "as the mind is cultivated, and taste gains ground, the passions become stronger, and rest on something more stable than the casual sympathies of the moment" (83). Conflicting impulses manifest themselves in the narrative through various ways. Wollstonecraft often writes of her restlessness, her frequent yearnings to go beyond the acceptable boundaries, both physically and emotionally, and shows somewhat contradictory, at times rather harsh views of the people of Scandinavia and of its landscape. The struggle between her wish to regulate her affections and desires and her longing to articulate what was in her heart at the time of her separation from her lover Gilbert Imlay creates the central tension in the collection of letters.

So what is this something more that Wollstonecraft wishes for? In the words of Freud, "the great question that has never been answered" is: "What does a woman want?" (letter to Marie Bonaparte, qtd. in Felman 2). *Letters from Norway* does not answer this question directly. Desire remains, as Belsey says, "unspoken in the utterance" (*Desire* 5). But Wollstonecraft does give her readers a number of ideas about what she does not want, and also clues about her vision of the possibilities for a woman. Part of the difficulty in articulating desire for Wollstonecraft comes from the more general problem of inscribing ourselves as women. According to Sidonie Smith, autobiography is essentially an "androcentric genre," which "demands the public story of the public life" (52). To write an autobiography forces a woman to identify with the father, with the "scenario of public achievement that apparently structures traditional autobiography, and the "myth of origins in the discourse of man" (52). As a woman "appropriates the story and the speaking posture of the representative man, she silences that part of herself that identifies her as a daughter of her mother" (Smith 53). Similarly, Shoshana Felman argues, "*none of us, as women, has as yet, precisely, an autobiography.* Trained to see ourselves as objects and to be positioned as the Other, estranged to ourselves, we have a story that by definition cannot be self-present to us, a story that, in other words, is not a story, but *must become* a story" (14).

Wollstonecraft was aware of the way women were trained to see themselves as objects, as the Other, and knew that, for a woman, becoming the subject of a story was not easy. In her *Rights of Woman,* she complained that "a false system of education, gathered from the books written . . . by men" has made women think of themselves more as "alluring mistresses than affectionate wives and rational mothers" (109). More than just advocating a less sexualized and less sensualized position for women in the same way as Jane West was to do in her writings, Wollstonecraft urged educational reform so that, as Claudia Johnson notes, women could "become fully rational and self-responsible citizens, moral agents, and family members" (24). But this process would involve changing the way both women and men viewed the "distinction of sexes" (see Johnson, Chap. 1). Theoretically, it would also mean encouraging women to use their reason as governing principles. However, by 1795-96, because of her recent experiences as Fanny's mother, Imlay's lover, and then his discarded mistress, Wollstonecraft's thoughts about the powers of pure reason as an infallible guide were evolving. *Letters from Norway* charts this evolution in her thinking about how women were to constitute their subjectivity, what their strengths were, and how to speak of their desires. Here she succeeds in writing an autobiographical narrative that does not efface her identity as a daughter, and as a mother.[4]

In terms of literary conventions, whether one considers *Letters from Norway* as autobiography, travelogue, or public letters, Wollstonecraft would have known of more precedents written by male than by female authors.[5] While recent studies in autobiography have uncovered a number of autobiographical narratives by women in the early modern period, such as those by Margaret Cavendish and Charlotte Charke (see S. Smith, Chap. 5, 6), the autobiographical example most readily available to Wollstonecraft would have been Rousseau's *Confessions*, which she reviewed favourably in 1790.[6] In his *Confessions,* as in *Emile,* Rousseau wrote about women, from simple chambermaids to the sophisticated wives of aristocrats, as creatures made for man's pleasure and comfort. Eighteenth-century travel narratives, with the exception of Lady Mary Wortley Montagu's Turkish letters, were written mostly by male travellers and adventurers, and the custom of a tour of Europe as part of a young gentleman's education often implied an initiation into sexual pleasures with French or Italian girls. In the latter cases, women, as much as the flora and fauna, were tourist attractions. Furthermore, as Bohls points out, it was difficult for women to participate in scenic tourism, which entailed "aesthetic and social distance between the aesthetic subject and the 'Vulgar,'" a problematic category which sometimes included women (13). In the revolutionary decade of the 1790s, the epistolary genre was used by various writers such as Edmund Burke, Joseph Priestley, and Helen Maria Williams to give a sense of the personal in a public debate. But *Reflections on the Revolution in France* and *Letters from France* are much less focused on the letter writer than on the political events being discussed (see Favret, Chap. 2, 3). With so few examples of woman as subject and looker, rather than as object in the landscape to be looked at, making herself the "little hero of each tale" (*LWSR* 62) was thus a complex and original enterprise for Wollstonecraft.

The ostensible reason for her voyage to Scandinavia was to recover a ship for Gilbert Imlay (see Holmes 21-26; Nyström). However, there were all sorts of underlying reasons for the trip. She departed on 6 June, only about a week after her attempted suicide. One could say that, in a sense, Wollstonecraft was travelling to flee the inescapable — an important element of which was her heart and passion.[7] In many of the letters, she makes references to escape, to breaking boundaries, and to going beyond the ordinary. Many of these are figured in terms of imagery of high and low, ascent and descent. For example, in her first letter, she speaks of the inhabitants of the little island off the coast of Sweden as "men who remain so near the brute creation, as only to exert themselves to find the food necessary to sustain life" (65). She complains that they "have little or no imagination to call forth the curiosity necessary to fructify the faint glimmerings of mind which entitles [*sic*] them to rank as lords of the creation" (65). Hence, they "contentedly remain rooted in the clods they so indolently cultivate" (65). Following a visit with some of these cottagers, she notes her desire to escape from their company: "Though my host amused me with an account of himself, which gave me an idea of the manners of the people I was about to visit, I was eager to climb the rocks to view the country" (67). Wollstonecraft's wish to go beyond the wants of "brute creation" is mirrored in her physical desire to find a higher elevation from which to see the landscape. From this point, she sees the commodious bay, and feels its "picturesque beauty" (67). As she describes it, "Rocks were piled on rocks, forming a suitable bulwark to the ocean" (67). She is attracted by expanse, the unlimited openness, as well as by the elevated prospect. Her desire for something more than a brutish existence manifests itself through her yearning for an aesthetically pleasing view, one that offers a sight of the contrasting elements of earth, water, and air. It is not only a picturesque scene, but one that traces a movement going outwards and upwards toward the sky.

In *Imperial Eyes*, Mary Louise Pratt notes that "promontory descriptions are . . . very common in Romantic and Victorian writing of all kinds" (202). Pratt remarks that in such "monarch-of-all-I-survey" scenes, the "landscape is estheticized" and is rendered into familiar terms through descriptions that use vocabulary from the explorer's home culture. In addition, the "relation of mastery" is "predicated between the seer and the seen," as the "scene is deictically ordered with reference to" the vantage point of the traveller (204-05). Wollstonecraft's description of the seascape follows the tradition of eighteenth- and nineteenth-century travel narratives, as she controls the scene aesthetically through her vocabulary. She writes of "still little patches of earth, of the most exquisite verdure, enamelled with the sweetest wild flowers" (67). These phrases make the Swedish landscape into something akin to an English countryside. The scene is "silent and peaceful" (67) and constitutes a moment of pleasure and reprieve from the "horrors" she had witnessed in France, as well as from her "disappointed affection" (68). As the viewer, she can control her relation and her responses to the landscape in a way that she cannot control her heart.

It is, of course, part of the quest of any hero to discover something above or out of the ordinary. But for Wollstonecraft, the discovery is a spiritual and emotional one, as well as a search for an external object or reward. Her desire for transcendence and freedom is expressed through her relation to landscapes of various kinds. At one point she notes that "[n]othing . . . can equal the beauty of the northern summer's evening and night," where night "only wants the glare of day, the full light, which frequently seems so impertinent" (69). As there is freedom in the expansive horizon, there is a different kind of latitude offered by the northern night, which provides light without the intrusion of a blinding glare. In her next letter, she is similarly enchanted by the twilight: "The cow's bell has ceased to tinkle the herd to rest; they have all paced across the heath. Is not this the witching time of night? The waters murmur, and fall with more than mortal music, and spirits of peace walk abroad to calm the agitated breast. Eternity is in these moments: worldly cares melt into the airy stuff that dreams are made of" (75). These descriptions of the borderline between conventional night and day suggest a desire for a place without boundaries, a state of in-betweenness. In this state she is able to see and feel what one cannot appreciate in the full light of day or the black of night. It is akin to the peace of "parting day" described by Thomas Gray in his "Elegy Written in a Country Churchyard." However, instead of evoking thoughts of the dead folk from the countryside, Wollstonecraft's reflections are more optimistic. These moments remind her of "reveries, mild and enchanting as the first hopes of love, or the recollection of lost enjoyment" (75). The pleasant sensations evoked by the liminality carry her out of her present situation to remembrances of things past or to a magical realm where everyday rules do not apply, as her reference to *The Tempest* suggests.

For Wollstonecraft, the imagination is an essential element of escape from the material world: "Without the aid of the imagination all the pleasures of the senses must sink into grossness" (72). Yet what she calls the imagination here is somewhat different from what Wordsworth was later to describe in his *Prelude*. For Wordsworth, a flash of the imagination reveals "[t]he invisible world" (*Prelude* 6.602), whereas for Wollstonecraft, the imagination is closer to the late-eighteenth-century conception of sensibility. As she says, "I never met with much imagination amongst people who had not acquired a habit of reflection; and in that state of society in which the judgment and taste are not called forth, and formed by the cultivation of the arts and sciences, little of that delicacy of feeling and thinking is to be found characterized by the word sentiment" (73). Wollstonecraft's idea of imagination is not a divine flash of inspiration, but a faculty that needs cultivation and development. As Conger notes, it is realigned with "qualities of mind: understanding, judgment, taste, sympathy, tenderness, genius, melancholy" (*Mary Wollstonecraft* 148). In *Letters from Norway* imagination compensates for loss and gives a "poignancy to [Wollstonecraft's] sensations" (*LWSR* 69). It is what makes her different from her fellow travellers. Returning to Stromstad near midnight after an excursion to Norway, Wollstonecraft uses language reminiscent of a lover's to describe the beauties of the sun rising: "I contemplated . . . a night such as I had never before seen or felt to charm the senses, and calm the heart. The very air was balmy, as it freshened into morn, producing the most voluptuous sensations. A vague pleasurable sentiment absorbed me, as I opened my bosom to the embraces of nature" (94). Her encounter with nature here is sensual and voluptuous, affecting her heart and bosom.[8] However, she is careful to distinguish herself from her companions on the ship, who "fell asleep," fortunately without snoring (94). The landscape and her contemplation of it are not only a way of escaping, at least in spirit, the more mundane world and the coarse-natured bodies around her, but they become the means by which Wollstonecraft expresses her desire for that "something more" not present in her immediate surroundings (cf. Belsey, *Desire* 7; *LWSR* 83). Her response, one of heightened sensibility to nature, suggests that that "something more" is a mixture of the erotic, the imaginative, and the intellectual.

In her next letter, she notices the association between her appreciation of nature and her desire for human love. She notes: "Nature is the nurse of sentiment,—the true source of taste;—yet what misery, as well as rapture, is produced by a quick perception of the beautiful and sublime, when it is exercised in observing animated nature, when every beauteous feeling and emotion excites responsive sympathy" (99). Such a link, however, has its hazards. Nature enables the soul to rise to "extasy" or to sink into "melancholy" (99). But, she remarks, "how dangerous is it to foster these sentiments in such an imperfect state of existence; and how difficult to eradicate them when an affection for mankind, a passion for an individual, is but the unfolding of that love which embraces all that is great and beautiful" (99). This passion, this desire that I have been exploring, is expressed obliquely through Wollstonecraft's response to the natural landscape, to the people around her, and to the culture of Scandinavia.

Through her reactions, her likes and dislikes of the people she encounters, we get an idea of the sense of isolation she feels and the fears that she dares not articulate, and we see a sketch of the ideal friend or companion she would like to have. In Norway, for instance, she reveals her vulnerability when she notes that people approached to assist her and to enquire after her wants, "as if they were afraid to hurt, and wished to protect" her (97). She attributes her "look of peculiar delicacy" to her weariness, but remarks that the sympathy affected her greatly because her spirits had "been harassed by various causes," by "much thinking," and by "a sort of weak melancholy that hung about [her] heart at parting with [her] daughter for the first time" (96-97). That she is so moved by the kindness of these strangers demonstrates her desire for a being or beings who can sympathize and care for her. Her wish for companionship is thus revealed by her reaction even though the persona she attempts to project in the *Letters from Norway* for the most part, is, a dignified and autonomous one, as Favret points out.[9] Relating her feeling of melancholy to her being female and a mother, she notes her ambivalence about women's keen sensibility and "delicacy of sentiment" (97), which sometimes force them to choose between their principles and their hearts. To deflect attention from her private grief, she generalizes on the state of woman by lamenting, "Hapless woman! what a fate is thine!" (97). This impassioned cry, though directed outwards rather than at her own miseries, nevertheless reveals her sense of anguish, her hope of seeing different ways of constructing a woman's subjectivity. The passage reveals a desire for a better integration of intellect and emotion, of what she calls a woman's "principles" and her "heart."

In another instance, while she attempts to demonstrate her strength, health, and good spirits to the reader, she ends up revealing her fear of death and her wish for an existence beyond the physical realm. In Tonsberg, she notes that the "air, exercise and change of scene" have been of great benefit to her health (111). Wishing to bathe in the sea, she meets a young woman who offers to row her across the water, among the rocks. But because the woman is pregnant, Wollstonecraft soon takes over the rowing and then discovers "a new pleasure" in the handling of the oars (111). What is interesting is the reflections that arise from her being "carried along by the current, indulging a pleasing forgetfulness" (112). Here, where one expects idle thoughts, Wollstonecraft thinks of "the fear of annihilation," the only thing of which she has "ever felt a dread" (112). She writes: "I cannot bear to think of being no more—of losing myself—though existence is often but a painful consciousness of misery; nay, it appears to me impossible that I should cease to exist. . . . Surely something resides in this heart that is not perishable—and life is more than a dream" (112). What starts out as a carefree jaunt across the water becomes a perfect mise-en-scène of the struggle between the life-giving forces of the maternal, in the figure of the pregnant woman, and the imminent danger of annihilation and oblivion. Wollstonecraft battles the temptation to succumb to death. Yet she values the tumultuous emotions of her heart. Instead of despair, her comments show her fierce desire for a belief in something that lasts beyond the mortal. Her contemplation reveals her attempts to convince herself that her "active, restless spirit, equally alive to joy and sorrow," is more than "organized dust" (112).

Another example of her anxieties about the maternal occurs in the same letter. She encounters a young woman who works as a wet nurse in order to support herself and her child. Wollstonecraft evidently identifies strongly with this woman, who has been abandoned by her partner, as she remarks on how "this most painful state of widowhood" has "excited" her "compassion" and led her to "reflections . . . that were painful in the extreme" (114-15).[10] Significantly, she does not sentimentalize motherhood, even though the tendency to do so was becoming increasingly pervasive by the middle and late eighteenth century. Ruth Perry points out that "the concept of bourgeois motherhood" became essential to a new "productive view of heterosexual relations," and that, consequently, "maternity came to be imagined as a counter to sexual feeling, opposing alike individual expression, desire, and agency in favor of a mother-self at the service of the family and the state" (187-88). For Wollstonecraft, however, maternity did not preclude sexuality or desire. The young woman's condition makes her wonder "whether this world was not created to exhibit every possible combination of wretchedness" (115). She notes that she asked "these questions of a heart writhing with anguish" (115). Her comments suggest that, to her, there is a synthesis between the maternal breast and female passion. Her anguished heart yearned for an amorous Other even as she was a mother. Unlike more conservative writers such as Jane West, who valorized the maternal but negated the sexual, Wollstonecraft desired a dialectical relationship between the two.

What is less evident in this passage is the strenuous effort Wollstonecraft made to conquer her aching heart. She records that soon after hearing the young woman's "melancholy ditty," she "hastened out of the house, to take [her] solitary evening's walk . . . to talk of any thing, but the pangs arising from the discovery of estranged affection, and the lonely sadness of a deserted heart" (115). In order to calm her broken heart and endure the temporary separation from Fanny at this point, Wollstonecraft takes on the imaginary figure of Rousseau's solitary walker. The reference to the *Reveries* at this point is significant. It is an effort not to identify too closely with the young woman who is represented by Wollstonecraft as a helpless victim and widow. Instead, she wishes to be the independent nature lover, at peace with herself. In his *Reveries*, Rousseau insists that his meditations were possible only in solitude, but that this solitude was also a means of escaping a hostile society and of discovering the self. While she was wary of his views on the education of women, Wollstonecraft was attracted to Rousseau's focus on his own subjectivity. The quick switch from the young woman to Wollstonecraft's "solitary evening's walk" demonstrates her desire not to fall into the same trap as the woman. It is perhaps not coincidental that Rousseau's own domestic arrangements were rather untraditional and problematic. In his *Reveries* he apologetically refers to leaving at the orphanage his children by Thérèse Levasseur, his longtime mistress and then wife. Becoming the solitary walker, then, was also a way of becoming the one who escapes the difficulties and responsibilities, rather than the victim who is left behind.

Finally, a sketch of the companion whom Wollstonecraft desires emerges from a number of the letters. Not surprisingly, it has some affinities with the portrait of Darnford in her last novel. In *The Wrongs of Woman,* Maria is initially attracted to Darnford's "marginal notes, in Dryden's Fables," which are written "with force and taste," along with a rather Jacobin-like fragment about the "enslaved state of the labouring majority" (85-86). The qualities that she admires in Darnford—that is, intelligence, an educated imagination, and sensitivity to the plight of the oppressed—are the same ones she writes about in her letters. In the novel, the narrator is aware that the ideal lover is something of an illusion, like those "ideal phantoms of love" after whom youths sigh, as

Maria represents Darnford as "the personification of Saint Preux" (99, 89). The unfinished ending suggests that he may not turn out to be as perfect as her painting of him. Wollstonecraft does not encounter a Saint Preux in her travels, but her repeated denigration of "commerce" and "speculation" (*LWSR* 143), "the tyranny of wealth" (150), and "men of business" (165) makes it clear that the man of commerce is abhorrent to her. As Mary Favret notes, Wollstonecraft underscores "the break between imagination and commerce, between the business of a woman writing and a man's 'business.'" *Letters from Norway* "construct[s] an economics of the imagination to rival that of capitalism" (119, 120).

Equally disappointing are the uncultivated men in the small towns who spend their days "smoking, drinking brandy, and driving bargains" (132). Wollstonecraft remarks, "They begin in the morning, and are rarely without their pipe till they go to bed. Nothing can be more disgusting than the rooms and men towards the evening: breath, teeth, clothes, and furniture, all are spoilt" (132). In this letter, the imagery of confinement appears again and again. She writes here that "the world appeared a vast prison" (130), that "[t]o be born here, was to be bastilled by nature—shut out from all that opens the understanding, or enlarges the heart," and that, upon walking along the rocks, she "felt the confinement, and wished for wings to reach still loftier cliffs" (131). Though her repulsion is ostensibly directed at the peasants, her anger and disappointment, and the extreme sense of imprisonment she feels, suggest that there are larger issues at work here. The aversion seems to be in excess of what the situation calls for, and is repeated when she quits Quistram, where again she sees a large party of men and women, "drinking, smoking, and laughing" (156). Of this scene of revelry, she comments, "I felt for the trees whose torn branches strewed the ground.—Hapless nymphs! thy haunts I fear were polluted by many an unhallowed flame; the casual burst of the moment!" (156). This strong lament is for more than the broken branches on the ground. I suggest that it is representative of a greater sense of loss—of the misuse of potential, of what could have been, but isn't. In many ways, these passages express the obverse of the desire that Wollstonecraft articulates indirectly through her descriptions and observations. Since her father was an alcoholic, Wollstonecraft is writing here from the perspective of the disappointed daughter.[11] The condemnation of drinking and smoking is a denunciation of all that is not right with the world, of those who have failed her, particularly the men—lovers, fathers, and father figures—in her life.

What she does desire in a domestic relationship seems to be just beyond precise symbolic representation. Like her aversion, her desire is in excess of what is expressed by her language at a given situation. I will focus my discussion on four short passages here to illustrate this last point. Reporting a conversation with a man about the "laws and regulations of Norway," she remarks that he "is a man with a great portion of common sense, and heart,—yes, a warm heart" (128). She then goes on to distinguish between "heart" and "sentiment." She writes, "The former depends on the rectitude of the feelings, on truth of sympathy: these characters have more tenderness than passion; the latter has a higher source; call it imagination, genius, or what you will, it is something very different" (128). Later, observing the lack of "taste and cultivation of mind" of the Swedes, she notes, "Affection requires a firmer foundation than sympathy; and few people have a principle of action sufficiently stable to produce rectitude of feeling; . . . even the most spontaneous sensations are more under the direction of principle than weak people are willing to allow" (161). These two passages seem to echo each other: they stress the importance of imagination, or taste and cultivation, in matters of the heart. However, what she terms "rectitude of feeling" is found in the heart in the first case, while it is something that needs "direction" and "principle" in the second, implying that one needs more than a sympathetic heart. These complementary requirements, as well as the many terms she employs for what is needed—imagination, genius, cultivation, taste, and principle—reveal her struggle with the articulation of her desire. Her desire is for someone who possesses that something more that is beyond what she can demand through language. In Lacanian terms, Wollstonecraft is substituting one signifier for another because desire is "endlessly metonymic and unsatisfiable" (Rajan, "Autonarration" 155). Her demand, here channelled through an unsatisfactory heterosexual love relationship mainly because of social and literary conventions, is only a partial articulation of her desire, which cannot be concretized through symbolic language.

Wollstonecraft herself realized how illusory this desire was. In at least two instances, she speaks of the difficulty of finding what Samuel Johnson called felicity in "private life" (*Rasselas*, chap. 26). She notes, "Friendship and domestic happiness are continually praised; yet how little is there of either in the world, because it requires more cultivation of mind to keep awake affection, even in our own hearts, than the common run of people suppose" (136). Yet for someone to have this "cultivation of mind" in its pure form is next to impossible. In her tour of Norway, Wollstonecraft searches for simplicity in the life of farmers, comparing their existence to the "fables of the golden age," where there was "independence and virtue; affluence without vice; cultivation of mind, without depravity of heart . . . " (149). However, she realizes that there are few chances of finding such an ideal because "the world is still the world, and man the same compound of weakness and folly, who must occasionally excite love and disgust, admiration and contempt" (149). Her practical and resigned conclusion about the state of the world, however, does not prevent her from continually hoping to find the object of her desire. It is this desire that makes *Letters from Norway* such an elusive, vibrant, and challenging text—one that breaks down boundaries between the literary and the social realms, between the acceptable and unacceptable, between the personal and the public, between life and art.

Notes

1   Conger notes that "in *Letters in Sweden* Wollstonecraft liberates sensibility from the inherited fictions that constrain it in her earlier writings" (*Mary Wollstonecraft* 145), and says that the work is distinctive because of "its public acknowledgement of feeling and the intense multiplicity of its personal revelation" (146). Bohls argues that "the new kind of pleasure that Wollstonecraft proposes depends on visible signs of social justice and material prosperity" (146).

2   Belsey suggests that one difficulty comes from the fact that "sexuality precisely calls into question that opposition between nature and culture." It is natural and yet "has to be *taught*—in sex education classes and popular handbooks" (*Desire* 5).

3   Poovey argues that the shadow of the Proper Lady is cast "across the careers of some of the women who became professional authors despite the strictures of propriety. The struggle each of these women waged to create a professional identity was in large measure defined by the social and psychological force of this idea of proper—or innate—femininity" (x).

4   Jeanne Moskal makes a similar point, but she focuses on the way Wollstonecraft revises aesthetic principles. Moskal argues that "the affectionate shapes the picturesque, that is, the affectionate tie between the traveling mother and daughter forms the conceptual center of Wollstonecraft's revision of the gendered aesthetic conventions of the picturesque and its concomitant terms, the beautiful and the sublime" ("Picturesque" 264).

5   Wollstonecraft reviewed more than a dozen travel books by male writers from 1788 to 1797 for the *Analytical Review*. The

only travel book by a woman listed in Todd and Butler's index is Hester Lynch Piozzi's *Observations and Reflections, Made in the Course of a Journey through France, Italy and Germany* (*Works* 7: 498).

6   Wollstonecraft reviewed the *Second Part of the Confessions* of J. J. Rousseau for the *Analytical Review*. She noted his "interesting account of his feelings and reveries" (*Works* 7: 228), and wrote that, "whether Rousseau was right or wrong, in thus exposing his weaknesses, and shewing himself just as he was, with all his imperfections on his head, to his frail fellow-creatures, it is only necessary to observe, that a description of what has actually passed in a human mind must ever be useful" (*Works* 7: 229).

7   Sunstein notes that Imlay and Wollstonecraft agreed that during the separation Imlay was to examine himself to see if he could settle with her. She was hopeful that the journey would bring her closer to him (*Different Face* 275-76).

8   In her analysis, Bohls notes that "Wollstonecraft's explicit and implicit departures from convention critique disinterested contemplation by destroying the distance between a perceiver and a statically framed scene" (151). Bohls argues that Wollstonecraft's descriptions disrupt conventional scenes, and remind us of practical conditions of life. Here, my emphasis is more on the way these descriptions express the unnameable.

9   Favret notes that "Wollstonecraft consciously reworks the struggle for self-control, so evident in the love letters, into a picture of self-reliance" (102).

10   Conger notes that "it is clear that Wollstonecraft sees many connections between her own situation and the young woman's" (*Mary Wollstonecraft* 157).

11   In Godwin's *Memoirs* as well as in Wollstonecraft's fiction, the father figure is negatively depicted as someone unstable and prone to inebriation. See, for example, the discussion in Sunstein, *Different Face*, Chap. 1.

(Un)Confinements: The Madness of Motherhood in Mary Wollstonecraft's *The Wrongs of Woman*

S. Leigh Matthews

Addressing these memoirs to you, my child, uncertain whether I shall ever have an opportunity of instructing you, many observations will probably flow from my heart, which only a mother—a mother schooled in misery, could make.

—Maria in *The Wrongs of Woman*

In her study *Bearing the Word: Language and Female Experience in Nineteenth-Century Women's Writing*, Margaret Homans notes that Western culture maintains a "dominant myth of language according to which women's experiences are unrepresentable" (xi), a myth in which women are "identified with the literal, the absent referent" of the "figurative structures of literature" (4). In a "predominantly androcentric culture" in which language and acts of representation are "constructed in this way," women writers struggle to represent the literal experiences of their lives, to engage in the system of language of their culture while aiming to inscribe a different point of view. Homans goes on to note that feminist reinterpretations of the "dominant myth of language" and the knowledge that "the Lacanian view of language is not a universal truth, but the psycholinguistic retelling of a myth to which our culture has long subscribed" (5-6)

Notes are on pp. 95-97.

allow modern readers of women's writing from past centuries to "be alert to" attempts to present textual resistance to the idea of the non-representability of women's experiences—to the idea that women writers both assumed that they *could* write about such experiences and "also subscribed to some version of the cultural myth of women's relation to and subordination within language" (xiii). What we often experience as readers of women's writing, then, is a dual voice: while what is represented in the text is a depiction, a further inscription, of female "subordination within language," that very depiction, accompanied as it often is by an implicit critique of women's subordination, constitutes a challenge to, a speaking out against, cultural myths. We see this duality in Mary Wollstonecraft's *The Wrongs of Woman; or, Maria: A Fragment* (1798), a text in which the author, by utilizing certain conventions of the literature of the period, manages, as Felicity Nussbaum suggests of women's self-writing in the eighteenth century, to "adopt positions available within the language at a given moment" as a means of allowing "alternative discourses of 'experience' to erupt at the margins of meanings" ("Autobiographical Commonplaces" 149).

Detecting these "eruptions" requires precisely that "alertness" that Homans suggests as a means to reading women's writing about "the relation between women and language" (xi). In her admonition, Homans points to the responsibility of the modern reader to acknowledge the reading contract that she makes with a text. In the case of Wollstonecraft's last work, that contract includes taking into account the author's position as philosopher and social critic and the necessity of reading *The Wrongs of Woman* through the events of the author's life to discern when the personal body of experience leaks into the public body of the text. Such a reading necessitates a revisioning of the traditional restricted definition of autobiographical texts as "trac[ing] the teleology of [the autobiographer's] life" (Bruss 1) to embrace Marlene Kadar's suggestion that the term "life writing" should encompass a "continuum that spreads unevenly and in combined forms from the so-called least fictive narration to the most fictive" ("Coming" 10). I would suggest that Wollstonecraft's final public representation of "the misery and oppression, peculiar to women, that arise out of the partial laws and customs of society" (*WWM* 73) in the late eighteenth century was born of her personal experience and philosophical beliefs regarding the social position of women. Although Wollstonecraft would have us believe that her story "ought rather to be considered, as of woman [the generic category], than of an individual" (73), the textual experiences of Maria reflect Wollstonecraft's own experiences with male-female relationships and with motherhood.

As noted elsewhere, *The Wrongs of Woman* opens with what Margaret Homans suggests is a particularly female way of representing women's experience: that is, with the "literalization" of a common figure of the dominant culture.[1] The text opens with Maria Venables incarcerated in a private madhouse, a trope that Wollstonecraft adapted from a popular literary form of the period, the novel of sensibility. I say "adapted" because, as noted by Janet Todd, from the "1780s onwards, sentimental literature and the principles behind it were bombarded with criticism and ridicule" (*Sensibility* 141). One popular point of attack was the connection between novel reading, selfishness, and passivity: indeed, Wollstonecraft herself, in the *Vindication* in particular, castigates the social apathy that she felt was induced in women by the reading of this type of literature. In *The Wrongs of Woman*, Wollstonecraft seeks to move the text of sensibility beyond the realm of the merely *affective* to being politically *effective*. She does so through her presentation of the wrongs perpetrated against women and her literalization of one of the common features of sentimental literature, namely, the female figure of madness. As Paul D. McGlynn suggests, eighteenth-century readers had a penchant for a combination of madness and femininity as "a particular catalyst for benevolence, pathos and irresistible pity" (39), as seen in the unnamed female inhabitant of Bedlam[2] in Henry Mackenzie's *The Man of Feeling* (1771), a figure whose countenance and situation move the protagonist Harley to "pity unmixed with horror" and result in his "tribute of some tears" (Mackenzie 21-22).[3] A more familiar example of such a figure is Laurence Sterne's Maria, who appears in both *Tristram Shandy* (1759-67) and *A Sentimental Journey* (1768). In the latter text, Sterne's Maria is an object of literary representation meant to illustrate Yorick's own acute sensibilities, moving him equally to tears and licentiousness: as he states it, "the story [Mr Shandy] had told of that disorder'd maid affect'd me not a little in the reading" (95).[4] If we read intertextually, Wollstonecraft's Maria is a literary descendant of Sterne's Maria, with a couple of key differences: whereas Sterne's Maria is figured as being mad through the representations of both Mr Shandy and Yorick, Wollstonecraft's Maria is an individual character with discursive agency, as she gives voice to the injustice of her incarceration and takes action against all the odds in the world to try to reform her situation. The silenced madwoman of both Mackenzie's and Sterne's texts does make an appearance in Wollstonecraft's *The Wrongs of Woman* in the figure of the "lovely maniac," who sings the "pathetic ballad of old Robin Gray" and who "had been married, against her inclination, to a rich old man" (88).[5] This figure works in Wollstonecraft's text in juxtaposition to Maria, whose situation of incarceration for (supposed) madness literalizes the experiences of those women who are defined and silenced by their culture and brings that history of definition and silence into question.

Descriptions of Wollstonecraft's "madwoman" make it quite clear why Maria Venables would be labelled as insane by the dominant discourse: we are told that "a whirlwind of *rage* and *indignation* roused her torpid pulse," that she suffers from "the heart heavings of *indignant* nature," and that she had "*raved* of injustice" on her entrance into the madhouse (75-77; emphasis added). In discussing women's life writing, Carolyn Heilbrun suggests that because they were "[f]orbidden anger, women could find no voice in which publicly to complain; they took refuge in depression or madness" (*Writing* 15). Yet in Wollstonecraft's text, it is precisely Maria's daring to express her anger and her indignation about her experiences of injustice in a patriarchal culture that results in that culture labelling her as insane; she does not willingly take refuge in madness but is, rather, labelled as mad because of her active disdain for patriarchal authority. We are told, in fact, that Maria's "type" of madness makes her particularly threatening or "mischievous," and that she must be "carefully watched" for she suffers from "lucid periods" during which "any vexation or caprice brought on the paroxysm of phrensy" (*WWM* 78-79). Clearly, it is only when the normally "lucid" Maria expresses her "vexation" or is "capricious" about her social position as a female—in short, whenever she refuses to be silenced—that the authorities figure her as mad. Indeed, Maria's "mischievous" nature, her refusal to suppress her anger and indignation, has caused her to perform what for a female of Wollstonecraft's period can be seen as the ultimate act of insanity: she has already made an utterance—a physical one—against patriarchal law in her flight from her husband's house with her child.

As Eleanor Ty suggests, for eighteenth-century patriarchs the "family becomes a microcosmic state, a basic political unit in its own right" (*Unsex'd Revolutionaries* 4-5); order at home ensures order in the state, and any attempt to subvert that "basic political unit" surely constitutes revolutionary madness.[6] It is especially significant, then, that Maria uses the terminology of the French Revolution when she states that "[m]arriage had bastilled [her] for life" (*WWM* 154-55), and it seems logical that, just as one of the first acts of the French Revolution was the storming of the Bastille prison, an icon of state institutional control, so too is Maria's first act of freedom an escape from the marriage bond. Such actions were not taken lightly, as seen in the text when the judge upholds the reasonableness of Maria Venables's confinement and states that he does not want "French principles in public or private life" and that the "conduct of the lady did not appear that of a person of sane mind" (199). In this action taken by Maria, we see Wollstonecraft's personal experience erupting into her text, for Maria's illness and flight represent the illness and flight of the author's sister Eliza from her husband in 1784. After the birth of her daughter on 10 August 1783, Eliza Bishop suffered a breakdown, the outward manifestation of which Wollstonecraft describes—in words evocative of Maria Venables's illness—to her sister Everina, in a letter of late 1783:

> She has not had a violent fit of *phrensy* since I saw you—but her mind is in a most unsettled state and attending to the constant *fluctuation* of it is far more harassing then the watching of those *raving* fits that had not the least tincture of reason— . . . I am so constantly forced to observe her (lest she runs into *mischief*) that my thought continual [*sic*] turn on the unaccountable wanderings of her mind—(*CLMW* 80; emphasis added)

Shortly after this, Wollstonecraft decided to effect the flight of her sister (by coach like Maria Venables, but without her daughter) from the home of her husband and a marital situation that she believed to be abusive (Tomalin 24-25). As she states it, Eliza's husband "would make a more determined person flinch—This quiet protends [*sic*] no good he will burst out at last and the calm will end in the usual manner" (*CLMW* 85).

Wollstonecraft's attack on the institution of marriage, both in her personal life and in her writings, targets the institution that best symbolizes patriarchy's need for an articulation of the absent mother, the absent referent of symbolic language. Conservatives such as Edmund Burke believed in the sanctity of the law as codified in the eighteenth century by Sir William Blackstone, including the principle of the feme covert, which made the wife "a hidden person, sunk into and merged with the personality of her husband" upon marriage (Perkin 2), or, as Wollstonecraft puts it, "make[s] an absurd unit of a man and his wife" and "reduce[s the wife] to a mere cypher" (*VRW* 282-83). By attacking the law of the feme covert and literalizing the female figure of madness, Wollstonecraft presents the reader of *The Wrongs of Woman* with a challenge to the Lacanian view of language by breaking down two of the powerful symbols of the dominant discourse of her culture, a challenge that she heightens by allowing Maria to articulate her complaints about her situation from a rather threatening alternative discursive position—a position of motherhood. Indeed, being labelled mad is not the only punishment for Maria's physical dissent from the bonds of marriage: for daring subjectivity and presence in a world in which she is meant to be merely an absent object, Maria suffers her child, "only four months old," being "torn from her, even while she was discharging the tenderest maternal office" (80). We are told that Maria's "malady [is] hereditary" (78) and the loss of her child prevents her, to borrow Homans's title, from "bearing the word" of rebellion down to her (very significantly) female child. The child having been taken literally from her breast, Maria is left "hear[ing] her speaking half cooing, and fe[eling] the little twinkling fingers on her burning bosom—a bosom bursting with the nutriment for which this cherished child might now be pining in vain" (75). Wollstonecraft thus articulates her critique of the dominant culture from Maria's participation, through the act of motherhood, within the realm of the presymbolic, a realm in which, as evidenced in the above quotation from the text, "the child shares with the mother what Julia Kristeva calls the semiotic, consisting of body language [the twinkling fingers and the burning/bursting bosom] and nonrepresentational sounds [the speaking half cooing]" (Homans 6). Indeed, as Domna Stanton points out, "the delineation of the subversive semiotic apparatus relies on a series of traditional images," one of which is the "topos of the child at the breast" ("Difference" 166).

However, both Margaret Homans and Domna Stanton qualify the usefulness that the Kristevan view of the semiotic presents for women writers by noting that, for theorists relying on the "patriarchal oedipal script," "the mother remains, as the phallotext defines her, a passive instinctual force that does not speak, but is spoken by the male" (Stanton, "Difference" 166-67). It is the male artist who is given the power to speak in the repressed discourse of the semiotic and so to present a temporary challenge to patriarchal dominance. Homans notes how feminist theorists of child development, such as Nancy Chodorow, have rearticulated the Freudian/Lacanian script from the daughter's point of view to suggest that she "has the positive experience of never having given up entirely the pre-symbolic communication" (13), which provides women writers with an alternative way of speaking out about silenced female experience. Eleanor Ty notes the existence of the semiotic in *The Wrongs of Woman* and makes a connection between Wollstonecraft's implied "distrust of the world dominated by the Father" and her position as a daughter, a position replicated in her "very close ties" with certain women friends (*Unsex'd Revolutionaries* 31-33). Wollstonecraft's position as a daughter, Ty argues, allows her to present an alternative discourse to the patriarchal one.

When we look at the text itself, however, we see that Maria's position as daughter, like Wollstonecraft's, is less than conducive to female agency: indeed, Maria makes apparent the neglect she suffered at the hands of her mother, who is so thoroughly entrapped in a world of male privilege that she gives preference to Maria's brother: "[t]he representative of [the] father, a being privileged by nature—a boy, and the darling of my mother, he did not fail to act like an heir apparent" (*WWM* 125). No semiotic tie can be said to have existed between mother and daughter, as Maria's mother "only suckled [Maria's] eldest brother, which might be the cause of her extraordinary partiality" (130). Similarly, as noted by Emily W. Sunstein, Wollstonecraft's own mother "apparently breast-fed only her oldest" child, a son, and the author did not experience "the kind of maternal care that delights in loving tattle, reminiscences, and infantile accomplishments" (*A Different Face* 9). To take their shared position as daughters one step further, we must examine the even stronger tie to semiotic discourse provided to both Wollstonecraft and Maria by motherhood, through which, as Homans notes, the daughter literally "attempts to recreate her symbiotic closeness with her mother, . . . to recreate that presymbolic language" (25). Rather than bearing a child as a *replacement* for the (supposedly lost) phallus in the Freudian sense, the mother gives birth as a means of "bypassing the phallus altogether," of reconnecting the umbilical tie of "presymbolic symbiosis" (24) that had been interrupted—or "socially and culturally suppressed and silenced" (19)—through the process of socialization.

Even stronger than her need to speak as a daughter, then, is Wollstonecraft's need to infuse into her text her maternal self, as a creator of an alternative way of speaking. For much of the time that she was working on her final text, Wollstonecraft was pregnant with her child by William Godwin, the future Mary Shelley; at the same time, she was already mother to her daughter, Fanny Imlay, who was just over two years old in the summer in which the author began writing this text. The importance of motherhood for Mary Wollstonecraft is evident in a letter dated 11 April 1797 to Amelia Alderson Opie, wherein she states—in words reminiscent of the language used to describe Maria Venables—that "many circumstances in my life have contributed to excite in my *bosom* an *indignant contempt* for the forms of a world I should have bade a long good night to, had I not been a *mother*" (*CLMW* 389-90; emphasis added). The truth of this statement, made while Wollstonecraft was pregnant with her second child, is evident in an earlier letter written to Gilbert Imlay on 12 June 1795, wherein she notes how she "looked at the sea, and at my child [Fanny Imlay], hardly daring to own to myself the secret wish, that it might become our tomb" (291). But Wollstonecraft's desire for death as an end to her personal misery is chastened by the language of maternal duty as she writes to Gilbert Imlay of her decision to choose life: "These are not common sorrows; nor can you perhaps *conceive*, how much active fortitude it requires to *labour* perpetually to blunt the shafts of disappointment" (292; emphasis added). To "labour," then, is to bear forth resistance, to speak out against, or, to use Wollstonecraft's own disfigured phallic image, to "blunt the shafts of disappointment." Wollstonecraft's own experience of motherhood is reflected in the most fully conceptualized sketch for an ending to *The Wrongs of Woman*: Maria, pregnant with her second child, has made the decision to escape "from this hell of *disappointment*" (202; emphasis added), but upon seeing her thought-to-be-dead daughter standing by her bedside, she suffers what appears to be a fit of madness, holds her child "to her bosom" and exclaims "The conflict is over!—I will live for my child!" (203). In this connection between Wollstonecraft's personal experience of being a mother and her representation of Maria's life, we see that the text embodies the author's (the creator's) potential for bearing an alternative discourse. In the Author's Preface she uses the following words: "[t]he sentiments I have embodied" (73), which, as Kelly's note tells us, means that she has "embodied personal feelings in the form of characters and a story" (*WWM* 215). But there may also be the suggestion that her text embodies the alternative discourse inherent to her body, the pregnant body, the mothering body; that her text makes present the absent mother, an*other* body of language and experience. Indeed, by presenting the maternal body in her text, Wollstonecraft refutes the usually disembodied production of female experience in the fiction of her time, wherein, as she states it in the Author's Preface, the heroines are "born immaculate" and made to "act like goddesses of wisdom, just come forth highly finished Minervas from the head of Jove" (73).

Wollstonecraft reinforces this alignment of childbirth and motherhood with the possibility of an alternative discourse of experience in her thematic presentation of mothering as madness, the latter being seen in this period as the "subterranean danger of unreason" (Foucault 84). In the text, the figure of the "lovely maniac" suggests that it is the experience of motherhood that makes women susceptible to madness, for we are told that—as with Eliza Wollstonecraft—it was "during her first lying-in" that she "lost her senses" (*WWM* 88). The term "lying-in" denotes the period of childbirth and recovery in that women were hidden away—absented—from public view, a period that was more commonly called "confinement"; thus, we seem to have a conflation in Wollstonecraft's text of the imagery of the confinement of motherhood and the confinement of madness. The confinement of the birthing mother and the mad person seemed to have had the same purpose: to suppress any discourse that posed a potential threat to the dominance of patriarchal authority. The female confined, whether in marriage, as previously suggested, or in childbirth, becomes the absent referent of symbolic discourse, then, as madness is the confined and absent referent of reason. But both the lovely maniac—who, we are told, had "something which hung on her mind" (88) after giving birth, possibly the ill-treatment of her husband—and especially Maria (who not only had something on her mind after childbirth, but acted upon it) resist the idea of being absent (mothers) and are confined a second time, now in the madhouse. Indeed, Wollstonecraft deliberately plays with patriarchal figurations by making the madhouse a metaphor for the womb itself, for its potential threat to the social order outside its walls, although she literalizes that threat by placing her reader not only inside the madhouse, but inside the mind of the mad mother as well. Wollstonecraft thus *un*confines both these symbols of patriarchal control and presents her reader with an alternative and "threatening space of an absolute freedom" (Foucault 84). With the image of the ruins outside the madhouse and the eventual disclosure of the madhouse proprietor's corruption, Wollstonecraft shows that the real madness exists in the very society that demands Maria's confinement.

While the alternative discourse of female experience uttered by both Wollstonecraft and Maria may seem intelligible to a modern audience enlightened by twentieth-century feminist theory, the view of the eighteenth-century patriarch was decidedly less positive, as we see when Maria attempts, for a second time, to articulate herself outside the madhouse walls. In response to her husband's suit against her lover, Maria composes a statement to the court delineating her abusive marriage and the circumstances of her wrongful incarceration: she "eagerly put[s] herself forward, instead of desiring to be absent" (*WWM* 195). In Maria's attempts to represent her life story to others, Wollstonecraft's writing becomes subversive of the dominant discourse and seeks to effect social change. To assert that Wollstonecraft and Maria speak their experiences from the presymbolic/semiotic realm is not to reinforce some essentialist notion of women's inherent position as Other for, as Allison Weir suggests, the symbolic and the semiotic do not function as exclusive and hierarchical categories:

> If the semiotic has an emancipatory force, it is not as an escape from or destruction of an unchangeable symbolic order, but as a constant reintroduction of heterogeneity into linguistic and social structures—a constant remembering and reassertion of difference, which produces conflict and change. (172)

Rather than presenting us with a true fiction, a utopian account of the legitimization of Maria's composed testament, Wollstonecraft, through the court's rejection of Maria's representation of female experience, effectively reinscribes the Law (and laws) of the Father and makes clear that "real life did not provide women with contrived endings. In real life women stayed imprisoned in their situation" (Figes 59).

Wollstonecraft was obviously also acutely aware that many eighteenth-century readers and critics would be unwilling to hear textual challenges to patriarchal authority and that Maria's revolutionary actions might be perceived as little short of madness: in her "Author's Preface," she wonders about the ability of her readers to "advance before the improvement of the age, and grant that [her] sketches are not the *abortion* of a *distempered* fancy" (*WWM* 73; emphasis added). Wollstonecraft's words are very carefully chosen, as both "abortion" and "distemper" encompass figurative and literal meanings that, in the context of *The Wrongs of Woman*, play against one another in the production of meaning. While "abortion" has the figurative meaning of "failure (of aim or promise)," [7] it also has the literal meaning of "the act of giving untimely birth . . . premature delivery" (*OED*), which results in the effective domination of human socialization by patriarchal norms. Meanwhile, "distemper" had both the concrete meaning of a "deranged or disordered condition of the body or mind," implying both anger and madness, and the figurative meaning of "derangement, disturbance, or disorder (*esp.* in a state or body politic)" (*OED*). Wollstonecraft knew that the perception of meaning and the reception of Maria's message would be informed largely by the gender of her readers. In a letter to George Dyson, to whom she had shown her manuscript, she writes: "I am vexed and surprised at your not thinking the situation of Maria sufficiently important, and can only account for this want of—shall I say it? delicacy of feeling by recollecting that you are a man" (*CLMW* 391-92). A lack of understanding of the importance of Maria's situation is evident also in a review of Wollstonecraft's *Posthumous Works*, which suggests that, although "the laws concerning [the institution of marriage] are far from being perfect, and might be much improved, we should beware of lessening the respect that is due to this legislated bond of love; and of so blackening the picture of married life, as to leave an impression on the public mind favourable to love unrecognized by the law" (Rev. of *Posthumous Works* 325-26).

Regardless of the rejection of Maria's appeal by the court and Wollstonecraft's own fears about reader perception, the embedded text that embodies Maria's story still forces the reader to question the status quo. Maria's story is told through her memoirs to her daughter, and she writes these memoirs because she is "uncertain whether [she] shall ever have an opportunity of instructing" her daughter personally (*WWM* 124). The memoirs are an active appropriation by Wollstonecraft of the very popular conduct and advice books of the period,[8] which were often written to orphaned girls and which, like Maria's narrative, were meant to constitute textual presences to replace the absent mother. Maria's "advice book" to her daughter illustrates that in this period the "auto-biographical impulse is often deflected into other forms," including "expository manuals of instruction and advice," which "may be even more revelatory, more demonstrative of a distinct and emphatic female voice, than autobiography proper" (Myers, "Pedagogy" 193-94). Maria's memoirs articulate just such a "distinct and emphatic female voice," for she is clearly not instructing her daughter to comply with an unjust society,[9] but rather is illustrating for her the "aggravated ills of life that her sex rendered almost inevitable" (*WWM* 76), as well as her own radical reaction against the subordinate position of women.[10] Maria's memoirs are meant to reconnect her with her "lost" daughter, and she hopes they "might perhaps instruct her daughter, and shield her from the misery, the tyranny, her mother knew not how to avoid," a thought that gives "life to her diction" as her "soul flow[s] into it" (82).

Wollstonecraft's final text is, I believe, a memoir for her own daughters, for all daughters, and she gives "life to her diction" by writing her life experience into her text. By thus writing her life, and writing for the life within her, she bears the word of an alternative discourse of female experience down through generations of readers who need only be alert enough to embrace the message. Like Fanny Imlay Godwin and Mary Godwin Shelley, the reader must respond to the "you" of Maria's narrative; we must, as Helen Buss suggests, be "mother, sister, and daughter to the text[s we] read" (*Mapping* 25); we must, in the case of *The Wrongs of Woman*, listen to the truth of Wollstonecraft's/Maria's madness and be moved to action by their appeal to the "justice and humanity of [us] the jury" (*WWM* 198).

Notes

1   In Chapter 1 of *Unsex'd Revolutionaries*, Eleanor Ty notes that Maria's imprisonment in the opening pages of *The Wrongs of Woman* is "one of the clearest instances" of Homans's concept of "literalization" (31), specifically as it realizes Maria's metaphorical query, "Was not the world a vast prison, and women born slaves?" (*WWM* 79).

2   Bedlam, or the hospital of St Mary of Bethlehem, which had become a mental hospital in the fourteenth century, was the "favourite resort for sight-seers" of London (Porter 122-23). As Gary Kelly points out in a note to the Oxford edition of *The Wrongs of Woman*, Wollstonecraft made a visit to Bedlam with William Godwin and her publisher, Joseph Johnson, on 6 February 1797, while she was in the middle of writing her last work and just seven months before she died (216).

3   Whether or not an actual visit to Bedlam was represented in a text, one of the conventions of the literature of sensibility seemed to be that the exuberant and indulgent passions of the characters are often expressed in the very language of madness: for example, words such as "frenzy," "melancholy," "mania," and "delirious," to give just a few, are rife within the literature of sensibility. This connection in the eighteenth century between extreme sensibility and madness is noted by Max Byrd, who looks at the history of the critical reception of Shakespeare's *King Lear* and notes that in 1784 a man named William Richardson wrote that Lear was "a man of 'ungoverned sensibility'" and that "to this undisciplined mind madness is inevitable" (8).

4   In *Tristram Shandy*, the narrator exclaims, "Adieu, Maria!—adieu, poor hapless damsel!—some time, but not *now*, I may hear thy sorrows from thy own lips—but I was deceived; for that moment she took her pipe and told me such a tale of woe with it, that I rose up, and with broken and irregular steps walked softly to my chaise" (601-02). Once again, Maria's own words are deferred in favour of the narrator's sensibilities.

5   Indeed, in Mackenzie's text we are told that the female inhabitant of Bedlam was "pressed by her father to marry a rich miserly fellow, who was old enough to be her grandfather" (22).

6   That revolution was seen as a form of madness is evident in an 1809 review of books about madness, wherein there is a section on something labelled "mania without delirium," which includes this example: during the French Revolution there was a release of inhabitants unlawfully confined by the state in the Asylum of Bicêtre. After one insane man convinced the revolutionaries that he was sane, they agreed to release him, but he was so overcome by the uproar that his mania surfaced and he began to murder them (Rev. of *Observations on Madness* 161-62). Although it is the madman who is being exemplified in the review, the revolutionaries are characterized as "brigands [who] . . . broke like

madmen into the hospital," and it is stated that, after learning of their mistake, they "yielded to the voice of justice and experience" and returned the inhabitants to their cells, and thus put things back to reason and right order.

7   It is interesting to note that the *Oxford English Dictionary* uses as one of its examples of the figurative meaning of the term "abortion" William Godwin's statement in *The Enquirer* — (February 1797) — that "Genius [may] terminate in an abortion" (35).

8   These are books written by both men and women that "prescribed the way in which a woman should behave in all circumstances, and often gave very detailed guides to personal conduct, from sexual behaviour to appropriate reading" (Buck 437).

9   It is interesting to note that after accompanying her sister, Eliza, in her flight from her husband, Wollstonecraft writes the following in a letter to her other sister, Everina: "in short 'tis contrary to all the rules of conduct that are published for the benefit of new married Ladies" (*CLMW* 86).

10 Wollstonecraft may well have been attempting to reproduce in fictional form the work of the "scandalous memoirists" of the eighteenth century, women such as Laetitia Pilkington, who "proclaimed their economic and sexual victimization," "recogniz[ed] their otherness within existing relations of production," and challenged the "intricate power relations of capital and patriarchy" from "outside the family" (Nussbaum, *Autobiographical Subject* 137).

Mary Wollstonecraft
and Harriet Jacobs:
Self Possessions

Jeanne Perreault

As she looks at the bill of sale for the thirteen-year-old "slave, female" who may have been her great-grandmother, law professor Patricia Williams wonders if or how one can be a self or have a self when one is the legal possession of another (16). Williams disconcerts notions of selfhood as abstract, psychological, or purely conceptual by claiming an "I" as material, as possession, even as property. She asserts the double authority of powerful possessor and valued possession, naming herself this way: "my most precious property, I" (Williams 128).[1] "I," usually the subject, is "I" the object here. Explicitly using the language of property in speaking of herself, Williams brings together the familiar if indeterminate notion of self-possession with the objectification implied in self (or any person) as property. The specific history of American slavery and her (unfixed) position as an African-American woman provide Williams with a way to examine "claims that make property of others beyond the self" (11). Mary Wollstonecraft, in both *A Vindication of the Rights of Woman* and *The Wrongs of Woman,* and Harriet Jacobs, in *Incidents in the Life of a Slave Girl* (1861), also examine such claims critically. Grappling with the different but linked problems of the legal possession of women by

---

Notes are on pp. 110-12.

men and the absence of rational and emotional self-possession of mis-educated women, Wollstonecraft relies heavily on the rhetoric, image, and idea of enslavement. Jacobs also makes use of enslavement as a trope, while the material, immediate, lived reality of being a slave, in law, in name, and in social practice, informs her text as it has shaped her life.

In Wollstonecraft's texts, cultural, class, and racial differences change only the terms of enslavement and not its principle. The white woman's body and its products, her children, are not vulnerable in the ways a slave woman's are, but they are not her own either.[2] Wollstonecraft and others of her generation have been criticized for using slavery exploitatively to give weight to their own arguments. Moira Ferguson insists that the "group response" of female solidarity, which is Wollstonecraft's primary (if ambivalent) commitment, can be posited only by looking at other oppressed groups, slaves in particular (*Colonialism* 31); hence Wollstonecraft's dependence on reference to slavery, either of the harem or the plantation (33). Markman Ellis looks at specific sentimental novels for their use of "the figure of slavery," which is, he says, "often replayed transferentially to discuss something else" (55), something he calls "gender relations," probably meaning marriage. Both writers are highly critical of white women's use of slavery as a trope for women's position.

The social reality of slave life makes the analogue between the material conditions of white women and enslaved black women tenable only in specifics of textual detail, not in general cases of social practice. Keeping in mind Hazel V. Carby's cautionary injunction that "any feminist history that seeks to establish the sisterhood of white and black women as allies in the struggle against the oppression of all women must also reveal the complexity of the social and economic differences between women" (30), my critical readings of Wollstonecraft and Jacobs will respect those profound differences. There can be no direct comparison of the position of women who are more or less protected commodities in ordinary social exchange and the position of women who are enslaved under the law by capture or from birth. Nevertheless, both Jacobs and Wollstonecraft seem to support the view Gerda Lerner puts forward in her investigation of the roots of slavery. Lerner argues that, "for women, sexual exploitation marked the very definition of enslavement" (89). The principle of ownership of one's own person is not a principle that women under any social system were (or in many contexts still are) able to assume. Slavery under law has a status in reality that no other experience of unfreedom, imprisonment, violation, consistency of abuse, or legalized exploitation shares. Focusing too narrowly on the use of the word "slavery," however, disrespects both the material and social evils of legal enslavement and the social and personal costs of being a female of any race where women are not legally entitled to self-determination.[3]

Wollstonecraft and Jacobs, paradoxically, insist that the subject position to which they are assigned, the interpellated self available, does not contain them. Whether the figure is the abstract woman in Wollstonecraft's argument, the suffering characters in her novel, or the "I" of Jacobs's narrative, the authors insist that something other than the abjected being is present. Each writer claims a female self-possession that refuses and refutes the view that, as a woman, she is "starve[d] . . . of her very being" (Griffin 304), or that as a slave she is a thing, not a person (Kawash 36). Resistance is not, these writers demonstrate, the only manifestation of selfhood, and subjectivity is not dependent upon some notion of pure control or authority over self.[4] The significance of *possession* on a sense of self, however, is repeatedly drawn.

Ferguson's treatment of Wollstonecraft's complexity and effectiveness in extending the discussion of (all) human(s') rights concludes with Ferguson's belief that Wollstonecraft's text cannot "ideologically fulfil itself" because it is mired in a "bourgeois project of liberation." She says: "Wollstonecraft's liberal, individualist perspective will not let her see that what is common to both white/black and male/female power relations is the concept of private property itself. Europeans see Africans as chattel; men own 'their women'" (*Colonialism* 32).

Despite Ferguson's view that this is an inadvertent flaw in Wollstonecraft's argument, the concept of private property is profoundly and fundamentally appropriated by Wollstonecraft for her ends. Indeed, both she and Harriet Jacobs have found in the apparent contradictions of property and power relations a lever to use against the weight of ownership. Tyranny, external pressure, is precisely a claim to possession of another, and both women's writings demonstrate tyranny's addiction to and dependence upon interior as well as exterior submission. The pressure of intolerable circumstances may dissolve the distinction between inner and outer, and Wollstonecraft's and Jacobs's texts repeatedly return to that point of pressure. There, the authors' belief in the right to self-possession is a necessary condition for their struggle against possession by someone else.

Ideas of self, property, and possession in Mary Wollstonecraft's description of English white women of the eighteenth century inform *The Wrongs of Woman*. In it, Maria is confined socially and legally in the narrow conventions of a middle-class marriage, imprisoned literally in the madhouse by her husband, who wishes to gain control of her inheritance, and enclosed as a fugitive after her escape. Jemima, the guard at the madhouse, is a prisoner of poverty and sexual vulnerability.

The struggles of those female characters and the exploration of issues of property and autonomy parallel those of the narrator in the autobiography of Harriet Jacobs. Jacobs, using the pseudonym Linda Brent, describes her life as a relatively privileged slave, granddaughter of a freed woman who is well respected and independent. Jacobs falls in love with a free black man but is deprived of the right to marry by her sexually obsessed owner. Interestingly, he does not rape her. He requires the submission of her will, not merely domination of her body. She must *agree* to sex with him. In self-defence and as a buffer against her master, she establishes a relationship with another respectable white man and has two children with him. When this strategy begins to fail and the sexual pressure increases, Jacobs hides in a tiny attic space in her grandmother's home, where she lives for seven years before escaping to the North. Harriet Jacobs, as an American slave, is a "possession" in the most blunt way: slavery is not a metaphor in her text or her life. Yet her "self," in the narrative and as she experienced it from childhood,[5] is not contained by legal definitions of chattel property.

For Jacobs, as for Wollstonecraft, issues of being property and having property are imbricated with ideas of selfhood. For both, the will to self-possession animates the very conception of subjectivity. The self as they articulate it textually (the "I" for Jacobs, the Maria and Jemima characters for Wollstonecraft) is an agent of action in the world, who chooses among alternatives, however grim, and who speaks with a will to be heard. It is also a mobile consciousness, feeling as well as thinking, registering passion, desire, and fear. Both women's texts acknowledge and demonstrate the tenuousness of reason and the fluidity of a feeling. In the novel, as in Jacobs's autobiography, a much more subtle and complex articulation of the relation of reason and will to emotion and circumstance is elaborated. For both writers, the loss of agency, will, or hope is registered as a loss in itself rather than as a voiding of selfhood. The "self" here is neither the absent, empty, linguistic construct that some postmodernist theories imagine self to be[6] nor the so-called sovereign subject of liberal tradition.[7]

Though the "sovereign" subject has been undone in a variety of ways, it continues to hold a grip on the imagination of critics if not autobiographers, and I fear I must take up the question here. I will make use of Samira Kawash's discussion of Frederick Douglass's most famous of slave narratives, where the "humanist subject" is the "modern liberal subject understood as individually autonomous, sovereign and rational" (32). Kawash notes that "the slave as slave by definition cannot be such a subject" (32) and argues through Douglass's narrative that it is precisely the existence of the slave and the exclusion of the slave from full humanity that informs definitions of subjectivity. She says, "Douglass remains firmly within the liberal tradition of thinking exemplified by Rousseau and Hegel, in which the relations of mastery and possession that define the relation between master and slave also define the relation of the sovereign subject to itself" (35).

Feminist theorists of subjectivity have long argued that this singular perpendicular "sovereign subject" never informed women's claims to subjectivity or to selfhood. The intersubjective, the maternal, the communitarian subject are all more congruent figures of female selfhood, and consequent self-to-self relations, than the hierarchical and tyrannical figure of sovereign and slave allows.[8] Patricia Williams, we note, says, "my most precious property, I," rather than using the objective case, *me*. The polarity of subject/object and its hierarchical implications for personhood are quite thoroughly messed up in the self-possessions of Wollstonecraft and Jacobs. While both examine critically the social constructions of women, neither will accept that an interpellated identity contains their whole being. And while both Wollstonecraft and Jacobs have an acute sense of the benefits of privilege, neither would support the belief that selfhood is one of them.

Both writers walk a cautious line, demonstrating that being abjected is damaging to spirit, character, and morality while showing the nobility, decency, and value of the person degraded by powerlessness. Morally and socially, the privileged are often represented as craven, vacuous, and vicious, degraded in body and mind—the dirty, drunken husband of Maria, for example, or the cold, vindictive, sexually obsessed master of Harriet Jacobs. The figure of the powerful male shows unequivocally that position does not ensure character any more than oppression necessarily negates it. Both Wollstonecraft and Jacobs were arguing desperately against legal and social systems that claimed the right first to *define* them and then to determine the conditions of life appropriate to the category in which they were placed. As writers they had to assert, and effectively construct for a reader, first the existence, then the value of the self that is contested territory both internally and externally.[9] Both writers build their narratives on a configuration of selfhood based on a paradox: to be free from being possessed by others, one must be possessed by self; to be fully a subject, one must also be an object.

Moira Ferguson comments that slavery's "injustice . . . underwrote middle-class women's dissatisfaction . . . with the status quo"

(*Subject* 108). The slightly dismissive tone Ferguson brings with the word "dissatisfaction" contrasts markedly with Wollstonecraft's insight into the subjugation of women. She says in the Dedication of *A Vindication of the Rights of Woman*, "They may be convenient slaves, but slavery will have its constant effect, degrading the master and the abject dependent" (104). Unlike the usual "diffidence of metaphor," which has no literal referent, to use Syndy Conger's nice phrasing (*Mary Wollstonecraft* xix), "slavery" as a figure has a most complex, long-reaching, and socially materialized referent. Wollstonecraft speaks doubly, to critique both the actual enslavement of Africans and the metaphorical enslavement of women. Making "property of others beyond the self" (Williams 11) brings degradation to all.

Harriet Jacobs is more graphic on the "constant effect" of slavery, marking the specific effects of gender as well as position. Jacobs says, "The slave girl is reared in an atmosphere of licentiousness and fear. The lash and the foul talk of her master and his sons are her teachers" (51). The female slave's body (taught by the lash) and mind (by foul talk) are equally vulnerable. But the costs of slavery to the slave owner ("pervading corruption" and "vitiated by unclean influences" [51-52]) are borne most by the character, spirit, or soul of the master and his family. Those who hold unjust power are more profoundly damaged in their personhood than is the victim of injustice, even though her body has been brutalized. Jacobs argues that "slavery is a curse to the whites as well as to the blacks" (52), but I do not mean to suggest that she equates the two positions. The damage to whites she can name: "it makes the white fathers cruel and sensual; the sons violent and licentious; it contaminates the daughters and makes the wives wretched" (52). For blacks, however, the horror is beyond her skill with language: "And for the coloured race, it needs an abler pen than mine to describe the extremity of their sufferings, the depth of their degradation" (52).[10]

Karen Sánchez-Eppler argues that "[f]eminists and abolitionists were acutely aware of the dependence of personhood on the condition of the human body" (93), and that the "human body" is "site and symbol of the self that links the struggles of feminists and abolitionists" (99). "Personhood" is necessarily an ambiguous term. I believe, however, that Jacobs' deepest argument is precisely the *separation* of personhood from the condition of the body rather than its dependence upon that condition. In fact, the arguments of pro-slavery forces work to demonstrate that the enslaved in body and name is subhuman in "nature." Of her mother, Jacobs says, "[she] had been a slave merely in name, but in nature was noble and womanly" (7).

Wollstonecraft's Jemima, though not a slave "in name," names herself enslaved. Her narrative parallels common African-American slave experience in several particulars and makes extensive use of enslavement as the appropriate term for the life Jemima lives. Paralleling the experience of many mixed-blood slaves (including that of Jacobs's daughter), Jemima as a child is required to serve her half-sister with, she says, "the servility of a slave" (103). Using the language available from the rhetoric of abolition, but not limited to it, Jemima explains that her stepmother was a "tyrant" (104), and that she laboured "under the lash" (105), and, like Harriet Jacobs, Jemima suppresses parts of her story. She says that she censors her tale "lest [Maria], who probably [has] never been drenched with the dregs of human misery, should think [she] exaggerate[s]" (105). Jemima names her own condition: "I was, in fact, born a slave, and chained by infamy to slavery during the whole of my existence" (106).

The "infamy" to which she alludes is, of course, sexual, reminding us of Lerner's view that "for women, sexual exploitation marked the very definition of enslavement" (89). Jemima's narrative outlines her desperation, confusion, and rage, and when she ends up on the street she names herself, tellingly, this way: "I was still a slave, a bastard, a common property" (109). She exists in a contradictory zone: unclaimed by patriarchy, she is therefore unpropertied, yet, unlike the respected wife and daughter, who are private property, she is "common property." The legal slave is ironically conditioned more like the wife than the street prostitute, but for Jemima the figure of slave speaks directly to her lack of choice. The men who use her sexually, from her first master who makes her "prey of his brutal appetite" (107) to the "desire of the brutes" (109) on the streets, to the "drunkards who abused [her]" (109), excite her loathing, disgust, anguish, and detestation (106-10).

Yet, like Jacobs, she holds fast to the small measure of freedom or independence she has, which, she explains, "only consisted in choosing the street in which [she] should wander" (109). Wollstonecraft interpolates Jemima's narrative, making the confessional narrative a centrepiece to the frame story of the privileged woman, the virtuous wife, and the beloved child. In giving Jemima her own story, and providing the tropes that bring Jemima's self-assessment into the revolution in feminist consciousness that Wollstonecraft wants, Wollstonecraft relies on the emotional effectiveness of all glimpses into the underside of life and enlists the shame, pity, and recognition that social change depends upon. By drawing Jemima's story so close to Maria's, Wollstonecraft reinforces Sánchez-Eppler's view of the dependence of "personhood on the condition of the human body" (93). But Wollstonecraft's use of Jemima's response to Maria and her own narrative also site the resilience of "personhood": it is very difficult to destroy, Jemima's renewal implies.

Maria, incarcerated, understands her alternatives, but that comprehension does not protect her: "Indulged sorrow, she perceived, must blunt or sharpen the faculties to the two opposite extremes; producing stupidity, the moping melancholy of indolence; or the restless activity of a disturbed imagination. She sunk into one state, after being fatigued by the other." It is while Maria is in this mental condition that Wollstonecraft speaks through her: "And to what purpose did she rally all her energy?—Was not the world a vast prison, and women born slaves?" (79). The reader is, I think, intended to answer both yes and no. The condition of the body can be, as Jacobs insists, reduced to the signifier—"a slave merely in name"—and the "nature," the signified, can "be noble and womanly." The division between the name and the named must be asserted; the despair that Maria suffers acknowledges that one's body's condition is a permeable membrane, but not a definitive (or over-determined) zone.

The "yes and no" answer to the question "Was not the world a vast prison, and women born slaves?" turns on the very permeability of selfhood and the instability of terms. In Maria's despair, no outside, no elsewhere to the female condition of enslavement, exists. Wollstonecraft grapples with this failure of imagination, of hope or will. Her refusal to allow the inner self of women to be utterly consumed makes her allegiance with Harriet Jacobs profound.

Jacobs consistently distinguishes between the perspective and perceptions of the slaveholders and the worth of the people whom they violate. Describing the occasion on which her grandmother is cheated of money she has loaned to her mistress, Jacobs explains, "The reader probably knows that no promise or writing given to a slave is legally binding; for according to Southern laws, a slave *being* property, can *hold* no property. When my grandmother lent her hard earnings to her mistress, she trusted solely to her honour. The honour of a slaveholder to a slave!" (6). This concluding exclamation point is left to speak the volumes of indignation and outrage that Jacobs feels. "Honour" is juxtaposed squarely against the machinery of the law, even the power of the written word. When honour is absent, as it must be when any slaveholder lives, the person cheated is the slave, but the person *dishonoured* is the slaveholder. The position in law (*being* property) is not incongruent with being honourable, nor does holding that property cohere with having honour.

Honour and trust, even a history of "kindness and attachment," are proven to be no substitute for material, property-based security:

"Never" Jacobs says, "should I know peace till my children were eman-
cipated with all due formalities of law" (138). Her daughter is indeed
treated as a slave by her Northern relatives, and Jacobs's bitterness
exposes something of the hope, if not trust, she had carried. She fears
the child's father has given her away "as a piece of property," and
reminds us that "slavery perverted all the natural feelings of the human
heart" (142). Jacobs, however, has been at pains to show that the "natural feelings," those born of touch, nurturance, kindness, and parenthood, are fully functioning in the beings designated as non-persons,
while the power of slavery to pervert falls much more heavily on those
who appear to be positioned as privileged and whose "personhood" is
never challenged by the slave system. Trust and honour are interactive,
and Jacobs' insistent recollection and reiteration of her trust are part of
the force of subjectivity that she claims. That she is betrayed in that
trust does not dishonour her in her own eyes but makes her compas-
sionate for her trusting younger self. She is hurt, troubled, damaged,
even maddened by the betrayals of trust (more than by the mechanics
of the slaveholder's power, it seems), but she is not degraded in her
own eyes. Resistance, here, is not the only route to subjectivity. Of
course, any autonomous thought, deed, or feeling can be construed as
"resistant," but I want to distinguish between resistance designed to
have an effect on the slaveholder and resistance focused elsewhere, in
the space of self-possession, capacity to respond, exercise of will for
one's own wishes and needs.

　　Harriet Jacobs, of course, resists the power of the slave master
with brilliant effectiveness, but at horrific cost to herself.[11] Her argument with herself about the nature of the system she is in and the kind
of "property" she is considered to be is informative here. Having finally escaped to the North and finding that her daughter is being treated as
a slave, she says, "In order to protect my children, it was necessary that
I should own myself. I called myself free, and sometimes felt so; but I
knew I was insecure" (166). Feeling one's self "free," naming one's
self so, and *owning* one's self are set in a strange triangularity here,
dominated by the necessities of the laws that hold authority over her
children. She unsuccessfully attempts to purchase herself and her children from the Flints.

　　For Jacobs, this need to "own" herself does not exist *in opposition*
to feeling free but alongside it, as part of the grotesque social reality she
must accommodate. The contradictions of her position and her
response to them appear in her reaction to the letter she gets from "[her]
friend and mistress" (187) inviting her to come to visit to work out the
terms of the sale. Jacobs explains to the reader that she wants to use her

income to educate her children and provide a home for them. The context in which she writes and the prevalence of the arguments about the rights of property holders are clear from her reaction: "It seemed not only hard but unjust, to pay for myself. I could not possibly regard myself as a piece of property" (187). She justifies her claiming of herself as her own property, imbricating contradictory positions and concluding with her judgment against the law: "I knew the law would decide I was his property . . . but I regarded such laws as the regulations of robbers, who had no rights that I was bound to respect" (187).

With the word "robbers," Jacobs is imaging the thieves of property: specifically, human bodies. She could not possibly regard herself as a "piece" of property, but she can imagine that she could be stolen, and the cruelty of this dilemma faces her when the Fugitive Slave Laws allow her to be hunted in New York. Her patron, Mrs Bruce, offers to buy her freedom. Jacobs says, "the idea was not so pleasant to me as might have been expected. The more my mind had become enlightened, the more difficult it was for me to consider myself an article of property" (199). Again, the specific reference to the "thingness" of property (a "piece," an "article") suggests what is intolerable to Jacobs. Though she rejects the offer, Mrs Bruce goes ahead, and Jacobs imagines the readers of the future examining the bill of sale of "a human being": "future generations will learn from it that women were articles of traffic in New York" (200). Jacobs claims the category "human being" for women, and "woman" for herself, and imagines a future in which neither race nor sex will mitigate the reader's horror—"A human being *sold* in the free city of New York!" (200). In this future, her femaleness will inform her unity with other women rather than her race marking her difference from the white women whom she addresses throughout this narrative. She then shifts the designation of that which has been sold: "I had objected to having my freedom bought, yet I must confess that when it was done I felt as if a heavy load had been lifted from my weary shoulders" (200). It is her *freedom* that has been bought, not her self. That possession has never been available for purchase.

Wollstonecraft and Jacobs have a deeply ambivalent relation to embodiment.[12] The condition of the body is not the determining factor in selfhood—yet, the body as self's own property informs their argument. The self must make itself into its own property, defined by the *OED* as "the right (esp. exclusive right) to the possession, use or disposal of anything (usually a tangible material thing)." For Wollstonecraft and for Jacobs, the concept of private property, rather than being a factor that works simply against them, in fact supports their belief in their right to self possession.[13] Self-possession, according to the *OED*, is an intellectual and/or emotional "action or condition" that has everything to do with "keeping (oneself, one's mind, etc.) under control." This definition implies a necessary restraint, a containment in defence of a self whose energies are intense and whose boundaries may be overwhelmed from within.

The definition of "possession" offered by the *OED* carries something of the dichotomy of property and possession: "The action or fact of possessing, or condition of being possessed; the holding or having something (material or immaterial) as one's own, or in one's control; actual holding or occupancy, as distinct from ownership." Under this first definition of "possession," both material and immaterial phenomena are named, and a distinction is established between "occupancy" and ownership, and between "control" and ownership. Legal ownership arises only in the second definition of possession, and there, property becomes central.

Discussing the entrenchment of slavery as the basis of economic production in the British colonies, Samira Kawash notes that "in relation to slavery, [the] color line was always also a property line, the boundary between a whiteness that could own but would never become property and a blackness that was defined in terms of its status as a (potential or actual) human property" (viii). Property, as conceived in the founding era,

> included not only external objects and people's relationships to them, but also all of those human rights, liberties, powers, and immunities that are important for human well-being, including: freedom of expression, freedom of conscience, freedom from bodily harm, and free and equal opportunities to use personal faculties. (Underkuffler 129; qtd. in Harris 1726)

Cheryl I. Harris argues that whiteness—"the right to white identity as embraced by the law—is property if by property one means all of a person's legal rights" (1726). A property or characteristic becomes "property" itself when the laws (and subsequent social practice) are determined on the basis of membership in a particular group. The colour line and the property line, as Kawash discerns, mark a boundary between having and being had, being in possession and being a possession.

Whiteness, however, was not in itself a guarantee against being property. Harriet Jacobs seems to suggest as much in her often-remarked conclusion to *Incidents in the Life of a Slave Girl*. Making a wry comment that reflects not only her text's difference from the genre of romance narratives, but also her life's distinction from the expectation that the life patterns of women progress toward marriage, she says, "Reader, my story ends with freedom; not in the usual way, with marriage" (201). Jacobs is asserting something about marriage for women as well as something about American slave life. Marriage offers no alternative to enslavement in this narrative. Maria, propertied with whiteness and class privilege, in her "memoirs" to her daughter names her status as property in law: "a wife being as much a man's property as his horse, or his ass, she has nothing she can call her own" (158). Blackness is the property that defines Harriet Jacobs (potentially or actually) as property. Her femaleness, like Wollstonecraft's, is the determining factor in how the conditions of being property will be manifested. Carla Kaplan says that, in the nineteenth century, marriage established "male possessive individuality through the exchange of women who mediated social relations not by being possessors of property but by being property" (109). In her urgent, even aggressive, insistence that women possess themselves,[14] Wollstonecraft demands that women take responsibility for themselves at the same time as she demands women's legal rights over themselves. In Wollstonecraft and Jacobs, the mind, the heart, and the body come together and come apart in the articulations of "self" whose hold on material and emotional self-possession is provisional, inconsistent, transgressive of specific laws, and contrary to convention. In contrast to William L. Andrews's argument that enslavement is a condition of "non-being" (65), the narratives I examine, whether of legal or social enslavement, have a common root in their claim to social justice grounded on the rights and responsibilities of self-possession. Just as privilege will not confer the intelligent engagement of emotion and reason—the passion and constraint that are characteristic of self-possession—oppression will not inevitably defeat it.

Notes

1 For a discussion of Williams's text, see my *Writing Selves*, 100-12. Jane Moore discusses Williams's analysis of the American Constitution in her Lacanian treatment of *A Vindication of the Rights of Woman* (30-33).

2 Note Fanny Kemble, who, when she protested the treatment of slave women on her husband's plantation, was denied access to her own children. As Diane Roberts notes, "She suffered a fate similar to that of so many slave women she pitied; her children were taken from her by their (and her) legal owner" (122).

3   Shipley's *The Origins of English Words* tells us: "The name *Slav* meant glory. . . . In A.D. 955 Holy Roman Emperor Otto the Great conquered the Slavs; hence E *slave, slavery.* Fr, *esclavage*: literally, slavery; used in 18th c. English of a necklace of several bands of gold resembling a slave's fetters but implying submission to a husband or lover" (187).

4   Despite Wollstonecraft's challenge to the "legal situation" (Ferguson, *Colonialism* 13) of slavery and the African slave trade, and despite her unequivocal support for abolition, Ferguson suggests negatively that Wollstonecraft believes that "reason [is] an even more important attribute to possess than physical freedom" (13). Since physical freedom without reason is a dubious "freedom" at best, Ferguson seems to be making a spurious argument here. Jacobs, like Wollstonecraft, cherishes her "reason" above all.

5   Despite the indeterminate status of "experience" as a validated and validator of autobiographical texts, Jacobs's actions allow us to infer the authority of her experienced self, feelings, decisions.

6   See my *Writing Selves* for a full discussion of feminist readings of subjectivity in a postmodern context.

7   See Jardine and Miller for important feminist interventions. I optimistically imagine that this fantastical figure (the sovereign subject) will be allowed to rest in peace, but even in so brilliant a book as Samira Kawash's it must be again deconstructed.

8   I need not belabour the too-obvious parallels of the relation between master and slave, husband and wife. I will mention, however, that these are legal and social roles and cannot wholly inform ontological or phenomenological relations between or within people.

9   Andrews, speaking in a critical language we might now rephrase, also asserts that it is in "the act of rebellion" that "the slave . . . claims . . . an existential authenticity and freedom while still in bondage" (65).

10 Describing the extremity of suffering, which Jacobs claims she cannot do, involves the highly ambiguous role of specularity. As Peter Brooks points out, the issues of "privacy and invasion," ultimately "the place and meaning of the body" (38), carry the narrative burden of significance. Privacy of the body is precisely a luxury that wives and enslaved women cannot enjoy.

11 Strong critical treatments of Jacobs's period in the attic crawl space, her strategies of resistance and escape, and her narrative, appear in Carby, Gwin, Kawash, and Mullen.

12   See Moira Ferguson's discussion of Wollstonecraft's complicated treatment of the question of "sexually abused female slaves"
(*Colonialism* 26-28).

13   I am aware that this is precisely the argument used by some
socialists to demonstrate that personalized feminism is a bourgeois concern. My own interest is in finding out how senses of
self are manifested in Wollstonecraft and Jacobs, what informs
them, and how they are functional in emancipatory discourses,
rather than in determining a correct feminism.

14   Some of this aggression Susan Gubar reads as "feminist
misogyny"—seeing in Wollstonecraft's critique of feminine
behaviours a hostility to women.

Memoirs Discourse and William Godwin's *Memoirs of the Author of* A Vindication of the Rights of Woman

Helen M. Buss

In her 1981 essay on Godwin's *Memoirs*, Mitzi Myers writes of the unruly intangibles of life writing, quoting Virginia Woolf's reference in *Orlando* to that riot and confusion of the passions and emotions that every good biographer detests ("Godwin's *Memoirs*" 309).[1] It is my purpose to make use of the theorization of life writing that has been taking place in the last two decades to show how the unruly aspects of Godwin's text have become less intangible to critical analysis. Explicating the subject position of a writer who may be seen to be in a difficult personal position as biographer, because of the riot and confusion of his passions, requires that we understand that a memoirist is not exactly the same thing as a biographer: differentiating more precisely between the two modes of writing is now possible, given that we live in a cultural moment when theoretical discussion of the varieties of life writing has become a preoccupation in the academy. The traditions of the spiritual and secular confessional and the developmental modes of mainstream autobiography,[2] the changing nature of the way biography "recognizes" its subjects,[3] and the (largely) feminist invention of words such as autogynography, autograph, and *testimonio*[4] are witness to a current critical activity of describing, both ideologi-

---

Notes are on pp. 123-25.

cally and generically, the differences that variously change the contract[5] readers make with any given auto/biographical account. My own interest has been with the memoir form, that slippery generic naming that insists on occupying the border spaces between fictional construction and claims of historical referentiality, between the making of the self and the memorialization of the other, between the generic contracts of biography and autobiography. Because of the wide variation that the form undertakes in different writers' hands, reviewers and readers have a difficult time deciding what a memoir should be.

Take, for example, a recent newspaper article that agonizes over the ethical status of a memoir that reveals an abusive marriage situation. The columnist reckons that "the classical memoir is written in hindsight, when objective assessment is theoretically possible, but the book under discussion show[s] more pain than perspective." Such "partisan dossiers for the defense," observes the regretful reviewer, "aim to tell only one side of the story" (Ross C1, C4).[6] The evocation of the term "classical memoir" strikes me ironically, because despite the efforts of critics such as Francis Russell Hart and Marcus Billson in the 1970s and Lee Quinby and myself in the 1990s, there seems to be no very sophisticated understanding of the generic and ideological positions occupied by the form,[7] not only by reviewers in the popular press, but also by many academic critics.[8] Indeed, far from being measured and reflective, some of the "classic" memoirs (if I can use that word to mean those republished over many years) are written "to tell one side of the story"; they are often written very close in time and/or passion to the events they relate and they are partisan, defensive, and almost always pained.

One of the reasons they are pained is that they chart the encounter of private person and public ideology, the life stories of individual human subjects who hardly ever fit current modes of subjectivity, in which the memoirist, sometimes desperately, sometimes with aesthetic élan, writes her/himself in and out of the reading contracts of novel, biography, autobiography, history, and assorted other recognizable discursive forms from philosophy to pornography. The memoir form is a heteromorphic bastardization of multiple generic borrowings. Perhaps that is why reading memoirs is often an ambiguous experience of page-turning intensity and squirming dissatisfaction. They both grip us with multiple generic appeals and disconcert us with their refusal to fulfill our generic expectations as readers of novels, of history, of biography, of autobiography.

I propose to read William Godwin's *Memoirs* of his wife, Mary Wollstonecraft, from a critical perspective that does not denigrate the partial, the personal, or the painful aspects of memoirs, but rather accounts for those aspects and others within a theory of the narrative positioning of the memoir writer as eyewitness, participant, and *histor* of the life story s/he is telling. In doing so, I will comment on the effect of Godwin's use of this autobiographical format that so intensely brings the personal and public worlds into interaction. Marcus Billson, in his 1977 article "The Memoir: New Perspectives on a Forgotten Genre," outlines this tripartite narrative position, and, attending to his observations, I hope to offer a reading contract with Godwin's text that helps to explain the very complex generic problems that Mary Wollstonecraft's husband took on when, shortly after her death, as William St Clair records, he hung her portrait up in her study, moved himself in, and began his memorial activity (180).

Billson proposes that from classical times the "eyewitness" stance "endow[ed] the narrative with an unchallengeable aura of authenticity" (272). In order to understand the epistemological and ethical processes involved in such a narrative stance, Billson draws on Hayden White's "ideographic" method of historical interpretation: "For some historians an explicated historical domain presents the aspect of a set of dispersed entities" that share "nothing more than their inhabitance of a single neighborhood of occurrences" (273). These entities cannot be subsumed under any "general rule, either of causation or of classificatory entailment" (274). This ideographic mode is the eyewitness stance, since the very vividness and immediacy of what is being witnessed is received as "scattered." Thus the epistemological positioning of the eyewitness implies a way of knowing in which interpretation must take place from a position of lack of distance, lack of overview, lack of generalizing capability. This narrative positioning, although implying a disadvantage because of what it lacks, is actually often productive of the most vivid and gripping accounts in literature. As Thomas Carlyle said of Boswell's *Life of Samuel Johnson*, a biography that has many aspects of the memoir form, "It was as if the curtains of the past were drawn aside . . . and we looked into a country . . . which had seemed forever hidden from our eyes . . . wondrously given back to us, there once more it lay" (qtd. in Hibbard 27).

Despite this special quality of authenticity that the eyewitness stance produces, in the actual post-event writing the inevitable ordering and selecting that takes place—what is detailed, what is cut short, what is given descriptive privilege, what is not—puts the eyewitness in a position in which stylistic and other practical choices entail ethical consequences. Perhaps I can best demonstrate this positioning and its ethical effects if we look at what is perhaps the most gripping eye-witnessing in

Godwin's memoirs, his account of Mary Wollstonecraft's labor and birthing, its complications, and her ultimate death from septicemia. At each stage of the tragedy we see Godwin observing the materiality of the situation as scattered, since he experiences each new turn as a step into the unknown: the course of the labour—during which Wollstonecraft in her practical low-key approach to birthing continued to write letters and move about until quite late in the process—followed by the presentation of the child to its father in a little ceremony of Wollstonecraft's creation, the sudden alarm caused by the failure of the placenta fully to come away, the midwife's advice to call a "male practitioner" (*MAV* [1987] 266), the intervention, which did not lessen the hemorrhage (and as we can surmise today, probably introduced the infection), the hours when the symptoms of infection grew alarmingly, the days of suffering, the momentary calm intervals when hope grew, the desperate rush for medical solutions, the ultimate concentration during the last hours on the dying woman, and the final exact recording of the fact, "She expired at twenty minutes before eight" (271).

While all of these exemplify the profound authenticating impact of the eyewitness stance, the epistemology of the "scattered field" is always already—whether it be in the minimal interpretive allowance given the witness in a court case or the wide latitude given the memoir writer—involved in an ethics of interpretation. I find in reading memoir that the most gripping accounts always offer a measure of interpretive interruption, but indeed it must be very measured to keep the vividness of the eyewitness stance intact. An interesting effect of this very delicate operation is that memoirists never seem to be able to keep it pure, one-dimensional; the stance is always dual: an interpretive position that serves to organize the events observed and one that serves the interests of the eyewitness. Godwin's stance does serve the events being witnessed in that he foregrounds Wollstonecraft's hands-off approach to childbirth as a labouring activity over a medicalized procedure; he works at accuracy in portraying the confusing philosophies of the various medical men who become involved; and he reinforces his respectful descriptions of his wife's decline by quoting her calm, intelligent, and sometimes humorous comments on her own situation. But from the beginning there is also the interpretive stance of the defendant. A terrible, irrational calamity has happened, and Godwin, like most of us in such a situation, needs to say that it is not his fault. From the very beginning of the chapter when he observes, "I cheerfully submitted in every point to her judgment and her wisdom" (265), through his distancing himself by calling her the "patient" (267) and his assurance that his efforts to find the best medical help made him "perfectly satisfied that every thing was safe" (267), to his appeals to Dr Carlisle's "maxim[s]" for dealing with the dying (271), much of the praised-filled memorialization of the other is also a defence of the self.

For those who consider the "classic" memoir to be one in which "objective assessment is theoretically possible" (Ross C1), Godwin's defensiveness would classify his memoir as not classic. I would argue the opposite, that it is the very impossibility of impartiality that makes it a "classic" memoir. And it is the reader's ability to observe the contestation between self-interest and the interest of serving the other that establishes the powerful and very active reading contract of the memoir form. As readers observing the ethical struggle of the memoirist — to be true to an accurate history of events, to be a true witness to the life of the other, to be true to his or her own self shaping itself in history — we experience an epistemological position similar to the writer's, we witness the witnessing, we move through our own ethical process in concert with the narrator. That is one reason why memoirs are so gripping, why reviewers find it hard to write objective reviews, why such accounts open the past in particularly effective ways. Like the memoirist, we cannot remain fully in the eyewitness mode; we inevitably become involved in a participatory stance: we participate by assessing the ethics of the memoirist's narrative position.

The slippage of eyewitnessing to self-witnessing in memoirs makes a participatory mode inevitably a part of the narrative stance. Billson observes that "as participant, the memorialist concentrates on himself and relates the course of his own role, however major or ancillary, in the story he has to tell. Acting as a participant in this narrative, the memoir-writer reinforces the authority of the eyewitness stance" (275). I have already implied that the participatory stance does not always reinforce the eyewitness's authority, but instead sometimes gives the reader the analytical tools with which to inquire into the self-making and, indeed, the self-justification that is always going on in the memoir form.

Godwin's participatory stance is a complex one. As Wollstonecraft's husband, editor, and philosophical soulmate, this man is intimately involved in the story he tells. But he also lives in a time when the writing contracts of memoir and biography were not as separate as we may think of them today. It is obvious in his preface to the memoirs that he does not draw clear lines between memoirs and biography: "It has always appeared to me, that to give the public some account of the life of a person of eminent merit deceased, is a duty incumbent on survivors." Despite the memoir implications contained in the word "survivors," Godwin sees his task as essentially that of the biographer. He must make an "industrious enquiry among the persons most intimately acquainted with her at the different periods of her life" and record "[t]he facts . . . taken from the mouth of the person to whom they relate" (204). Godwin sees himself as biographer (as does his twentieth-century advocate, Richard Holmes, who names the *Memoirs* "biography" [16]). However, Godwin takes up the participant dimension of the memoir's form almost immediately, when, five pages into the *Memoirs*, he recounts the coincidence that his stay in the town of Hoxton occurred at the same time as the Wollstonecraft family was there. In doing so, he makes what I see as a participatory observation (one that is imaginary, but certainly desirous of participation):

> It is perhaps a question of curious speculation to enquire, what would have been the amount of the difference in the pursuits and enjoyments of each party [Godwin and Wollstonecraft], if they had met, and considered each other with the same distinguishing regard in 1776, as they were afterwards impressed with in the year 1796. The writer had then completed the twentieth, and Mary the seventeenth year of her age. Which would have been predominant; the disadvantages of obscurity, and the pressure of a family; or the gratifications and improvement that might have flowed from their intercourse? (209)

This observation alerts readers early, as memoir writers often do, either deliberately or unconsciously, that the memoir text, while not able to exist without the significant other, is always also about the self.

Several aspects of Godwin's self are involved in his participatory stance. Sometimes he is the stern judge of other significant others as when, after informing us that Wollstonecraft "may be said to have been, in a great degree, the victim of a desire to promote the benefit of others" (214), he adds that the recipient of much of this "benefit," her best friend Fanny Blood, "was a woman of a timid and irresolute nature, accustomed to yield to difficulties" (217). Sometimes he is the grieving husband and father who cannot help but admit: "While I thus enumerate her more than maternal qualities, it is impossible not to feel a pang at the recollection of her orphan children!" (219). Sometimes he is the literary critic who, as he critiques the "homily-language" of her early work, confesses that "to speak *from my own feelings*," such a style "is calculated to damp the moral courage it was intended to awaken" (227; emphasis added).

What happens in the interplay of witnessing and participating is that although the writer tends to set up distinctions among his identities as writer, as narrating eyewitness, and as participant—for example, by using the third person, a choice that may disguise his participation—the very construction of the different narrative positions, as Billson observes, allows "the reader . . . to gauge the validity of an account by judging the memorialist's physical relationship to events. The memorialist's participation determines his relations to the world. . . . The reader often finds the rationale for those values that pervade the memoir in the lineaments and motivations of the memorialist's actions in society" (275). By traditional standards of discourses that claim objectivity—such as history and biography—a writer who puts in doubt his or her authenticity as eyewitness by confusing or self-serving stances as participant is a bad writer, but the memoir is the genre for those who cannot get past partiality, cannot get past the intricate implication of the self in all of his or her readings of the world. The memoir allows this highly complex, often unsatisfying, but very materially real human condition to exist without resolution, and in doing so it empowers readers to participate in the struggle of the contradictory but coexisting stances, and to read themselves powerfully into the text as participant in the role of mediator between those stances.

One of the ways in which Godwin's memoir continues to fascinate me is the way his fear of full participation as lover, husband, and father causes his suppressed participatory imperatives to erupt in inappropriate ways. For example, when describing the terrible experience of hope revived and hope crushed during the final days of Wollstonecraft's life, he writes:

> But I now sought to suppress every idea of hope. The greatest anguish I have any conception of, consists in that crushing of a newborn hope which I had already two or three times experienced. If Mary recovered, it was well, and I should see it time enough. But it was too mighty a thought to bear being trifled with, and turned out and admitted in this abrupt way. (269-70)

He then adds, in the kind of excruciatingly inappropriate phrase that makes it necessary for this reader to realize her full responsibility as mediator of this volatile genre: "I had reason *to rejoice* in the firmness of my gloomy thoughts, when, about ten o'clock . . . Mr Carlisle told us to prepare ourselves, for we had reason to expect the fatal event every moment" (270; emphasis added).[9] Certainly, he might have reason to be *relieved* that both Wollstonecraft and those who loved her were soon to be spared more suffering by the fact of her death, but it is interesting to see such an imprecise use of language from a man so practised in language making. The philosopher whose favourite mode of verbal expression is the double negative—which, as William St Clair observes, gives his writing a "tone of lofty imperturbability" and a "latinate gravity" (21)—is here driven by the multiple demands of the memoir form to drop his reserve and try for a more positive verbal expression, but instead lands on the inappropriate infinitive, "to rejoice." I do not dwell so long on such a minor choice to undermine Godwin's authority as memoirist, but rather to insist on the authenticity of his effort, caught up as he was in a memorial, biographical, and autobiographical writing event, in the pained and partisan act of memoir writing. Part of the effect of such a writing act is that language often betrays our intentions and writes more or less than we would wish.

The complexity and ambiguity of Godwin's role as participant empower the reader to interrogate the third role of the tripartite narrator: the role of *histor*. Billson borrows this word from Robert Scholes and Robert Kellogg, who in *The Nature of Narrative* describe the effect of the *histor* role as one in which the writer/narrator

> establish[es] himself with the reader as the repository of fact, a tireless investigator and sorter, a sober and impartial judge—a man in short, of authority, who is entitled not only to present the facts as he has established them but to comment on them, to tell the reader what to think and even to suggest what he should do. (266)

It is my experience that although other genres may encourage such trust in the narrator, the memoir writer rarely has this kind of power over the reader. The often contending and ambiguous roles the narrator performs as eyewitness and participant tend to give the reader permission to seek below the smooth surface of the *histor*'s construction of the facts of the life story.

Godwin's chief authority as *histor* is in his role as the philosopher who brings the theories of deterministic "necessity" and human "perfectibility" to bear on the telling of his wife's life story. St Clair summarizes Godwin's rational reconciliation of these two philosophical principles:

> The universe is . . . a chain in which everything is connected with everything else. If you tug the end of a chain, there will be repercussions all along its length. . . . The operations of the mind . . . can be regarded as a similar series of events. . . . But although the mind may be governed by laws of causation, this does not mean, according to Godwin, that human beings are totally pre-programmed. The key to the apparent contradiction lies in the application of perception, reason and motive. . . . [If human beings] succeed in making an improved perception, that itself is a mental event as a result of which the subsequent chain of mental—and therefore

physical—events is different from what it would otherwise have been. In practice, this admits a limited free will element into a generally determinist theory. (71-72)

Godwin's approach as the sorter of the facts of Mary Wollstonecraft's life is indeed governed by his belief in the idea that the chain of events and influences in early life dictates the broad lines of the character. In sketching these out in the first several chapters of the *Memoirs*, he accurately predicts the future directions of Western auto/biography in terms of the importance of parents, family, place, class, and education in the making of the self.[10]

He also posits a doctrine of perfectibility, taking it up in his critique of Wollstonecraft's work not in terms of the social perfection that he writes about as a philosopher, but in terms of her theme of personal perfectibility. For example, he proposes that *A Vindication of the Rights of Woman* is "a very unequal performance, and eminently deficient in method and arrangement" (232), while he finds Wollstonecraft much improved by the time she writes *A Short Residence* (249). In this and a number of other interpretations and in the ordering of biographical detail, he posits a progressive theory of human character, very much like the one Wollstonecraft advocated. This is a typical strategy of memoir writers and generally honours the person being memorialized. Yet it is at such moments that Godwin's role as authoritative *histor* can once more be interrogated by his material position as husband of the deceased. Praising her progress as a writer he comments that in *A Short Residence*, "[t]he occasional harshness and ruggedness of character, that diversify her *Vindication of the Rights of Woman*, . . . totally disappear. If ever there was a book calculated to make a man in love with its author, this appears to me to be the book" (249). The desire to have "harshness and ruggedness" (qualities considered masculine) removed from a woman's work, and a narrative positioning that judges the ability to make people fall in love with her as a noteworthy achievement of a woman writer, focuses this reader's attention on a consideration of the ways in which culture "recognizes" the female subject.

William Epstein defines biographical "recognition" as "the conceptual process of classifying within conventional categories" and proposes that "recognition is an activity generated by the relationship between analysis and genre" (*Recognizing* 2). Certainly, recognition through a biographical process was an increasingly popular form of memorialization in Godwin's historical moment, as biographical formats "participated in the shift from a sacred to a secular form . . . and thereby became an individualizing tactic through which the mass consumer market of the modern state could materially reproduce the individual" (71).[11] I propose that it was exactly this process of individualization of the person he meant to honour that Godwin attempted to use in his *Memoirs*. However, his attempt led not to an honouring of his dead wife and the institutionalization of her works and ideas, as he must have desired, but rather to the intellectual banning of her work that lasted through many decades of the next century.[12] Indeed, the *Memoirs* caused even friends like Southey to accuse Godwin of "stripping his dead wife naked" (qtd. in St Clair 224).

Part of the reason for Godwin's ethical failure (one that I would argue is an inadvertent failure) lies in the fact that his subject was female and not male. Epstein has proposed that "biographical recognition" works differently when the subject is female, or for the other "cultural outlaws" that cannot fit the generic format ("(Post)Modern" 227). The female subject cannot fit the "pattern" of public (male) subject, and so she cannot receive a public honouring and institutionalization of her intellectual legacy. As a woman she can have only a private existence, a fact that Godwin himself seems to recognize indirectly when he says that Wollstonecraft wrote so well that *A Short Residence* made "a man fall in love" with her. To cast a woman into a public script is to risk making her a "cultural outlaw" ("(Post)Modern" 226), a figure much like the writers of the "scandalous memoirs" (Nussbaum, *Autobiographical Subject* 178), women of questionable reputation writing earlier in the eighteenth century. Since women could occupy only highly limited and often negative public roles, the contemporary reader's focus would have moved inevitably to their behaviour as private persons. Another reason for Godwin's ethical failure lies in the intimacy of the memoir form of biography, which encouraged this shift to the private, especially since the writer was a husband who entered the text as participant and eyewitness, thus focusing more intensely on the private life of the subject. When the woman subject's private life has broken the accepted moral boundaries for her gender, as Wollstonecraft's did, no public accomplishment can redeem her "outlaw" status, since such an accomplishment is then seen as further proof of her inappropriate behaviour. Godwin's mistake was a generic one: he seems to have genuinely believed that he could make a public "life" of a female person in the new mode of biography/memoir, one that embraced the theory that character grows through the "the application of perception, reason and motive" to the lived life. However, as Godwin's *Memoirs* proved, in public situations women, unlike men, were not seen as characters who could progress; they were seen only as having reputations that could be defended or destroyed.

Certainly, it was possible to write about Wollstonecraft in a manner that did not open her to public ridicule and censorship. For example, by adopting a policy of declaring and not describing her "triumph over malignant destiny" and emphasizing her move to the "hope [and] promise" of the condition of wife and mother (233), the obituary published in *The Monthly Magazine and British Register for 1797* avoids direct reference to the portions of Wollstonecraft's life that would be found most objectionable. However, such an account lacks the keen personal involvement of the participant stance that is essential to the memoir form as I have described it, as does Mary Hays's longer memorial in the *Annual Necrology, 1797-1798*. While these may offer us atypical examples of how biographical art is developing in the eighteenth century, they are not major contributions to the memoir form as it will evolve in the next two centuries.[13]

I would argue that Godwin's memoir is a paradigmatic text for the study of the memoir form. It may well have been a serious break in conventional morality for him to take up his habit of total frankness of discussion in writing this memoir, obviously not realizing that such frankness would work differently in the memoir format than in other discursive practices, and differently for a woman than for a man. Normally, such a policy would help guarantee the sincerity of the writer, but such frankness in memoir is often seen as self-serving, or sometimes interpreted as character assassination. However, new approaches to writing lives are not accomplished by taking safe paths. Although in writing publicly about his wife as if she were the equivalent of a male, Godwin unwittingly "stripped her" (as Southey put it) of any power she might have had in public discourse as a writer and feminist, in the longer run he gives us a more valuable book by doing so. While the memoir form was a risky, perhaps calamitous, generic choice for Godwin to take up in the late eighteenth century, we inherit a text that for the reader of the present moment can, in Carlyle's words (qtd. in Hibbard 27), draw aside "the curtains of the past" and "wondrously" reveal the author of *A Vindication of the Rights of Woman* as well as her husband.

———

Notes

1   Myers's positive evaluation of Godwin's intellectual and personal learning process is one I agree with, especially when she acknowledges that the complexity of the work results from its generic location as an unusual hybrid that unites autobiographical

and biographical reference. However, throughout her article Myers calls *Memoirs* a biography.

2   See Paul Jay's *Being in the Text* for an examination of how men have represented their subjectivity from romantic to postmodern times.

3   See William H. Epstein's *Recognizing Biography* for an examination of how ideology affects the way we "recognize" (and therefore construct) the biographical subject. Epstein deals with writers from Walton through Johnson to Strachey.

4   Domna C. Stanton used the term "autogynography" in her introduction to *The Female Autograph,* replacing the "bio" in traditional theorization's "facile presumption of referentiality" ("Autogynography" vii). In *Writing Selves,* Jeanne Perreault takes up "autograph" to assert that there is no genre classification for feminist self-writing. The exploration of the Spanish term *testimonio* is a critical and theoretical response to the growing body of autobiographical literature by Latin American women who engage in self-referential accounts that are part memoir, part history, part biography, and part political manifesto, and that are generally written in co-operation with a transcriber and translator. See Sommer, Beverley, and Caren Kaplan.

5   In describing the "autobiographical pact" between author and reader, Philippe Lejeune suggests a double process of "contract" in autobiography: "the agreement and the system of presentation chosen by the author, and the mode of reading chosen by the reader" (126). Since both processes are often more implicit than explicit, there is much more room for contractual misunderstanding in life writing than in other genres.

6   Val Ross compares Elspeth Cameron's memoir, *No Previous Experience,* to other recent memoirs.

7   Billson's "The Memoir" is the only consideration that I can find of the memoir form as a genre, marking out its difference from history (the genre it was generally associated with before the twentieth century) and from autobiography (the genre it is generally associated with after 1900). Hart takes up the memoir's tendency to write the human subject into a group identity, which is then problematized by the "self-alienation" (209) that results. Quinby, using a Foucauldian approach, takes up the ability of the memoir form to refuse "the totalizing individuality of the modern era" (297) and construct an "ideographic" selfhood. I summarize and extend these critics' contributions in my article "Memoir with an Attitude."

8   In "Memoir with an Attitude," I note that although there are
    many scholarly articles on Kingston's text, none gives attention
    to the importance of the fact that it is a memoir. As it does with
    most books that are named memoirs, the critical community
    tends not to see the memoir form as different from traditional
    autobiography.

9   The *OED* defines *rejoice* as to enjoy by possessing or to have
    full possession and use of; however, none of the many usage
    examples suggests that Godwin's reference to such a negative
    reason to rejoice would be a common or even acceptable usage.

10 Godwin is already working in a modern tradition that begins
    with Rousseau's *Confessions*. William St Clair records that
    Godwin read the book in 1790 and that Wollstonecraft later
    encouraged him to read more of Rousseau's work (184).

11 Epstein names the publication of Roger North's General Preface
    to his *Lives* of his brothers, written between 1718 and 1722, as
    the beginning of this shift to secular biographical formats from
    hagiographical forms, a shift that is generically well developed
    by Godwin's time (*Recognizing* 71)

12 See St Clair 182-88 for an account of the effects of the *Memoirs*.

13 It could certainly be argued that Hays's treatment of Wollstonecraft
    offers a more feminist defence of her life than does Godwin's book,
    but it is doubtful if that it did her public reputation any service.

A Mother's Daughter: An Intersection of Mary Shelley's *Frankenstein* and Mary Wollstonecraft's *A Vindication of the Rights of Woman*

Charles E. Robinson

We often forget that Mary Wollstonecraft Shelley was a biographer: she wrote lives of many eminent writers and scientists from Italy, Spain, Portugal, and France for Dionysius Lardner's *Cabinet Cyclopaedia*; and she undertook but never finished lives of her husband, Percy Bysshe Shelley, and her father, William Godwin. We wish, of course, that she had written or at least sketched out a life of her mother. Had she done so, we would have had not only a window into the life and works of Mary Wollstonecraft but also a mirror by which to see Mary Shelley's own self-reflection in a biographical memoir of her mother. In one way, Mary Shelley herself was able to see some of that self-reflection in the John Opie portrait of her mother that hung over the mantle in the Godwin home: because Mary Wollstonecraft was pregnant with Mary Shelley when that portrait was taken in 1797, the daughter could witness her own effect on her mother.

Although Mary Shelley never directly knew her mother, she could at least experience Mary Wollstonecraft by means of indirect representations. The Opie portrait, for example, gave the daughter a sense of her

---

Notes are on pp. 137-38.

mother's physical characteristics, and the more elusive character of her mother could be discovered in what Godwin, Maria Reveley (later, Maria Gisborne), and others told her, as well as in the letters and published works of her mother. The extant documents, of course, provide a record of the mother that Mary Wollstonecraft became to Mary Shelley—and the daughter's response to those documents in turn can inform us of the kind of daughter that Mary Shelley became to her mother. In short, although Mary Shelley did not write a biography of her mother, we can partially reconstruct what that biography might have been by the study of the surviving documents, especially now that we have the new Pickering and Chatto *Novels and Selected Works of Mary Shelley* that, together with the older Pickering and Chatto *Works of Mary Wollstonecraft*, makes the task possible. The task is all the more possible because of the publication in recent years of *The Letters of Mary Wollstonecraft Shelley*, *The Journals of Mary Shelley*, *Shelley and His Circle*, and (as we shall see) *The* Frankenstein *Notebooks*. Indeed, there is a book begging to be written on mother and daughter, a study of the ways in which Mary Wollstonecraft and her literary texts play out in the lights and shadows of Mary Shelley's life and works. If only Godwin's manuscript diaries and/or letters were published in full, we could more readily gather evidence on the two Marys.

The full relationship between the mother and daughter awaits other scholars and other discoveries, but I propose to explore at least one aspect of that relationship, one small intersection of Mary Wollstonecraft's *A Vindication of the Rights of Woman* (1792) and Mary Shelley's *Frankenstein* (1818), two radically different English romantic works that nevertheless address similar issues about education and parenting. Mary Shelley may have been denied direct advice and nurturing from her mother, but she could at least indirectly seek that parent's wisdom by reading her works.

We usually assume that Mary Shelley was an early and avid student of her mother's life and works, but we really do not have the evidence to assert, for example, that the *Vindication* was "a text Mary Shelley read and reread during her childhood" (Zonana 172). In fact, we know very little about Mary Shelley's reading of her mother's works prior to her meeting with Shelley in 1814; even after 1814, she did not leave behind many direct reflections on her mother. Not until 1831 did Mary Shelley write an extended (and public) paragraph to be found in the "Memoirs of William Godwin" that she prefaced to the Colburn and Bentley edition of *Caleb Williams* (1831). After misrepresenting the facts about the elapsed time between her parents' marriage and her own birth, Mary Shelley offered the following remarks on her mother:

The writings of this celebrated woman are monuments of her moral and intellectual superiority. Her lofty spirit, her eager assertion of the claims of her sex, animate the "Vindication of the Rights of Woman"; while the sweetness and taste displayed in her "Letters from Norway" depict the softer qualities of her admirable character. Even now, those who have survived her so many years, never speak of her but with uncontrollable enthusiasm. Her unwearied exertions for the benefit of others, her rectitude, her independence, joined to a warm affectionate heart, and the most refined softness of manners, made her the *idol* of all who knew her. (ix; my emphasis)

There is no reason to doubt that these words accurately reflect Mary Shelley's judgment about her mother at this time, a judgment similarly expressed four years earlier in an 1827 letter to Frances Wright: "The memory of my Mother has always been the pride & delight of my life; & the admiration of others for her, has been the cause of most of the happiness . . . I have enjoyed. Her *greatness of soul* . . . [has] perpetually reminded me that I ought to degenerate as little as I could from those from whom I *derived my being*" (*LMWS* 2: 3-4, my emphasis).

A similar hagiographical enthusiasm characterizes some of Mary Shelley's other reflections on this "idol" from whom she "derived [her] being." Consider, for example, the following statement that she made about her mother in a fragmentary biography that she wrote in the 1830s about her father. The original manuscript of these remarks may no longer be among the Abinger papers, but C. Kegan Paul published this extract in *William Godwin: His Friends and Contemporaries* (1876):

Mary Wollstonecraft was one of those beings who appear once perhaps in a generation, to gild humanity with a ray which no difference of opinion nor chance of circumstances can cloud. Her genius was undeniable. She had been bred in the hard school of adversity, and having experienced the sorrows entailed on the poor and the oppressed, an earnest desire was kindled within her to diminish these sorrows. Her sound understanding, her intrepidity, her sensibility and eager sympathy, stamped all her writings with force and truth, and endowed them with a tender charm that enchants while it enlightens. She was one whom all loved who had ever seen her. Many years are passed since that beating heart has been laid in the cold still grave, but no one who has ever seen her speaks of her without *enthusiastic veneration*.[1] Did she witness an act of injustice, she boldly came forward to point it out, and induce its reparation. Was there discord among friends or relatives, she stood by the weaker party, and by her earnest appeals and kindliness awoke latent affection, and *healed all wounds*. "Open as day to melting charity" [*2 Henry IV*, 4.4.32], with a heart brimful of generous affection, yearning for sympathy, she had fallen on evil days [*Paradise Lost* 7.25], and her life had been one course of hardship, poverty, lonely struggle, and bitter disappointment.

Godwin met her at the moment when she was deeply depressed by the ingratitude of one utterly incapable of appreciating her excellence; who had stolen her heart, and availed himself of her excessive and thoughtless generosity, and lofty independence of character, to plunge her in difficulties and then desert her. Difficulties, worldly difficulties, indeed, she set at nought, compared with her despair of good, her confidence betrayed, and when once she could conquer the misery that clung to her heart, she struggled cheerfully to meet the poverty that was her inheritance, and to do her duty by her darling child [Fanny Imlay]. It was at this time that Godwin again met her, at the house of her friend Miss Hayes. (1: 231-32)

These remarks certainly suggest the devotion that Mary Shelley had for her mother, and it would be fascinating to speculate what might have been Mary Wollstonecraft's nineteenth-century reputation if Mary Shelley had turned her hand to redeeming her mother rather than her husband by her editorial and biographical work; but instead I turn to the facts of the letters and journals in order to document what knowledge Mary Shelley had of her mother and her works (including Godwin's *Memoirs of the Author of* A Vindication of the Rights of Woman).

The documentary evidence tells the following narrative about Mary Shelley reading her mother's texts, beginning just after she eloped in late July 1814 with Percy Shelley for their six weeks' tour:

Mary: A Fiction: Mary and Percy Shelley read "part" of this novel on **17 August 1814**, Percy finished reading it on **31 August**, and Mary read it again on **7 June 1820** (*JMS* 15, 22, 320).

Letters Written during a Short Residence in Sweden, Norway and Denmark (known as "Letters from Norway"): Percy read this aloud to Mary and to her stepsister Claire Clairmont on **30-31 August** and **1 September 1814** (*JCC* 33-34; *JMS* 22; see also *History of a Six Weeks' Tour* [*NSW* 8 34], where Mary Shelley wrote that "S*** read aloud to us Mary Wollstonecraft's Letters from Norway," marking what appears to have been the first time Mary Shelley "publicly" referred to her mother in print). The sixteen-year-old Claire Clairmont's remark that "Letters from Norway . . . is one of my very favorite Books" (*JCC* 33) suggests that she (and possibly Mary Shelley) had previously read it. Claire Clairmont read it again on **1-2, 4 June 1820** (*JCC* 149), and Mary Shelley reread it on **4-6 June**

1820 (*JMS* 319-20) and then requested another or replacement copy on **30 November 1821** (*LMWS* 1: 211).[2]

The Wrongs of Woman; or, Maria, A Fragment (from Vols. 1-2 of *Posthumous Works*—see below): Mary Shelley read this fragmentary novel on **8-9 October 1814** and again on **25-26 February 1822** (*JMS* 33, 400).[3] Charles Clairmont indicated how much he loved this novel in a letter to Claire Clairmont on **20 September 1815** (*CC* 1: 15).

Posthumous Works of the Author of A Vindication of the Rights of Woman, 4 vols. (containing *The Wrongs of Woman* in Vols. 1-2 as well as "the first book of a series of lessons for children" [*Posthumous Works* 1: iii], "Letters [to Imlay] and miscellaneous pieces [including 'The Cave of Fancy']"): Mary Shelley continued to read in this four-volume edition on **10 October 1814** (*JMS* 34) shortly after Percy requested a copy from his first wife Harriet on ?3 October 1814. He canceled his request on 5 October, writing that he had "committed an oversight in requesting [it]" and that he could "easily procure another copy" (*LPBS* 1: 400, 405), possibly the copy that Mary Shelley began to read on 8-9 October when she read *The Wrongs of Woman* therein. Mary Shelley read *Posthumous Works* again on **1-2 June 1820** (*JMS* 319), and she requested another or a replacement copy on **30 November 1821** (*LMWS* 1: 211).

Elements of Morality, for the Use of Children: Mary Shelley read this children's book on **25 October 1814** (*JMS* 38-39).

An Historical and Moral View of the Origin and Progress of the French Revolution: Percy Shelley read this volume aloud on **23 December 1814**, and Mary Shelley continued to read it on **23-24** and **27-29 December 1814** (*JMS* 55-56).

A Vindication of the Rights of Woman: Mary Shelley read this volume on **6-9 December 1816** and again in Pisa on **21-22 May 1820** (*JMS* 149, 318). Claire Clairmont apparently read the same copy in Pisa on **29-31 May** and **2-4 June 1820** (*JCC* 149). Percy Shelley had ordered his own copy of *Vindication* as early as **29 July 1812** (*LPBS* 1: 319).

Memoirs of the Author of A Vindication of the Rights of Woman: Mary Shelley read her father's memoir of her mother on **3 June 1820** (*JMS* 319).[4]

Original Stories from Real Life: Mary Shelley asked that this children's book be sent to her in Italy on **12 January 1823** (*LMWS* 1: 306).

This list, of course, does not preclude there having been other times when Mary Shelley read her mother's works between 1814 and

1823 (or, for that matter, before 1814), but we have evidence only for the above list, most of which involved two extended periods: one during and shortly after the six weeks' tour in 1814; and the other in May/June of 1820. We can supplement this list by noting the few places where Mary Shelley directly quoted or alluded to her mother's works. But with the exception of a few quotations from *Letters Written during a Short Residence*,[5] there are almost no direct references to (or even echoes of) her mother's works in the works of Mary Shelley.[6] This is a bit surprising, given the latter's propensity to sprinkle her texts with quotations from and allusions to other writers.[7] In *Frankenstein*, for example, the novel is dedicated to Godwin, and there are quotations from Byron, Coleridge, Wordsworth, Leigh Hunt, and (of course) Percy Shelley (in one case Mary Shelley appropriated a sixty-word description from Percy's fragmentary journal of his tour round Lake Geneva with Lord Byron [Robinson 1: lxxix, 561]), but there appears to be no direct quotation from or reference to her mother's life and works in *Frankenstein*.

If we look with care, however, we can find Mary Wollstonecraft lurking in the corners of Mary Shelley's most famous novel. Syndy Conger, for example, persuasively argues that Mary Wollstonecraft can be seen in many of the characters in *Frankenstein*, and that the number of motherless daughters (and sons) in *Frankenstein* recalls Mary Shelley's birth and Mary Wollstonecraft's death ("Prophecy"). We might even suspect that the *Frankenstein* trial scene, in which Elizabeth's eloquent defence of Justine is ignored by the court (*FMP* 60-61), is indebted to the trial scene in Chapter 17 of *The Wrongs of Woman,* in which Maria's defence of Darnford is rejected by the court. Or we might use a perpetual calendar and discover that Walton's Journal in *Frankenstein* begins on 11 December 17[96] and concludes on 12 September 17[97], a period of 276 gestation days that points to the time of Mary Shelley's own conception and birth. The novel ends thirteen days after Mary Shelley was born and two days after her mother died, and it appears to begin thirteen days after she was conceived (probably on 28 November 1796—the date suggested by William St Clair).[8] I do not wish to reject these possibilities, but I prefer to ground suggestions of influence on stronger evidence, since, of course, motherlessness is a cliché in fiction at this time, the similar court scenes may be merely coincidental, and the gestation parallels may have been created by us rather than by Mary Shelley.

We can only speculate why Mary Shelley did not publicly acknowledge her mother's life or works in *Frankenstein*: possibly because she feared such naming or quoting might not benefit her mother's reputation, a reputation that had not yet recovered from the effects of Godwin's 1798 confessional *Memoirs* of his wife. But it is equally possible that Mary Shelley felt unworthy of or unequal to her mother with respect to women's rights. We know that twenty years later, in the privacy of an 1838 journal entry, she confessed that she was reluctant to publicly serve the "'good Cause' . . . of the advancement of freedom & knowledge — of the Rights of Women" (*JMS* 553). She had "respect" for her "Parents & Shelley," who had "a passion for reforming the world," but she was not a person to cling to such opinions. This is not to say that Mary Shelley was a Byronic fatalist; on the contrary, she "earnestly desire[d] the good & enlightenment of my fellow creatures"; she never wrote "a word in disfavour of liberalism"; but she never wrote for it openly because she doubted her argumentative powers and even felt the counter-arguments too strongly. In effect, Mary Shelley had a different approach to the fever and fret of the world, aligning herself more with Keats's view of the vale of soul making when she wrote in this same journal entry, "I beleive [*sic*] that we are sent here to *educate* ourselves & that self denial & disappointment & self controul are a part of our *education*" (*JMS* 2: 554; my emphasis).

Keats is useful here, for the very word "education" tolls me back to my sole subject of the intersection of *Frankenstein* and *A Vindication of the Rights of Woman*, two works that directly address the question of education. Mary Shelley could not have failed to notice that her mother's overtly didactic and argumentative *Vindication* (which advocated a national and free education for "all classes" and "both sexes") addressed the same issues that Mary Shelley herself was addressing in *Frankenstein*, a novel about the dangerous consequences of education and the pursuit of knowledge. Education pursued to an extreme (either too public or too private) was represented as the cause or at least the occasion of moral disaster in both of these works. In the case of *Frankenstein*, Mary Shelley subsumed and conflated three Western myths (from Genesis, from Greek mythology, and from Plato's *Symposium*) about the dangers of knowledge, each of which was gendered in ways that reflect her mother's teaching:

1. Eve ate of the apple first but somehow forsook her intellectual primogeniture;
2. Prometheus brought the sorrow of knowledge into the world, as did his brother Epimetheus, who also brought the evils of Pandora's box;
3. the circular, androgynous, and primal being from Aristophanes' myth in the *Symposium* presumed so much that s/he fell into

distinct genders ("we are unfashioned creatures, but half made up," Victor explained in the 1831 revised edition of *Frankenstein* [16; *FMP* 187]).

In effect, on a mythic level Mary Shelley addressed larger issues than her mother did—and, at the same time, she empiricized the theme of education (and its dangers and limits) in her novel: Walton's "education was neglected" we are told (*FMP* 11), but he was self-educated by reading travels, poetry, mathematics, medicine, and physical science; Victor's education at home, at school (with Clerval), and at university is central to the plot; Elizabeth learned Latin and English, took over the instruction of Victor's brothers, and "regretted that she had not the same opportunities of . . . cultivating her understanding" by accompanying Victor and Clerval for their two years in England (118); even Justine was given an "education superior" (46) to the one that had been originally intended by Caroline Frankenstein; the monster was educated in the "godlike science" of language (83), and he increased his knowledge (and his sorrow) by reading Volney, Milton, Plutarch, Goethe, and Victor's journal; and, finally, at the centre of this novel dealing with the consequences of the pursuit of knowledge, we and the monster encounter Safie (whose name suggests "Wisdom"), who was educated by her mother at home, a mother who "*instructed* her daughter in the tenets of her [Christian] religion, and *taught* her to aspire to higher powers of intellect, and an independence of spirit, forbidden to the female followers of Mahomet. This lady died; but her *lessons* were indelibly impressed on the mind of Safie, . . . now accustomed to grand ideas and a noble emulation for virtue" (92; my emphasis).

A number of critics, most notably Joyce Zonana in her fine 1991 article on Safie's letters, have used this important paragraph on Safie's education to argue for Mary Wollstonecraft's presence in *Frankenstein*: briefly put, the Christian mother educating her daughter Safie in the tenets of Christianity in a land of Islam may be allegorized as the feminist Mary Wollstonecraft educating her daughter Mary Shelley in the tenets of revolutionary feminism in the oppressive patriarchal climate of England and Europe. In the *Vindication*, Mary Wollstonecraft had specifically condemned "Mahometanism" as well as British educational practices for subordinating women and treating them as creatures without souls or rational faculties (see Zonana 173-74). In effect, both Safie and Mary Shelley had been educated in "grand ideas" by their mothers. For Safie, her mother's Christianity—and for Mary Shelley, her mother's rational religion—could help redeem daughters (and sons) from an ideology of oppression. At another level of meaning, the redemptive *Vindication* itself could have offered *Frankenstein* a redemptive heroine in the form of Safie, whose "Wisdom" was recorded in her letters that passed through the hands of Felix, Agatha, the monster, Victor, Walton, and presumably that other MWS, Margaret Walton Saville—or should we say, with a French pronunciation, "*Saville*," to show how Mary represents herself as both the motherless Safie and the motherless (and homophonically equivalent) Saville in the innermost and outermost tales of the novel.

We are encouraged to read the Safie episode in this way because we can now prove that Mary Shelley wrote this section on Safie's education at the exact time that she was reading the *Vindication* in December 1816. Here, in digest, is how I have reconstructed the composition of the novel: a novella-length and now lost ur-text of *Frankenstein* was completed in the summer of 1816; that ur-text contained neither Walton's outermost frame nor Safie's innermost tale, but it did contain most of the other parts of the novel; this novella was being transformed into a novel in October and November 1816 (we now know, for example, that Mary Shelley finished drafting the Justine episode on 20 November); by 5 December, she had completed a long but now missing chapter on Safie (what eventually became the chapter where the monster began to learn the "science of letters" [88] when he overheard Felix teaching Safie to read Volney's *Ruins of Empire*); for the next four days, from 6 through 9 December, Mary Shelley read the *Vindication* at the same time she revised that now missing chapter and also wrote and revised the next chapters on Safie, including the passage on Safie's education quoted above. So textual scholarship can serve as a handmaiden to the feminist hypothesizing that has already pointed to an intersection of the mother's *Vindication* and the daughter's *Frankenstein*.[9]

Textual scholarship, however, can cast doubt on one other part of this intersection of the *Vindication* and *Frankenstein*. A number of critics have hypothesized that Safie gets her name by way of Sophie in Rousseau's *Emile*, his treatise on education. Mary Wollstonecraft, it will be recalled, went to considerable lengths in the *Vindication* to attack the foundation of Sophie's education, and it is possible that Mary Shelley's more nobly educated Safie may intertextually take us back to Rousseau by way of Wollstonecraft. One major caution, however, about this *Emile* connection: when Mary Shelley wrote the Safie chapters in December 1816, the Arabian was first called Maimouna; Maimouna then became Amina—and only in April 1817 was the Arabian denominated Safie.[10]

Also, before we idealize Safie too much, we should, finally, look at one important action in the Safie episode—an action sometimes overlooked in the discussion of this Arabian. Despite all of her admirable qualities, Safie redeemed neither the monster nor the text of this novel: in fact, she "rushed out of the [De Laceys'] cottage" (*FMP* 101) in that terrible scene of confrontation between the De Laceys and the monster. We could argue that Safie's action was fated by circumstances beyond her or even Mary Shelley's control: she was a late addition to the narrative and therefore had to act in accordance with the already conceived and partly written conclusion to the novel—the conclusion to the novella-length ur-text that Mary Shelley had drafted in the summer of 1816. So it could be argued that it was too late for Safie to do any good. But it is also possible that even in December 1816 Mary Shelley was, as she said in that 1838 journal entry, "far from making up [her own] mind" about the practical results of an enlightened education and was more content to show the world as it was than to falsify human experience by adopting "a passion for reforming the world," as her parents and her husband had done (*JMS* 554, 553). If that were the case in 1816-17, then Safie's final action—her abandonment of the monster and of the De Laceys who had befriended her—did little more than reveal her humanity in a fallen world and Mary Shelley's acknowledgement of that fallen human condition. The last thing we know about Safie is that she "will never recover [her] horror" (103). The wise Safie and the good Agatha and the happy Felix were all culpable in their response to the monster. And if Felix's name invokes the redemptive context of the *felix culpa,* we can only conclude that Mary Shelley, more like Byron (or even Keats) than like Mary Wollstonecraft (or Percy Shelley), was certainly ironic in her choice of names for these three youths in the De Lacey cottage, where all best things (wisdom, goodness, and happiness) were thus confused to ill. And in that irony was Mary Shelley's own evaluation of her relationship to her mother: Mary Shelley was her mother's daughter only to the same extent that Safie was her mother's daughter.

Notes

1   If, as I argue later in this essay, Mary Shelley and her mother are figured in Safie and her mother in *Frankenstein*, then compare this remark with Safie speaking "in high and enthusiastic terms of her mother" (*FMP* 92).

2   Incidentally, the first U.S. publication of this volume was in 1796 in Wilmington, Delaware, a state with a sizable Swedish population.

3   Mary Shelley alluded to this novel when she referred to her "Mother's heroine" in a letter to Jane Williams on 10 April 1823 (*LMWS* 1: 330, 332n).

4   Incidentally, the University of Delaware Library owns William Michael Rossetti's copy of this volume.

5   In *The Last Man*, for example, Mary Shelley quoted her mother's famous description of rocks as "the bones of the world waiting to be clothed with every thing necessary to give life and beauty" (from Letter V of *Letters Written during a Short Residence*)—and in this instance actually named her mother and the text with the footnote of "Mary Wollstonecraft's Letters from Norway" (*LM* 328n). This same quotation was used more cleverly and subtly to link mother and father in Mary Shelley's 1830 review of her father's novel *Cloudesley*, where she remarked on the uniqueness of the novel: "Comparing this book with others, we felt as if we had quitted gardens and parks, and tamer landscapes, for a scene on nature's grandest scale; that we wandered among giants' rocks, 'the naked bones of the world waiting to be clothed'" (*NSW* 2: 204). See also an allusion to this same passage in *Rambles in Germany and Italy* (145).

6   One possible echo of *Maria* is pointed out in the new Pickering and Chatto edition of Mary Shelley's *Lodore* (146 and n.).

7   These quotations and allusions most often provide important thematic emphasis—see, for example, the discussion of the incest references in my essay, "Mathilda as Dramatic Actress," in Bennett and Curran, *Mary Shelley in Her Times* 76-87.

8   See St Clair's "Appendix I: Godwin's Sexual Relationship with Mary Wollstonecraft" (497-503), especially 502.

9   For a fuller discussion of the compositional history of this novel, see Robinson, especially his "*Frankenstein* Chronology," lxxvii-xci.

10   The name Maimouna, however, may have offered homage to another woman of intellect, for Maimouna was Percy Shelley's nickname (borrowed from the wise woman in Robert Southey's

Islamic epic, *Thalaba the Destroyer* [8.23ff; see Robinson 1: lix]) for Mrs Boinville, whose "understanding & affections" (*LPBS* 2: 92) came close to realizing the ideals that were described in Mary Wollstonecraft's *Vindication*. And these ideals by themselves may have led Mary Shelley in April 1817 to choose Safie or "Wisdom"as the name of her Arabian.

Mary Shelley: Writing/
Other Women in
Godwin's "Life"

Judith Barbour

I am now writing a novel "Falkner"—My best it will be—I
believe

Others write—my Father did—in peace of heart—the imagination at work alone—some warmth imparted to them by the strong
conjuring up of fictitious woes—but tranquil in their own bos-
oms—

But I! O my God—what a lot is mine—marked by tragedy &
death—tracked by disappointment & unutterable wretchedness—
blow after blow—my heart dies within me—I say—["]would I
might die." that is wicked—but life is a struggle & a burthen
beyond my strength. My health is irremediably shattered—my
hopes entirely low—day after day—& if a joy come it is so inex-
tricably & above all so closely linked with misery—that I feel it
only to know that it is gone—I have lost my dear darling Father—
What I then went through—watching alone his dying hours!

My Percy—my adored child remains—Protect him, heaven!—
rain evil & pain upon me but spare him! . . .

Was I ever rewarded? O My God—I am too miserable to write . . .

London, 7 June 1836[1]

Mary Shelley's journal is an untidy repository of unofficial
secrets, worries, and gripes, and the borderline between literary romance fiction and quotidian family affairs is porous. Her father,
William Godwin, had died on 7 April 1836, leaving Shelley as the only

---

Notes are on pp. 153-57.

writer and the only breadwinner in a family consisting of herself and Mary Jane Godwin, both widows, and Percy Florence Shelley, still a schoolboy at Harrow. In her journal of this period, money and writing oscillate as objects of desire and dread. The impassivity of a writer self-warmed by "imagination at work alone" is chided and envied by one whose lot is to "[watch] alone [Godwin's] dying hours!" Women's work, whether watching or writing, is never ("was I ever?") rewarded. Mary Shelley writes in ressentimental loops between graveside and cradleside: "I have lost my dear darling Father," "My Percy—my adored child remains."[2] Godwin's name of Father and status as writer are lodged in the niche reserved for the phallus, by definition the scarce good that launches a rising line of posterity. Cast into flux below the tide mark, a woman writer is all but wrecked, and her call for even more "rain" invokes a sublimely prolific flux. Adventitiously she throws up a spar on the flood, an intercession on behalf of her son, Percy Florence, "Protect him . . . spare him!" In case this is too much for "heaven" to spare, she braces herself to pay a penalty, a punishment, a set of sanctions of the law of diminishing returns: "rain evil & pain upon me but spare him!"

No less jealously than Hamlet, Mary Shelley defends the exclusive act of procreation within the exclusive matrimony of her writer parents, William Godwin and Mary Wollstonecraft. "[W]atching alone" the dying Godwin accrues a credit that is now presented, an "entry" in the double sense, confessional journal and moralistic account book. It cuts widow Mary Jane Godwin out of William Godwin's death scene, and their son William Godwin Jr out of his paternity, in order to have "my . . . Father" answer to an only child's witness.

The law of Scarcity (Ananke), Malthus's law of population pressure, permanently discounts female reproductive energy as (if it were) a natural self-replenishing source. A woman writer cites her own maternity and a maternal grandfather's authorial canonical genealogy as a (small) hoard of fossil fuel, soliciting, as only mother of an "adored child," for these connections to be counted as assets for her child. In her writings of the 1830s Mary Shelley pursued an intricate genealogical romance of her own poetic election and exceptional parentage, over and under the undramatic commonplaces of securing her only surviving child a place in English "good society." Ultimately, young Percy Florence represents a libidinal spur to writing, as well as a guilt-inducing obstacle to getting on with it.

Mary Shelley's concentration in the 1830s on Johnsonian biography of Eminent Men and scholarly editing has been construed by her biographer Emily Sunstein as a deliberate shutdown of emotion-charged fiction, in order to avoid "rousing bitter depths" (336): depths of jealousy among Percy Bysshe Shelley's former intimates, and of antagonism from Godwin's old enemies in the Tory press. After Percy Florence became a baronet in 1844,[3] Mary Shelley not only stopped writing for publication, but also left off the journal she had kept since 28 June 1814, elopement day. Mary Shelley's letters glumly mock the "stultified" demeanour of the inadequate object of her vicarious ambitions, when Sir Percy Shelley is presented as a baronet to Queen Victoria and Prince Albert in 1845.[4]

On 19 July 1836 Mary Shelley was commissioned by publisher Henry Colburn to write a "Memoirs and Correspondence of the late William Godwin," for the sole benefit of his widow, Mary Jane Godwin.[5] In his will Godwin had tasked his daughter with publishing his last testament, a polemical treatise on religious freedom.[6] "The Genius of Christianity Unveiled" is an atopic effusion, rather than a utopian synthesis of Godwin's religious views. Godwin kept it by him, under wraps, where its heartfelt defiance of established authority and its desire for its own authorization were protected and prolonged. Its implicit antagonist-reader and protagonist-editor are his Roman Catholic wife Mary Jane, and his troubled agnostic daughter, Mary Shelley: the latter's decision to suppress it is covered by her undertaking to write and publish an idealized Godwin of the 1790s. Mary Jane's contract with Colburn gave Mary Shelley an alternative to the "Genius," composing a decorous biography of Godwin's life in literature. And ultimately, it gave her the option of shelving both scripts and enduring the private resentment of William Godwin's admirers rather than a public onslaught from the powerful press of the orthodox Right.

Six months after its conception, the gestation of Godwin's "Life" is proceeding slowly and Mary Shelley is under attack from a rival writer as well as besieged by writer's nerves. Edward Trelawny is Mary Shelley's rival—one of a pack—for the legacy of the poet Percy Bysshe Shelley, and she has to move quickly past the death of Godwin to establish her investment in Percy's future:

> With regard to my Father's life—I certainly could not answer it to my conscience to give it up—I shall therefore do it—but I must wait. This year I have to fight my poor Percy's battle—to try to get him sent to College without further dilapidation on his ruined prospects—& he has to enter life at College—that this should be undertaken at a moment when a cry was raised against his Mother— & that not on the question of _politics_ but _religion_, would mar all— I must see him fairly launched, before I commit myself to the fury of the waves.[7]

The extravagant final image — fired Viking longboat or Adonais's spirit bark? — might have relieved the writer's feelings more than it frightened Trelawny, who had a tough hide. Trelawny was the psychopomp in Mary Shelley's tragic scene: it was he who brought the dreadful news to the two women who waited at Lerici after the storm that sank Shelley's and Edward Williams's boat, and it was he who had designed the unstable thing, although he continued forever to bluff and lie about his hand in it. Convention had decreed that only men attended Godwin's funeral, and Mary Shelley stayed at home. Among the stragglers who composed Godwin's posterity, Trelawny was portentously present in the bystander role, as in 1822 at Shelley's beachside cremation. The decent interment of a patriarch amid his "following" requires a pact among the survivors, and sixteen-year-old Percy Florence Shelley was there as chief mourner of his maternal, and prospective heir to his paternal, grandfather. The newspaper obits tolled for literary genius on both sides of the male line and noted that Mary Shelley would compose a memorial biography.[8]

Mary Shelley began work on the "Life of William Godwin" by writing to request return of Godwin's letters and memorabilia from a circle of people[9] who had known Godwin in his heyday of the 1780s and 1790s. Betty T. Bennett lists Mary Hays, Henry Crabb Robinson, Henry Colburn, Thomas Abthorpe Cooper, Josiah Wedgwood, William Hazlitt Jr (for his father's papers), and Edward Lytton Bulwer. Mary Shelley searched out Tom Cooper and successfully petitioned Josiah Wedgwood for letters and further information about his late brother. Bennett notes (*LMWS* 2: 272n.) that Mary Shelley was unsuccessful with Crabb Robinson and Bulwer, who had in any case known Godwin only in later life. This may have confirmed Shelley's decision to treat only the events of Godwin's early life.

The only woman on Bennett's list is Mary Hays, to whom Mary Shelley wrote (in answer to a request from Hays): "[Y]our most reasonable request will be complied with. There is nothing more detestable or cruel than the publication of letters meant for one eye only. I have no idea whether any of yours will be found among my Father's papers — any that I find shall be returned to you" (*LMWS* 2: 270; 20 April 1836). Sure enough, I have found none of Hays's letters to Godwin among the manuscripts pertaining to Mary Shelley's "Life" of Godwin. Shelley took the opportunity, when copying selectively from Wollstonecraft's and Godwin's correspondence, to snip out references to Hays. At her own request, it would appear, Hays is disappeared from the Wollstonecraft and Godwin story. By the same stroke, Mary Shelley spared herself any decision respecting

Godwin's breathtakingly cold letters to Hays after Wollstonecraft's death.[10]

Women friends and fellow-authors who survived Godwin were Maria Gisborne (by two weeks, died in April 1836), Mary Hays (d. 1843), Harriet Lee (d. 1851), and Amelia (Alderson) Opie (d. 1853). Non-survivors included Elizabeth Inchbald (d. 1821) and Sophia Lee (d. 1824). In the years when Shelley was at work on the "Life," Mary Hays, Amelia Opie, and Harriet Lee were all alive still, Lee surviving till 1851, when Mary Shelley herself died, and Opie outliving them all. Yet, Mary Shelley did not attempt to contact any of the women (Lee, we guess, least of all). Of the three women, only Harriet Lee is presented in her own writing in the "Life."

Whereas publishers and editors Leigh Hunt, Dionysius Lardner, and best of them all Edward Moxon,[11] had made their expertise available to Mary Shelley throughout the 1830s, for the unfashionable project of Godwin's "Life" she could call only on the help of her stepmother, Mary Jane, and neither woman cared much for this unaccustomed proximity. Mary Jane was involved from the start: she signed the Colburn contract in July 1836; profits were to go to her; she owned the papers, but not the copyright; and she had been Godwin's scribe and second hand for nearly twenty years, so she could read his drafts better than anyone, and she wrote a clear elegant round hand, whereas Mary Shelley's is a spiky scrawl. Mary Jane was set to work transcribing passages from Godwin's early novel *Damon and Delia* (1784) and almost the entire Chapters 9 and 10 of Godwin's January 1798 first edition of the *Memoirs of the Author of* A Vindication. Shelley kept Mary Jane under tight control, assigning her simple copyist's tasks, and curtailing the scope of the narrative to the 1790s, before her stepmother entered Godwin's personal history. Only at the last stage of writing did she drop her guard somewhat, admitting Mary Jane's reminiscences of Godwin to his official story.[12] But this thaw in the co-writers' relations also marked the onset of Mary Jane's last illness, which called Claire Clairmont back to London in 1840 to nurse her mother. With Claire back on the scene, Trelawny's desultory sniping over Godwin's radical legacy, and Jeff Hogg's bitter jealousy of her claims to Percy Bysshe Shelley, the pressures on Mary Shelley escalated. John Hobart Caunter, Mary Jane's co-signatory on Colburn's contract, was apparently trustworthy but inexperienced in publishing. Mary Shelley's somewhat desperate memo to him in May 1840[13] staves off the presses while she reconsiders her decision to include certain letters (I suspect these were the letters of Godwin and Harriet Lee in 1798, but only because they are still there. Who knows what else might have been jettisoned?). In 1841 Mary Jane died, and Colburn had paid nothing, so he left well alone when the "Life" was shelved. Four years of Mary Shelley's intermittent work between July 1836 and May 1840[14] culminated in a provisional format for a "vol. i" only. In the Abinger MSS at the Bodleian,[15] it is filed under the inelegant rubric, "Mary Shelley's abortive biography of her father, William Godwin."

In "Life of William Godwin," Shelley intertwines her first-person narrative with selected contemporary documents, mostly letters written by Godwin himself, contextualizing and historicizing the fictional genre of the passage from youth to maturity, *Bildungsroman*. Godwin's vigorous campaigns of private and public letter-writing, and occasional responses in kind from his correspondents, complement the simple chronological line with clusters of personal intercourse and significant social interaction. His autobiographical essays, including the unpublished three chapters on his childhood up to 1772,[16] make a scantily furnished baseline. Shelley conjures up 1772, the year his father died and the date at which Godwin's autobiography switches from consecutive narrative to journal jottings, as the starting post for her story.[17] The semi-autobiographical essays of his late years, published in *Thoughts on Man* (1831),[18] present a mellow sage, especially when reinforced by Mary Shelley's brief eulogistic portrait of both Godwin and Wollstonecraft in her "Memoirs of the Author," also published in 1831 as a preface to the fourth edition of *Caleb Williams*.[19] This creates an uneasy mixture of radical active youth and paternalistic commentator. Mary Shelley's telling of Godwin's life story to the age of forty-two is characterized by early-Victorian niceness. By contrast, her open showing of personal and informal documents arrests the narrative tenor, and when it is Godwin's letters that she shows, the effect can be startling.

Concurrently with Godwin's "Life," Shelley was composing a complete edition,[20] with biographical notes, of Percy Bysshe Shelley's work; the daughter's commission from Godwin kept pace with the widow's retrospect of Shelley. As recently as 1835, her father-in-law had again frustrated her plans to publish her Shelley book. In 1832, she had generously conceded priority to Jeff Hogg to write of his and Shelley's student days,[21] as Hogg was less susceptible to the old baronet's anger. Yet this depleted her creative resources, for Shelley's youth is the damaged crucible of Victor Frankenstein, the malformed sprig of doomed aristocracy thwarting the elitist story of ruling-class patronage. Godwin had been deprived of one story by his dissenter provincial origins, and had taken pains to insert himself into another by assiduous pedagogic interventions. An "early life" of Godwin could rehearse the romance genealogy of talent, ambition, and defiance of tyranny, while the Shelley story waited in the wings. No longer "Victor," the petted scion of aristocracy, the protagonist of Godwin's *Bildungsroman* is a parvenu, but one with "merit, talents, ardour." In 1838 Sir Timothy nodded at last, and whatever "lights astral and shelleyan"[22] had been borrowed by Godwin's draft memorials were returned to Shelley with interest. There is a probable but unverifiable gap in composition of the Godwin "Life," corresponding to the absence of manuscripts between those on 1835 and 1837 paper and those on 1839 paper. A romantic poetics of biography produced one monumental inscription, "Mrs Shelley's Notes" to Shelley's *Poetical Works;* an attempt to cast Godwin, too, as the capable hero of his own writing shapes the "Life of William Godwin." The pretextual dictate that personal biography should be appended to literary canonicity is turned into text.

What remains constant in the moves between the Godwin and Shelley commissions is that Mary Shelley's writer-I is always older, by survival and by hindsight reflection, than the young men of whom she writes. She seeks occasions for personal signature in her overlapping *Bildungsromane* of young Shelley and young Godwin. Ironic time shifts evade the gender imbalance in the genealogical chart. The male subject's action entails effacement of the reproductive female line from which his power to act derives. Everything depends on a young man's initiation story culminating, in the "Life," in the death of Mary Wollstonecraft and a widower and wiser Godwin.

I want now to tease out the structural implications, for the "Life," of Mary Shelley's vantage point on the women in Godwin's bachelor life, a string of pearls on love, marriage, virtuous life, and the pursuit of happiness, successively revisited by Mary Shelley's script in the course of its composition over four years, 1836-40. Mary Wollstonecraft came into Godwin's life in 1796, and Mary Shelley's account of Wollstonecraft's long year of marriage and her death is to be found among the latest-written sections of the "Life of William Godwin," on paper watermarked 1839 (chiefly in deposits c.606/4 and c.532/8). My procedure, reflecting on the streaming tendency of romance in Mary Shelley's project, follows toward and over the starred figure of Mary Wollstonecraft.

In the earliest-written sections[23] of the "Life of William Godwin," Mary Shelley disposes (the word is not too harsh) of the provincial womenfolk who nurtured the future author:

> The first letter in the series is from his mother who, as he mentioned
> in his Life, had after losing her husband become uncomfortable in
> mind, through association with Methodists. The primitive tone of the

letter, its mixture of religious precept with a warning not to walk in the dark, renders it a precious relic of the good old times. Following this is a letter from Godwin to his mother. I do not know whether it was written in answer—but as to a great degree it is an answer it can be inserted with as great propriety as in any other place. (c.606/2)[24]

Thus begins Shelley's account of the women of Godwin's family: Ann, his mother; Hannah, his only sister; and Miss Godwin, later Mrs Sothren, who was his father's cousin (St Clair 1-2). Mary Shelley never met her grandmother Godwin, who resided in rural Norfolk and died in 1809. Godwin's fragmentary autobiography is kinder to his mother than to his father, as Kegan Paul noted,[25] no doubt because he had nego-tiated his freedom from her without a qualm. The Godwin women are placed by Mary Shelley on a ragged join where Godwin's first-person autobiography ends, in the year his father died, so the "Life" opens with the provincial family already lacking a male head. Mary Shelley from the outset colluded with Godwin's evasion of his father's claims and the "Life" compounds this evasion in fine detail. Shelley endorses Godwin's pedagogical ventures into younger people's "minds," and his lifelong (filial) protest against arbitrary (paternal) authority. From dis-senter tradition Godwin inherited Milton's rejection of priestly power (this is branded "stiff-necked contumacy" in Samuel Johnson's *Life of Milton* [1779]), and absorbed into it the anticolonialism of his American contemporaries. The autogenesis of literature and its over-writing of patrilineal succession are registered by the index of early works Shelley draws up from one of Godwin's many lists to mark off the cenotaph, or vacated tomb, of paternity.[26]

Mary Shelley's "Life" script contains only early materials relating to Godwin's mother, Ann, and the other female relatives in Dalling, Norfolk, and even within that time frame there are notable gaps, like Ann Godwin's welcome to the news of his marriage to Wollstonecraft,[27] her many grumbling gifts and loans of money, and her letters after Wollstonecraft's death. Ann Godwin's relationship with Mary Jane Godwin after 1801 is subsumed in the script's larger neglect of the very existence of this second wife, whom Ann addressed as her "dear daugh-ter" (as she did the other wives of her sons). A characteristic letter dated 27 April 1803, from Ann Godwin to "my dear Wm" reads: "Doubtless I should be glad to see you and your wife ^as she is part of yrself^ or any of your Children."[28] "Your wife" in 1803 is, of course, Mary Jane, and this falls outside the time frame of the "Life."

Shelley attaches one Ann Godwin letter in 1792, as a specimen of old-fashioned provincial prejudices. Ann's anxieties about the lack of religious observance in Godwin's London household are tactlessly pursued over long pages of admonition and reproach. Shelley collocates this letter with a brusque letter from Godwin to his mother (it is undated and internal evidence places it at an earlier date than 1792). Godwin fends off his mother's solicitations on two troublesome topics, money and religious adherence. Mary Shelley's judgment that this was typical of many such exchanges over the years is probably right. As usual, once she has placed a Godwin letter before her reader, Mary Shelley absolves herself of further comment. Here is a sample of Godwin's self-justification:

> I am exceedingly sorry that you should suffer yourself to form so unfavourable an opinion of my sentiments & character as you express in your last letter. Not that I am anxious so far as relates to myself what opinion may be formed of me by any human being; I am answerable only to God & conscience. But I am sorry even without deserving it to occasion you the smallest uneasiness. . . .
> I am in every respect, so far as I am able to follow the dictates of my own mind, perfectly indifferent to all personal gratification. I know of nothing worth living for but usefulness & the service of my fellow creatures. The only object I pursue is to increase as far as lies in my power the quantity of their knowledge & goodness & happiness.[29]

Mary Shelley sets Ann Godwin's superstitious "Methodism" against Godwin's intellectual freedom, the classic mother-son tug o'war. Ann Godwin is trying to hold control over a man aged thirty-six, and Godwin at thirty-six is using rhetorical muscle against an unsophisticated opponent.

Ann writes in May 1797 to Godwin congratulating him on his first marriage, albeit in terms that Mary Shelley would certainly have wished away from her carefully crafted history of that event: "Dear William/Your broken resolution in regard to matrimony incourages me to hope that you will ere long embrace the Gospel. . . . [Y]ou might have been so good as told me a few more particulars about your conjugal state as when you were married as being a father as well as husband, I hope you will fill up your place with propriety in both relations." The reference to Godwin's being a father is probably to his new stepdaughter, three-year-old Fanny Imlay.

Two seductively entwined romances haunt Mary Shelley's script of Mary Wollstonecraft, revolutionary virago and penitent whore. Godwin's *Memoirs of the Author of* A Vindication of the Rights of Woman and posthumous edition of Wollstonecraft's *The Wrongs of*

Woman had set these romantic legends on the obverse and reverse of a memorial tablet. Mary Shelley dictates a further dichotomy, that between private family women—womenfolk—and women writers, artists, and performers in the public eye.[30] The troubled lives and works of Wollstonecraft and her female fellow-writers are diverted by Mary Shelley's script into tributary streams, as Shelley pays out Wollstonecraft's talents in tribute to Godwin. She romances a circle of "other women" to hide Wollstonecraft where Godwin will find her, as in a comedy of courtship, "the laughter coming from the corner where the young girl is hiding."[31] While Godwin freely crisscrosses modern metropolitan London in pursuit of diverse career goals, his steps are traced and ritually supported, first by a standing or (better still) sitting circle of eligible waiting women, and next by Mary Shelley's writing as she guides his traverse toward Mary Wollstonecraft as his bride. His reluctant backward march into wedlock—though I think writing it (and reading him) cost her pain—is excused by Godwin's wish to reform sexual mores and break the established church's hold over marriage. In late 1839 and into 1840, Mary Shelley laboured to clothe the gritty details of her parents' marriage in shelleyan rainbow colours. Perhaps she found the double load of a twice-told tale too much; or perhaps the fragile idealized defence of her marriage to Shelley, published in December 1839, looked the more fragile in her eyes when she tried to write it again in her mother's name.

Mary Wollstonecraft, praised for her "sweetness" to "all who knew her," and her defence "of her own sex," is isolated from all particular female friendships. Nor is there any evidence of a network of female-authored textual exchanges or of women as progenitors of literary culture. Wollstonecraft may be elevated as a feminine nonpareil, helpmeet, spouse, and mother, but her isolation and silence in this elevated position are almost absolute.

Meanwhile, Godwin is surrounded by a bevy of Wollstonecraft's contemporaries, women writers such as Amelia Alderson[32] and Elizabeth Inchbald,[33] whose acquaintance Godwin cultivated, all to a lukewarm degree, during the five years (1791 to 1796) that he served a willing apprenticeship to literature. Mary Hays, who introduced the couple, and who was uniquely the intimate of both Godwin and Wollstonecraft, is reduced to a name. Maria Reveley (later Gisborne), Mary "Perdita" Robinson, and Sarah-Anne Parr are also placed by Mary Shelley as Godwin's friends, not Wollstonecraft's. This was accurate only in the case of Godwin's relationship with Sarah-Anne, the daughter of Rev. Samuel Parr, of Hatton. Mary Shelley drew up a one-page potted history of this young woman's less than fortunate life, with the evident purpose of scotching any suggestion of sexual interest on Godwin's part. On the ascent to Wollstonecraft, Shelley treats similarly each and every "other woman" in turn, but for Sarah-Anne she omits the sympathetic vignettes that accompany the others; and Mary Wollstonecraft's sour letter to a vacationing Godwin in May 1797— when Sarah-Anne eloped with her father's student—which compromises the accuracy of Shelley's presentation even in this case, is, of course, omitted from notice.

Elizabeth Inchbald makes a more graceful appearance before she too bows out. She is represented as a notable beauty, an actress, and a successful writer, Shelley noting her correspondence with Godwin about his books. Godwin quarrelled bitterly with Inchbald immediately after Wollstonecraft's death.[34] Mary Shelley suppresses the quarrel itself but, more importantly, she erases from her account of Godwin's "sincere admiration" for Inchbald his own behaviour, which had precipitated the very public breach between Inchbald and Wollstonecraft in the spring of 1797. Maria Reveley's brief memoir of her girlhood in Constantinople, written at Godwin's request in 1832, is among the papers in the Bodleian,[35] and Mary Shelley has drawn on it for her account of Reveley's *relationship* with Godwin and her *picture* of Wollstonecraft. My emphasis is deliberate; in spite of Mary Shelley's insistence on Wollstonecraft's tender regard for her own sex, there is no sign of her female friendships, and all traces of dissension or dislike among women are systematically expunged from the record. Wollstonecraft is encircled by women but not shown in relation to any of them, as each in turn comes before Godwin to be *not* chosen by him. A large bundle of loquacious letters written by Amelia Alderson in Norfolk to Godwin in London between late summer 1795 and early 1797 was arranged, numbered, and annotated by Mary Jane Godwin, undoubtedly at Mary Shelley's behest and with a view to attaching some of them to the body of the "Life." Alderson is a mine of gossip about personalities, and Mary Jane Godwin's sub-acid marginalia show that some of the barbs stuck forty years on. It is doubtful where (or whether) Mary Shelley would have introduced Alderson's effusions into her design, their tone toward Godwin being so unlike her own.

On the topic of her parents' courtship, Mary Shelley picks out and rearranges a few passages from the intimate notes that passed almost daily between Wollstonecraft and Godwin before the December discovery of Wollstonecraft's pregnancy (which is never mentioned). She culls from each note, excising Wollstonecraft's confidential remarks about Mary Hays and Mary Robinson from one, retaining a charming detail about three-year-old Fanny in another. The original scribbles reveal an easily dispirited Wollstonecraft, and a Godwin prone to pomposity. Checked against these originals, Shelley's excerpts are seen to decontextualize the notes and compress their tenor to exclusively lover-like sentiments. She emphasizes the harmony of the courting pair, no hint given of disquietude (Wollstonecraft's) or cold feet (Godwin's).

Mary Shelley's account of 1797 does whatever it can to lengthen out the months of marriage before the fatal childbirth. It pictures Godwin as a married man:

> As time proceeds a considerable change appears to have been operated in Mr. Godwin's mind; more in manner than in substance certainly—but there was a softening attendant on his having quitted his independant position & making one of the family of mankind. His cares encreased on him at the same time, & there is more of pecuniary struggle to be traced in his correspondance. (c.606/4)

Shelley draws on Godwin's account of Wollstonecraft's "increasing sweetness" and "softening" by marriage and maternity, in *Memoirs* (1798), for a kind of osmosis between the married pair that naturalizes her decline and his survival. Maternal softening is a dead weight unless paternal law carries it forward. Mary Shelley's Godwin has no organic softening "substance," but she wants to figure him in the family way, softening (not his demands for money: these, as she correctly notes, increase, but) his doxa on marriage, an ideological climb down tantamount to the surrender of selfish individualism.

At the date of Wollstonecraft's death, Mary Shelley signals a moratorium, announcing that letters to and from Godwin in the later months of 1797 will be included elsewhere in the biography. "I commence this year [1798] with a few letters dated at the conclusion of the last [1797], but which would have interfered with the subject that set its dark seal on that year."[36] Her decision to relocate Tom Wedgwood's letters, "written towards the conclusion of the last [year 1797]," is of particular interest for Wedgwood's letter from Wales on 31 July 1797,[37] expounding his scheme of founding "a nursery of genius," and conveying his somewhat frigid respects to "Mrs. Godwin" (Mary Wollstonecraft). This is the earlier of the two letters in the Abinger archive in which Wedgwood acknowledges Godwin's marriage—the second offers condolences for her death six weeks after the first. Wedgwood had lent money to Godwin in February 1797 for a purpose that Godwin had declined to name, and his reaction to the discovery that Godwin had used it to pay out Wollstonecraft's debts can only be guessed at between the lines of these and other letters.[38] I am unable to say whether it was these two letters in particular that Mary Shelley had at hand when she announced her decision to move them away from her account of Wollstonecraft's marriage and death.

Continuing her narrative[39] past Wollstonecraft's death, Mary Shelley's script carries Maria Reveley's story forward to 1799, when Godwin proposed marriage to her immediately after the death of her first husband, Willy Reveley. For Reveley's story Shelley draws on the autobiographical memoir written by Reveley at Godwin's suggestion in 1832. In this memoir, and her letters and journals, Reveley writes with a discerning critical eye, especially tart on the topic of men, and particularly on the topic of Godwin. Liking to leave this side of Reveley dark, Mary Shelley improvises a scene for Godwin to enter upon, after Willy Reveley's sudden death in 1799. Maria's grief, mingled with guilt because her married life was less than happy, becomes frantic; but when Godwin declares his love, she abstains from a second chance of happiness, still unabsolved from the failure of her first. There is no precedent for this hysterical heroinism in any of Maria Reveley's writings. Godwin's virile gesture toward Reveley proves, while it puts a strain on, his fidelity to the husband role. The wasteful machinery of family romance dictates that Godwin should master the late Willy Reveley, while survivor guilt proves too strong for Maria Reveley.[40]

The last section of Shelley script, again on 1839 paper, narrates Godwin's unsuccessful wooing of Miss Harriet Lee of Bath from March to August 1798; that is, within a year of Wollstonecraft's death. At the latest stage of composition, and probably after Mary Jane had to beg off further copyist work, Mary Shelley discovered a bundle of letters from Godwin in 1798 to the writer and schoolmistress Harriet Lee, whom he had met on his visit to Bath after the publication of *Memoirs*. He proposed marriage to her, she refused him, he would not take no for an answer. In the space of five months an epistolary siege ensued, but in the end it was still no. These papers have been placed in a separate folder (b.228/4), and Mary Shelley's commentary on them is not continuous with her long section on Wollstonecraft in 1797 and Maria Reveley in 1799. The coldly furnished wooing and the lapsed correspondence between Godwin and Lee resided in the Godwin archive with the polemical essay on religious freedom that grew out of it, both awaiting Mary Shelley's imprimatur, in the end withheld from both.

In the Harriet Lee incident, Godwin's ebullience on paper gives the lie to Shelley's description of the "softened" widower of the previous year. Godwin puts up a barrage of arguments for his emotional independence and liberty of conscience. And crucially, Harriet Lee speaks up for herself in four letters, the sole dissenting voice heard in the "Life."[41]

Shelley's manipulations of women other than Wollstonecraft entangle themselves with figures of men other than Godwin.[42] Godwin's *Memoirs of the Author* had included unflattering references to Imlay and Fuseli, omitted Holcroft, and given equivocal testimony to Wollstonecraft's publisher, Joseph Johnson, for his fostering of her intellectual and emotional development. Mary Shelley further depresses Holcroft's and Johnson's roles, and emphasizes the commemorative piety of *Memoirs*, of "Godwin's incomparable wife," "the treasure he had lost." According to Shelley's script, Godwin's rushed courtships of Harriet Lee and Maria Reveley are misadventures of a widower father of "two infants of the opposite sex." Godwin always avoided attachments to women under male authority; he was not keen to be a son-in-law in a Radcliffe romance. He was deaf and blind to the girlish wiles of Amelia Alderson and Sarah-Anne Parr, eligible not-so-young daughters of leading men of dissenter and Anglican provincial communities. He married two divorcees, Mary Wollstonecraft Imlay and Mary Jane Vial Clairmont, and courted a handsome widow, Elizabeth Inchbald, from a safe distance. Harriet Lee was an established author and taught at a fashionable girls' school in Bath, where her elder sister Sophia, Miss Lee, was headmistress. During his epistolary wooing of Harriet for six months of 1798, Godwin displayed intense annoyance at Sophia's liberty to read his words over Harriet's shoulder. He was unused to having personal authority asserted by anyone except himself. His resentment of being crowded and looked over by the sisterhood on this occasion begs the questions of rightful authority and rightful resistance to it, canvassed throughout his writings.

The last written sections of the "Life" include a transcription from the final chapters of Godwin's *Memoirs of the Author of* A Vindication of the Rights of Woman (1798) in Mary Jane Godwin's hand on watermarked 1839 paper. Mary Jane occasionally slips up. She alters the spelling of Tom Paine's surname to Payne—which was how her American acquaintance Howard Payne spelt his name. She substitutes the 1798 text's "removed the placenta by hand," with "removed *parts of* the placenta by hand"; supplementing the discreet published account with the known terrible fact. It is an accident (one of many such) that the final pages of the transcription have gone missing from the Bodleian folder. The missing section corresponds to the final pages of Chapter 10 of the first edition of *Memoirs,* where Godwin famously attributes *no* last words of religious belief or repentance to the dying Wollstonecraft.[43] Their disappearance shows up the flimsiness of paper and ink, and the vagaries of private owners and official biographers.

Notes

1 "Mary Shelley's Journal, 1826 intermittently till 1844," Duke University mfm reel 11, Abinger Collection. First published selectively in *Mary Shelley's Journal*, ed. Frederick L. Jones (Norman: U of Oklahoma P, 1947). Entries for the years 1826-44 are in *JMS*, vol. 2.

2 Shelley's simultaneous gestures toward dying father and infantilized son suggest the relevance of two articles by Luce Irigaray. "The Eternal Irony of the Community" treats women's role as bearers of group memory, and what Joseph Roach has termed surrogates, in the reproduction of the male ruling group. "Women, the Sacred, and Money" posits the waste of the mother in the heterosexual economy: "It is clear that our societies assume that *the mother should feed her child for free*, before and after the birth, and that she should remain the nurse of man and of society. She is *the totem before any totem is designated*, identified, represented. . . . How old must these children . . . be? . . . How much will they cost? . . . Calculating how much a child costs is enough to shock anyone, or almost" (75, 83; emphases in original).

3 Account of Sir Timothy Shelley's death, Sunstein, *Mary Shelley* 363-64.

4 Sunstein, *Mary Shelley* 336-69. Mary Shelley's interest in Victoria is evident in the second and third volumes of *LMWS*. See, for instance: "our pretty little Queen" (?March 1840; 2: 342-43); "What an abominable thing is this attack on the Queen—she is a brave little thing" (June [1842]; 3: 29-30); "like our little Queen she had no trouble or pain at last at all & has a boy" (October [1843]; 3: 100-01).

5 The MS contract with Colburn, for "Memoirs and Correspondence of the late William Godwin," in "not less than two volumes," is in Oxford, Bodleian Library (Abinger deposit), MS Eng. lett. c.461 f. 153, dated 19 July 1836, co-signatories John Hobart Caunter and Mary Jane Godwin. Quotations in this arti-

cle from Lord Abinger's Shelley-Godwin Papers in the Bodleian Library, Oxford and MS microfilms in the Perkins Library, Duke University, Durham, are published by kind permission of Lord Abinger.

6   Duke reel 5. Godwin MS note to "My Literary Executor," dated 30 June 1834. Letter from William Godwin to Mary Shelley, undated, c. 1835, lacking signature: "My dear Mary/ I am devolving on you an arduous duty, which I am afraid will cause you often to think of me with disapprobation & pain. But I have no alternative./ I leave behind me a manuscript in a considerable state of forwardness for the press, entitled, 'The Genius of Christianity Unveiled: In a Series of Essays.'" Godwin's pamphlet was later edited anonymously by Charles Kegan Paul as *Essays by the Late William Godwin: Never Before Published.* See also Godwin, *Political and Philosophical Writings,* Vol. 7.

7   Mary Shelley to Edward Trelawny, 26 January 1837 (*LMWS* 2: 280-81). Sunstein comments: "Trelawny accused her of being afraid to publish Godwin's political views. . . . It was not a question of '*politics,* but *religion,*' she wrote him" (*Mary Shelley* 335).

8   Pollin, *Godwin Criticism,* "Necrologies" 267n.: "It is believed he has left several unpublished MSS"; 320n.: "Mrs Shelley inherits his genius"; 459n.: "Funeral mourners include young Shelley"; 510n.: "In the Memoirs [*of the Author of* A Vindication of the Rights of Woman], Mary [*sic*] appears to have been grossly irreligious, indelicate, and dissolute. . . . Mrs Shelley is about to publish his autobiography."

9   The list of Mary Shelley's addressees and the text of her letters to several of them are in *LMWS* 2: 269-77.

10   Letter-press copies of Godwin's letters to Hays of 5, 10, 22, and 27 October 1797 are in b.227/8 and Duke reel 5. Godwin's letter to Hays of 26 December 1797, completing the sequence, is in MS Pforzheimer (WG322), New York Public Library.

11   Details of Mary Shelley's negotiations on her own and Godwin's behalfs, with publishers and editors, including Lardner, publisher of *Cabinet Cyclopaedia,* are in my article "Among the Dead Men."

12   In the section of c.532/8 headed "Mrs G's Letters," on watermark 1839 paper. Mary Jane Godwin died in 1841.

13   C.606/4 Richmond, 6 May 1840. See also *JMS* 564-65. Mary Shelley left for Italy with Percy and two of his Cambridge friends on 13 June 1840, 564 n.4.

14 Dep. c.606/4, Mary Shelley's note headed "Richmond/ 6 May 1840," on watermark Joynson 1839 paper, is the latest positive dating for work ongoing for "Life of William Godwin."

15 See also microfilm reels of the Abinger Shelley-Godwin collection at Duke University.

16 Godwin's "regular autobiography," composed in 1796-97, and a few fragments and "notes," were first published in William Godwin, *Collected Novels and Memoirs* 1: 3-38; "Autobiographical Fragments and Reflections, 1772-9," 1:41-51.

17 Mary Shelley certainly read and annotated the pre-1772 materials. Cf. Duke reel 2, MWS marginalia on Godwin's pre-1772 autobiography: "temper of his father—desires to run away—the Cat—Schoolmaster—Mrs Sothren—visit to Norwich—*the* seat on the top of the organ."

18 Autobiographical "particulars" are in Essays 7, 9, 14, 18.

19 "Memoirs of the Author," prefixed to Godwin, *Things* [iii]-xiii.

20 Published by Edward Moxon in 1839, in four volumes of poetry and two of prose essays and letters.

21 In 1832 Mary Shelley gave Jeff Hogg bundles of her notes and Shelley's to assist him in research for his brief biography, "Shelley at Eton." In 1834 Lady Blessington and in 1833 Thomas Medwin published memoirs of Bysshe Shelley distasteful to Mary. She announced that she would not read either work, "as was her practice with publications she disapproved" (Sunstein, *Mary Shelley* 318).

22 Wallace Stevens, "Mr. Burnshaw and the Statue," *Opus Posthumous* 47.

23 Deps. c.606/1, c.606/2, c.606/5, some leaves are 1835 and 1837 watermark paper.

24 Ann Godwin's letters are in c.516, together with one undated draft letter from Godwin to his mother. Another Ann Godwin letter dated 1801 is in b.214/3.

25 Paul (1876), 1: 6-7. Ann Godwin's letters to Godwin in c.516/1.

26 Mary Shelley's transcription of Godwin's chronological lists of his early works is in c.606/1.

27 Ann Godwin letter [3] May 1797, c.516/1. The marriage took place on 29 March 1797.

28 C.516/1, another letter from Ann Godwin in November 1803 shows that Godwin and Mary Jane, but none of the children, did visit her that year.

29 MWS script in c.606/2. Ann Godwin's letter (dated from Dalling, Norfolk, April 1792) and Godwin's undated letter are both in c.516/1.

30   Mary Poovey's classic statement of the opposition between "proper lady and woman writer" casts a psychological burden and ritual role on individual women writers, engaged over their heads in gendered dominance struggle.

31   Horace, *Odes* 2.3.

32   Alderson's letters to Godwin 1795-97, annotated by Mary Jane Godwin, are in b.210/6.

33   Mary Shelley's account of Godwin's relations with Amelia Alderson and Elizabeth Inchbald is in c.532/8.

34   Letter-press copy in b.227/8(a), Godwin to Inchbald, dated 13 September 1797: "I must endeavour to be understood as to the unworthy behaviour with which I charge you towards my wife."

35   In c.607 Mary Shelley's commentary on Godwin's friendship and later his courtship with Reveley is in c.532/8 (on 1839 paper).

36   A more detailed discussion of Mary Shelley's editorial decisions is Clara Tuite, "William and Mary" 102-03, citing Mary Shelley's script in c.532/8 and c.606/4.

37   In Duke reel 12.

38   Cf. St Clair, Chapter 12, "Mary Wollstonecraft."

39   In Deps. c.606/4 and c.532/8, both on 1839 paper throughout.

40   Mary Shelley script in c.532/8. Maria Gisborne's 1832 memoir of her girlhood in Constantinople, c.607. Cf. Mary Shelley's "Journal of Sorrow" entries after Bysshe Shelley's sudden death in Italy in July 1822. Then, Jane Williams was Mary Shelley's confidante, Trelawny the subaltern male, Bysshe the lost bridegroom.

41   The manuscripts are (for once) grouped together in a single Bodleian folder, dep. b.228/4, and the letters of both Godwin and Harriet Lee to which the commentary refers are all present and accounted for. Mary Shelley's commentary on the Harriet Lee affair is written on watermark "Joynson 1839" paper identical to the paper in c.606/4 and c.532/8. The Harriet Lee affair was canvassed in 1876 by Charles Kegan Paul in the first volume of Godwin's authorized biography. It seems probable that Paul's work on the manuscripts has been instrumental in keeping this element of Mary Shelley's text intact.

42   "Mary Shelley's romance of marriage idealizes Wollstonecraft, and explains Godwin's liaisons with other women after her death as contingencies predicated on his desire to 'regain a portion of the treasure he had lost.'" Tuite, citing b.228/4, Mary Shelley's script on Godwin's courtship of Harriet Lee in 1798.

43   Transcription from the January 1798 first edition of Godwin's *Memoirs* ends on the words "His [Dr. Carlisle's] conduct was uniformly tender and anxious," and below that, the drop word "ever." This corresponds to page 187 in Godwin's published text; on page 190 of the first edition we read: "On these two days her faculties were in too decayed a state, to be able to follow any train of ideas with force or any accuracy of connection. Her religion, as I have already shown, was not calculated to be the torment of a sick bed; and, in fact, during her whole illness, not a word of a religious cast fell from her lips." The missing pages of Mary Jane's transcription correspond to pages 187-90 of the first edition. This version ends on page 199.

"Unconceiving Marble": Anatomy and Animation in *Frankenstein* and *The Last Man*

Anne McWhir

To write a novel whose hero brings a creature to life is to write life twice—once in the narrative events, and once in the authorial labour that mirrors dissection, obsession, and construction. In *Frankenstein*, Mary Shelley writes her "hideous progeny"[1] into textual life, while her modern Prometheus constructs an artificial creature out of the body of death. Recognizing the parallel between these creative acts, however, one also recognizes the difference between a metaphor of birth and one of construction: Shelley implies that she has given birth to a monstrous text; her Prometheus, like his classical prototype (though using different materials), constructs his creature. Through her metaphor, Shelley reminds us that reproduction is primarily a physical process, not just the mass-production or replication of artifacts. Whereas creating life can be a labour of the will (like Frankenstein's construction of the creature) or of the imagination (as in most romantic aesthetic theory), it is most fundamentally a labour of the body bound to time. Considering the creature in *Frankenstein* as a product of life writing, this essay will explore the limits of artificial creation and its relation to the time-bound processes of conception, gestation, and birth. Further, it will consider the conclusion of *The Last Man*, amid the stat-

Notes are on pp. 173-75.

ues of Rome in a world where reproduction is no longer possible, as a meditation on the limits of representation.

In relation to *Frankenstein*, much has been written about the creative work of Prometheus, rebel and man-maker. In *The Pantheon, or Ancient History of the Gods of Greece and Rome* (1806), William Godwin retells Hesiod's story in terms that emphasize Prometheus's role as artist. His daughter, however, presents a far more complicated version. Her modern Prometheus is a grave-robbing anatomist whose creation falls short of his prototype's "exquisite workmanship" (Godwin, *Pantheon* 76); "Minerva, the Goddess of arts" (76) helps Hesiod's Prometheus, the model for Godwin's, to steal celestial fire, an advantage Shelley's isolated, obsessed hero conspicuously lacks. Far from moving, thinking, and speaking to fulfill the creator's fondest wishes, as Godwin describes "the man of Prometheus" (77) doing, Frankenstein's initially inarticulate creature fills his creator with horror and despair.

The sequel to this familiar story is, however, equally relevant to *Frankenstein*. Godwin, following Hesiod, continues as follows:

> Jupiter became still more exasperated than ever with this new specimen of Prometheus's ability and artifice [the making of a man]: he ordered Vulcan, the great artificer of Heaven, to make a woman of clay, that should be still more consummate and beautiful of structure than Prometheus's man: with this alluring present Jupiter determined to tempt Prometheus to his ruin: all the Gods of the Saturnian race, eager to abet the project of their chief, gave her each one a several gift, from which circumstance she obtained the name of Pandora, *all gifts*. (77)

Designed by the gods to ensnare men, Hesiod's Pandora is a *kalon kakon* or beautiful evil gifted to curse rather than bless by bringing into the world sexual reproduction and its contingent institution, marriage. Godwin censors the worst of Hesiod's misogyny: "Women are bad for men, and they conspire / In wrong, and Zeus the Thunderer made it so" (*Theogony* 42). In the well-known version of the story in the *Works and Days*, Epimetheus, Prometheus's foolish brother, takes Pandora in, she opens the vase or jar, and the world's sorrows fly out, leaving only Hope in the jar as a palliative for human suffering (62).

According to the earliest, pre-Hesiodic version of the story, Pandora was made not by Hephaestos (Vulcan), but by Prometheus himself. Andrew Tooke tells this story: "some say, that [Prometheus] was not punish'd because he stole Fire from Heaven, but because he had made Woman, which is the most pernicious Creature in the World" (363-64). This (without that last clause) is the version that informs

Calderón and Voltaire, both of whom present a Pandora more like one of Percy Shelley's "Phidian forms" (*Prometheus Unbound* 3.4.112) than like the moulded clay of Hesiod. Pandora, like Pygmalion's statue (Ovid, *Metamorphoses* 10.243), is the marble artifact wakened into life. In his discussion of James Barry's painting *Pandora*, John Barrell argues that Pandora typifies the neoclassical body, defining the community of male culture by providing it with a focal object (158). However, the idealized form of female beauty, presented to the male gaze, is shadowed by woman's pernicious nature; the idealized body of Pandora the all-gifted, moulded from earth by Hephaestos or Prometheus, seems inseparable from her fatal effect: she is the "lovely curse," the "hopeless trap" (*Theogony* 32) whose gifts are fatal.

While Mary Shelley's subtitle alone justifies the critical attention Prometheus and his creature have received, Pandora also deserves attention in discussions of *Frankenstein*. Shelley introduces her obliquely and abortively, emphasizing the reproductive threat she embodies for Frankenstein. Knowing Pandora's stories and roles, Shelley's hero chooses to deny the female creature the spark of life. Half-made and then torn to pieces, the draft of an unwritable text, Pandora inhabits the novel as an ambiguous possibility — the creature's hope of redemption, the creator's monstrous nightmare. Given her history, Pandora seems to demand a female champion;[2] and, indeed, the unrealized possibilities of her ambiguous beauty haunt *Frankenstein*. Yet the story of the first woman as animated artifact is overwhelmed by the negative connotations of her jar of ills. Exercising Promethean foresight, Frankenstein recognizes the danger the creature's female companion might pose to humankind:

> Even if they [the creature and his desired companion] were to leave Europe, and inhabit the deserts of the new world, yet one of the first results of those sympathies for which the daemon thirsted would be children, and a race of devils would be propagated upon the earth, who might make the very existence of the species of man a condition precarious and full of terror. (128)

Frankenstein destroys his Pandora because he shares Hesiod's distrust of woman and Hesiod's preference for a self-contained male order over the reproductive potential of female sexuality. As he tears apart his artificial woman, Frankenstein prefigures the creature's murder of Elizabeth on her wedding-night: "The remains of the half-finished creature, whom I had destroyed, lay scattered on the floor, and I almost felt as if I had mangled the living flesh of a human being" (132). This act of violent dismemberment, described in language evoking abortion as well as murder, goes beyond the creature's stranglehold, leaving Shelley's modern Pandora broken and nameless, an unwritten life and text weighted with stones and cast into the sea. Frankenstein's fear of monstrous reproduction can be generalized as a fear of all reproduction outside his control: even in his most euphoric moments, he prefers the role of father-god (the receiver of worship, the maker of creatures who stay in their place) to the risks of biological fatherhood.

Based on his reading and his observations of the De Laceys, Frankenstein's creature has a view of reproduction different from his creator's:

> I heard of the difference of sexes; of the birth and growth of children; how the father doated on the smiles of the infant, and the lively sallies of the older child; how all the life and cares of the mother were wrapt up in the precious charge; how the mind of youth expanded and gained knowledge; of brother, sister, and all the various relationships which bind one human being to another in mutual bonds. (90)

Given many discouraging examples of parenthood within the novel (and his own disillusionment when he confronts the De Laceys), the creature's enduring desire for a mate is particularly significant. The novel shows on the one hand a resistance to sexual reproduction and on the other hand an insistence on it as a human longing and, indeed, necessity. Perhaps Frankenstein, but neither Mary Shelley nor the creature, resists the interdependence of parents and children, an interdependence that presses relentlessly into the future and refuses the illusion of stasis or any respite from history.

If Pandora's jar, box, or urn-like vase represents the specifically sexual temptation she offers Epimetheus, it can also be read reproductively as a version of the womb. This is made explicit in a 1920 drawing by Paul Klee, *Die Büchse der Pandora als Stilleben* (Pandora's Box as Still-Life), where the word "Pandora" names a womb-like metonymic vase "emitting evil vapors from an opening clearly suggestive of the female genitals."[3] Yet the association of womb with Pandora's jar or vase is sufficiently evident even in Hesiod. Out of such an urn/womb come all the ills of the world—"Thousands of troubles, wandering the earth" (*Works and Days* 62)—represented in illustrations to Charles Abraham Elton's translation (engraved after John Flaxman) as miniature creatures (including a tiny skeleton) escaping as Pandora lifts the lid.[4] Hope alone, unreleased in Hesiod or, in other versions of the story, sent forth with all the rest, compensates for (or intensifies) the curse of Pandora's gifts.

When Shelley returns to Pandora's story in *The Last Man*, she does so in the context of a novel about the failure of reproduction. She introduces Pandora obliquely, alluding to her box of evils and speculating about their source. Having described the ravages of plague, her narrator, Lionel Verney, quotes from Elton's translation of Hesiod's *Works and Days*:

> With ills the land is rife, with ills the sea,
> Diseases haunt our frail humanity,
> Through noon, through night, on casual wing they glide,
> Silent,—a voice the power all-wise denied.
> (*LM* 248; Hesiod, trans. Elton 16)

In the original context, Hesiod is describing the evils let loose from Pandora's jar, which in *The Last Man* correspond to plague (itself associated with female agency through Evadne's curse on Raymond and the subsequent personification of plague as female). If Shelley's use of this passage from Hesiod seems too indirect an allusion to Pandora, a couple of pages earlier, at the end of Volume 2, Lionel has made the source of the novel's ills explicit, lamenting that in the plague-ravaged world hope has given way to resignation and despair:

> Old fable tells us, that [hope] sprung from the box of Pandora, else crammed with evils; but these were unseen and null, while all admired the inspiriting loveliness of young Hope; each man's heart became her home; she was enthroned sovereign of our lives, here and hereafter; she was deified and worshipped, declared incorruptible and everlasting. But like all other gifts of the Creator to Man, she is mortal; her life has attained its last hour. . . . Hope is dead!
> (243-44)

Implying that Pandora's box is the source of evils, Lionel focuses on Hope—here springing forth in compensation for suffering, only to die along with humanity (and specifically prefiguring the death of Lionel's son, Evelyn, and wife, Idris, early in Volume 3). Disease, blight, and death have no amelioration except, perhaps, the hint that they are mortal like their victims.

Shelley's emphasis here is no longer on Pandora as "manufactured maiden" (Hesiod, *Theogony* 32), but on Hope, the offspring of Pandora's mythical function. In a novel of depopulation, in which the multitudes become multitudes of corpses and, finally, are subsumed by the sculptured forms of Rome, the death of Hope signifies the end of reproduction as anything but a replication of death and disease. All the future possibilities promised by the "birth and growth of children"

(*FMP* 90) fade with the death of Hope. In this sense, it is appropriate that Hope's funeral procession ends Volume 2 of *The Last Man*, prefiguring Lionel's final desolation.

The story of Pandora grants the marble woman life; but Mary Shelley's account of her own experience, like several passages in *The Last Man*, shows the living woman turned to marble.[5] In October 1822, a few months after Shelley's death, Mary wrote in her journal: "fill me, my chosen one, with a part of your energy, & angelic nobility of spirit. . . . I am not unfeeling—my hourly agonies prove that, yet the presence of those who do not love me, makes me feel as if I were of marble" (441). Obscuring the distinction between life and death, the marble woman recalls the vitality of those she has lost, whose physical presence is like a remembered dream: "My William, Clara, Allegra are all talked of [in old letters]—They lived then—They breathed this air & their voices struck on my sense, their feet trod the earth beside me—& their hands were warm with blood & life when clasped in mine. Where are they all?" (435). Shortly before this, she has transcribed into her journal Trelawny's account of burying Edward Williams's body: "it was dreadfully mutilated—both legs seperating [*sic*] on our attempting to move it—the hands & one foot had been entirely eaten—with all the flesh of the face—by fish" (423). Haunted by both cherished and horrific images of the loved dead, it is no wonder that she presents herself as hardly alive: "I am in the valley of the shadow of death & soon shall be a clod" (435).

Both the marble woman and the "clod," the disintegrating body of clay, are versions of death; yet they are very different models for what it means to write life. The first, lacking subjectivity, is nevertheless a familiar expression of that universal order which, in "A Defence of Poetry," poets (including sculptors) "imagine and express" (*SPP* 482). The marble woman animated by passion or artifice is, of course, a familiar mythic figure, typified by Pandora and Pygmalion's statue: the statue is lifeless until she is awakened by the gazer as, in Mary Shelley's story "The Dream," Constance, like a "statue hewn of marble in monumental effigy" (*Collected Tales* 163), "open[s] her eyes and beh[olds] her lover, who ha[s] watched over her dream of fate, and who ha[s] saved her" from plunging over a chasm as she suddenly comes to consciousness (164). The second model, the disintegrating body of death, represents defunct life from the perspective of the kind of science that may murder to dissect. Both the marble woman and the clod of clay are equally inanimate and unresponsive—and equally models for versions of "life." Yet if the marble woman is one product of what

Percy Shelley calls in "Defence of Poetry" "τὸ ποιειν, or the principle of synthesis," which he goes on to identify with imagination, she is less distinct than he might wish from the body as clod of clay, one object of "the τὸ λογιζειν, or principle of analysis" (*SPP* 480).

Contrasting "the form and the splendour of unfaded beauty," emerging out of an inspired creative process, with "the secrets of anatomy and corruption" (503), understood through dissection and analysis, Percy Shelley elsewhere praises the statue of an athlete by remarking that the "muscles are represented how differently from a statue since anatomy has corrupted it" ("Notes on Sculptures," 315), an interesting aesthetic judgment that puns on the connection between knowledge of anatomy and knowledge of death and decay. At the Royal Academy of Arts in London, he may have seen the cast of a man hanged at Tyburn, who was flayed and placed in a sculpture-like posture by the anatomist William Hunter in 1775.[6] Yet Percy Shelley's notions of the corrupting influence of anatomy on beauty (not to mention his opposition to the death penalty)[7] suggest that he would not have admired such a grotesque representation of the human body and that he would have consistently drawn a clearer distinction between art and anatomy than some of his contemporaries were willing to do.

Yet both Shelleys celebrated the artist's passage through a conjunction of birth and death, leading either to the "diviner day" of *Prometheus Unbound* (2.5.103) or to daemonic terrors of flight and pursuit. Birth and death meet in the scientist's world, too; and the scientist and artist collaborate in that meeting. William Hunter, professor of anatomy at the Royal Academy of Arts, was also a famous obstetrician, "physician extraordinary" to Queen Charlotte.[8] His multiple yet interconnected roles emphasize the close interdependence of art and anatomy, creativity and dissection, in the late eighteenth century. Sir Anthony Carlisle, in 1808 one of Hunter's successors as professor of anatomy, had been a student at the Royal Academy. His paper "on the 'Connection between Anatomy and the Fine Arts,'" argued "that minute knowledge of anatomy was not necessary to the historical painter and sculptor";[9] yet his own example as someone trained in both art and anatomy indicates that many artists did have such knowledge. Frankenstein's prototype, Prometheus, had produced a closed work of art, animated by divine fire; Frankenstein, in contrast, pieces together a version of the grotesque body, composition in decomposition, its interior visible like that of a body on a dissection slab: "[h]is yellow skin scarce covered the work of muscles and arteries beneath" (39). The creature comes to life like an anatomical drawing, animated so as to emphasize with every movement his difference from ordinary life. Yet in the moment before animation the creature also lies before his creator like an effigy: "I had selected his features as beautiful." (39). Two distinct models—one focused on the inner workings, the other on the smooth surface—govern Mary Shelley's representation of life, and the transformation of artifact into nightmare echoes the meaning of the myth of Pandora.

Frankenstein and *The Last Man* both explore the anatomy and the statue as transformations and representations of the living body. The first is bound to death and corruption, whereas the second readily signifies transcendence and ideality. The first dabbles in death and even seeks to "renew life where death ha[s] apparently devoted the body to corruption" (37); the second provides an illusion of life. Yet Mary Shelley demonstrates that the two are less dissimilar than they might appear to be, thereby challenging a romantic aesthetic that urges their separation. Frankenstein is artist as well as scientist, bound on creating a beautiful creature—though he describes himself as "rather like one doomed by slavery to toil in the mines, or any other unwholesome trade, than an artist occupied by his favourite employment" (39).

Through his double role, he confirms that the dissection room provides material for both art and science, a point that is illustrated by the popularity of both art galleries and museums of science in this period.[10] One of William Hunter's most famous art students at the Royal Academy was John Flaxman, who paints an early self-portrait with his hand resting on a skull (Irwin 7, plate 6), and who paid for an anatomy course in Rome in 1792 (Irwin 47). Self-knowledge evidently includes scientific knowledge of the body's death. The charming smoothness of Flaxman's drawings for Elton's Hesiod, like the smooth neoclassical finish of his monumental sculptures, demonstrates a deliberate choice of polished, idealizing images. Yet Flaxman, like many contemporary artists, also produced anatomical drawings based on dissection: his drawings of bones and muscles are detailed and particular, emphasizing specific function rather than the general effect of line and surface. Similarly, the painter George Stubbs performed dissections of horses and other animals and published beautifully detailed drawings based on his anatomical work. Less well known is his work on human anatomy, including drawings of human fetuses *in utero* surrounded, in some cases, by the obstetric instruments that must have failed the subjects of those particular dissections.[11]

Far beyond Pandora's curiosity, dissection is the ultimate disclosure of the body's secrets. William Hunter's ground-breaking *Anatomy of the Human Gravid Uterus* (1774, with etchings by Robert Strange based on drawings by Jan van Rymsdyck) withdraws the veil in a disturbingly literal fashion. We confront images not of general human anatomy, but of a particular woman's body. At first, the subject's legs seem decorously covered; then, as the surgeon's scalpel, through a series of successive plates, peels back layer upon layer of skin, fat, and muscle, revealing the fetus within the womb, then removing the fetus to reveal the internal organs, the cloth disappears and the observer can see the trunk of what was once a woman, cut apart through the thighs (and, a note explains, below the breasts). An early plate, in which one looks at the pregnant abdomen from between the subject's thighs, gives way to a later representation of the mutilated subject, clitoris and labia excised, cross-section of the femur meticulously represented—emptied of human dignity and reproductive significance and rendered merely a fragment of a dead object. All this is represented with extraordinary technical skill: pubic hair, the texture of the skin, the shading of the internal organs, the moulding of the dead unborn child's head—all are perfect. Reproduction, halted by death and penetrated by analysis, is systematically reduced to a series of beautifully represented but increasingly useless parts.[12]

In this case, art and science together dismantle the integrity of the subject. Hunter's truncated body parts, once the cloth is removed, allow for no illusions. In this respect they are very different from Leonardo da Vinci's anatomical drawings—in which parts are still the highlighted fragments of an implied whole—or from Stubbs's complete human figures captured in motion, flayed to show the muscular structure but still representations of integrated form. The romantic aesthetic of wholeness represented by John Keats's Grecian urn or Percy Bysshe Shelley's Neoplatonism evidently challenges representation of the body as an accretion of inanimate parts subdued by science. Percy Shelley's poetry generally subordinates fact to a perception of general truth, to what Shelley describes in the Preface to *Prometheus Unbound* as "beautiful idealisms of moral excellence" (*SPP* 135). According to this view, dissection and anatomy can decipher *only* facts, not a truth that must be glimpsed imaginatively rather than understood rationally. "[T]he perfect and consummate surface and bloom of things" in *Defence of Poetry* is a better representation of meaning than "the secrets of anatomy and corruption" (503) that preoccupy William Hunter and other surgeons of his day.

However, the flayed figure in motion, the animated corpse, the tomb effigy that evokes breath, the marble statue that softens into speech, all have in common their defiance of such oppositions as art and nature, death and life, stasis and movement. Each is an attempt to represent that "mystery of our being" which, according to Percy Shelley, words cannot "penetrate" ("On Life," *SPP* 475). If poets are makers and sculptors are poets, as Percy Shelley claims in his *Defence of Poetry*, both are able to animate senseless clay and bring cold marble to life. Thus Mary Shelley seems in 1822 to regard *herself* as inanimate marble, rendered senseless through the loss of her artist-lover. Yet Percy Shelley implies that life is wholly available in its general truth only when it is not the life of particular bodies; as James A. W. Heffernan puts it, "[t]he moment sculpture pants, it loses its transcendent superiority to the narratable contingencies of breathing human life" (114). In spite of the "vast and trunkless legs of stone" in "Ozymandias," then (*SPP* 103), Percy Shelley insists on the transcendence of art, its inviolability to penetration, analysis, and fragmentation.

Mary, however, demonstrates in the urgency of her life writing in *Frankenstein* the relationship between Life in its general truth and the particularities of the body. Frankenstein constructs his creature as if he were reversing the process of William Hunter's successive dissection plates, replacing veils and layers and stitching together amputated parts of hewn cadavers in the hope of reassembling wholeness and reversing decay. To shift from metaphorical to literal process, writing into being the life of Frankenstein's "new species" (37) becomes possible through ordering fragments of text and memory, relics of physical and intellectual experience. The life writer no less than the anatomist, in Frankenstein's words, "bestow[s] animation upon lifeless matter" (36). In *The Last Man*, the fictional editor's project becomes a work of monumental life writing, an attempt to embody the world by giving coherent form to its fragments and relics in the womb-space of the sibyl's cave. The result is an attempt to undo dissection by reading and writing backwards—Lionel's monumental goal—which clashes with the relentless anatomizing of the world that characterizes the novel's plot.

Whereas Frankenstein's fear of monstrous reproduction and his need to control it lead to an act of violent dismemberment, in *The Last Man* reproduction fails and Lionel Verney's world becomes one of replicated death. Mass destruction replaces reproduction; in response, Lionel focuses on the particular details of experience, as if to pluck from individual stories the elusive principle of life. "Now each life was a gem," he asserts, "each human breathing form of far, O! far more worth than subtlest imagery of sculptured stone" (251).

This discovery of "life" in the particular rather than the universal is an implicit challenge to Percy Bysshe Shelley's aesthetic theory. Having edited his poetry, Mary must have questioned not only his privileging of Life over lives, but his insistence that variant readings and textual revisions are unpoetical ("Compositions so produced are to poetry what mosaic is to painting" ["A Defence of Poetry," *SPP* 504]). *The Last Man* is an explicitly mosaic text, the leaves of the Cumaean sibyl deciphered by a particular editor.[13] Yet at the same time as her novel seems to challenge the notion of universal truth, Mary seems drawn to Percy's sense that art transcends life. While *The Last Man* illustrates the body's value on almost every page, Lionel Verney repeatedly laments his betrayal of the ideal of art. The body is valuable as a temple of the spirit, not for its own sake, he insists. Body without spirit is of value only to the materialist; art embodies spirit, pointing beyond itself. Even at the very end of the novel, Lionel still finds consolation for his own "insignificance" in considering "the poetry eternized in these statues [of Castor and Pollux, which] took the sting from the thought, arraying it only in poetic ideality" (357). The paradox of his predicament, however, is that art, including textual art, depends for its life on an incarnate spectator. For this reason, art is less valuable as life becomes more so: "farewell to sculpture," Lionel writes, "where the pure marble mocks human flesh, and in the plastic expression of the culled excellencies of the human shape, shines forth the god!" (252). The body, Mary Shelley's novel demonstrates (sometimes in spite of Verney's explicit claims to the contrary), is the condition that lends meaning to all seemingly transcendent ideals and values.

Yet the novel is itself a gallery of artifacts, from the busts of ancient philosophers that adorn Adrian's study, through the descriptions of particular characters and the references to particular works of art, to Lionel Verney's tour of depopulated Rome at the end of volume 3. The narrative frame alludes to Raphael's *Transfiguration* (8), the subject of which draws particular attention to the relation of body and spirit; but the first specific artifact mentioned in the text is the *Apollo Belvedere*, a copy of which Lionel keeps in his London lodgings and to which Raymond compares himself: "the head will serve for my new coinage, and be an omen to all dutiful subjects of my future success" (52). As David Irwin points out in his discussion of Flaxman, plaster casts of artifacts, including the *Apollo*, were much in demand in England during this period (46; and see *LMWS* 1: 38 and n.4). Immaterial significance resides as well in a copy as in the original, so that plaster is as good as marble or bronze: Raymond sees the resemblance to himself in the archetype of the victor, not in the physical peculiarities of a particular statue.

The Last Man traces the disintegration of such archetypes and the failure of Lionel's attempt to reconstruct them. The words of his story thus take on a double meaning, for they record the painful particularities of experience while they also construct a monument that points beyond the material world. "If I were to dissect each incident," Lionel writes, "every small fragment of a second would contain an harrowing tale, whose minutest word would curdle the blood" (310). While many episodes of his narrative seem the results of such dissection, the novel ends among statues that ought to be impervious to death and corruption:

> I passed long hours in the various galleries—I gazed at each statue, and lost myself in a reverie before many a fair Madonna or beauteous nymph. I haunted the Vatican, and stood surrounded by marble forms of divine beauty. Each stone deity was possessed by sacred gladness, and the eternal fruition of love. They looked on me with unsympathizing complacency, and often in wild accents I reproached them for their supreme indifference—for they were human shapes, the human form divine was manifest in each fairest limb and lineament. The perfect moulding brought with it the idea of colour and motion; often, half in bitter mockery, half in self-delusion, I clasped their icy proportions, and, coming between Cupid and his Psyche's lips, pressed the unconceiving marble. (360-61)

The marble forms point to the identity of divine and human beauty, yet their ideality is also their deficiency of sympathy. The representation of Cupid and Psyche is inadequate *because* it is "perfect" in its illusion of life. Colour and motion are lent by the spectator; but the life of Cupid and Psyche remains an illusion because it is "unconceiving"—incapable of conception either in the reproductive sense associated with the god of love or in the intellectual, imaginative, and spiritual senses appropriate to Psyche, whose name means "soul." Like the dead, who disappear from the narrative while these marble multitudes remain, stone deities elude the life of the body and offer no certainty of imaginative or spiritual solace. More than a vision of transcendence, unconceiving beauty offers an image of despair in a world where the only hope of continuing life and art is in reproduction, not in the enduring representations of the past.

As if to emphasize the importance of artifacts in this novel, Evadne becomes reacquainted with Raymond through her design for a national gallery. In the first volume of *The Last Man*, Raymond visits her in a London tenement, where she lives alone trying to survive as an artist: "her dark hair was braided and twined in thick knots like the head-dress of a Grecian statue" (87). But this moment of idealization, before Evadne and Raymond recognize each other, is a kind of illusion. Later in the novel, dying on a battlefield in Constantinople, Evadne has been utterly transformed by "twelve years of change, sorrow and hard-ship; her brilliant complexion had become worn and dark, her limbs had lost the roundness of youth and womanhood; her eyes had sunk deep" (144-45). No longer a statue, she has become a "monument of human passion," grotesque in her delirious *danse macabre* and in her Gothic cursing of Raymond. Finally given over to mortality, she is transformed from an image of ideal beauty into a dead body that Lionel must guard from "birds and beasts of prey" (145).

Such transformations of artifacts into bodies and bodies into arti-facts recur in *The Last Man*. Idris, sleeping, recalls the image of death, so that Lionel asks himself, "If she were dead, . . . what difference?" (267). The difference is, he claims, mind or spirit, which inhabits the living body until the moment of death. Later, having placed his wife's body in the vault at Windsor, Lionel confronts the Ex-Queen, Idris's mother: "her tall form slowly rose upwards from the vault, a living stat-ue, instinct with hate, and human, passionate strife" (280). Yet Lionel starts to see in his mother-in-law an unfamiliar resemblance to her daughter. The Ex-Queen's transformation from someone consumed by rigidity and pride—a condition in which "[h]er passions had subdued her appetites" so that "her body was evidently considered by her as a mere machine" (61)—into a woman capable of love is figured as the animation of a statue rising out of the grave. As the Ex-Queen's resem-blance to her dead daughter becomes apparent—"the force of blood manifested in likeness of look and movement" (281)—flashes of recognition make Lionel aware at once of the immateriality of life *and* of its immanence in the body. Life, giving rise to countless particular stories and ending in countless horrific and pathetic images, is both specific and generic: Lionel's quest at the end of the novel is to find a human "companion" (364) *and* to embody in his text the Life he rec-ognizes in "virtues" (362) and other spectral presences.

Archetypal and biological views of life and art contend with each other. On the one hand, *The Last Man* strives to write life within the context of romantic aesthetics. Sculptured forms come alive ambigu-ously—given life by their creators long ago but, even at the end of the world, animated by the beholder whom they both console and disturb. Contemplating sculpted forms rather than the anatomist's fragments, Lionel, a latter-day Prometheus, begins to write his narrative, comfort-ed only by the "poetic ideality" of "the voice of dead time" "breathed from . . . dumb things, animated and glorified . . . by man" (357). Yet Lionel's readers, those "other spirits, other minds, other perceptive beings, sightless to [him and his contemporaries]" (267), who either have not yet been born or will be "of race spiritual," without dependence on biological reproduction, will nevertheless share the human qualities of "frail flesh and soft organization" (310). Even straining against the body, imagining a spirit-world of beauty, virtue, and truth beyond the death of humanity, Shelley's narrator conceives of readers no less human than himself.[14]

In keeping with the logic of the reader's position, then, we might expect Lionel to place human life—breathing physical existence— above all artistic expression. In Rome, a city of undead statuary, "marble forms of divine beauty" gaze back at him with "supreme indifference" (360). Lionel's response is to turn inward, to examine his own particular experience. Self-examination, which Mary Shelley exemplifies in "Giovanni Villani" by Robert Burton's *Anatomy of Melancholy* (130), is an exploration of the "workings" of the heart as scientific in its way as the postmortem examination of any physical anatomist. Near the end of *The Last Man*, an anatomical text in genre as well as subject, Lionel Verney emphasizes one way in which his celebration of extinct life has been an act of dissection:

> Ah! while I streak this paper with the tale of what my so named occupations were—while I shape the skeleton of my days—my hand trembles—my heart pants, and my brain refuses to lend expression, or phrase, or idea, by which to image forth the veil of unutterable woe that clothed these bare realities. O, worn and beating heart, may I dissect thy fibres, and tell how in each unmitigable misery, sadness dire, repinings, and despair, existed? (361)

"[S]hap[ing] the skeleton of [his] days," Lionel writes the life he has known, which is both his own life and the history of the world.

Yet the last word is the editor's, who releases from the sibyl's cave of the frame, like plagues from Pandora's box, mosaic fragments, broken artifacts, allusions separated from their original contexts, contagious ideas, specimens of the dissected heart, and risky pieces of untold stories. Having deciphered one of their possible meanings, the editor writes an anatomy of life beyond the death of Hope, an anatomy that is also an answer to Lionel's despair. Generated by the womb-space of the cave, Lionel is a human being searching hopelessly for "the children of a saved pair of lovers" (362) or for a "companion" (364), in a world where artifacts are inanimate monuments to the anatomized body, no longer reproductive. Yet the stirrings and transformations within a text that contains the twenty-first century—and its own imagined future readers—within the shell of the nineteenth century and the womb of the mythical past characterize a reproductive work of art in which past and present generate futurity. Shelley's twentieth-first-century readers already stir in her sibyl's cave, hideous progeny of those ideas about nature and art she popularized in her fiction. Emerging from the sibyl's womb-cave, a version of Pandora's box, they consider, by the light of a science that goes well beyond dissection, new ways of writing and creating life.

Notes

1 Introduction to the 1831 edition of *FMP* 180.

2 Wollstonecraft champions Pandora when she suggests that inequality of rank has caused human suffering, which men have then conveniently blamed on women and the gods: "the vengeance of heaven, lurking in the subtile flame [of Prometheus], like Pandora's pent up mischiefs, sufficiently punished [man's] temerity, by introducing evil into the world" (*VRW* 119). In the Dedication to *A Vindication of the Rights of Woman* she argues that men—not Pandora as female scapegoat—must take responsibility for "[t]he box of mischief . . . opened in society" (104) by women deprived of proper education who are persuaded that their identity is entirely a sexual one. However, Naomi Wolf notes the persistence of Pandora's crudely negative reputation: "as a future woman, the little girl learns [from her school reader] that the most beautiful woman in the world was man-made, and that *her* intellectual daring brought the first sickness and death onto men" (610).

3 Panofsky and Panofsky 113, also qtd. by Laura Mulvey in support of her argument that "[a] seductive appearance that is appealing and charming to man generates its polar opposite, an interior that is harmful and dangerous to man" (6), and that "the sexualized image [represented by Pandora] becomes tinged with repulsion and disgust" (8). On page 112, the Panofskys reproduce Klee's drawing, one of many representations of Pandora that emphasize the specifically sexual nature of the temptation and threat she represents.

4 The Panofskys reproduce these illustrations: 98 ("Pandora Brought to Earth"), 100 ("Pandora Brought to Epimetheus"), and 101 ("Pandora Opening the Vase").

5 On hearing his son, Charles, praise his mother, Godwin's St Leon says that he "stood there, as the statue of Prometheus might

have done, if, after being informed with a living soul, the Gods had seen fit to chain its limbs in everlasting marble" (*St. Leon* 438). Thanks to Lorne Macdonald for pointing out this passage.

6   See Richardson 37, 38.

7   See the fragment "On the Punishment of Death" (1815?) in *Complete Works* 6: 185-90.

8   See the title-page of his *Anatomia* (1774).

9   *Dictionary of National Biography* 3: 1013. The source for this reference seems to be an obituary of Carlisle in the *Gentleman's Magazine* NS 14 (December 1840): 660-61. According to this obituary, the essay on anatomy and the arts appeared in a periodical called *The Artist*, which I have been unable to trace.

10   Mary Shelley's journals record visits to the galleries of Italy and to such museums as the Gabinetto Fisico in Florence, where—according to Joseph Forsyth, *Remarks on Antiqities, Arts, and Letters, during an Excursion in Italy, in the Years 1802 and 1803*, qtd. by Paula Feldman and Diana Scott-Kilvert, *JMS* 306 n.2—"the very apartment where the gravid uterus and its processes lie unveiled, is a favourite lounge of the ladies, who criticise aloud all the mysteries of sex."

11   David Irwin cites Flaxman's *Anatomical Studies of the Bones and Muscles for the Use of Artists* (1833) and has a brief discussion of Flaxman's anatomical drawings (118-19). Stubbs's work is reprinted by Doherty.

12   A passage from Hunter's Preface is worth quoting to illustrate the way in which his language mirrors the progression in the plates from "woman" to dissected fragments illustrating "truth": "in the year of 1751 the author met with the first favourable opportunity of examining, in the human species, what before he had been studying in brutes. A woman died suddenly, when very near the end of her pregnancy; the body was procured before any sensible putrefaction had begun; the season of the year was favourable to dissection; the injection of the blood-vessels proved successful; a very able painter, in this way, was found; every part was examined in the most public manner, and the truth was thereby well authenticated."

13   "As if we should give to another artist, the painted fragments which form the mosaic copy of Raphael's Transfiguration in St. Peter's; he would put them together in a form, whose mode would be fashioned by his own peculiar mind and talent" (*LM* 8).

14   *Prometheus Unbound* is a strong influence here, as Prometheus imagines being visited in his cave by "the progeny immortal / Of

Painting, Sculpture and rapt Poesy" (3.3.54-55). Yet Lionel's—
and Mary's—future readers are far less idealized, because they
can be only human readers like ourselves.

Further Thoughts on the Education of Daughters: *Lodore* as an Imagined Conversation with Mary Wollstonecraft

Lisa Vargo

That *Lodore* (1835) contains autobiographical elements has never been in dispute. "Have you read Lodore," Mary Shelley asked Maria Gisborne in a letter. "If you did read it, did you recognize any of Shelley's & my early adventures—when we were in danger of being starved in Switzerland—& could get no dinner at an inn in London?" (*LMWS* 2: 260-61). When Claire Clairmont read the novel, she voiced her ambivalent feelings in a letter to Mary: "Mrs. Hare admired *Lodore* amazingly—so do I or should I, if it were not for that <beastly> modification of the beastly character of Lord Byron <which you> of which you have composed Lodore" (*CC* 2: 341). It was Edward Dowden's so-called "fortunate discovery" that brought these matters to a larger audience in his 1886 life of Percy Bysshe Shelley, where he notes "some important passages of biography" in the novel (1: 436-38).[1] In particular, "the narrative of the troubles which beset the early wedded life of Edward and Ethel Villiers is a genuine piece of autobiography" (1: 486). Following Dowden's lead, Florence Marshall, Mary Shelley's biographer, suggests "the fact that some of the incidents are taken from actual occurrences in her early life" adds "a special interest of its own" (2: 264). But this "special interest" needn't obscure

Notes are on p. 187.

other possible readings; after all, autobiography is a subgroup of the larger practice of life writing. In this privileging of autobiography, other forms of life writing, which might lead to a deeper understanding of *Lodore*, have been overlooked. Such is the case when William Walling argues that an "absence of ideas" in its pages means the novel's "concealed significance" is that it provides biographers with "a promising source for filling in the lacunae of certain passages of their subject's life" (104).[2] To conceive of life writing, in Marlene Kadar's words, "as a continuum that spreads unevenly and in combined forms from the so-called least fictive narration to the most fictive" (10) is to recognize that the novel can be read as containing serious ideas. While other critics have concerned themselves with the autobiographical aspects of the parent-daughter relationship in the novel,[3] I wish to tease out another strand—how *Lodore* may be conceived of as an imaginary conversation with Mary Wollstonecraft. Mary Shelley draws upon the methods and ideas of her mother's writings to speak to her mother as she contemplates the writing of two daughters' lives in the novel.

Shelley was ever conscious of the fact that her own life as a daughter was read through her parents' "distinguished literary celebrity." She comments in her 1831 Introduction to *Frankenstein*, a densely layered example of life writing, "My husband . . . was from the first, very anxious that I should prove myself worthy of my parentage, and enrol myself on the page of fame" (*FMP* 176). Her response to Frances Wright's letter of introduction in 1827 further glosses her feelings of filial obligation: "The memory of my Mother has been always the pride & delight of my life; & the admiration of others for her, has been the cause of most of the happiness < . . . > I have enjoyed. Her greatness of soul & my father['s] high talents have perpetually reminded me that I ought to degenerate as little as I could from those from whom I derived my being" (*LMWS* 2: 3-4). The phrase "memory of my Mother" erases the boundaries between fact and fiction; memory of the mother Shelley never knew is recuperated from Wollstonecraft's writings.[4] In turn, through writing, Shelley can symbolically speak to her mother and demonstrate that she has not degenerated from Wollstonecraft's example. As the "Author of *Frankenstein*," Shelley recognizes that regeneration means more than the animation of mere parts. *Lodore* serves Shelley as a workshop in which the ideas and principles that formed her self are cast in a fictionalized form to challenge the putative "facts" of women's place with respect to domestic ideology.[5] Life writing, then, is deeply ingrained in the writing of the novel.

It is not only in *Lodore* that Mary Shelley practised life writing as an imagined conversation with individuals who shaped her life. A desire to speak to and on behalf of those dear to her informed Mary Shelley's diverse literary practices as travel writer, diarist, reviewer, novelist, and editor, but in the 1830s imagined conversation seems to have especially preoccupied her, and the circumstances of her relations with Sir Timothy Shelley and the nineteenth-century attitudes toward the proprieties of biography meant her practice had to be circumspect. She tellingly suggests in her 1831 Introduction that conversation inspired the writing of *Frankenstein*: "Many and long were the conversations between Lord Byron and Shelley, to which I was a devout but nearly silent listener" (179); and she reflects in retrospect how its "pages speak of many a walk, many a drive, and many a conversation" (180). Byron and Percy Shelley were never far from Mary Shelley's thoughts, and in the 1830s giving life to their works formed part of her literary activities. Shelley assisted Thomas Moore with his *Letters and Journals of Lord Byron* (1830) and edited Edward John Trelawny's Byronic fictionalized autobiography, *Adventures of a Younger Son* (1831).[6] The end of the decade saw the publication of her annotated editions of Percy Shelley's poetry and prose.

If Sir Timothy constrained her from writing a biography of Percy by threatening to cut off her allowance, a different set of concerns inspired her life writing about Wollstonecraft. The problematic precedent for conversation with her mother was her father's *Memoirs of the Author of* A Vindication of the Rights of Woman (1798). In his Preface, William Godwin suggests that the "facts detailed in the following pages, are principally taken from the mouth of the person to whom they relate" (*MAV* 204). Godwin's *Memoirs* was unlikely to have provided Shelley with a useful model because of the outrage it evoked.[7] Instead she looked to her mother's writings to redress the notoriety of her father's text in its frank account of Wollstonecraft's life.

It was "from the mouth" of Wollstonecraft's works that her daughter was provided with examples of life writing as a vehicle for women's expression. As is characteristic of life writing, Mary Wollstonecraft's works blend many genres and forms of lesser and more fictive narration. Wollstonecraft practised life writing on a number of levels, the most obvious being *Letters Written during a Short Residence in Sweden, Norway, and Denmark* (1796), which Shelley used as a model for her own travel writings. Gary Kelly points out that *Thoughts on the Education of Daughters* (1787) and *A Vindication of the Rights of Woman* (1792) employ autobiography by way of "sustaining the authority of a woman writing on women" (*Revolutionary Feminism* 33). When Wollstonecraft observes about matrimony in *Thoughts on the Education of Daughters* that "Nothing, I am sure, calls forth the faculties so much as the being obliged to struggle with the world; and this is not a woman's province in a married state" (*TED* 100), she infuses the text with the conviction that comes of personal experience.

At the same time as she makes use of autobiography, Wollstonecraft also draws upon techniques of the novel. Wollstonecraft was wary of "the reveries of the stupid novelists," whose "stale tales" work "to corrupt the taste, and draw the heart aside from its daily duties" (*VRW* 330); nevertheless, she recognized fiction's power to show women their lives. Kelly argues that the novel can "represent within itself an entire culture's order of discourses or cultural practices, 'novelizing' this order and thereby relativizing, subverting or even revolutionizing it" (*Revolutionary Feminism* 115). In *A Vindication of the Rights of Woman*, Wollstonecraft applies novelistic discourse to communicate the world of the public sphere to women and to demonstrate how fictions construct the social order. As "novelized polemic," the *Vindication* "uses the confessional first-person mode to create a self-validating text addressed to the reader as an equal," and "novelizes" the "discursive order of professional middle-class culture in order to show that this order is hierarchally gendered" (Kelly, *Revolutionary Feminism* 114-15). Wollstonecraft's narratives of the widow who kept novels from her daughters and the father who educated his niece and daughter under different plans (*VRW* 331-32) represent to the reader the power of the novel to influence the order of discourse.

A careful reader of her mother's writings, Shelley does not degenerate from Wollstonecraft's practice of "a bricolage of sub-literary 'women's' writing to emancipate its readers from the intellectual and cultural subordination usually associated with and reproduced by such writing" (Kelly, *Revolutionary Feminism* 112). Shelley works within the form of fiction in vogue in the 1830s to question cultural assumptions about women. The plot of *Lodore* with its focus on high society, a duel, marriage, and inheritance makes clear its similarities with the fashionable or "silver fork" novel popular in the 1820s and 1830s. Henry Fitzhenry, Lord Lodore, has fled England with his three-year-old daughter Ethel and settled in Illinois. He was unwilling to fight a duel with his son, the product of an affair with a Polish countess, and has left England without his proud and much younger wife, Cornelia. Ethel is educated by her father in exile, and when she reaches fifteen, he decides to return to England and attempt to reconcile himself with his wife. He is killed en route in a duel with a witness to the earlier challenge. A will made out of spite at the time of his separation from Cornelia ties his wife's maintenance to keeping her separated from her daughter. Ethel lives with her aunt, and a chance meeting reintroduces

her to Edward Villiers, who was her father's second in the duel. Edward
and Ethel fall in love and marry; their marriage is tested by Edward's
arrest for debt, as his wastrel father has gambled away his son's inheritance. Ethel is aided by Fanny Derham, the daughter of her father's
boyhood friend, but her salvation comes when Cornelia sacrifices her
fortune to her daughter and retires to obscurity. The mother and daughter are reunited and a humbled Cornelia marries Fitzhenry's cousin,
widowed after an unwise marriage to an Italian woman. The resemblances between *Lodore* and the novel of fashion are a sign that Shelley
is aware of what will gain readers, yet she employs popular culture of
the 1830s to revive her mother's 1792 call for a "REVOLUTION in female
manners" (*VRW* 341). Shelley's novel animates her mother's ideas as
arguments counter to British society's discourses of domestic ideology.

But there seems a significant difference between Shelley's conception of life writing and that of her mother. Mitzi Myers points out
that Wollstonecraft "is a very personal writer in both theory and practice; from her first novel to her last essays, the individual vision is central to her work" ("Mary Wollstonecraft's *Letters*" 167). Mary Shelley
writes from a desire to capture the collective voices around her; the
novel is an apt genre for her multivocal discourse. Her writings come
closest to the world of Wollstonecraft in the sense that they are dialog-
ical, incorporating many voices (Kelly, *Revolutionary Feminism* 115).
Prose fiction likewise suits her purpose of questioning social practices,
which she shares with her parents, who used the Jacobin novel as a
vehicle for their ideas. Although the *Vindication* and the *Letters from
Norway* are the texts by Wollstonecraft with which Shelley was most
familiar, I am also tempted to look to their precursor for a model on
which Mary Shelley perhaps unwittingly draws. *Lodore* might be sub-
titled "Further Thoughts on the Education of Daughters," in tribute to
her mother's response to Rousseau's *Emile* and to the conduct literature
of James Fordyce and John Gregory, *Thoughts on the Education of
Daughters: With Reflections on Female Conduct, in the More Important
Duties of Life*. In the novel, Shelley introduces a number of mothers and
daughters whose lives represent the problems with women's education
that Wollstonecraft herself contemplated: Cornelia and Ethel, Lady
Santerre and Cornelia, Mrs. Derham and Fanny, Countess Lyzinski,
Saville's cousins, Elizabeth Fitzhenry, and Clorinda Saville. But it is in
the portraits of the educations of two daughters, Ethel and Fanny, that
Shelley most clearly converses with her mother's words to regenerate
revolutionary principles in the 1830s: the harm of poor education, the
need for women to be independent, and the creation of alternatives for
women besides marriage and family.

In the first volume of the novel, Shelley's portrait of Ethel's life enables the novelist to converse with her own mother's analysis of women's education. Perhaps most central to Wollstonecraft's own life writing is her belief that weakness and a lack of understanding enslave women. The summary of her argument in her Introduction to *A Vindication of the Rights of Woman* is illustrative of her ability to analyze the language of social discourse: "I wish to persuade women to endeavour to acquire strength, both of mind and body, and to convince them that the soft phrases, susceptibility of heart, delicacy of sentiment, and refinement of taste, are almost synonymous with epithets of weakness, and that those beings who are only the objects of pity and that kind of love, which has been termed its sister, will soon become objects of contempt" (111). In the first volume of Shelley's novel, Ethel is introduced as representing what the emergent Victorian culture of the 1830s idealizes in women, yet the voice of the narrator challenges that ideal from the perspective of Wollstonecraft's thought. Shelley creates a heroine whom she compares with Shakespeare's Miranda, Campbell's Gertrude of Wyoming, and Byron's Haidée, in order that she might demonstrate how such figures embody male fantasies of feminine passivity and weakness. In describing Ethel's education in exile, the narrator critiques the patriarchal values of domestic ideology: "Fitzhenry drew his chief ideas from Milton's Eve, and adding to this the romance of chivalry, he satisfied himself that his daughter would be the embodied ideal of all that is adorable and estimable in her sex" (*L* 18). The allusion to Milton's Eve evokes Wollstonecraft's discussion of *Paradise Lost* in the *Vindication*, including her wry observation that great men are often led by their senses to inconsistencies (*VRW* 127). In the Eden of Illinois, "Ethel was taught to know herself dependent; the support of another was to be as necessary to her as her daily food" (*L* 19). It is clear that for Shelley, as for Wollstonecraft, dependency in women is a weakness: "A lofty sense of independence is, in man, the best privilege of his nature. It cannot be doubted, but that it were for the happiness of the other sex that she were taught more to rely on and act for herself. But in the cultivation of this feeling, the education of Fitzhenry was lamentably deficient" (*L* 19). Shelley's narrator speaks in a voice that echoes Wollstonecraft's rational and ironic perspective in presenting an account of the life of an inadequately educated daughter.

Ethel's "sexual education" in the name of an "ideal of what a woman ought to be" (*L* 218) evokes Wollstonecraft's use of "sexual" to refer to gender (*VRW* 103 and n.). Ethel's life is used by Shelley to define women's potential in spite of the limitations placed upon them by social expectation: "active in person, in mind she was too often indolent, and apt to think that while she was docile to the injunctions of her parent, all her duties were fulfilled. She seldom thought, and never acted, for herself" (*L* 19). Certainly Shelley writes through her own life experience to speak to her mother's principles. Ethel is left to call upon her own resources after the death of her father, as Mary Shelley herself was after the death of her husband. The similarities with Shelley's life narrative end there. Ethel finds another protector in her husband, yet his own helplessness, a sign of his privileged class position, means that she must think and act for herself. But her education to be dependent prepares her insufficiently for her role. When Ethel acts or asserts her will, her body suffers as she trembles, faints, or wastes away with anxiety experienced on behalf of her husband. Like her mother, Shelley uses a narrative of one life to represent the ideological position of middle-class women. The story she would tell is that such weakness is a threat to the health of the social body if obedience and dependence in women are valued at the expense of their understanding and self-reliance.

Ethel's life narrative shows how straightforward examples of life writing give way to more subtle engagements with the genre. The education of a daughter by her father in the absence of a mother is another aspect of the plot that clearly echoes Shelley's own life.[8] But in novelizing Wollstonecraft's ideas about independence, Shelley demonstrates that she was perhaps even more profoundly instructed by her dead mother's principles, with which she readily converses in *Lodore*. Wollstonecraft believed that women need to be independent and should be presented with practical alternatives to marriage and family, and Shelley responds with her own versions of these beliefs through the figure of Fanny Derham, who embodies Wollstonecraft's ideals. In naming a character Fanny, Shelley invokes the memory of Wollstonecraft's other daughter, Fanny Imlay, as well as of Fanny Blood, the beloved friend who, through their correspondence, taught Wollstonecraft to write (*MAV* 211). When in *Letters from Norway* Wollstonecraft addresses her estranged lover, Gilbert Imlay, concerning her prognostications for the future of their daughter, Fanny, she confesses to "more than a mother's fondness and anxiety, when I reflect on the dependent and oppressed state of her sex" (*LWSR* 97). Fiction enables Shelley to respond to Wollstonecraft's impassioned cry, "Hapless woman! what a fate is thine!" (97), in giving her character a happier fate than either Fanny Imlay or Fanny Blood.[9]

Wollstonecraft wonders about the fate of daughters when she suggests of Fanny, "I dread lest she should be forced to sacrifice her heart to her principles, or principles to her heart. . . . I dread to unfold her mind, lest it should render her unfit for the world she is to inhabit" (97). Her daughter Mary responds to her mother's meditations on heart and mind with her portraits of the lives of Ethel and Fanny, who are educated by their fathers' beliefs in the contrasting ideals of sensibility and reason: "The one fashioned his offspring to be the wife of a frail human being, and instructed her to be yielding, and to make it her duty to devote herself to his happiness, and to obey his will. The other sought to guard his from all weakness, to make her complete in herself, and to render her independent and self-sufficing" (*L* 218). If Ethel is guided by her heart, Fanny is guided by her understanding. Both women are to be admired, but Shelley questions the wisdom of cultural values that generate such aphorisms as "Man rules the mind of the world: woman its heart" (Rowton 1). In so doing, Shelley seems to respond to the voice of her mother's narrative in *Letters from Norway*, in which, Mitzi Myers argues, Wollstonecraft "reaches toward integrations" with a narrative mode that "endorses reason and justifies imagination" ("Mary Wollstonecraft's *Letters*" 182). Shelley's text suggests how far apart these selves are for women in the 1830s by creating two figures who have the potential to appreciate the other's qualities, but who cannot imagine leading one another's lives, each "wondering at a mechanism of mind so different from her own" (*L* 217-18).

In this division of mind Shelley provides an alternative to the sorts of lives that are available for bourgeois women and represented in popular forms of writing. Like her mother, Shelley uncovers the kinds of subordination written into such narratives. Romance is symptomatic of society's desire to keep women from ruling the mind; accordingly, Fanny Derham, who was so atypical of popular fiction that she was ignored by contemporary reviewers, lays bare the inadequacies of romance by her placement in the narrative as an outsider. Her incongruity is meant to awaken the reader to the forms of control that romance exercises over women: "Such a woman as Fanny was more made to be loved by her own sex than by the opposite one. Superiority of intellect, joined to acquisitions beyond those usual even to men; and both announced with frankness, though without pretension, forms a kind of anomaly little in accord with masculine taste" (*L* 214). Fanny offers an alternative to submissive womanhood: "Fanny could not be the rival of women, and, therefore, all her merits were appreciated by them. They love to look up to a superior being, to rest on a firmer support than their own minds can afford; and they are glad to find such in one of their own sex, and thus destitute of those dangers which usually attend any services conferred by men" (*L* 214). Not only do women appreciate Fanny; in turn, Fanny is able to value Ethel's mother,

Cornelia, as more than a society beauty, and she instigates Cornelia's embrace of a "sense of right" with her decision to act for herself "unsupported" (*L* 271) on behalf of her daughter. Fanny's life story enables Mary Shelley to point to the wrongs of women that Wollstonecraft herself discloses in cultural practices.

In addressing her mother's hopes and fears for women, Shelley's portrait of Fanny Derham revolutionizes fiction in representing an alternative model for women, one that includes justice for the lower orders that domestic ideology would control. As she reflects on her experiences among the poor in her clergyman father's parish, Fanny provides a foil for Ethel's weakness and dependency: "'Words have more power than any one can guess; it is by words that the world's great fight, now in these civilized times, is carried on; I never hesitated to use them, when I fought any battle for the miserable and oppressed. People are so afraid to speak, it would seem as if half our fellow-creatures were born with deficient organs; like parrots they can repeat a lesson, but their voice fails them, when that alone is wanting to make the tyrant quail'" (*L* 213). But for Fanny's reminder, the poorer classes are not part of a novel set in the world of the privileged. Fanny is used by Shelley to name those who are missing from the life stories told in romance. Her words are a powerful translation of the doctrines of necessity from an earlier generation to the era of the Reform Bill and Chartism. Fanny's Wollstonecraftian ideals disclose a network of acts of kindness on the part of women that go against the prevailing ideology that the modern subject need be shaped by the principles of a "nation of shopkeepers" connected with trade and merchandise (Ellis 13).

After her brief introduction in the first volume, Fanny's reappearance in Volume 3 facilitates the recognition that it is women and not men who act for the good of others in the novel. Ethel, rather than Villiers, takes action with respect to his money problems. Cornelia provides for her daughter, after Lodore and Villiers have failed. And Elizabeth Fitzhenry, Lodore's spinster sister, finds the missing Cornelia and effects a reconciliation between mother and daughter. Shelley points to the power women have as domestic managers, but she would have that power used in a different way than to perpetuate the injustices of capitalism.

Like her mother, who used fiction and novelized polemic to tell how discourse can oppress people, Shelley contemplates in *Lodore* the kinds of narrative available for women. The novel ends with a characteristic that Carolyn Heilbrun identifies in *Writing a Woman's Life* as women's life stories' necessary weighing of the erotic plot of love and marriage against the quest plot of knowledge and selfhood that is usually restricted to men (48). Wollstonecraft explored these plots in her writings and in her life, as Shelley's evocation of them attests. While Wollstonecraft viewed sensibility and understanding as "varied selves" (Myers, "Mary Wollstonecraft's *Letters*" 182), Shelley's conviction that lives need dialogue with one another leads her to create two separate figures who can befriend one another and converse. Both voices speak at the end of the novel, but it is clear that Shelley privileges one over the other in a manner that goes against the narrative that society would write for women. The concluding chapter predictably focuses on the happiness of Ethel and Cornelia in married life but also moves to another life story that raises the possibility of alternatives for women. The novel's most radical gesture is to end with the quest plot of Fanny Derham, who "has entered upon life." "Deceit, and selfishness, and the whole web of human passion must envelope her, and occasion her many sorrows," yet "in her love of truth and in her integrity, she will find support and reward in her various fortunes" (*L* 313). The narrator suggests, "it would require the gift of prophecy to foretell the conclusion," but "the life of Fanny Derham" can "be presented as a useful lesson, at once to teach what goodness and genius can achieve in palliating the woes of life, and to encourage those, who would in any way imitate her" (*L* 313). The final lines of *Lodore* regenerate the voice of Wollstonecraft's writings as Shelley imagines a woman's life—and not a man's—as the model for social transformation through "a love of truth in ourselves, and a sincere sympathy with our fellow-creatures" (313).

It seems to be difficult to undo the received notions of the "special interest" of biography (Marshall 2: 264), no matter how compelling other forms of life writing may be in revising our thoughts about the significance of *Lodore*. It was not so long ago that Emily Sunstein felt compelled to lament that Frances Kemble Butler's story about Mary Shelley's wishing her son "to think like everyone else" is "the exemplary Mary Shelley quotation down to today" (*Mary Shelley* 396). In her later life and writings, Shelley did not abandon the political beliefs she inherited from her parents. In a novel so concerned with the consequences of legacy, the most significant inheritance reflected by *Lodore* is the intellectual one bestowed to its author by her circle. Mary Shelley's novel is an imagined conversation with her mother, a life-writing practice that allows her to speak to and through her mother's beliefs. In *Lodore*, which concludes with the reunion of a mother and daughter, it is fitting that the voice of Mary Wollstonecraft is heard along with that of Mary Shelley.

Notes

1   The phrase "fortunate discovery" comes from Richard Garnett's Introduction to *Tales and Stories* vii. Garnett was keeper of printed books at the British Library. He published a collection of Percy Shelley's literary remains, the *Relics of Shelley* (1862), and assisted Lady Jane Shelley in finding biographers for Percy and Mary Shelley.

2   Jean de Palacio is another critic who reads *Lodore* for its autobiography, as does Emily Sunstein in her biography *Mary Shelley*. Another prevailing view is represented by Jane Blumberg, who suggests that in her later fiction Shelley abandoned "new or complex ideas" and "was finished with the intellectual and emotional struggle that had characterized all her previous work and she settled into an artistically unchallenging but emotionally tranquil life" (223). Anne Mellor (*Mary Shelley*) and Mary Poovey are more positive about the novel, but they read it as more or less complicit with the bourgeois project of domestic ideology.

3   For a reading of the father-daughter relationship in the novel, see Hill-Miller. A different approach than I wish to take here with respect to the mother-daughter relationship is pursued by Jowell.

4   Charles E. Robinson presents an enormously helpful catalogue of Mary Shelley's recorded reading of Wollstonecraft's works in his essay in the present volume, 130-31.

5   See Langland 1-23.

6   See P. Feldman.

7   For a summary of the reception of the work, see Richard Holmes's Introduction to his edition of the *Memoirs* (1987) 43-50. As Robinson points out in his essay, the first recorded evidence for Mary Shelley reading the *Memoirs* is 3 June 1820. Whether she read the work before 1820 is a matter of speculation.

8   For an account of Shelley's education by Godwin, see Sunstein, *Mary Shelley* 37-45.

9   Fanny Blood, whose health, Godwin says, "had been materially injured by her incessant labours for the maintenance of her family" (*MAV* 216), died in childbirth in Portugal in 1785, attended by Wollstonecraft. Fanny Imlay committed suicide in 1816.

Speaking the Unspeakable: Art Criticism as Life Writing in Mary Shelley's *Rambles in Germany and Italy*

Jeanne Moskal

Victorian literature frequently offers us a scene of a pensive woman in an art gallery. In Charlotte Brontë's *Villette* (1853), Lucy Snowe contemplates in the painting of Cleopatra everything that is forbidden and repulsive to her; in George Eliot's *Middlemarch* (1871-72), Dorothea Brooke is intrigued but mystified by Roman art just as the disappointment sets in over her marriage to Mr Casaubon; Sigmund Freud's case study of "Dora" (1905) records that his patient, a young woman betrayed by her beloved Frau K., gazed for two rapturous hours on Raphael's *Sistine Madonna* (Freud 222).[1] In each of these scenes, paintings speak what is, as yet, unspeakable about the heroine's life, by performing a kind of dream-work in which a disruptive truth about that life is presented in figural language, partly revealed, partly concealed, rising to visibility just below the surface of consciousness, but not yet breaking the surface to demand full recognition.[2] Here I should like to propose that in her last published work, *Rambles in Germany and Italy* (1844), Mary Shelley as both author and heroine of her own work—that is, as autobiographer—anticipates these Victorian works in employing her art criticism as autobiographical dream-work, simultaneously revealing and concealing those unspeak-

Notes are on pp. 213-16.

able portions of her autobiography that disrupt her roles as the beloved wife and faithful widow of the poet Percy Bysshe Shelley, the editor of his works, and the mother of his son.

In making the analogy between dream-work and life writing, the crucial common ground is their work to protect the self by distortion if necessary. Mary Shelley acknowledges the importance of self-protection in life writing in her biography of Cervantes (1837).[3] Noting that Cervantes wrote about his captivity in Algeria only in fictionalized form, she muses:

> As Cervantes often alludes to himself, it is strange that he did not write an account of his years of captivity; but the truth is, that, though we may be led to mention ourselves, it is ever a tedious task to write at length on the subject: recollections come by crowds; hopes baffled, our dearest memories discovered to have a taint, our lives wasted and fallen into contempt even in our own eyes; so that we readily turn from dispiriting realities to such creatures of the imagination as we can fashion according to our liking. (Italian *Lives* 3: 133)

Though Mary Shelley at first dismisses autobiography ("writ[ing] at length [about ourselves]") as "tedious," her subsequent observations suggest turbulence and conflict, not tedium: flooding of memory ("recollections come by crowds"); retrospection coloured by contempt and guilt (in which "our dearest memories [are] discovered to have a taint"); and confusion ("hopes baffled"). Protecting themselves against such an onslaught, autobiographers understandably turn toward "such creatures of the imagination as [they] can fashion according to [their] liking." This model anticipates present-day feminist life-writing theory in that it concedes that the autobiographer may possess only partial self-knowledge,[4] proposing, indeed, that autobiography itself may be a defence against full knowledge.

Moreover, Mary Shelley's remark about turning from "dispiriting realities" to "the imagination" provides a rough analogy for the switch from the dominant verbal mode of *Rambles* to the figural mode of (describing) paintings in which the dream-work occurs. Freud writes, contrasting the adequate formulation of the dreamer's latent desire with the incomplete, mendacious manifest content of the dream, that the two versions are "presented to us like two versions of the same subject-matter *in two different languages*, or more properly, the dream-content seems like *a transcript of dream-thoughts into another mode of expression, whose characters and syntactic laws it is our business to discover*" (qtd. in LaPlanche and Pontalis, *s.v.* "latent content"; emphasis added).

It is just such a change of language that interests me here. Paintings provide a similar change of language because "there is no definite unit to the experience, no particular duration of time one must linger" and no set stopping-point (Spitz 13), and a written meditation on a painting can create the illusion of stopping narrative sequence. Mary Shelley's oddly lyrical, dreamy passages of art criticism, several of them responses to paintings of the Madonna, defy her own repeated denigration of her skill as an art critic (e.g., *RGI* 302). They also challenge what is conventional and easily speakable—the early Victorian roles of widow and mother—with a figural representation that speaks the unspeakable portions of her life in a different language.

For readers unfamiliar with *Rambles*, a brief summary may be in order. This epistolary travel book recounts two journeys Mary Shelley made in the early 1840s with her son, Percy Florence, and his friends, the first journey prompted by her desire to revisit Italy, where she had lived several years with Shelley, and where he and two of her children, William and Clara, had died. The travellers boated down the Rhine, spent six weeks at Como, and briefly visited Milan. Two years later, Mary Shelley sought a cure for her headaches at German spas and made "a pious pilgrimage" to Rome, the site of Shelley's grave (*RGI* 348; Dolan Kautz). In addition to its autobiographical interest, her book advocates Italian nationalism and was published to raise money for one of its partisans (Moskal, "Gender, Italian Nationalism").

In *Rambles*, Mary Shelley crafted a persona that stressed her relational roles as a widow and mother, eschewing the persona of autonomous celebrity author used by some of her contemporaries (Campbell Orr) and exemplifying Mary Jean Corbett's generalization that "most secular women autobiographers . . . can master their anxiety about being circulated, read, and interpreted only by carefully shaping the personae they present and, more especially, by subordinating their histories of themselves to others' histories" (97). Accordingly, the book begins by designating the travellers' destination, Italy, as the place where "I left the mortal remains of those beloved—my husband and my children, whose loss changed my whole existence" (75-76). As her own mother had done in *Letters from Norway* (Moskal, "Picturesque"; see also Schor), Mary Shelley foregrounds her role as a mother, stressing her delight in her son's companionship, and trying to suppress her worries when his boating expeditions summon memories of Shelley's drowning. Campbell Orr has noted the shaping of this material into conventional channels: Mary Shelley stresses Percy Florence's accession to adulthood and to his inherited titles, and thus their respectable place among English gentry who attended Oxford and Cambridge, and disguises her lingering disreputability as a fallen woman who, as a teenager, had eloped with a married man.

Reviewers of *Rambles* strongly approved of Mary Shelley's autobiographical presentation in the roles of Shelley's widow and the mother of his children. The *Critic*, for example, celebrated the production of "the widow of the poet, and the author of *Frankenstein*," to whom Italy is "ever sadly memorable as the grave of the true genius that it was her boast to call by the holy name of husband"; and the *Globe* noted that the volumes' "powerful interest" lies in the authorship of "the widow of the gifted and lamented Shelley." The *Examiner*, too, sounded an approving note: "Mrs Shelley has profited by time, and experience, and sympathetic memories of her husband." The *Literary Examiner* praises her in both roles: "It is affecting to see how at one time she suffers under the recollection of her husband's death, and at the other does all she can to enjoy society and gaiety of her younger companions. Her son inherits his father's love of boating, which occasions her anxiety, yet she is wise enough to approve what is useful to his health" (467).[5] The *Sunday Times* praised her "power to give utterance to a pleasing melancholy, to recollections of sorrows hushed by time, but still with a sharp and vital sting in them, capable, at any moment, of being roused into activity." The preponderance of the reviews' evidence shows Mary Shelley's tact in presenting the "pleasing melancholy" appropriate to her widowhood and the anxious, affectionate wisdom suited to her maternal role.

As art critic, too, Mary Shelley worked within the gendered constraints of her time, accepting the role of amateur commentator allotted to women. In particular, she followed the lead of her friend Anna Jameson.[6] Jameson focused on art criticism in her travel book *Sketches of Germany* (1834), and scored a major success with her *Handbook to the Public Galleries of Art in and near London* (1842), reviewed in all the major journals of the day (Johnston 154). Jameson went on to become an eminent Victorian art critic, prolific and popular, but was always excluded from the professional museum-based work monopolized by men. In addition, Mary Shelley worked within the tradition of expounding on the "spiritual content" of art (Gombrich 33), a tradition powerfully represented in the 1840s by John Ruskin's first book, *Modern Painters* (1843), and continued in our own day by writers such as Sister Wendy Beckett. Mary Shelley's acquaintance with this tradition is crystallized in her friendship with the liberal Catholic art critic Alexis-François Rio, whom she met through her father's friend Samuel Rogers (*LMSW* 3:

37 and n.; Palacio 552).[7] She read Rio's *De la poésie chrétienne dans son matière et dans ses formes* (1836), an anti-academic work that makes "inspiration," not style, the criterion of aesthetic judgment; elides the distinction between the artist's "inspiration" and the spectator's response; and in effect defines artistic inspiration in terms of religious content, reserving its highest praise for Raphael's Madonnas.[8] Though Mary Shelley dissented in important ways from Rio, the intellectual influence was reinforced *in situ* when Mary Shelley toured the galleries of Dresden and Rome accompanied by Rio and his wife. Mary Shelley's mastery of the art-critical discourse is attested by reviews. The *Examiner* notes that "she has acquired no mean taste in the Fine Arts" (467), and the *Eclectic Review* concludes: "[I]t is a great merit in all Mrs. Shelley's criticisms on works of art, that though unpretending, they always direct attention to that wherein the true character of the work consists" (702).[9] Mary Shelley thus played well the woman's role of amateur commentator, with her "unpretending" acquisition of "no mean taste," but within those limits gratified her audience's expectations of "spiritual content" by "always direct[ing] attention to . . . the true character of the work." The reviews further suggest that her art criticism, while perceived as powerful writing in its own right, did its job in maintaining the equilibrium of the roles it could potentially disrupt.

Suicide and Titian's Assumption of the Virgin

While visiting the Accademia delle Belle Arti in Venice in 1843, Mary Shelley saw Titian's *Assumption of the Virgin* (1516-18; see fig. 1), already regarded as a masterpiece of the Renaissance for the strong upward motion with which it depicts the Virgin Mary, at her death, taken up into heaven (Wethey 1: 75; Crowe and Cavalcaselle 1: 215-17).[10] Shelley writes:

> In another large apartment is the Assumption of Titian. The upper part is indeed glorious. The Virgin is rapt in a paradisiacal ecstasy as she ascends, surrounded by a galaxy of radiant beings, whose faces are beaming with love and joy, to live among whom were in itself Elysium. Such a picture, and the "Paradiso" of Dante as a commentary, is the sublimest achievement of Catholicism. Not, indeed, as a commentary did Dante write, but as the originator of much we see. The Italian painters drank deep at the inspiration of his verses when they sought to give a visible image of Heaven and the beatitude of the saints, on their canvass. (277)

Figure 1. Titian. *Assumption of the Virgin*, 1516-18. Santa Maria Gloriosa dei Frari, Venice. Copyright Archivi Alinari, 1990.

In the autobiographical dream-work that paintings perform in *Rambles*, Titian's *Assumption of the Virgin* provides a figure onto which Mary Shelley condensed several important but unspeakable feelings about her own death. As Marina Warner observes, the doctrine of the Assumption is essentially a vindication of the Virgin Mary's worthiness and sexual purity throughout her life; as a special mark of divine favour, God spared the Virgin any mortal decay (92). The same idea, of being vindicated at death, pervades Mary Shelley's journals and her works. One journal entry reads, "I wish I were worthy to die. As yet I am not, but after a few years of toil perhaps I may disappear as he" (*JMS* 438), thus giving voice to the guilt about her perception that she had failed Shelley because of her "coldness"—a guilt that she could not or would not voice explicitly. A similar sentiment is expressed in her poem "The Choice," an *apologia pro vita sua*, dated July 1823, but not published until 1876. There she declares:

> I have a faith that I must earn
> By suffering & by patience, a return
> Of that companionship & love, which first
> Upon my young life's cloud, like sunlight burst.
> (*JMS* 490 and n.).

Mary Shelley's character Despina in "A Tale of the Passions" (1823) observes, "All the good depart from this strange earth; and I doubt not that when I am sufficiently elevated above human weaknesses, it will also be my turn to leave this scene of woe" (13).[11] In both instances, human life is seen as a vale of soul-making, in which the moral achievement of worthiness or "elevation" is made visible by a vindicating death, a theme only a hair's breadth away from Catholicism's assertion that the Virgin Mary maintained her worthiness rather than achieving it over time.

In her responses to the *Assumption of the Virgin* (the doctrine, this painting of it, and the Murillo), Mary Shelley makes two interesting modifications. The first one is that in responding to Titian, she ecumenizes the Virgin Mary's death, draining it of its specifically Catholic references: "The Virgin is rapt in a paradisiacal ecstasy as she ascends, surrounded by a galaxy of radiant beings, whose faces are beaming with love, and joy, to live among whom were in itself Elysium." Even though she praises the work as one of the "sublimest achievement[s] of Catholicism," she de-emphasizes the Catholic idea that the Virgin Mary was reunited with Christ, Hellenizing the paradise as "Elysium." And she designates the putti as "a galaxy of radiant beings," an astronomical metaphor that avoids the question of belief in angels. Drained of its sectarian provenance, the paradise depicted by Titian might be hospitable to another Mary, one with a freethinking and Anglican religious education.[12]

A second, more important modification is to make the Assumption approach what her father, William Godwin, called a "voluntary death" (*PJ* 1: 92). According to Catholic teaching, the Virgin Mary died of natural causes but assented joyfully to her death. However, in an earlier response to a painting of the Assumption, Mary Shelley describes the Assumed Virgin as a martyr. After viewing Bartolomé Murillo's *Assumption of the Virgin* (1678; see fig. 2)[13] in Paris in 1840, she writes,

> [It is] worth ten thousand pictures such as one usually sees. She does not look so beautiful as Raphael's. She looks more like a martyr received into heaven; her almost tearful eyes, soft, upturned, imploring, her parted lips full of sensibility, all appear expressive of painful impressions of horror and death, and gratitude at the reward she is rising to receive. . . . [T]he colouring is glowing, and, like all Murillo's, is as satisfactory to the eye as harmonious music to the ear. (*LMWS* 3: 8; my emphasis)

Mary Shelley's characterization of the Assumed Virgin as a martyr, in the dream-logic of the art criticism, refers to a loophole in Godwin's prohibition of suicide in *Political Justice*. In general, Godwin condemns suicide, but martyrdom appears to be an exception to the rule. "The difficulty," Godwin writes,

> is to decide in any instance whether the recourse to a voluntary death can overbalance the usefulness I may exert in twenty or thirty more years of additional life. But surely it would be precipitate to decide that there is no such instance. There is a proverb which affirms, "that the blood of the martyrs is the seed of the church.". . . Let it be observed that all martyrs are suicides by the very signification of the term. They die for a testimony; that is, they have a motive for dying. But motives respect only our voluntary acts, not the violence put upon us by another. (1: 93; my emphasis)

Godwin's logic—granted, a bit twisted—seems to run like this: if there is an instance in which our usefulness in courting a voluntary death outweighs our usefulness in living, martyrdom is that instance, because of its benevolent motive. Because the martyr, like the suicide, seeks death, martyrdom is a species of suicide. Then Godwin qualifies his drastic equation by making the crucial distinction between martyrs and suicides (as usually understood): strictly speaking, martyrs will only their testimony, which may bring about their death, but they do not will the violent means and therefore do not will the death itself. In spite of his later qualification, the clarity of the equation rings out—"all martyrs are suicides"—adding a step in the rebus of the dream-work of the painting.

For in the chain of signification "Assumed Virgin Mary = martyr = suicide," Mary Shelley's painterly dream-work found a circuitous way of venting her own suicidal ideation, expressed in her journals in the conditional mode ("my life is a burthen I *would fain throw* on one side"

and "O my God . . . I say—[']would I might die'") and as an imperative addressed to God ("My God— . . . Grant that I may return to
Italy . . . or *make me die*") (*JMS* 531, 548, 571n; emphasis added in
both examples). In the latter two entries, the request for death is
addressed to God, and if it were granted, Mary Shelley's death would
fall into the category of "martyrdom"—or fall close to it, anyway—and
thus qualify for the loophole in Godwin's prohibition against suicide.
Her awareness of her father's prohibition follows closely on one of
those prayers: after praying, "O my God . . . I say—[']would I might
die,'" she follows quickly with the censorship: "that is wicked—but life
is a struggle & a burthen beyond my strength" (548).

Figure 2. Murillo. *Our Lady of the Immaculate Conception,* c. 1678.
Prado, Madrid.

This final comment—that the wish to die is "wicked"—registers Mary Shelley's conscious censorship of suicidal ideation, censorship associated with both parents: Godwin prohibited it (though with equivocations, as we have seen),[14] and Wollstonecraft was pilloried for "deserting her helpless offspring, disgracefully brought into the world by herself, by an intended act of suicide" (*European Magazine* 246). Mary Shelley, the "helpless offspring" Wollstonecraft later "desert[ed]," would have felt this condemnation more keenly. Suicide (as usually conceived) was the ultimate negation of maternal responsibility and a sign of an ungodwinian lack of stoicism.

Figure 3. Raphael. *Sistine Madonna*, c. 1513-14. Dresden Gallery, Dresden. Bildarchiv Foto Marburg 661891.

Mixed in with the prohibitions, however, were numerous signals of permission. Contemplating suicide was easier for Mary Shelley than for most people because so many family members had committed it, and others had threatened to do so. Her half-sister, Fanny Imlay, and Shelley's first wife, Harriet Westbrook, both killed themselves in 1816. Godwin evidently threatened suicide to force Shelley to marry his daughter (Sunstein, *Mary Shelley* 129). Wollstonecraft made two suicide attempts. Shelley had courted death more than once: he took laudanum to persuade Mary to elope with him (N. I. White 1: 344-45); and, when a boat trip on Lake Geneva turned dangerous, "Shelley, unable to swim and knowing that Byron would attempt to save him, caught hold of a locker and determined to sink with it rather than endanger another life by accepting Byron's aid" (N. I. White 1: 445). Moreover, he advocated suicide more or less explicitly in *Adonais*: "'Tis Adonais calls! oh, hasten thither, / No more let Life divide what Death can join together" (476-77). Thus, the characterization of the Virgin Mary, in the response to Murillo, as a "martyr" still marked with "powerful impressions of horror and death" approximates Mary Shelley's prayer for herself, "God . . . make me die," for martyrs actively seek death rather than just resigning to natural causes. But, in the response to Titian, her rhapsodic identification with the Virgin Mary as a model of worthiness, a grateful recipient of violent death, comes close to the suicidal ideation, but does not cross the line into articulating the "wicked" desire.

Emilia Viviani, *Epipsychidion,* and Raphael's *Sistine Madonna*

In Dresden, Mary Shelley saw Raphael's *Madonna di San Sisto*, commonly called the *Sistine Madonna* (1514; see fig. 3), so named from its original location at the Convent of San Sisto at Piacenza.[15] She records her awe at its solemnity:

> Entering this [room], we are at once commanded and awed by the "Madonna di San Sisto," the Virgin bearing the Infant God in her arms, by Raphael. As a painting, technically speaking, I believe there are faults found with it: worst of all, it has been retouched and restored; but no criticism can check the solemn impression it inspires. The Madonna is not the lowly wife of Joseph the carpenter: she is the Queen of Heaven; she advances surrounded by celestial rays, all formed of innumerable cherubim, from whose countenances beam the glory that surrounds her. The majesty of her countenance, "severe in youthful beauty" [*Paradise Lost* 4.845],

demands worship for her as the mother of the Infant Saviour, whom she holds in her arms. And he, the Godhead (as well as feeble mortals can conceive the inconceivable, and yet which once it is believed was visible) sits enthroned on his brow, and looks out from eyes full of lofty command and conscious power. With one hand, he makes the sign of blessing, as in Catholic countries this is bestowed. Below are two angels—both lovely; one inexpressibly so—who are looking up. I have seen copies and engravings from this picture; I have seen these angels well imitated, but never the mother and child. In some, the angelic beauty is sacrificed in the endeavour to portray the majestic glance, which thus becomes stern; or the dignity fades, that the beauty, which thus becomes inexpressive, may be preserved. (198)

Mary Shelley's response to the *Sistine Madonna,* interestingly, leaves behind technical considerations and begins to pick up speed and intensity with a rejection of what she is not—"The Madonna is not the lowly wife of Joseph the carpenter: she is the Queen of Heaven"—even though the painting itself offers no clue about Joseph's presence and thus no prompting for such an association. With this excess—mentioning Joseph when he is not there—the dream-work performed by the painting translates into another language a sentence Mary Shelley wrote about her own marriage in "The Choice." Addressing Shelley, she writes,

> —No more! No more! What tho' that form be fled
> My trembling hands shall never write thee—dead—
> Thou livst in Nature—love—my Memory,
> With deathless faith for aye adoring thee—
> The wife of time no more—I wed Eternity—
> (*JMS* 493; my emphasis)

Reduced to a kind of rebus, the sentences are roughly equivalent: Mary (both the Virgin and Mary Shelley) ≠ an earthly wife, but = a heavenly wife. After the dismissal of the earthly spouse, Mary Shelley affirms, with an almost excessive elaboration, the divinity of the one to whom the Virgin Mary is now united, the Christ Child, who with "Godhead . . . sit[ting] enthroned on his brow, . . . eyes full of lofty command and conscious power" assumes the attributes of an adult, command and power, and thus is more an equal or a spouse to the Virgin than her child. In the same way, "The Choice" had protested, perhaps too much, Shelley's eternal endurance: "Thou livst in Nature—love—my Memory." The *Sistine Madonna* dream-work thus translates into a figural language the defence of the Shelleys' marriage against the threat of

Shelley's death by asserting the eternal power of the one to whom each Mary is united. In using the Madonna to ratify her own marriage's eternal status, Mary Shelley exemplifies Jacques Lacan's observation that Christianity mediates the woman's cultural problem of accepting herself as an object of desire for the man rather than being able to attain the status of desiring agent by making the Virgin Mary, a symbol for all women, "the object of a divine desire, or else, a transcendent object of desire" ("Intervention" 99). Accordingly, Mary Shelley found vicarious consolation in the *Sistine Madonna* for her wounded claim to what Lacan calls divine desire from Shelley, now divinized as one of the benevolent dead (*Rambles* 123).

There is evidence, as well, that the *Sistine Madonna* defends the Shelleys' marriage against the memory of Shelley's infidelities. This chain of associations begins with a comment in Anna Jameson's 1834 book, *Sketches of Art, Literature, and Character*, which Mary Shelley quoted and consulted in *Rambles*.[16] Of the *Sistine Madonna*, Jameson writes:

> While I stood in contemplation of this all-perfect work, I felt the impression of its loveliness in my deepest heart, not only without the power, but without the thought or wish to give it voice or words, till some lines of Shelley's—lines which were not, but, methinks, ought to have been, inspired by the Madonna—came, uncalled, floating through my memory. (351-52; my emphasis)

Epipsychidion, from which the "lines of Shelley's" are derived, was a major source of pain to Jameson's friend Mary Shelley, because it celebrates Shelley's 1821 involvement with Emilia Viviani,[17] and allegorizes Mary Shelley as a Moon "in the sickness of eclipse" (310), denouncing her as "cold chaste Moon" (281). The affair with Emilia was one of the infidelities festering in Mary Shelley's mind due to the suddenness of Shelley's death (Sunstein, *Mary Shelley* 233). The pain it caused is evident because, while editing Shelley's *Poetical Works*, Mary Shelley wrote substantial notes on *Queen Mab*, *Alastor*, *The Revolt of Islam*, *Prometheus Unbound*, *The Cenci*, and *Hellas*,[18] but provided almost no information on *Epipsychidion*, leaving readers to infer what they may about Shelley's "intimate friends" from her evasive notes on poems written in 1820 and 1821.[19] Thus, despite Mary Shelley's commitment to uncensored presentation of her husband's works, her silence in the annotation demonstrates an unspeakable pain, which she described in her journal, as she was preparing the edition: "I am torn to pieces by Memory" (*JMS* 559). She repeatedly vented her jealousy of Emilia in veiled ways, for example, in "The Bride of

Modern Italy" (1824) and in the frivolous Clorinda in *Lodore* (1835). Moreover, the fact that this poem praises Emilia and not the poet's wife was obvious from a section Jameson tactfully omits, in which Shelley writes, "I never thought before my death to see / Youth's vision thus made perfect. Emily, / I love thee" (41-43). Thus Jameson, and all readers of Shelley's *Poetical Works*, would know of Shelley's emotional, if not sexual, unfaithfulness. Jameson wrenches the lines from their obviously intended referent, by saying that they were not, but ought to have been, inspired by someone named Mary.

Figure 4. Ghirlandaio. *Adoration of the Magi,* 1488. Ospedale degli Innocenti, Florence. Copyright Fratelli Alinari, 1996.

Jameson goes on to quote the description of Emilia as the perfection of youth's vision, a passage early in *Epipsychidion*:

Seraph of Heaven! too gentle to be human,
Veiling beneath that radiant form of woman
All that is insupportable in thee
Of light, and love, and immortality!
Sweet Benediction in the eternal curse!
Veil'd Glory of this lampless Universe! . . .
Thou Harmony of Nature's Art!
. . . I measure the world of fancies, seeking one like thee,
And find—alas! mine own infirmity!
(*Epipsychidion* 21-26, 30, 69-71, as quoted in *Sketches* 352)

Though Jameson does not say so, her reading of these lines of Shelley's as ideally inspired by the Madonna probably depends on the allusion in "Sweet Benediction in the eternal curse" to the Hail Mary's praise of the Virgin, *Benedicta tu in mulieribus* ("Blessed art thou among women") and to the Salve Regina, which declares Mary exempt from the fate of *exiles filii Evae* ("exiled children of Eve"). In addition, several epithets in the section Jameson skips allude to the cult of the Madonna:

Thou Moon beyond the clouds! Thou living Form
Among the Dead! Thou Star above the Storm!
Thou Wonder, and thou Beauty, and thou Terror!
Thou Harmony of Nature's art! Thou Mirror
In whom, as in the splendour of the Sun,
All shapes look glorious which thou gazest on! (27-32)

Shelley here gives new life to several of the Virgin Mary's traditional epithets: *stella maris* ("star of the sea"), is echoed in Shelley's "Thou star above the storm"; and "mirror of grace" is elaborated in "Thou Mirror / In whom, as in the splendour of the Sun / All shapes look glorious which thou gazest on!" Moreover, the Virgin Mary in her role as Immaculate Conception is often depicted standing on or over the moon, a motif sounded in Shelley's line "Thou Moon beyond the clouds." Jameson's link of the *Sistine Madonna* to *Epipsychidion* thus springs from associations any Catholic, or anyone trained in Catholic iconography, would make to Shelley's poem. In fact, within the logic of *Epipsychidion* itself, Jameson's transferring the reference of the vision of perfection from Emilia to the Virgin Mary makes a certain amount of sense, because, later in the poem, Mary Shelley is equated with the moon while Emilia is called "Soft as an Incarnation of the Sun" (335). Jameson, oddly, forces a certain consistency on Shelley, then, to suggest that the vision of perfection once called "Thou Moon beyond the clouds" might have the same name as the one later called "cold chaste Moon."[20] Nonetheless, by performing what Harold Bloom would call a strong misreading of the painting, Jameson removes from *Epipsychidion* the taint of Shelley's infidelity by suggesting the appropriateness of a Mary to receive this homage.

Mary Shelley had struggled for such a redirection of homage. Shortly after Shelley's death, she accepts the negative assessment in the poem, writing "now I am truly *cold moonshine*" (*LMWS* 1: 284; emphasis in original). But in revising *History of a Six Weeks' Tour* in the late 1830s, she places a benevolent and joyous moon over the couple's passage to Switzerland (388), and closes *Rambles* with a lunar blessing: "above us bends a sky—in whose pure depths ship-like clouds glide— and the moon hangs luminous, a pendant sphere of silver fire" (386).[21] Her struggle with Shelley's love of Emilia—to which Jameson's reading of the *Sistine Madonna* contributed—took place on this metaphoric ground.

"Poor Harriet" and Ghirlandaio's *Adoration of the Magi*

Mary Shelley registers "happiness" as her first response to Ghirlandaio's *Adoration of the Magi* (1488), exhibited in the Ospedale degli Innocenti in Florence (see fig. 4):[22]

> There is another picture of this age, which to see, is to feel the happiness which the soul receives from objects presented to the eye, that kindle and elevate the imagination. It represents the Adoration of the Magi, by Ghirlandajo, in the chapel of an hospital in the Piazza della Annunziata. There is one of the Kings standing on one side of the Virgin, which might (as the Apollo Belvidere is said to have done), create a passion in a woman's heart. Where on earth find a man so full of majesty, gentleness, and feeling? There is a charming accessory to this picture. In the back-ground is represented the Murder of the Innocents, in all its terror; but immediately in the fore-ground, on each side of the Virgin, kneel two children—the souls of the Innocents who died for Christ, and are redeemed by him. The attitude of these babes, especially of one, has that inexpressible charm of innocence which words cannot convey, and which since the creation of man, the pencil has seldom been able to depict.
>
> Led by the admiration which this picture excited, I visited every other in Florence by Ghirlandajo. (*RGI* 304)

Figure 5. Detail from Ghirlandaio's *Adoration of the Magi*, 1488. Ospedale degli Innocenti, Florence. Copyright Fratelli Alinari, 1996.

The lyrical tone of this passage suggests the stirring of deep waters: in the quiet acknowledgement of sexual passion, when she notes that one of the Magi "creates a passion in a woman's heart" (see fig. 5). Tactfully, Mary Shelley alludes to an erotic passage on the Apollo Belvedere from *Childe Harold's Pilgrimage* (4.162), so as not to attribute the passion too directly to herself. Indeed, she lingers on his beauty, elegiacally asking, "Where on earth find a man so full of majesty, gentleness, and feeling?" And Mary Shelley attests to the picture's enduring impact: "Led by the admiration which this picture excited, I visited every other in Florence by Ghirlandajo." It would have been a considerable undertaking just to see all of Ghirlandaio's

Madonnas in Florence, let alone his other paintings, for his Madonnas adorn the Uffizi and the churches of Ognissanti, Sant' Andrea, and Santa Trinita; the church of Santa Maria Novella devotes an entire wall to Ghirlandaio's frescoes on the life of the Virgin (Micheletti 38-46). What about this painting prompted Mary Shelley's admiration and energetic response? Unlike Titian's *Assumption of the Virgin* and Raphael's *Sistine Madonna*, the other two paintings that evoke almost universal acclaim, Ghirlandaio's has a narrower, more eccentric claim.

The answer lies, I think, in Ghirlandaio's bold departure from convention in juxtaposing the Madonna with the Massacre of the Innocents. (The fact that the painting was commissioned for an orphanage may explain Ghirlandaio's choice.) The convention it defies is explained by Jameson: "as an event, [the Massacre of the Innocents] belongs properly to the life of Christ; it is not included in a series of the Life of the Virgin, perhaps from a feeling that the contrast between the most blessed of women and mothers and those who wept distracted for their children was too painful" (*Legends* 269).

This juxtaposition, however, tapped the guilt at the heart of Mary Shelley's greatest sorrow, the loss of her children: three-year old William, "my eldest born, my loveliest, [and] my dearest" (*JMS* 492), after whose death in June 1819, she wrote, "this world seemed only a quicksand, sinking beneath me" (*JMS* 438); and one-year-old Clara, whose death upon arrival in Venice the previous September brought forth "those [passions] the deepest a woman's heart can harbour—a dread to see her child even at that instant expire" (*Rambles* 269). Mingled with these sorrows was a deep sense of just retribution for her own part in the betrayal of Harriet Westbrook, Shelley's wife since 1812, and the mother of his infant daughter Ianthe when, in July 1814, Shelley and Mary Godwin eloped to the Continent. (Harriet had another child, Charles, in November 1814.) After prolonged pleas for Shelley to return, Harriet committed suicide in December 1816 by drowning herself in the Serpentine. Shelley and Mary Godwin were married on 29 December; as Emily Sunstein aptly says, they married over Harriet's dead body (*Mary Shelley* 140).

The spectre of their responsibility for Harriet's death thus stood over their marriage and their family. In fact, in a letter to Harriet's sister Eliza, Shelley seems to blame Mary outright, conceding that Eliza "may excusably regard [Mary] as the cause of [her] sister's ruin," a letter that Mary saw during the custody battle over Harriet's children (*LPBS* 1: 523; Sunstein, *Mary Shelley* 130).[23] Mary Shelley's assumption of responsibility—however realistic or unrealistic that assumption might be—emerges in a journal entry of 1822. Before William's death, "I was, as another, the Mother of beautiful children. But these staid not by me" (*JMS* 438). Harriet Shelley, called merely "another [Mother]" in 1822, returns in fuller force by February 1839, when, writing of the dedication to *Queen Mab*, she mourns "Poor Harriet to whose sad fate I attribute so many of my own heavy sorrows as the atonement claimed by fate for her death" (*JMS* 560). Since all of her children were born after Shelley's betrayal of Harriet (with Mary Shelley's collusion), guilt coloured her retrospection, contaminating the remembrance of even those moments of pleasure and joy in William, Clara, Shelley, and Claire Clairmont's daughter Allegra. As Mary Shelley wrote in her life of Cervantes, "our dearest memories [are] discovered to have a taint," the taint of ill-gotten goods. The Shelley legend, however, demanded the suppression of Harriet's betrayal by Shelley in favour of his generosity and other-worldliness. Mary Shelley's guilt over her part in precipitating Harriet's death may also have reawakened guilt over "causing" her own mother's death from puerperal fever.[24] Melanie Klein observes that mothers of dead children can experience their loss as punishment wielded by their own mothers (156, 158); Mary Shelley displays a variant of this pattern of maternal punishment in the connection she drew between her guilt over Harriet Shelley and her children's deaths. Ghirlandaio's inclusion of the Massacre of the Holy Innocents displaces the punitive character Mary Shelley attributed to Harriet onto Herod, the evil king and father, and his soldiers, and propitiates them while still finding them despicable.

This propitiation is not the final word. Mary Shelley draws attention to "a charming accessory," the fact that, "in the fore-ground, on each side of the Virgin, kneel two children." The horror of the massacre recedes as two babies return from the dead to kneel in front of their new mother, the Virgin Mary, effecting a restoration of maternal gladness, and allowing the maternal spectator to feel a happiness that is attributed to "objects . . . that kindle and elevate the imagination." Thus the Ghirlandaio *Adoration of the Magi* satisfies two contradictory urges: on the one side, it acknowledges the justice of Harriet's claim, the "atonement" demanded of Mary Shelley (the deaths of William and Clara); but on the other, it assuages her bereavement by, imaginatively, restoring to life and to their mother the two babies who have "that inexpressible charm of innocence which words cannot convey." The children are declared innocent despite the guilty circumstances of their parents' marriage.

In addition to the specific power of Ghirlandaio's painting, the city of Florence and its art works had a powerful hold on Mary Shelley's understanding of the loss of her children. She records her reluctance, in the 1840s, to revisit a major Florentine art gallery, the Uffizi:

> With slow steps my feet almost unwillingly first moved to the collection in the Reali Uffizi. As I entered the Tribune I felt a crowd of associations rise up around me, gifted with painful vitality. I was long lost in tears. But novelty seems all in all to us weak mortals; and when I revisited these rooms, these saddest ghosts were laid; the affliction calmed, and my mind was free to receive new impressions. (*RGI* 308)

The associations "gifted with painful vitality" arose from the memory of her first visit to the Uffizi in 1819, when Mary Shelley was pregnant again after having lost Clara and William.[25] Then she and Shelley first saw the huge statue of Niobe, acknowledged as the gem of the gallery, which Shelley had described in a long and passionate fragment as "a mother in the act of sheltering from some divine and inevitable peril, the last, we will imagine, of her surviving children" ("Notes on Sculptures" 330), a description far too close to his own wife for comfort. After repeated visits to the Uffizi in the 1840s, visits that were probably interspersed with the Ghirlandaio pilgrimages, Mary Shelley records the general response that "these saddest ghosts were laid; the affliction calmed" and adds a less tempestuous response than Shelley's to the Niobe, "whose maternal, remediless grief sheds a solemn sadness around" (*RGI* 310). In my view, Ghirlandaio's juxtaposition of massacre and Madonna triggered the calming of her affliction of guilt, transformed her perception of the Niobe, and laid to rest "these saddest ghosts," including the ghost of Harriet Shelley. In all the instances of dream-work performed by the paintings, this purgation, calming of affliction, and renewed energy in viewing paintings, suggest the successful working-through of the material brought to consciousness in the art criticism.

The Politics of Mary Shelley's Religion

What conclusions can we draw from the autobiographical dream-work performed by Mary Shelley's art-critical writings in *Rambles*? At first glance, Mary Shelley's reverent treatment of the Virgin Mary may disappoint those enamored of the iconoclastic teenager who wrote *Frankenstein* and serve to confirm the long-standing feminist disillusionment with Mary Shelley, articulated by Mary Poovey, as one who succumbed to the deadly power of propriety. However, the treatment of the Virgin Mary in the 1840s reveals political courage and substantive continuities with the young writer as well. When Mary Shelley wrote of the *Sistine Madonna* that "the majesty of her countenance . . . demands *worship* for her *as the mother* of the Infant Saviour" (emphasis added), we see an echo of the mother-religion daringly expounded in her 1823 novel, *Valperga*. In that novel, the religion is explained, and the history of its founder, Wilhelmina of Bohemia, is given by one its opponents:

> Outwardly professing the Catholic religion, and conforming in the strictest manner to its rules, she secretly formed a sect, founded on the absurd and damnable belief, that she was the Holy Ghost incarnate upon earth for the salvation of the female sex. . . . Her tenets were intended entirely to supersede those of our beloved Lord Jesus, and her friend Magfreda was to be papess, and to succeed to all the power and privileges of the Roman pontiff. (*NSW* 3: 130-31)

Mary Shelley's source for the heresy, Lodovico Muratori, unsympathetically notes Wilhelmina's woman-centred twist on the heretical antinomian view of the coming "Third Age" of the Holy Spirit, one in which women subvert that quintessential institution of Catholicism, the Papacy. Mary Shelley's novel stresses this woman-centredness by giving Wilhelmina a daughter "through whom the spirit of heresy survives and mutates" (Rajan, *Valperga* 457 n.10). It does seem a long distance from the mother-worshipping heresy of *Valperga* to the apparently conventional statement regarding worshipping the Virgin Mary, whose worship (from a feminist point of view, such as Warner's) is always circumscribed by the orthodox assertions of her perpetual virginity and of her perfect submission to God the Father.

However, the links with Wollstonecraft remain clear in both cases. Wilhelmina echoes Wollstonecraft both in her name and in bearing an illegitimate child (Mary Shelley's addition to Muratori). And the Virgin Mary, who shares Shelley's mother's name (as well as her own), provides the occasion for Mary Shelley to experience herself as the daughter of both Marys, exemplifying Nancy Chodorow's observation that "Mothering . . . involves a double identification for women, both as mother *and* as child . . . Women take both parts in it. Women have capacities for primary identification with their child through regression to primary love and empathy. Through their mother identification, they have ego capacities and the sense of responsibility which go into caring for children" (Chodorow 204; emphasis in original). This mother-daughter doubleness is especially easy to project onto images of the Virgin Mary because of the Catholic tradition that she is the daughter of her own son, as attested in Dante's phrase *figlia del tuo figlio*, "daughter of thy son" (*Paradiso* 33.1). Finally, Mary Shelley had more practice than most people in using paintings as substitutes for mothers. When Wollstonecraft died, Godwin moved into her study and hung John Opie's portrait of her above the fireplace (St Clair 180). Mary Shelley, then, grew up knowing her mother through a painting as well as, in later life, through her texts.

In addition to its reference to her own mother, Mary Shelley's statement that the Virgin Mary demanded "worship" was a risky one in 1840s British culture. Catholic Emancipation, passed in 1829, generated widespread petitions and protests, as many Britons "saw themselves, quite consciously, as being part of a native tradition of resistance to Catholicism" (Colley 330). In 1833, the Tractarian movement, which restored many Catholic elements to the Church of England, began with John Keble's preaching on "National Apostasy" and John Henry Newman's inauguration of *Tracts for the Times*. National controversy reached a peak in 1840-41; in 1841, Newman's *Tract 90*, which suggested the compatibility of the Thirty-Nine Articles and the Church of Rome, caused indignation in Oxford, whose bishop demanded cessation of the *Tracts*. In 1845, the year of Newman's conversion to Catholicism, a question about government subsidies of Catholic seminaries was declared by Harriet Martineau to be "the great political controversy of the year—the subject on which society seemed to be going mad" (Norman 23).[26] In response to the "popishness" of the Tractarians (and perhaps also to increased devotion to the Immaculate Conception in France [Carroll 148]), some English Protestants vilified "worship" of the Virgin Mary. For example, Thomas Horne Hartwell's *Mariolatry: or, Facts and evidences demonstrating the worship of the Blessed Virgin Mary, by the Church of Rome, derived from the testimonies of her reputed saints and doctors* (like *Rambles*, published in 1844) attacks the very idea broached by Mary Shelley, that the Virgin Mary deserves "worship," by comparing it, in the term "Mariolatry," to the worship of idols. Published the next year, Benjamin Disraeli's novel *Tancred* illustrates the contestedness of the territory. At their first meeting, Eva asks Tancred what kind of a Christian he is: "Pray, are you of those Franks [European Christians] who worship a Jewess; or of those who revile her, break her images, and blaspheme her pictures?" (194). Tancred's careful response is, "I venerate, though I do not adore, the mother of God." Such subtle distinctions among the terms "worship," "adoration," and "veneration" in regard to the Virgin Mary suggest the stormy nature of the controversy Mary Shelley entered. Indeed, *Rambles* was denounced as pro-Catholic in its day.[27]

In addition, Mary Shelley's reveries on the Virgin Mary form part of a generally sympathetic treatment of Catholicism, one strategy in her advocacy of Italian nationalism. While this sympathy toward Catholicism looks indeed as if Poovey's "proper lady" has retreated from the death-wish to the Papacy expressed in *Valperga*, in fact, Catholicism too had changed in relation to Italian nationalism.[28] In the 1820s, the sole spokespersons for Italian nationalism were the Carbonari, who "first taught the Italians to consider themselves as forming a nation" (*RGI* 323); the Catholic Church, in collusion with the Austrians who governed most of Italy, declared any connection with Carbonarism a sin and attempted to extirpate it by means of the confessional and the threat of excommunication. Since the Catholic Church had declared war on the cause of liberty and republicanism that she held dear, it makes sense that in *Valperga* Mary Shelley would seek to supplant it with a mother-religion.

By the 1840s Catholicism and the Papacy had assumed roles different from those of the 1820s and also differentiated from each other.[29] The torch of nationalism had passed from the unsuccessful Carbonari to "Young Italy," founded by Giuseppe Mazzini in the 1830s. Like the Carbonari, Mazzini advocated insurrection, but his opposition to religion was more nuanced than that of his predecessors. Even though Mazzini's motto was "God and the People," he opposed the Papacy, and by "God" meant a nonsectarian sense of Italy's divine mission rather than one sanctioned by the forms of Catholicism. In 1843, Vincenzo Gioberti published *On the Moral and Civic Primacy of the Italian People*, a work that outlined the "Neo-Guelph" position. Gioberti thought that Italy should be a confederation of states, presided over by the Pope, and his brilliance lay in divorcing Italian nationalism from its revolutionary origins, to which Mazzini clung, thus making nationalism available for the consideration of moderates and the clergy. (Gioberti himself was a priest.) The movement was so powerful for a time that it influenced the election of Pius IX, a sympathizer, to the papacy in 1846. Though Mary Shelley does not mention the Neo-Guelph movement explicitly in *Rambles*, her praise for Massimo d'Azeglio, son-in-law of novelist Alessandro Manzoni and later the prime minster of Piedmont (*RGI* 334-35 and n.) gives a substantial clue to her own position. D'Azeglio rejected both the insurrectionary means of Young Italy and the endorsement of papal leadership held by the Neo-Guelphs in favour of "a conspiracy in the sunlight" to influence public opinion.[30]

Mary Shelley's presentation of Catholicism in *Rambles* is inflected by these subtleties. She highly praises the religious faith of Manzoni, whose novel *The Betrothed* gave prominence to the Tuscan dialect's claim to become the language of the emerging Italian nation. She notes that Manzoni is "a devout Catholic" and praises the "exquisite finish and poetic fire that adorns the fervent piety of his poetry" (334). And she praises his integration of politics and religion in *The Betrothed*: "It is not the vulgar notion of bringing forward the Pope, with his army of priests and monks, as the regenerators of society, at which he aims; it is the Christian spirit of resignation and self-denial that he wishes to revive, and render the master-feeling of the world" (333).[31] Thus Manzoni's position forges a middle way, in which Catholicism still has a leading role in promulgating "the Christian spirit of resignation and self-denial," but in which the Papacy has no political or military role, no "army of priests and monks." In keeping with this strong but limited endorsement of Catholicism's role in politics, she praises Catholicism's charitable institutions, to the detriment of England's: "It must be added, that wherever the Catholic religion prevails, great works of charity subsist. During the time of Catholicism, charitable institutions, as is well known, abounded all over England—in some few obscure corners such still survive" (354). Thus, her imaginative reveries on paintings of the Virgin Mary, while full of biographical resonances, also form part of a consistently favourable presentation of Catholicism[32] and, with it, Italian culture and national aspirations. In them, Mary Shelley sounds a note of political courage and fidelity to the republican principles she had held in her youth.

The case of Mary Shelley's use of religious material suggests a wider application. As we have seen, careful historical reconstruction of the relations between politics and religion can help us reassess the relationships among women, religion, and conventionality. Romantic-period scholarship has traditionally taken women and religion as components of the "conventional" background, against which iconoclastic male writers cut a dramatic figure. Jane Tompkins, in a now-classic essay, revealed an analogous prejudice among scholars of American romanticism. Tompkins attributes the neglect of Harriet Beecher Stowe to the contrast between the writers Nathaniel Hawthorne called "a damned mob of scribbling women" and "a few giant intellects, unappreciated and misunderstood in their time, struggling manfully against a flood of sentimental rubbish" (22). In contrast to this traditional drawing of figure and ground, the personages of Stowe and, as I have shown, of Mary Shelley suggest that religious material did not relegate all women writers to the eddies of mere conventionality. Instead, religious material offered them occasions of bravery, liberty from convention, and creativity.[33]

Earlier versions of this paper were given at the University of Calgary's conference on "Mary Wollstonecraft/Mary Shelley: Writing Lives," the

Eighteenth- and Nineteenth-Century British Women Writers Conference at the University of North Carolina at Chapel Hill, the Institute for Research on Women and Gender at Columbia University, and the New School for Social Research. The author thanks Isobel Armstrong, Helen Buss, Betty T. Bennett, Ellen Chirelstein, Pamela Clemit, Charles L. Cooper, Nora Crook, Daniel Dibbern, Doucet Devin Fischer, Mark Hansen, Jean Howard, Linda K. Hughes, Anne K. Mellor, Charles E. Robinson, Amy Rambow, Esther H. Schor, Maura L. Spiegel, Lisa Vargo, Gina Luria Walker, Marina Warner, Deborah Elise White, and Carolyn Wood for their responses to previous drafts of this essay; Clarissa Campbell Orr, Beth Dolan Kautz, and Constance Walker for making their work available to me in typescript; William L. Andrews, Janet Beizer, Maria LaMonaca, Marsha Manns, Steven Marcus, Alan J. Stern, and Halbert Weidner for helpful information; Erin Core for translations from Palacio's French and Stan Ridgeway for Spanish translation; and Elizabeth Denlinger, Claire M. Giordano, Tamara Graham-Voelker, Mark T. Katuz, and Shelley Wunder Smith for their research assistance.

Notes

1 For a justification of a literary reading of the Dora case, see S. Marcus.

2 LaPlanche and Pontalis define dream-work as "The whole of the operations which transform the raw materials of the dream—bodily stimuli, day's residues, dream-thoughts—so as to produce the manifest dream. Distortion is the result of dream-work" (*s.v.* "dream-work").

3 For the personal and political meanings of Cervantes to Mary Shelley, see Moskal, "Cervantes." "The Captive," the fictional account of Cervantes's captivity, is found in *Don Quixote* 1.4.12-14.

4 For example, see Benstock (1141), whose model is productive here for broadening the discussion of life writing to include travel books and other genres besides the full-dress monograph.

5 The presence of Percy Florence is also mentioned in the *New Monthly*, the *Atlas*, and the *Globe*. The *Spectator* sounds the only disapproval of Mary Shelley as mother, complaining that she responded to her son's sailing with "morbid dread" (782).

6 For Mary Shelley's friendship with Jameson see *LMWS* 2: 12 and Palacio 549. Mary Shelley had reviewed two of Jameson's previous works, and praised *Sketches in Germany* (*RGI* 202); Jameson's interest in Mary Shelley is suggested by a letter of Maria Jane Jewsbury's to Jameson in 1830 (*LMWS* 2: 112n.).

7   William Godwin, too, spent considerable time with artists, including John Martin (Pamela Clemit, personal communication to the author).

8   Rio's work was thus a conservative reaction against a new trend toward scientific method in cataloguing, attribution, and analysis of art, which began in the 1830s (Sherman 3-7). Venerable authorities such as Giorgio Vasari's *Lives of the Most Eminent Italian Painters, Sculptors, and Architects* (2nd ed. 1568) and J. J. Winckelmann's *History of Ancient Art* (1764) were challenged in the 1830s by Karl Friedrich von Rumohr's work on Vasari and Johann David Passavant's work on Raphael. Franz Kugler's *Handbuch der Geschischte der Malerei* (1837) brought this movement to England as *A Handbook of the History of Painting*. The increased rigour in art history and criticism reached the universities of what are now Germany and Austria, where the first professors of the subject were appointed, and the museums, where art historians began to be approved as directors: Passavant at Frankfurt in 1840, and Gustav Waagen, in 1830, at the Berlin Gallery (Sherman 5-6), which Mary Shelley visited. In addition, Giovanni Morelli, trained in comparative anatomy, challenged traditional methods of attribution in evaluating museums' purchases, by using photography as the basis for scientific connoisseurship (Sherman 6-7).

9   The *Eclectic Review* also praises her rejection of Rio's "artistic bigotry" (702)—a code word for Catholicism.

10   The painting was exhibited at the Accademia from 1817 until 1918, when it was returned to the church of Santa Maria dei Frari, for which it was commissioned (Wethey 1: 75).

11   On the more general theme of being worthy in God's eyes, the narrator of *The Last Man* describes Clara's first desire as "[t]o make herself acceptable to the power she worshipped" (300); and, in her life of Pascal, Mary Shelley asserts the value of "a spirit of pious resignation, and a wish to be acceptable to God" (French *Lives* 1: 195).

12   For Mary Shelley's childhood religious education, see Claire Clairmont's recollections (*CC* 2: 627).

13   Now restored to the Prado, it is called *La Inmaculada Soult* in indignant reference to Napoleon's Marshal Soult, who in 1813 took it from Spain to Paris (Gaya Nuño n. 311), where Mary Shelley viewed it. Scholars debate whether several Murillo paintings, including this one, represent the Immaculate Conception or the Assumption (Gaya Nuño).

14   There is also a fragment of an essay on suicide in Godwin's papers, one which I have not yet seen.

15   It was moved to the Dresden Gallery in the eighteenth century (Pope-Hennessey 211-12).

16   Judith Johnston helpfully sorts the various titles of Jameson's volume (237). Mary Shelley may have purchased the 1837 edition, published in Frankfurt under a different title, when she visited Frankfurt in 1840 (Palacio 564n; Moskal, Introductory Note 55 n.17). She definitely had access to this work in writing *Rambles*, if not during the journey, for she relies on Jameson's remarks on Titian's *Cristo della Moneta* (202 and n.).

17   Her real name was Teresa; Emilia was the name used by the Shelleys and Claire Clairmont.

18   In the second edition she added a note on *Oedipus Tyrannus*.

19   The note for the poems of 1820 mentions that "his solitude was enlivened by an intercourse with several intimate friends"; the 1821 note mentions "others" who "found in Shelley's society . . . delight, instruction and solace." (Shelley, *Complete Works* 4: 79, 122).

20   For biographical interpretation of *Epipsychidion*, see Cameron.

21   Mary Shelley's mention of St Joseph, who is excluded from the *Sistine Madonna*, may also serve to vent a fantasy that would make sense of her blame of Shelley for her children's deaths: "We came to Italy thinking to do Shelley's health good—but the Climate is not any means warm enough to be of benefit to him & yet it is that that has destroyed my two children. . . . May you my dear Marianne [Hunt] never know what it is to loose [*sic*] two only & lovely children in one year" (*LMWS* 1: 101). Scapegoating the climate barely disguises Shelley as the target for blame, since his health prompted the family to move. Moreover, Raphael's evocation of the cultural fantasy of conception without a man reinstates the child exclusively as the mother's, covertly enacting Mary Shelley's maternal rage and blame by erasing Shelley completely from the picture. Moreover, the figure—not just in Raphael's version, but archetypally—denies the father through the myth of a virgin mother. Ramas notes that this is a fantasy of "a conception in which the phallus and the 'primal scene' play no role" (172-73).

22   This painting is not to be confused with another *Adoration of the Magi* by Ghirlandaio in the Uffizi (Micheletti 3).

23   Shelley writes, "I cannot expect that your feelings towards the lady whose union with me you may excusably regard as the

cause of your sister's ruin should permit you to mention her with the honor [*sic*] with which Ianthe must be accustomed to regard the wife of her father's heart" (*LPBS* 1: 523). Thus there is some ambiguity whether "union" or "lady" (i.e., Mary Shelley) is the referent of what Eliza may regard as the "cause."

24   Cf. Constance Walker's characterization of Mary Shelley as a double mourner, whose "real loss of her mother was arguably embedded in each of her subsequent losses" (143) (cf. Segal 390).

25   The toll of her losses rises to three if one counts the unnamed girl born in 1815.

26   This was the "Maynooth Question." Anti-Catholic sentiment crystallized around annual Parliamentary debates over subsidizing a Roman Catholic seminary in Maynooth, Ireland, debates that "fill[ed] a larger space than [any other] in Hansard's Parliamentary Debates of the first half of the nineteenth century" (Hogan).

27   The *Observer*'s review noted "the religious tendency of the book" with its "reverence for . . . the glories of Catholicism in the churches of France and Italy," a tendency it attributes to "an evident leaning—the leaning of all minds which begin with pyrrhonism [skepticism] and end with implicit faith—to the calm and consolatory doctrines of the 'old faith.'"

28   I discuss this in full in "Gender and Italian Nationalism."

29   Throughout this paragraph and the next I rely on Duggan (112) and Di Scala (63-89).

30   D'Azeglio's ideas were already known in Italy, even though his book, *On the Last Incidents of the Romagna,* was published two years after *Rambles* (Di Scala 79).

31   A contrasting view of Manzoni's religion appears in "Modern Italian Romances," which has not been definitively attributed to Mary Shelley (*RGI* 333n.).

32   It is true that she praises "the intellectual liberty gained" by Protestantism and looks forward to its spread to "those countries which are still subject to Papacy" (*RGI* 182). Palacio's landmark 1969 study accurately characterizes her religion as humanism touched with "elegiac and profoundly Christian resignation" (301), but, in my view, overstates her antipathy to Catholicism.

∽

Biographical Imaginings and Mary Shelley's (Extant and Missing) Correspondence

Betty T. Bennett

In her review of a life of Virginia Woolf, Carolyn G. Heilbrun sums up a critical truth about biography: "Biographies are fictions we contrive about lives we find meaningful. Facts are interpretable, and become available to the biographer with a certain randomness." Biography, then, is a construct of experiences selected from self-reports, reports of others, and various contextual material, linked together through the biographer's imagination. This imagination necessarily operates within an assumed relationship to the subject's life that may or may not become apparent in the work itself. The reliability of any biography, defined as the extent to which it accurately depicts what can be verified, is therefore open to question. But, of necessity, the facts about any life remain, to a minor or major degree untestable. Perhaps this challenge in part accounts for the enthusiastic reviews of so many recent fictionalized biographies—reviews that are all the more extraordinary in an age of almost overwhelming data accessibility.

Editions of letters, however, have the potential to reduce materially such biographical randomness. As important, because the letters incrementally establish the story of a subject's life, these editions may also serve to encourage the privileging of subject over biographer or

---

Notes are on pp. 230-31.

editor. But letters themselves represent a complex amalgam of influences. Self-consciousness, audience-orientation, politics, time, place, and frame of mind of the letter-writer, or even whether a stamp or stationery is handy, can impinge on the collected shape of a correspondence. Perhaps this is never more so than in the case of letters written by those who, like Mary Shelley, self-identify as authors, for whom writing itself forms a customary and critical segment of life. Moreover, all collections of letters have been influenced by three problem areas: editorial perspective; the veracity of subject and correspondents; and the spaces left by missing letters.

Mary Shelley's discussion of the component parts of her creature in the introduction to *Frankenstein* suggests a model for approaching these three particular quandaries in editing letters as biography: "Invention, it must be humbly admitted, does not consist in creating out of void, but out of chaos; the materials must, in the first place, be afforded." My paper will explore Mary Shelley's letters not to resolve the quandaries, but rather to recognize how they are critical "component parts of a creature" we call biography (*Frankenstein* [1831]: ix, x).

Mary Shelley faced those same quandaries herself. Her novels *Valperga* and *Perkin Warbeck* include historical characters and actions that represent her nineteenth-century agenda of socio-political reform in a medium she expected to be received as fiction. On the other hand, her collected letters indicate her interest in writing actual biographies,[1] an intent realized in her five volumes of *Lives* and in the notes to her monumental 1839 editions of P. B. Shelley's works.

Her correspondence demonstrates that she did extensive research for fictionalized as well as actual biography, but that the imaginative freedom she inscribed in her fiction was restrained by facts in her biographies. When Edward Moxon, publisher of the 1839 editions, pressured her to omit atheistical passages in P. B. Shelley's works for fear of legal prosecution, she struggled to make a decision that took into account what she believed to be P. B. Shelley's wishes as well as the publisher's and her own. Her conflicted feelings as editor are explicit in a series of letters to friends, in which she asks advice: "I dont like mutilations—& would not leave out a word in favour of liberty. But I have no partiality to irreligion & much doubt the benefit of disputing the existence of the Creator"; "I dislike Atheism but I shrink from Mutilation—"; "Except that I do not like the idea of a mutilated edition, I have no scruple of conscience in leaving out the expressions which Shelley would never have printed in after <life Life>" (*LMWS* 2: 301, 303, 305; 11, 12, [14] Dec. 1838). She first acquiesced to the publisher's wishes. When severely criticized for the excisions, however, she reinstated the deleted passages in the second, one-volume edition—at which point Moxon was indeed prosecuted for blasphemous libel (*LMWS* 2: 301, 3: 9; 11 Dec. 1838, 30 Nov. [1840]). Not surprisingly, during and since her time, her own editing has been the subject of extensive commentary (Fraistat 420 n.11).

Despite their complexities, letters may serve as an important objectifying agent in biographical constructs. The obstacles often reside less in the materials available than in the first of the three editorial quandaries: a particular editor's outlook and the context (time and place) of an edition. The editorial perspective of scholars remains as important today as it has been throughout the publishing history of letters and biographies. In Mary Shelley's case as a biographical subject, for instance, it encouraged me to question whether her significance as a romantic had been insufficiently recognized "not because her works lacked a philosophic basis but rather because we had not noticed or understood it" (Bennett, "Finding" 291).

The most significant biographical difference between my edition and earlier editions of Mary Shelley's letters emanates from the basic premise guiding the research encapsulated in my footnotes: the importance of Mary Shelley as an author, in her own period and ours. This principle led to digging in libraries, record offices, and private holdings for details that elucidated the letters in themselves and as they cast light on her life and works. This search was necessarily limited by the edition's publication date and by the number of pages allocated by the press, two factors that seem reasonable only at the beginning of a project. At times one may resent both restrictions, but no individual or team can ever find all the details that make up any subject's life. The goal is to locate everything conceivable within a reasonable frame of time and space and, most important, to emphasize the salient perspectives of the subject rather than of the editor. It is safe to say, no responsible editor of letters leaves a project without reams of unused contextual material.

New editions obviously allow for corrections, sometimes minute, but important in terms of biography. Just one example of this kind: a letter of Mary Shelley's about the education of her son, Percy Florence Shelley, was misread by an earlier editor to read, "the bustle of a school would develop his chances better." Quoting this has led to the impression she was rather mercenary in directing her son's future. She actually wrote that the bustle "would develop his character better" (*LMWS* 2: 134; 5 May 1831).

Handwriting also offers important information about Mary Shelley's life. Her earliest found writing resembles Godwin's. After her elopement with P. B. Shelley, her script looks more and more like his, to the degree that sometimes it seems impossible to know which of the two Shelleys wrote a particular word or phrase. Finally, in the last eleven years of her life her script flattens, at times becoming no more than a wavy tail at the end of a word, evidence of the duration of the recurrent illness that ended with her death on 1 February 1851. Cycles of illness reflected in her handwriting shed light on Mary Shelley's career in the last eleven years of her life, as well as on her courage as she resisted that illness, generally glossed over in past biographies.

Many studies of Mary Shelley's works have argued that those works were accidental or were written with little or no artistic commitment. Her letters prove otherwise. Whether she wrote books or shorter works; corrected Sir Walter Scott's impression that P. B. Shelley wrote *Frankenstein*, or later, presumed on his positive review of her first novel to write to him for information for *Perkin Warbeck*; negotiated after P. B. Shelley's death with publishers and editors for her own works and his; or served as editor and agent for friends, her letters over the course of her career profile her ambitions, frustrations, and engagement in the "business" of writing, as well as the aspirations expressed in her comment that "After all Valperga is merely a book of promise, another landing place in the staircase I am climbing" (*LMWS* 1: 361; 3-5 August [1823]).

Her professionalism also shows itself in her confidence that she can meet her financial needs through her writing. When she advised Leigh Hunt to write for magazines to earn the money he needed, she characterized her own situation: "I write bad articles which help to make me miserable—but I am going to plunge into a novel, and hope that its clear water will wash off the <dirt> mud of the magazines" (*LMWS* 1: 412; 9 Feb. [1824]). While writing her last work, *Rambles in Germany and Italy* (1844), between bouts of illness, she confidently asserted that her first, *History of a Six Weeks' Tour* (1817), had brought her many compliments and she had no doubt this new work would "procure [her] many more" (*LMWS* 3: 96; 27 Sept. [1843]). The letters also confirm her intellectual habits of research and extensive reading for her fiction and non-fiction writing. They show that she remained in locations in order to do research, wrote to experts for suggestions of additional sources of information, and visited sites she wished to incorporate into her fiction.[2]

The second editorial quandary—about the veracity of the subject and her correspondents—follows directly from the question of fiction. What if the letters themselves are works of fiction? For example, P. B. Shelley wrote a number of letters about being physically attacked while he was in Wales, and over the years continued to refer to that attack

(*LPBS* 1: 355-56). Most biographers doubt the attack ever occurred (*CC* 2: 597). This story, and others, have been accounted for by his friends as examples of P. B. Shelley's extremely active imagination. Enough "active imagination" incidents occur in his letters and life to raise, for the editor and biographer, the question of his veracity. In an 1834 letter to Mary Shelley, Claire Clairmont described him as "zealous when writing for his cause, but tolerably insincere in his private affairs" (*CC* 1: 314). Mary Shelley, however, as editor of his letters, wrote: "it may be argued that truth and frankness produce better fruits than the most generous deceit. But when we consider the difficulty of keeping our best virtues free from self-blindness and self-love, and recollect the intolerance and fault-finding that usually blots social intercourse; and compare such with the degree of forbearance and imaginative sympathy, so to speak, which such a system necessitates, we must think highly of the generosity and self-abnegation of the man who regulated his conduct undeviatingly by it" (P. B. Shelley, *Essays*, 1: xxiv-xxv)

Are there like examples of "active imagination" in Mary Shelley's letters? If one were to accept the gossip of Lady Blessington (Byron 371-72), who did not personally know Mary Shelley, there certainly would be. Take, for example, the case in which Isabella and Richard Hoppner[3] believed a former servant's accusations that an affair between P. B. Shelley and Claire Clairmont resulted in the birth of the "Neapolitan child" (*LMWS* 1: 7 n.1, 147; 1 Jan. 1815, 18 June 1820). Mary Shelley absolutely denied the accusation and earnestly defended both Shelley and Clairmont in her two letters of 10 August 1821 (*LMWS* 1: 204-08), and in 1843, when she met the Hoppners again, she cut them entirely (*LMWS* 3: 58; 20 Feb. 1843). Speculation continues about the Neapolitan child and its mother, even suggesting that Mary Shelley was complicit in a cover-up. But evidence in support of Mary Shelley's truthfulness exists in a variety of sources, including the letters themselves. In 1843, while revisiting Naples, Mary Shelley wrote to Claire Clairmont of being comfortable there—except that the place "reminds me too much of Lerici for me not to feel a weight on my spirits" (*LMWS* 3: 73; 17 May 1843). We understand why reminders of Lerici where P. B. Shelley had drowned, would be "a weight" on her spirits. But certainly, if she associated Naples with scandalous conduct by Shelley and Clairmont, it would have been the source of unhappy memories in its own right.

Furthermore, both Godwin and Claire Clairmont (*CC* 2: 598) attested to Mary Shelley's fundamental truthfulness. Just as accumulated incidents raise doubts regarding P. B. Shelley's truthfulness, so they build confidence in Mary Shelley's. Her letters build a case for her candour about others and herself. Indeed, her occasional requests for the destruction of her letters demonstrate, if in a backhanded way, her candour within personal correspondence (as opposed to her writing for public consumption). The general reliability of letters obviously offers the editor significant insights into a subject's life and data for contextualizing her letters. The biographer benefits even more because the materials gained can be given far wider scope in a biography than in the editing of letters.

The question of truth, reliability, and fictionalization leads almost in a continuum to the third editorial quandary: the paradox of spaces. It exists alongside the four recognized components of editions: author, editor, reader, and publishing process, but the existence of this fifth component of editions of letters is seldom discussed. As I edited Mary Shelley's letters, and now, as I write a critical biography of her, the orneriness of the fifth component has insistently posed essential questions about the construction of an author's life: what is the impact of absent material on the comprehensive story, and how do editors deal with the gaps? In approaching the category of the missing letters, the editor must continue to be guided by what actually exists but also must find the means to acknowledge in some way letters that do not exist.

This fifth component is invariably present, and invariably baffling to editor and biographer because of its intangibility. It shadows, as surely as a copy-editor's blue ink, every collection of letters. The other challenges to any edition of letters are generally more tangible. The editor obtains permissions of heirs and libraries; locates letters (which may be in one collection or in a number of major and minor collections worldwide, as are Mary Shelley's); transcribes the letters, a process that entails any number of problems, including handwriting, deletions, missing dates, and unknown recipients; and finally analyzes their meaning and annotates them to the extent that he or she is able—and that space permits. But beyond these traditional challenges, each editor must at one point, or many, deal with the paradox of spaces. By this I mean that no matter how extensive a collection of letters may be, one may be sure that some letters, possibly as crucial as any of the materials located, have not been, or cannot be, found. In Mary Shelley's case, a large number of letters—or perhaps I should say "wordless letters"—exist in these spaces.

To detail the problem of this component, I will not only address my experience of editing the 1,267 Mary Shelley letters in *The Letters of Mary Wollstonecraft Shelley* and the twenty-four new Mary Shelley letters published in the *Keats-Shelley Journal* in 1997 but also draw on correspondence to Mary Shelley, auction records, and any number of blank spaces that feel as palpable as actual letters. Earlier, I explained the basic premise guiding the editing of Mary Shelley's "found" letters. When we approach the category of the missing letters, this guiding principle plays an equally important role.

I have identified four subgroups within the fifth component, which I will examine in turn:

1. Formerly missing letters that have surfaced
2. Large collections of letters that were written to major figures in a subject's life and can be demonstrated to have existed but— to date—remain unlocated
3. Small numbers of letters that were written to momentary friends or enemies and can be demonstrated to have existed but—to date—remain unlocated
4. Letters that can be demonstrated to have been destroyed.

As this list derives from the particular process of editing Mary Shelley's letters, there may well exist other missing categories, which should be included in a general consideration of the problem of missing letters.

1. Formerly Missing Letters

The most obvious and reassuring category of missing letters is that of the letters that surface, to an editor's chagrin, *after* publication of an edition, an occurrence as inevitable as manuscript words that are indecipherable or letter-owners who refuse publication. The twenty-four new Mary Shelley letters or segments published in the *Keats-Shelley Journal* illustrate the potential impact of such finds, even of letters that do not contain startling information that requires major reconsideration of the narrative of Mary Shelley's life.

The new letters, written between 1820 and 1846, allow corrections of earlier letters taken from copies and provide a variety of new details about Mary Shelley and her circle. The article canvasses these contributions, but it is useful to include here just a few examples: Mary Shelley's 7 March 1820 letter to Sophia Stacey, published in *LMWS* from a previously published version, here more fully sketches the Shelleys' daily lives and provides more information about Claire Clairmont; her new 1828 letters to John Bowring, editor of the *Westminster Review*, again demonstrate her intelligence and assertiveness as an author, profile the interaction of an author of the day and her publisher, and offer further details about the part she played in gathering information for Thomas Moore's *Life of Byron*. Letters to the Rev. Dionysius Lardner suggest that the essay on "Ercilla" in *Lives* may in fact have been written by Mary Shelley, adding one more work to her oeuvre. A number of letters illustrate her support of women whose own lives were marginalized through fiscal need or societal mores, which serves to confirm the self-depiction in her journal (561; 11 Feb. [1839]). In addition to these letters, a number have surfaced but have been resold into holdings in which they again have disappeared, leaving only auction catalogue snippets.

In total, the new letters unquestionably amplify what we know about Mary Shelley's life, particularly as an author. This first subcategory has the daily potential to be expanded through the appearance of letters in the remaining three categories of the fifth component, which might alter at least elements of Mary Shelley's story—even possibly restructure it—although the great quantity of materials already in the published letters and journals and other primary sources suggests that even dramatic information would recontextualize and/or shift some aspect of our understanding rather than prompt an overall reevaluation.

2. Unlocated Letters to Significant Correspondents

From the security of newly discovered letters, let us move on to consider unlocated letters to correspondents who were significant in her life. In each instance, either Mary Shelley's own letters or other sources give ample evidence that she corresponded extensively with Teresa Emilia Viviani; the Beauclerk family; the Robinson family; and, not the least significant, her father, William Godwin.

The close relationship of Viviani (*LMWS* 1: 162-66; 3 Dec. 1820) and the Shelleys has been documented by Mary Shelley's and P. B. Shelley's correspondence and other sources. Biographers have conjectured about the extent of P. B. Shelley's involvement with Viviani, some taking *Epipsychidion* as proof that he was in love with her and out of love with Mary Shelley. Mary Shelley appears to have summed up her own final feelings about "*la Italiana*" in a nursery rhyme that ends: "I gave her sugar candy, / But oh! the little naughty girl! / She asked me for some brandy[.] / Now turn . . . brandy into that wherewithall to buy brandy (& that no small sum *pero*) & you have [the] whole story of Shelley['s] Italian platonics" (*LMWS* 1: 223; 7 March 1822). This, and Mary Shelley's satirical short story "The Bride of Modern Italy" (*Tales* 32-42), has been characterized by critics as a jealous wife's reaction to her husband's new favourite. But Mary Shelley's initial reaction to Viviani was as favourable, and as affectionate, as P. B. Shelley's. She described the nineteen-year-old Viviani to Leigh

Hunt as a "beautiful" young girl "of great genius—who writes Italian with an elegance and delicacy to equal the best authors of the best Italian age" (*LMWS* 1: 165; 3 Dec. 1820).

For her part, Viviani's eleven or so located letters to Mary Shelley address her affectionately as "my beautiful Mary. / My dearest Sister," "My beloved Mary," and "My dear Sister and Friend," and refer to Mary Shelley's letters to her.[4] What might we learn from Mary Shelley's missing letters to Viviani? Almost certainly, they would shed new light on "The Bride of Modern Italy" and *Epipsychidion*. They would also amplify Mary Shelley's relationship with Viviani, her attitudes toward other women, and especially her attitude toward P. B. Shelley and other women; and they would possibly reveal more about both Shelleys' unconventional perspectives on the meaning of love and on love relationships.

The missing Beauclerk correspondence would be fascinating from a number of points of view. Correspondence with Gertrude Paul, née Beauclerk, might fill in the story of Mary Shelley's support of this friend, whose love affair defied convention but who ultimately reunited with her husband. Correspondence with George Beauclerk would tell more about Mary Shelley's friendships with men. The most significant correspondence would be that to and from Aubrey Beauclerk, with whom the widowed Mary Shelley apparently had a love relationship. Because Aubrey Beauclerk married Julia Robinson, it might also tell more about the Robinson family.

The Robinson documents are among the most important of those unlocated. For many years, Mary Shelley was a close friend of a number of the Robinsons, including Isabella Robinson, alias Mrs Walter Sholto Douglas. Locating correspondence from, to, or about Isabella Douglas could well tell us more about her "marriage" to Mary Diana Dods, in which Dods successfully posed as Mr Sholto Douglas, Robinson's "sposo," in an elite Anglo-French circle in Paris. Prosper Mérimée's letters to Mary Shelley that include information about "Mr. and Mrs. Douglas" are an example in point (Bennett and Little). While my edition of the letters (1: 533ff) and my book-length study, *Mary Diana Dods: A Gentleman and a Scholar,* discuss the details of this relationship, in which Mary Shelley's prominent involvement discloses so much about her, important unresolved questions await new evidence.

The last significant group of missing Mary Shelley letters is her letters to her father. We have only a handful of her many letters to Godwin. One is actually not to Godwin at all, but rather a postscript to a P. B. Shelley letter to Godwin asking for "Mamma to be so kind" as to purchase some gold band for "Willy's hat" (*LMWS* 1: 59; 7 Dec. 1817). The second is merely a quotation of one and a half lines in one of Godwin's letters (*LMWS* 1: 134; 14 March 1820). The third is once again a quotation, in one of Godwin's letters, from her letter of c. 20 July 1822, in which Mary Shelley discusses her feelings following P. B. Shelley's death (Henry Sotheran Catalogue [1923] 3: 401). The fourth is a brief note about Mary Shelley's fiscal straits, thus illustrating that even as she struggles to earn money, she is nevertheless lending it to others, in this case to Claire and Charles Clairmont, and undoubtedly continuing to supplement Godwin's own income (*LMWS* 2: 101; [?17 Jan. 1830]). The fifth is another brief note, written to Godwin and Mary Jane Godwin, regarding Mary Shelley's recovering health (*LMWS* 2: 187; [?April or June 1833]). Godwin made notes on this letter for his *Lives of the Necromancers*, which one suspects is the reason he preserved it. The sixth asks Godwin if he will return to Harrow with her the next day. Godwin jotted notes on "Speculations [Observations] on Man his Faculties and Their Operation" on this letter, again suggesting the reason it was kept (*LMWS* 2: 194; [?27 Sept. 1833]).

Godwin's many extant letters to Mary Shelley make it clear that they had an active interchange. What is missing? Not only her many letters to him from Italy but letters she almost certainly wrote between 17 May and 19 December 1811 when she attended Miss Caroline Petman's school at Ramsgate[5] and during 1812 and 1813-14[6] while she resided with the Baxter family in Dundee.

3. Unlocated Letters to Minor Figures

The category of missing letters also includes letters to momentary friends or enemies who received attention through one or two letters. An example is Col. Jeremiah Ratcliffe, with whom Mary Shelley apparently had a brief friendship in 1840. Her few letters referring to him indicate how deeply she became engaged in trying to aid him in the period in which he tragically lost his sanity.[7] And sometimes, a letter or two, such as the two written by Mary Diana Dods, or Mary Shelley's two letters referring to "David Lyndsay," Dods's literary pseudonym, can be the key to opening a biographical locked closet.

4. Destroyed Letters

The last category is letters known to have been destroyed, purposely or casually. Mary Shelley's letters to Godwin may well be in this category. It appears that Godwin, with few exceptions, simply didn't keep letters from his children. Moreover, only a few of Percy Florence Shelley's letters to his mother are extant. This fact raises the question of whether Mary Shelley, like the father whom she emulated in so many ways, did not keep them, or whether they were destroyed later, perhaps by Percy Florence or his wife, Jane Shelley.

The category of destroyed material obviously depends on evidence of existence in the first place, which often disappears along with the document. How many instances are there, for example, like those in which P. B. Shelley "rigged out a flotilla" of paper boats "from any unfortunate letters he happened to have in his pocket" (Peacock 2: 338)?

Some material leaves a trail. For example, in May 1851, Percy Florence Shelley's attorney, John Gregson, sent him sheets of a Sotheby catalogue announcing the sale of Mary Shelley and P. B. Shelley materials, with the judgment that nine of the letters, but particularly three, should be purchased and burned.[8] At the auction on 19 May, Gregson purchased eleven letters on behalf of the Shelleys for £57.15.0, which he described as an exorbitant cost, but less than the price of an injunction. Several of these do appear to be missing, while others that he recommended for destruction are extant.

Unquestionably, Mary Shelley, and then her son and daughter-in-law, attempted to remove family letters, some of which were illegally obtained, from the public forum. Her 1846 letter to Thomas Medwin expresses her determination to keep certain matters private in the interests of Ianthe Esdaile (P. B. Shelley and Harriet Shelley's daughter)— and tacitly, of Percy Florence Shelley. She repeated to Medwin what she had written in the Preface to the *Poetical Works*: "the time has not yet come to recount the events of my husband's life." Her reflections on "the time" also reveal the narrowness of early Victorian society. (In fact, English society was "Victorian" even before Queen Victoria came to the throne, a judgment that Mary Shelley's letters support as early as the 1820s.) She asserts, "In modern society there is no injury so great as dragging private names and private life before the world. . . . In these publishing, inquisitive, scandalmongering days, one feels called upon for a double exercise of delicacy, forbearance—and reserve" (*LMWS* 3: 284; [?13-16 May 1846]). In this example of familial censorship, there is a clear conflict between the public desire for knowledge and the personal desire for privacy, an issue that is often shaped by the mores of the age—and one that each editor and biographer must face.

Obviously, Mary Shelley's correspondence to and from Aubrey Beauclerk, Isabella Robinson, and Mary Diana Dods, among others, may have been destroyed because of the secrets it might have revealed to the embarrassment of their Victorian families. Certainly we have evidence that biographers of the Shelleys who worked with Percy Florence and Jane Shelley made suggestions about materials they believed *should* be destroyed.[9] Still, it is also possible that in some attic. . . .

The clearest instances of destroyed Mary Shelley letters were the work of Mary Shelley herself. She asked Claire Clairmont on several occasions to burn her letters about matters she considered particularly troubling, and Clairmont assured her she had done so—but she didn't (*LMWS* 3: 255; 10 Nov. 1845). And in the most notorious destruction, at Mary Shelley's behest, the French police raided the home of the Italian expatriate Ferdinand Gatteschi in 1845, when he tried to use her letters to blackmail her (*LMWS* 3: 233-39; [13-14, 14, 15-16 Oct. 1845]). The police confiscated her letters and turned them over to Alexander Knox, her friend, who burned them. Or did he?

It seems appropriate to consider forgeries of letters along with letters that have disappeared, because although some forgeries may be complete fabrications, evidence points to the fact that a number of forgeries of Mary Shelley's letters are copies made from originals that have disappeared. Among these, we can identify the handiwork of George "Byron," whose career as a forger included letters allegedly by Byron (who he claimed was his father), Mary Shelley, and P. B. Shelley. In 1845-46, George Byron attempted to sell to Mary Shelley a series of letters purportedly by P. B. Shelley. Her eleven letters to Thomas Hookham, who represented her in dealing with George Byron, document a process whereby she attempted to purchase what she had reason to believe were actual P. B. Shelley letters that came into George Byron's possession on the death of a bookseller named John Wright on 25 February 1844.[10] Difficulty arose because he forged copies of the letters, including some already published, and successfully sold them to Mary Shelley; Percy Florence Shelley; William White, a bookseller, who sold some to the publisher John Murray; and Edward Moxon, who bought some at auction. In 1852, Moxon published a number of the purported "Shelley letters" with an introduction by Robert Browning. Upon the discovery that the letters were forgeries, Moxon removed the volume from circulation.

George Byron's abilities as a forger have resulted in much confusion about the authenticity of a number of P. B. Shelley and Byron letters, and at least one Mary Shelley letter, dated 17 December 1816. Theodore G. Ehrsam[11] contended that this letter was a total forgery (189). In contrast, Kenneth Neill Cameron argued the letter was genuine, based on someone else's careful examination of the manuscript at the Bodleian (White et al. 99). I was pleased to verify its authenticity through first-hand examination (*LMWS* 1: 24-26).

The challenge of forged letters for editors and biographers is obvious. In the case of the Shelley letters, including those of the collector and expert (and forger!) Thomas J. Wise himself, the forgeries add further to the question of which letters are missing and which never existed in the first place. For example, some forgeries go unnoted, passing into the corpus of accepted, authentic letters. Two such letters are at the Henry Ransom Center for Research at Austin. These letters appear to be in accord with Mary Shelley's interaction with the publisher William Galignani in 1829, when he was preparing his edition of *The Works of Coleridge, Shelley, and Keats*, with Mary Shelley's secret assistance (*LMWS* 2: 86, 99; [?3 Sept. 1829], 8 Jan. [1830]). Galignani, as with his other publications, used pirated materials. One might assume that Mary Shelley would be resistant to the project, but from her perspective, it allowed the publication and dissemination of Shelley's works that his father's injunction had forbidden her to publish (*LMWS* 1: 386-87 n.2; 18 Sept. [1823]). Her role in the 1829 volume included commenting on the introduction, with its rather frank depiction of her elopement with P. B. Shelley, and supplying her own pencil sketch of P. B. Shelley. Correspondence exists regarding the edition from Mary Shelley to Cyrus Redding, who served as intermediary, and to Galignani. The difficulty is that the two known letters to Galignani are, despite their authentic postage marks and contemporary watermarks, not written by Mary Shelley. Their script suggests they may have been traced from the originals. The letters remain at the Research Center as by Mary Shelley, but accompanied by a note suggesting that I question their authenticity; and after all, they may, despite their inauthenticity as originals, be useful to the biographer as authentic copies.

To all this, I am tempted to add a passing reference to all of the letters I imagine Mary Shelley thought to write, but changed her mind about because she felt too strongly, or not strongly enough, about the subject. But this is to wander off into the realm of fiction, a terrain pleasant enough to visit but quicksand for an editor or biographer.

Let us, then, return to the initial question of letters and biography, and the problems of candour and of absent material that are vital challenges for the editor of letters and for the biographer. Mary Shelley, as editor and in her biographical notes to her 1839 editions of P. B. Shelley, was acutely aware of those challenges. Her letters following Shelley's death trace her own efforts throughout the remainder of her life to collect his letters, some of which she later included in *Essays*. She also drew on those letters as an archival resource; for example, when writing *The History of a Six Weeks' Tour* and *Rambles*, she specifically asked for the return of letters for that purpose.[12] After Godwin's death, when she agreed to prepare a (never completed) biography of her father to benefit her stepmother, she corresponded with a network of his friends to gather those letters as well.[13] She was obviously aware both of the facts that letters reveal and of their importance in suggesting an individual's interactions with his or her correspondents. Furthermore, for biographies of authors, letters may also work as an index of an author's progress on a project, efforts to publish, joys, ambitions, and frustrations, about individual works and his or her career in general. Certainly, this is true of both Shelleys' letters. But even more than this, an edition of letters can provide great insights into the psyche of an author, consciously and unconsciously revealed.

In the end, then, letters provide an invaluable biographical infrastructure for understanding the works and life of an author. But only if editors and biographers manage, in a sense, to "go missing" themselves can the letters serve their purpose. Only through striving to explore the subject's intelligence, perspectives, sensibilities, oddities, and flaws objectively, through a complete reading of available sources—as Mary Shelley said, with all the correctness possible[14]—will an edition or biography reflect the complexity of a life, documented, proven, incongruous, and finally, biographically imagined. In one of her letters, Mary Shelley made a self-revealing statement about correctness that seems an appropriate last word for editor and biographer: "although I bestow little value on correctness by itself, I like it united to the genius and spirit of poetry" (*LMWS* 1: 76; 26 July 1818).

Notes

1   See, for example, *LMWS* 2: 89; 12 Nov. 1829.

2   For example, in 1819, the Shelleys remained in Florence for her research on *Valperga* (*LMWS* 1: 120-21 n.4; c. 13 Dec. 1819); when writing *Perkin Warbeck* she wrote to Thomas Crofton Croker for Irish sources (2: 65; 30 Oct. 1828) and to Sir Walter Scott for references to Scottish source material (2: 77-78; 25 May 1829). In 1825, she attended Parliament and revisited Virginia Water at Windsor for *The Last Man*. For her five volumes in Lardner's *Lives*, she wrote many letters to contemporaries, including Sir John Bowring and Gabriele Rossetti. And her editions of P. B. Shelley's work tell a story in themselves of her networking and her determination to present the public with volumes constructed largely from P. B. Shelley's very difficult handwriting, preserved in "Manuscript books—full of scraps of

finished or unfinished poems—half illegible" (*LMWS* 2: 330; 11 Nov. [1839]).

3   Richard Belgrave Hoppner (1786-1872) had been English consul general at Venice since 1814; Isabella was his Swiss-born wife. P. B. Shelley had met the Hoppners when he and Claire Clairmont went to see Allegra Byron, who, either at the Hoppners' suggestion or at Byron's request, was staying with them (*LMWS* 1: 79; [c. 13] Sept. 1818).

4   Eight letters appear in White, *Shelley* 2: 466-84, drawn from *Shelley and Mary,* Lady Jane Shelley, ed. and Dowden. The manuscript letters are in the Bodleian.

5   Godwin's journal indicates he wrote to her on 20 July, 28 August, and 13 September 1811.

6   For her first visit, she left London on 7 June 1812 and returned on 10 November 1812. She left for her second visit on 3 June 1813 and returned on 30 March 1814.

7   *LMWS* 2: 341-42, 3: 5; 10-12 March 1840, 26 Oct. [1840], respectively.

8   Abinger Manuscripts, Bodleian Library, Shelley Adds. c. 11.

9   See Metcalf; White et al.; and Thurman.

10   See *LMWS* 3: 245, 248, 250-51, 258, 278-79, 280, 282-83, 297; 28 Oct. [1845], 30 Oct. [1845], [?3 Nov. 1845], [20-22 Nov. 1845], [?27 Feb. 1846], [?3 March 1846], [?11 March 1846], 12 Sept. [1846], respectively.

11   See Smith with Schlegel et al. 109-12; Ehrsam 189.

12   See for example, *LMWS* 1: 19n1; 17 May 1816; and 3: 1-4; 20 July [1840].

13   See Judith Barbour's essay in this volume, pp. 139-57.

14   P. B. Shelley, *Poetical Works* 1: vii.

Reflections on Writing
Mary Shelley's Life

Anne K. Mellor

In 1988, in my biographical study of the life and fiction of Mary Shelley, *Mary Shelley: Her Life, Her Fiction, Her Monsters*, I argued that we could best understand Shelley's fiction, and in particular her most famous novel, *Frankenstein*, by placing it in the context of her specific historical and psychological experiences. I also argued that we could read her life and her fiction as, in some meaningful way, "representative" of the specific constraints and concerns imposed upon the women of Britain by the social construction of gender in the early nineteenth century. Here I would like to reflect upon the problematic assumptions that lay behind these two arguments.

First, I would like to ask whether it is ever possible to determine the "particular historical and psychological experiences" that constitute the actual life of the biographical subject. Can the biographer ever achieve what Marc Pachter calls for in his introduction to *Telling Lives: The Biographer's Art*, the ability "to know the true shape of another's experience, to capture it in the face of all resistance" (7-8)? Or, as Hayden White has argued most vigorously in his *Metahistory*, are historical "facts" always already encoded within a master narrative or plot? Since I am not competent to address this question at a general level, I would like to respond to it only in relation to my ways of accounting for Mary Shelley's life and its reflection in her fiction. Specifically, I want to explore the degree to which my personal experiences and current ideological commitments framed the context and determined my interpretation of Shelley's life and fiction.

My description of Shelley's life was based on as much archival and published material as I could consult—on her journal, letters, unpublished and hitherto unanalyzed manuscripts in the Abinger Shelley Collection in the Bodleian Library, and all her published work (stories, essays, travel writings, poems, and novels), as well as on the published and unpublished documents of her father, William Godwin, her mother, Mary Wollstonecraft, her husband, Percy Shelley, and such members of their circle as Claire Clairmont, Edward Trelawny, Lord Byron, Leigh Hunt, and Maria Reveley. I argued that, as a child, Mary Wollstonecraft Godwin felt an "excessive & romantic attachment" (her words) to her father and was tormented by the fear that he would abandon her. As she later confessed to Jane Williams, "Until I knew Shelley I may justly say that [my father] was my God—& I remember many childish instances of the excess of attachment I bore for him" (*LMWS* 2: 215, 1: 296). Mary Shelley's intense devotion to her father may be explained in part by the fact that her mother died in childbirth, and her primary caregiver during her infancy, her nanny Louisa Jones, was abruptly dismissed by Godwin when Mary was three years old. But even before Louisa's departure, Mary's anxiety about Godwin's love for her surfaces in a revealing comment Godwin wrote to Louisa on 11 July 1800, when he was away in Ireland: "Tell Mary I will not give her away, and she shall be nobody's little girl but papa's" (11 July 1800, qtd. in Paul 1: 364-65). Mary's fear of abandonment was further intensified during her childhood, I suggested, by her estrangement from her step-mother, who favoured her own children over Mary in the Godwin household, and by her father's decision to send her, when she was fourteen years old, to Scotland to stay for two years with a family she did not know, the William Baxters of Dundee.

I argued in my book that this childhood experience of abandonment, both by mother and by father, was autobiographically encoded in the life of Victor Frankenstein's creature. From this perspective, *Frankenstein* can be read as the story of what happens when a man like Godwin tries to have a baby without a woman, of his failure to parent his child, and of the consequences, of the ways in which his abandoned child becomes a monster. The creature, rejected by all whom he has tried to serve—from the drowning girl to the De Lacey family to the small boy he wished to adopt—either inadvertently or deliberately kills the innocent, blue-eyed, blond-haired William Frankenstein.

I have argued that this narrative is Mary Shelley's psycho-autobiography, a retelling of her own childhood experience of paternal abandonment, of her personal conviction that she had been forever shut out from a loving family (whether the Godwin household or the Baxter family, whose warm mutual love she so envied), and of her most painful recognition—to use a modern idiom—that an abandoned, abused, and battered child can easily become a battering parent. The name of the Creature's first victim, William, must have been powerfully resonant for Mary: it is the name of the half-brother who displaced her as the favoured child in the Godwin household, it is the name of the father who abandoned her, and—most troubling—it is the name she had given only one year earlier to her own son, who possessed the same blue eyes and blond curls she assigned to William Frankenstein. At the psychological level, I suggested, the murder of William Frankenstein—in which Mary Shelley in effect imagines murdering her own son—records her horrified recognition that an unloved child can become an adult capable of destroying his or her own child.

After Mary Godwin's elopement at the age of sixteen with the married poet Percy Shelley, Godwin became even more estranged from his daughter. He accused her of "committing a crime" (even though he had himself married two unwed mothers) and refused to see or correspond with her (even though he continued to write to Percy Shelley to demand money). He did not communicate with her directly for two and a half years, not until after her marriage to Percy in December 1816. And when Mary Shelley's three-year-old son William died in Rome of malaria—he was the third of her three children to die, and his death cast her into a deep and enduring depression—Godwin took up his pen to write her what must be one of the most heartless letters on record:

> I cannot but consider it as lowering your character in a memorable degree, and putting you among the commonality and mob of your sex, when I had thought you to be ranked among those noble spirits that do honour to our nature. Oh! what a falling off is here! . . . you have lost a child; and all the rest of the world, all that is beautiful, and all that has a claim upon your kindness, is nothing, because a child of three years old is dead! (9 Sept. 1819; Jane Shelley 1: 410A)

Mary Shelley responded to Godwin's cruelty, I have suggested, by writing "Mathilda," her story of father-daughter incest, in which the incestuous father, after declaring his irresistible passion for his eighteen-year-old daughter, commits suicide, an act anticipated by Mathilda in her dream the night before. In this tale Mary Shelley articulated her profound ambivalence toward her father: her contradictory and deeply repressed desires both to possess her father's love completely and at the same time to punish him to the death for his abandonment of her.

The question that I now wish to pose is this. Did I emphasize Mary Shelley's passionate but frustrated love for her father, and Godwin's lack of paternal love for his only biological daughter—an emphasis that earlier accounts of Mary Shelley's life and especially of Godwin's life had not given (or even allowed as a possibility)—*because* of my own experiences? Did I respond overly intensely—and perhaps disproportionately—to the documented instances of Godwin's unconcern for or hostility to Mary, and wilfully ignore other instances of his paternal love and support for her? Godwin did compliment Mary, for instance, on the "vigour" of her writing in *Frankenstein*—even as he kept the profits from the novel for himself. As that last comment indicates, I have a very hard time seeing Godwin in a positive light as the father of this daughter, however kind he may have been to Fanny Imlay and his other children. Did I respond in this way because my own childhood relationship with my father was extremely conflicted? Because my father clearly preferred my sibling, my younger sister? Because after my father divorced my mother when I was eighteen in order to marry his mistress, he intentionally abandoned his first family and has seen me only three times in the last thirty years? As a close friend and former colleague once said to me, "A woman who loved and felt close to her father would write a different book on Mary Shelley."

If this is the case, then perhaps we need to revise Roland Barthes's trenchant statement about biography. Barthes called biography "a novel that dare not speak its name" (*Mythologies* 73), and Carolyn Heilbrun, in *Writing a Woman's Life*, has insistently reminded us that all biographies are fictions. But perhaps it would be more accurate to say that all biographies are *autobiographies* that dare not speak their name.

I want to return to the theoretical implications of this, but let me first consider another question. To what degree was my account of Mary Shelley's life further shaped by my political commitment to feminism? My involvement in the academic discipline of women's studies was the determining factor in my initial decision to write a study of Mary Shelley's life and fiction. I had been trained as a specialist in British romanticism, and had before 1980 worked exclusively on male writers. Inspired by the successes of the women's movement in the United States both in the political and the social spheres, in 1980 I decided to devote the rest of my career to studying and teaching feminist theory and women writers in my field of specialization. I chose Mary Shelley rather than Jane Austen or Mary Wollstonecraft because in 1980 far less was known about Shelley's life and writing career; *Frankenstein* was rarely taught in colleges and universities, except in isolated classes on science fiction. And the manuscript of *Frankenstein* had never been edited, hardly even looked at by scholars. My decision to explore Shelley's life and fiction was thus motivated by a wish to broaden the canon of British romantic literature taught in the academic curriculum. I also wanted to understand better what it was like to be an intelligent woman living and writing in the early nineteenth century.

But did these self-consciously feminist motivations also produce in me an increased—and, some might say, unwarranted—sensitivity to the ways in which the power of the father might have manifested itself even in Mary Shelley's avowedly radical and unorthodox family? Did my political concern with the subtle coercions of patriarchal social institutions—many of which I had encountered in my own academic career—overly bias my response to Godwin's interactions with his daughter? Did this feminist engagement predetermine my reading of *Frankenstein* as the failure of *fathering* rather than, as male psychoanalytic critics such as Paul Sherwin and Neil Rudenstein had argued, the failure of *mothering*? Was this why I devoted the final section of my book to a study of father-daughter relationships in all of Shelley's fiction, focusing especially on the incestuous patterns revealed in "Mathilda," *Lodore,* and *Falkner*?

Obviously, the answer is yes. My contemporary awareness of the high degree of child abuse and father-daughter incest in families across all class and ethnic groups in Britain and North America sensitized me to the recurrent pattern of dominant fathers and motherless daughters who feel compelled to play the loving wife as well as daughter in these three novels. Nonetheless, I would argue that Mary Shelley's version of the courtship plot, in which an older man who is separated from his wife or mistress becomes obsessively fond of a young girl (either his daughter or an adopted child) who then grows up to marry a younger version of this man, accurately represents the fundamental structure of the bourgeois family in early-nineteenth-century England. By reading Shelley's later novels, which in 1996 were reprinted in toto for the first time by Pickering and Chatto, we can see that, with remarkable clarity and prescience, she uncovered the historical existence of what Freud would later call the family romance, the dynamic through which infant boys and girls learn to map their sexual desires onto their parents, thus eroticizing the patriarchal structure of the bourgeois nuclear family.

I would now ground this argument not so much on Freud's writings as on the large body of sociological research published by both British social historians and women's historians in the last decade. I am thinking in particular of the superb work done by J. H. Plumb and his disciples John Brewer, Colin Campbell, and Jonathan Barry on the growth of a capitalist consumer culture in England in the eighteenth century; of Gerald Newman's and Linda Colley's work on the development of a British national identity; and of Leonore Davidoff and Catherine Hall's trackings in *Family Fortunes,* and Hall's in *White, Male and Middle-Class*, of the increasing dominance of a bourgeois domestic ideology that relegated women to a private sphere as mothers, homemakers, and consumers of household goods. This historical research has provided extensive documentary evidence that early-nineteenth-century British women were socialized to be economically and psychologically dependent on men. We now have ample evidence that many daughters were the product of what Mary Shelley in *Lodore* so revealingly called "a sexual education" (218). As Shelley's Lord Lodore articulates this Rousseauistic theory of female education, he "fashioned his offspring to be the wife of a frail human being, and instructed her to be yielding, and to make it her duty to devote herself to his happiness, and to obey his will" (218).

Moreover, Mary Shelley's own life-long dependence on men—first on William Godwin, then on Percy Shelley and, after his death, on his sacred memory—itself becomes another historical example of the pervasiveness of this domestic ideology. As she insisted, she possessed "the woman's love of looking up & being guided, & being willing to do anything if any one supported & brought me forward" (15 Oct. 1838, *JMS* 555). Her novels can thus be read not only as psychological explorations but also as social facts, as further historical evidence for the existence of a cultural ideology that advocated male dominance of the public sphere.

As I reflect here upon the degree to which my political commitment to feminism influenced my interpretation of Mary Shelley's relationships and creative work, I turn finally to what may be the most lasting contribution of feminist theory to human knowledge, what is now called stand-point theory, a form of feminist epistemology. In brief, stand-point theory assumes that no individual human being can attain "objective" truth. This theory accepts the argument of Marxist and postmodernist theory, the neo-Kantian argument that all human perceptions are linguistically mediated, shaped by what Foucault has called the discourse of the episteme or what Thomas Kuhn has called the "matrix" of our culture. We can phrase our questions and our answers only in terms of the linguistic usages available to us in a particular time and place; no absolute ontological truth expressed in a perfectly transparent language is possible.

Feminist epistemologists such as Nancy Hartsock, Sandra Harding, Mary Hawkesworth, Evelyn Fox Keller, and Genevieve Lloyd have taken this argument one step further. Our apprehensions of the external world are mediated, not just by language, but more precisely by the sum total of our uniquely individual experiences of the material world, by the specific ideological investments we embody as the consequence of our particular gender, class, ethnicity, sexual orientation, age, education, personality, and so forth. As Sandra Harding has argued most trenchantly, the scientific claim that a value-neutral and empirically verifiable "objectivity" can be achieved is at best a claim for what she tellingly calls "weak" objectivity. It rests on the mere repeatability of certain experiments or thought processes according to rules or methods that are themselves the product of a particular group of historically and socially situated agents, for instance scientists, usually male, with the academic credentials required to gain access to private or state-supported funding, expensive research labs, and highly developed technology.

In opposition, she argues, one is able to achieve a "strong" objectivity with far greater explanatory power by recognizing that "the subject of knowledge" must "be placed on the same critical, causal plane as the objects of knowledge" (Harding 69). In other words, we must subject our selves to the same rigorous analysis that we bring to the texts and historical lives that we study. We must acknowledge our own ideological investments and life experiences as we write. That her view has now gained wide academic acceptance is witnessed by the explosion of recent autobiographical criticism by literary scholars and art historians, from Alice Kaplan's *French Lessons: A Memoir* (1993) to Frank Lentricchia's *The Edge of Night* (1994), from Marianna De Marco Torgovnick's *Crossing Ocean Parkway: Readings by an Italian American Daughter* (1994) to Eunice Lipton's *Alias Olympia* (1994). As David Simpson has recently observed, we now have a historical "culture" of autobiographical criticism that is "inescapable, and not at all open to dismissal from some high point of disinterested inspection" (82).

But this establishment of what the academic journal *Lingua Franca* in 1996 called "the *Moi* school of criticism" has raised as many theoretical and pragmatic problems as it has solved. As Aram Veeser commented in his Introduction to *Confessions of the Critics*, a distinguished collection of essays on this topic, we now need "new rules" for such confessional criticism (xi). The practice of such criticism has to date consistently revealed a great deal more about the writer than about the supposed "subject" of his or her investigations. In writing what Kathryn Kendall has termed a "duography" of the eighteenth-century British woman of letters and possible lesbian Catherine Trotter Cockburn, Kendall in fact—as is typical in this genre—tells us much about what this writer has meant to her, but relatively little about what the same writer might mean to other readers. As she rightly concludes, "I have taken Catherine Trotter Cockburn into myself and merged with her" (Kendall 281).

How then might we write a "feminist literary biography" that would respect and preserve the *otherness* of the biographical subject while at the same time acknowledging the positionality of the biographer? Rather than "abducting" the biographical subject—the metaphor of violent and narcissistic appropriation explored by William H. Epstein in his analysis both of Norman Mailer's *Marilyn* and his own use of Marilyn Monroe to further his academic career—we must always remember that the reader cares, not about us or our (often rather predictable, even boring) lives and emotions, but about our subject's life and works ("(Post)Modern Lives"). At the same time, however, we must reveal to readers enough about our own subjective experiences and responses to enable them to *evaluate* our interpretations of the subject's life. We should do this as tersely as possible, with rhetorical tact, and without indulging a narcissistic desire for complete or unnecessary self-disclosure. We might in fact limit such personal revelations to the notes, to an introductory or, perhaps better yet, a concluding section, or at most to an occasional interruption in the text of the biography.

If we do this, we make it possible for readers with different life experiences and political commitments to reshape the lives we have written as they read. This is what I have been trying to do in this essay, perhaps belatedly, although I think attentive readers of my book on Mary Shelley might well have done it for themselves. What I am now defending as the ground of the most honest and useful social knowledge that we as biographers, literary critics, and scholars can produce is a *dialogic* model of biographical writing, similar to the model of feminist dialogic *reading* so brilliantly developed by Patrocinio Schweickart. As we work we must sustain an ongoing, never-ending dialogue between the object of knowledge, our selves, and the reader, exercising the same dialogic imagination that Bakhtin located at the heart of the nineteenth-century novel.

I hope it is clear that I am promoting not a wilful "subjectivity" but rather a "strong objectivity" grounded on the recognition that *all* accounts of the external world, of material reality, of the "other," are positional, situated, and culturally mediated. What we as scholars and critics owe that other, in this case the biographical object or literary text, is intellectual honesty. As biographers, we must never knowingly suppress evidence that does not fit the shape of the life we are constructing. We must acknowledge that other interpretations, developed from other positions, are plausible. And we must present as much of the evidence as is practicable within the constraints of publishers' word-limits and coherent narratives. In Clifford Geertz's terms, we must give as thick a description as is possible of our biographical object (6-28). That description will tell a life/story and thus, to return to Hayden White's claim, will always already be shaped by the culturally determined conventions that govern narrative structure, plausible characterization, and the representation of a reliable narrator. I would qualify Hayden White's arguments in only two ways. The new convention of the reliable narrator, in contemporary biographical and critical writing, now requires that we be as openly self-revealing as possible with our readers, telling them what they need to know *about us* so that they can evaluate our judgments within the context of *their* different experiences and commitments. Secondly, as Sharon O'Brien has perceptively noted, such a "double-voiced" conversation precludes narrative closure: other tellings of the same life/story are not only possible but inevitable. Yet I believe that only out of this double dialogue, between biographer and biographical object on the one side, and between biographer and reader on the other, can come the shaping of a life that seems both honest and meaningful.

Caves of Fancy[1]

Rose Scollard

Act One

The stage is draped over with grey, filmy material. The effect is abstract and dreamy, the furniture under the drapery making unidentifiable but provocative shapes. Laughter off. MARY *runs on, followed by her half-sister* FANNY *and her stepsister* CLAIRE. *They enter exuberantly but quickly assume a solemn demeanour. There is a quality of ceremony to their speech and movements as* MARY *draws them into her fantasy.*

The First Resurrection

MARY   It's a descent, that's how I think of it, a tunnelling down to that sweet treasure dome. I find nourishment there. No matter what misfortune may strike, there will be consolation and strength, I'm sure of that. My mother is the key—my way down.

FANNY   Mother.

MARY   The torch of self-knowledge by which I rout my demons.

CLAIRE   Mother.

MARY   My phantasmagoria.

CLAIRE   She said, "I love man as my fellow, but his sceptre does not extend to me."

Notes are on pp. 292-93.

FANNY   She said, "Strengthen the female mind and there will be an
           end to blind obedience."
MARY   She said, "It is time for a revolution in female manners—
           time to restore their lost dignity and make them a part of the
           human species."[2]
MARY   Because of her, we will never be slaves or sexual playthings.
CLAIRE   Because of her, we will never give up freedom and inde-
           pendence for the sake of reputation.
MARY   In the name of Romance—
FANNY   Adventure—
CLAIRE   Passion—

*They appear by their gestures to be conjuring something or some-
one. Nothing happens.*

FANNY   It didn't work.
CLAIRE   It's been too long.
MARY   No! Wait! She said, "Imagination is the true fire, stolen from
           heaven, to animate this cold creature of clay."
CLAIRE   In the name of imagination!
MARY   Imagination!
FANNY   Imagination!

*As they murmur repeatedly the word "imagination" there is a
stirring, and the drapery covering the set begins to rise. It forms
a tent-like canopy over the stage and creates for the audience the
effect of being in a tent or airy cavern. The stage area is a simple
rectangle surrounded on three sides by the audience. The fourth
recedes off into the darkness of the backstage area. The furnish-
ings are simple: a chaise longue at the front; two chairs; a clothes
rack holding costume changes at the back; a large trunk beside
the rack; a small make-up table with mirror, also at the back.
There is a large, grey table centre stage and as the canopy rises
we discover stretched out on it the figure of the CREATURE. The
young women warily approach this figure.*

FANNY   *[Pause]* Is it?
MARY   I'm not sure.
CLAIRE   Then who?
MARY   I don't know.

*The CREATURE groans, struggles, and lurches to a half-sitting posi-
tion. The women retreat a little as the CREATURE sits up. He is*

wearing a ragged military redcoat over stays and blue trousers. He groans again.

FANNY   It's her. I *know* it is.

CREATURE   Half revived, half rotting away. . . .

FANNY   Mother?

CLAIRE   It's gone wrong, hasn't it.

CREATURE   This is your father's fault. He made a monster of me.

FANNY   He made you an angel in our midst.

CREATURE   A cadaver in your midst.

CLAIRE   We learned everything from you.

CREATURE   Yes. I showed you how to be good little corpses. The cadaverously silent little Godwins.

FANNY   Are you really our mother?

CREATURE   Don't I look motherly?

FANNY   You're too raggedy.

CREATURE   As if she wasn't raggedy. Stitched together out of decaying memories, little scraps of writing, furtive hopes. Your first fabrication. A raggedy lie.

MARY   Come away from him, Fanny!

CREATURE   And you were counterfeit as well *[overrides their objections]*, put-together little girls in the image of a dead mother—a pastiche of little temptations, little weaknesses, things that hardly matter. Little desires. *[Touches* MARY's *hair]*

MARY   Don't!

CREATURE   Your mother knew all about desires. Your father was a monk until he met her, a celibate, naive fool. He wore a yellow waistcoat and blushed when a woman came into the room. But she awakened his appetites.

MARY draws back in distaste.

CREATURE   Yes, she did. Again and again. He loved it so much he kept a record of it. Mary knows, don't you, Mary? You figured out all those mysterious ciphers in his journals, every last pinch and tweak.[3] That's why he churned out his memoir, to revive those juicy feelings.

MARY   He wrote it to inform the public about a great woman.

CREATURE   He wrote it to get an erection, and the public knew it. They saw that what he had brought to life was a monster, a whore in blue stockings.

FANNY   You're making my head ache!

MARY   We don't need that disgusting kind of talk.

CREATURE   And you're such a little nun, I suppose? All that gallivanting in St Pancras churchyard,[4] chasing Shelley round my headstone.

MARY   *Your* headstone! You're not my mother!

CREATURE   I'm not?

MARY   *[Uncertain]* Well, if you are, I wasn't gallivanting. I went there to read your books and honour your memory.

CREATURE   And fuck Shelley.

MARY   No!

CREATURE   He seduced you on my grave, didn't he?

MARY   Shelley *adored* you.

CREATURE   Of course he did. It was really me he was trying to fuck. And I wanted it. I reached up from the grave and held you while he did it to you.

MARY   Don't!

CREATURE   And to complete the picture—your Papa riding his back. A rampant eight-legged beast, the four of us panting together, panting and writhing, and panting and . . .

MARY   You're disgusting!

CLAIRE   Imposter!

The CREATURE notices the audience.

CREATURE   Ah! I knew you couldn't stay away. You heard the word *phantasmagoria* and your minds immediately dipped into horrid and delicious suppositions. Am I right? You came to see what I would be like, made up from all those horrid bits and pieces, those charnel-house scraps resurrected.

MARY   And for your information I am not a counterfeit. I'm real and up to the minute! Shelley chose me, didn't he? All the lovers he could have had and he chose *me*!

I remember the exact moment he asked me to go away with him. I was wearing a new dress, green and red tartan, and I felt so alive underneath it, just shivering with life, as if my skin had eyes, my skin seeing the soft honeyed marble and the green dancing grass and Shelley looking at me. I shivered and there was a hot rushing sound in my ears. It was my destiny.

CREATURE   And you acted out your destiny right there on your mother's grave.

MARY   Get out of here! Leave us alone!

CREATURE   Scrappy little thing, isn't she? It's true—Shelley fell for her the minute he set eyes on her. But it wasn't for her sleek head and saucy manner. It was her incandescent parents—Godwin and Wollstonecraft, the Philosopher and the Feminist. To an up-and-coming young poet, like Shelley, in-laws like that were an irresistible dowry.

MARY   Shelley loved me for myself.

FANNY   It was me he came to see those first visits.

CLAIRE   He wrote a poem about me. "Thy voice slow rising like a Spirit lingers / O'ershadowing it with soft and lulling wings."

FANNY   I had special things to tell him. Going to Sweden with my mother.

CLAIRE   That's in her book. Shelley can read.

FANNY   But I *remember* it. Standing with my mother on that lonely shore.[5]

CLAIRE   All in the book. Nobody needs *you* to picture it, Fanny. The romantic mother with child in a wild landscape. The wind disarranging her hair.

CREATURE   Ah yes, they all want to be that mother. To claim her glory. . . .

CLAIRE   To claim her strength.

CREATURE   But Fanny was Wollstonecraft's love child, her pedigree stained. And Claire was no relation at all to the great woman, except in her mind—a sort of self-declared, posthumous stepchild.

CLAIRE   She taught me to love the word *woman*.

FANNY   She taught me to love the word *mother*.

MARY   *[Gathering them in]* She taught me that anything is possible. We will resurrect her in our hearts and we will dare to claim everything we can imagine.

CREATURE   Dreamers every one. No money, no power, too studious and outspoken for their own good, and yet they still hope to achieve all those things young women long for.

Forgetting the CREATURE, MARY, CLAIRE and FANNY fling themselves on the chaise longue and imagine their futures.
While they speculate the CREATURE takes a white cloak from the costume rack and folds it into a small baby-like bundle.

FANNY   Romance.

CLAIRE   Adventure.

FANNY   Children.

MARY	Fame.
CLAIRE	And sex.
MARY	All of it. Adventure, children, fame . . .
CLAIRE	Adventure, children, fame, and sex.
FANNY	You can't have it all, though.
MARY	Why not?
FANNY	Well . . . because.
MARY	I will. By the time I'm twenty at the latest. I already have Shelley, Europe, our book nearly finished . . .
CREATURE	*[Moving closer]* A paltry little travelogue.
MARY	My baby almost here *[pats her stomach]*.
FANNY	Mother died having you.
MARY	Well I don't mean to die. Adventure, children, fame . . .
CLAIRE	Sex . . .
FANNY	*[Looking at the* CREATURE, *who has moved very close]* And . . . death.

The CREATURE *steps forward with the bundle and, reaching over* MARY's *head, places it in her arms.*

Death of an Unnamed Daughter[6]

FANNY and CLAIRE are conversing. MARY *has moved away and sits apart, holding her little bundle, lost in grief and introspection.*

MARY	Death.
CREATURE	Her first baby.
MARY	She was perfectly well when I went to bed.
CREATURE	They think it was convulsions.
MARY	I dreamt it came to life again. We rubbed it by the fire and it lived.
CREATURE	The reversal of death—a dizzying thought. To renew life where death has consigned the body to corruption. *[Takes the bundle from* MARY's *arms]*
MARY	I keep thinking if there was some little thing you could put into it, some little functioning part, my baby would turn over and smile up at me.

The CREATURE *shakes out the bundle with a flourish. It's empty.*

FANNY	How is she?
CLAIRE	Brooding in her room, filling her journal with gloomy thoughts.

FANNY	I brought a cake *[keeping it from CLAIRE]*, for Shelley.
CLAIRE	Fanny! You're not wearing stays!
FANNY	I found them in Mother's trunk. They're exactly my size. Everyone says I'm just like her.
CLAIRE	So be like her. Ride horses! Row boats. Impress your intellect on strangers. But stays!
FANNY	There's nothing wrong with being neat and trim. You could tidy yourself up a bit.
CLAIRE	Freedom. It's about *freedom*, Fanny.
FANNY	It's not respectable going about half dressed.
CLAIRE	It's not respectable to be such a stick in the mud either. Oh I don't blame you. How can anyone be romantic in London! How can anyone be *remotely* romantic. Debts and riots and unrest and the wretched weather. Well, I'm going to escape it all, thank God.
FANNY	What are you talking about?
CLAIRE	Didn't they tell you? I'm going to Linley for a while.
FANNY	We don't know anyone in Linley. Who are you staying with?
CLAIRE	No one. I'm to live in a seaside cottage with jessamine and honeysuckle twining over the window, and a little downhill garden full of roses.
FANNY	You're making it up.
CLAIRE	The moon will shine in at my solitary window and I shall devote myself to philosophy and write my book.
FANNY	You're not writing a book.
CLAIRE	It's about a woman who commits every violence against received opinion.
FANNY	Sounds like you.
CLAIRE	Shelley thinks it's a wonderful idea.
FANNY	I'm sure.
CLAIRE	Why else would he arrange my retreat?
FANNY	*Shelley's* arranging it?
CLAIRE	He chose the cottage himself.
FANNY	But . . . *[Takes CLAIRE's news in, slowly and painfully]* It's not *fair*. Well it isn't! I have to be responsible for everything while you get cottages and roses and Shelley watching out for you.
CLAIRE	He only wants me to be happy.
FANNY	I'm twenty years old and all the doors are closing. Not that they ever opened.
CLAIRE	Oh Fanny, always so melancholy.
FANNY	It's not *fair*. *[Flings down her parcel and rushes out]*

CLAIRE picks up parcel as MARY *enters.*

MARY	I thought I heard Fanny.
CLAIRE	She's just run off in one of her fits. *[Opens cake]*
MARY	Poor Fanny.
CLAIRE	She thrives on gloom. *[Breaks off a piece of cake, pops it in her mouth]*
MARY	*[Sharing the cake]* Don't be so hard on her. She's taken on all the burdens we've abandoned. All of father's financial woes, the household tasks. And your mother isn't the kindest person in the world to her.
CLAIRE	And Shelley doesn't love her. *[Takes more cake]* That's the real cause of her woe.
MARY	Oh I hardly think so.
CLAIRE	She's obsessed with him. "I'm cross with Shelley for not mentioning his health." "What does Shelley think of the weather?" She's like a lovesick goose, running about, bringing him little sweets and cups of tea, hanging on every word just because he encourages her.
MARY	And how are you so different? Always clinging, always whispering.
CLAIRE	We joke with each other. I'm ruled by the comic muse. We can't all be sad sacks.
MARY	You go out with him every day. You walk to heaps of places while I have to stay here alone. Even today. This *morning*.
CLAIRE	*[Gently]* We were arranging the burial.
MARY	You have no idea what I'm going through.
CLAIRE	I do. I know what a loss you've had. I do know.
MARY	I can't wait till Friday.
CLAIRE	Friday. . . . No . . . you need me to take care of you, Mary.
MARY	Shelley will take care of me.
CLAIRE	How can you send me off like this? I wouldn't do it to you.
MARY	We've talked about it, Shelley and I. . . .
CLAIRE	*Ad nauseam.* I hear you up there in your room. Your little whining voice. "She's got to go! I can't bear it. Give me a garden and the absence of Claire or I will die!"
MARY	It will be good for you. You might meet someone or get a position.
CLAIRE	I don't want a position. I want *life*. And I'm not going to find it in some rain-soaked, gloomy town.
MARY	What happened to the honeysuckle and roses? And the little downhill garden?

CLAIRE   You were eavesdropping!

MARY   Honestly, the way you tormented poor Fanny.

CLAIRE   I didn't notice you coming in to take her part. Self-righteous prig! I don't know how Shelley puts up with you!

MARY   Shelley and I are soul-mates. We dream together; we write together.

CLAIRE   You don't realize that Shelley can't be bound to just one woman. He is a creature of the air. Of the universe. He's a spirit of the ether.

MARY   I am perfectly aware of Shelley's nature

CLAIRE   Then you know he'd be just as happy with twenty women gathered about him as one.

MARY   But we've never actually tested out the one, have we? You've been with us ever since we eloped together. You're always there. You never leave us alone for a minute.

CLAIRE   I just hope you'll find out one day how cruel it is to be without anyone.

MARY   I don't want you to be without anyone. I just want you to be without Shelley. Why don't you get your own poet. *[Sweeps out]*

CLAIRE   I intend to!

CREATURE   Poor Mary. Launched on her life of destiny and already things are going very wrong—a baby dead, her romantic lover writing poems to other women, her stepsister always in the way. Claire will be disposed of for a while, but she won't stay disposed of.

Assignation   ●

The CREATURE assumes a Byronic pose. CLAIRE is writing a letter.

CLAIRE   Claire Clairmont to Lord Byron. Sunday morning, April 1816, London.

    Lord Byron is requested to state whether seven o'clock this evening will be convenient to receive a lady on business of peculiar importance. She desires to be admitted alone and with the utmost privacy.

CREATURE   Lord Byron is not aware of any *importance* which can be attached by any person to an interview with him—and more particularly by one with whom he is not acquainted—He will, however, be at home at the hour mentioned.

FANNY enters and CLAIRE shows her the letter.

CLAIRE   Byron! Only the most romantic poet in all of England. I just bombarded him with fascinating letters till he gave in.

FANNY   You make it sound so easy.

CREATURE   That odd-headed girl? I wasn't really in love with her.

CLAIRE   *[Looks only at FANNY during the scene]* At first he . . . might have been.

CREATURE   No. I never loved nor pretended to love her—but a man is a man and if a girl of eighteen comes prancing to you at all hours, there is but one way.

CLAIRE   He always was a liar.

CREATURE   It was simple lust. Nothing else.

CLAIRE   I didn't enjoy that part of it much, to tell you the truth.

CREATURE   Now who's lying?

CLAIRE   He got me pregnant.

FANNY   Claire! Have you told him?

CLAIRE   I can't, can I? He's in Switzerland.

FANNY   And Shelley?

CLAIRE   Shelley is scared to death that people will think it's his.

FANNY   What are you going to do?

CLAIRE   We're going to Switzerland. Shelley's going to try to talk to him.

FANNY   Switzerland. Can I come with you?

CLAIRE   Not this time Fanny. Oooh! *[Clutches her stomach and runs off]*

FANNY   Not fair! It isn't. Mary has another baby. Claire is pregnant. And now they're going off again. When will it be my turn? *[Runs off in despair]*

Inspiration

CREATURE   And now we come to the relevant part of this story. How many of you here can name the moment of your own conception? I can, to the exact minute. I still shudder with ecstasy to think how simply it happened. Picture it. Europe is having the darkest, wettest summer in all history and our young adventurers *[sets out a couple of chairs as though round a fire]*, Shelley, Byron or, as they nicknamed him, *Albé*, Mary and Claire and Byron's physician Polidori, holed in by the weather, have been huddled round the fire reading each other ghost stories. The general mood, to say the least, is volatile. Hysteria, nightmares, and visions, shrieks and thumps in the night. Shelley is the most affected. He jumped up in one of their fireside sessions pointing with horror at Mary. "The White Witch!" he cried. "That's not a witch," they assured him. "Just your own Mary." "No, a witch, unbound to the waist! Look! Look at her breasts—she has eyes where her nipples should be!"

That was two days ago. They've settled down a bit, now. Found themselves a task. They're having a contest as to who can write the most hair-raising story.

CLAIRE enters, very pregnant, wrapped in a shawl.

CLAIRE   Albé has a lot to answer for. *We will each of us write a ghost story*, he declares, and ever since there's been no rest. It's depressing. Every morning to be taxed with the same question: *Have you thought of a story?* I always get so anxious and then find that everyone else is as blank as I am.

MARY enters, lost in thought.

CLAIRE   Mary. *[Strokes stomach]* Do you think I'm starting to show? We missed you at breakfast.
MARY   What happened?
CLAIRE   Nothing. Well, Polidori produced his skull-headed woman again. But no. Everyone's at a stalemate.
           A ghost story. It should be the easiest thing in the world, in this weather, this incessant rain. Just looking out the window is pure horror. Look down there. The lake is writhing about like a beast hungry for flesh. *[Turns to MARY, who's been very quiet]* Mary? Are you all right?
MARY   I had a . . . restless night.
CLAIRE   You're shivering! Here take this. *[Wraps her own shawl round MARY]*
MARY   *[Draws shawl close]* I couldn't sleep for the images flooding my brain. Image after image after image. It went on all night. And then, I saw . . .
CLAIRE   What? What did you see?
MARY   A young man, a student, very pale, tired, kneeling over a thing stretched out beside him.

The CREATURE moves to the table and stretches out like a corpse.

CLAIRE   A *thing*.

MARY   A hideous man, made out of bits and pieces of corpses.

CLAIRE   Oh Mary!

MARY   The student brings it to life. But it's so horrible, so unspeakably repulsive, that he runs away, praying that the spark of life will fade and that the thing will subside again into dead matter.

CLAIRE   It's terrifying! You're a genius!

CREATURE   Solitary and detested.

MARY   *[Very softly]* Solitary and detested.

CLAIRE   What?

MARY   Someone walking on my grave.

CLAIRE   I should think so. I wouldn't write that story after dark if I were you. *[Exits]*

MARY   *[To herself or to some imagined audience]* I set out to tell a story that would speak to the mysterious fears of our nature and awaken thrilling horror. I wanted to curdle the blood and quicken the beatings of the heart. I wanted to make the reader dread to look around.

CREATURE   *[Comes slowly to life]* My first memories are a confusion of light, hunger, thirst, and darkness. But by degrees I began to distinguish one sensation from another. I savoured the taste of berries, the songs of birds. I rejoiced in the moon. But I did not know what manner of creature I was.

MARY   I had my plans. But sometimes, descending into that subterranean gloom, plans can take unexpected turns.

CREATURE   I did not know what manner of creature I was. Then, one day, bending over a pond to quench my thirst . . . I saw myself. At first I could not believe that it was I who was reflected there. I was . . . *unspeakable.*

MARY   You can never predict. You haul something hideous out of the shadows but, instead of recoiling from it in horror, you find something.

CREATURE   She should never have given me the power of speech. But her little William was lisping his first words, and it just seemed natural to allow me to do the same.[7] She just couldn't deny me. *[Moves over to* MARY *and crouches before her]*

MARY   Fire.

CREATURE   *Fire.*

MARY   Milk.

CREATURE   *Milk.*

MARY   Bread.

CREATURE　*Bread.*

MARY　　Wood.

CREATURE　*Wood. [Goes on by himself] Good, dearest, unhappy.*

MARY　　You find something that interrogates you and calls you to account.

CREATURE　Saying words made me feel powerful. I felt if I could become master of their language people might overlook the deformity of my figure. *Sister, brother . . . father.*

MARY　　Mother.

CREATURE　She allowed me reading, too. *[Savours each name]* Volney. Goethe. Plutarch. Milton. There never was such an educated monster.

　　　　　I read of the rise and fall of empires. I read of love and honour, of vice and bloodshed, how man could perform the most saintly acts and then go forth to murder his fellow.

　　　　　I read of the difference of the sexes, of the birth and growth of children, and all the various relationships which bind one human being to another.[8]

　　　　　But where were *my* friends and relations? No father had watched my infant days; no mother had blessed me with smiles and caresses. What was I? Where I had come from?

MARY　　What's that on your hands?

CREATURE　And then I found the journal of my accursed origin.

MARY　　It's blood, isn't it.

CREATURE　Every detail of the disgusting circumstances which produced me was carefully recorded.

MARY　　Whose blood? Whose blood is it?

CREATURE　I sickened as I read of the hateful day when I received life. Cursed creator! Why did you form a monster so hideous that even you turned from me in disgust? Why did you leave me solitary and detested?

He grasps her hands. She looks at his hands in horror.

MARY　　*Whose blood?*

The CREATURE's mood changes, his anger dissipates, he smiles up at her and she pulls away. She moves off in distress, but meets CLAIRE carrying William wrapped in a shawl. The sight of the baby soothes her. She moves to the chest, where she takes pen and paper and works on her book.

Fanny's Prenuptials

FANNY enters dressed for travel, carrying a small portmanteau.

FANNY   Solitary and detested.

CREATURE   Ah, Fanny. Poor Fanny. She has at last taken matters into her own hands and has set out on her dark honeymoon. All she lacks is a bridegroom.

The CREATURE takes her portmanteau and sets it down and helps her remove her pelisse. She is wearing her mother's stays. He leads FANNY in a courtly manner back to the make-up table and chair, where he unbinds and brushes her hair.
CLAIRE moves forward to the central table where she sets William down while she writes a letter to Byron.

CLAIRE   My dearest Albé, I'm writing this to you to cheer myself up. Fanny has written a stupid letter to Shelley and frightened us all to death.

It's such a cozy evening. I'm taking care of Willmouse while Mary writes her book. I just stooped down to ask *itty babe* if I should send his love to you and he replied by putting his heel with great composure into my eye.

I expect it's because we've been using your portrait to frighten him when he's naughty. You'd better be good, we say, for the great poet is coming. Now he's lying in his cradle like a little angel. I hope my little girl will be half as pretty. Now don't frown. It's going to be a girl—it's all settled. I don't plan to have anything but daughters.

I'm not supposed to be writing letters at this moment.

Holds up a misshapen little shirt.

I'm supposed to be sewing little garments. Thank God, you can't see my handiwork or you'd never take me seriously again. I was given the makings of six bodies all cut out and I've ended up with four and a half. Somehow, I've got the legs attached to the shoulder holes and the back is upside down altogether. Mary's going to murder me.

I know you don't want to hear this, but I've been so lonely since we came back from Switzerland. I've missed you so much. If you would write me to say how you are, if you will say that you think of me sometimes without anger and that you will love and take care of our baby, I would be so happy.

MARY cries out, crushes the page in her hand. CLAIRE rushes to her.

CLAIRE   What is it? You're deathly white.
MARY   It was so *real*.

CLAIRE pulls the paper from MARY's hand and smooths it out.

CLAIRE   Give me that. It's a page of your story. Why have you crumpled it?
MARY   It frightened me.

The CREATURE bends down, pulls FANNY close, and takes a long deep kiss. She pulls away.

CLAIRE   *[Reads]* "I thought I saw my beloved walking in the streets of Ingolstadt. I embraced her but as I imprinted the first kiss on her lips, they became livid with the hue of death; her features changed and I beheld the corpse of my dead mother in my arms, and I saw the grave worms crawling in the folds of her shroud." Oh God!
MARY   It's too horrible! What have I unleashed?
CLAIRE   Come and look at Willmouse. That will cheer you up.
MARY   I fear for him.
CLAIRE   It was that stupid letter from Fanny. That's what's upset you. Shelley will fix it. He'll talk some sense into her
MARY   Fanny will come and live with us when we get a house. It will be much better for her.
CLAIRE   Yes. It will.

The CREATURE leads FANNY down stage to a chair, where he continues arranging her hair.

FANNY   It's all so distressing. There they are, writing books, having babies, travelling. Their lives are like the pages of a romance. It's the babies mostly. Holding them, bathing them, sewing little things for them. All those things you do. I can't look at a baby, any more, without wanting to cry. . . . I've tried everything. I educate myself, I make myself pleasing and agreeable and I don't complain. And yet no one ever says, "Bring Fanny along." "Let's ask Fanny what she thinks." "How can we conceive of doing anything without our beloved Fanny!"

CREATURE *[Gathering up her hair and piling it in a crown]* How's this?

FANNY   *[Shaking it out with pleasure]* It's lovely. How clever you are. All in all, I'm quite satisfied. It's all come together so well. The coach ride here was an adventure. And this is such a charming place, everyone so concerned for my comfort. *[Strokes her stays]* Something old.

CREATURE *[Touches her watch]* Something new?

FANNY   My watch? It's pure gold. Shelley and Mary bought it for me in Geneva. They were feeling guilty about me. The blue is in my skirt. I always liked this blue. I chose everything I'm wearing with great care.

CREATURE Like a trousseau. Something borrowed? *[Pulls a scarlet handkerchief out of his pocket]*

FANNY   Thank you. This is silk, isn't it. Such a glorious red. *[Holds it to her face.]* If I could see ahead. If I could imagine something more. But I look into the future and I can't see myself. All I can see is . . . you. *[Frightened, she moves away from the CREATURE]* I . . . I meant to be like my mother. I had all these pictures in my head of her. So many pictures. But now I can't seem to see any of them. Just the last—that cold dreadful room that will never be blotted out. It's as if I am that room and everything in that room. The bed my mother lay in, I am that bed stained with her blood and pain. I am the cool sheets they wrapped her in, linen with a hint of lavender. And I am Mrs Fenwick's gentle hands shifting her up in the bed and setting the pillows under her. I am the cold sweat on her face and I am the thin cold hands of the doctor—I am unwashed hands with dirt under the nails.[9]

I was there, wasn't I? The bed, the walls, the little green-winged fly that buzzed in the window. The fever that gripped her and the chill that rattled her bones. And I heard that rattle and I heard my father's collapsing breath, and the little baby in the next room crying, my sister crying, because the puppies had pushed her away from my mother's breast and taken her place.

The light is harsh, glaring—she stands, staring into endless space.

CREATURE *[Opening a drawer and taking out a clipping]* Something from my scrapbook.

CLAIRE   Is that the paper? What does it say?

MARY   I'm sure it isn't her.

CLAIRE   *[Reads]* "A melancholy discovery was made in Swansea yesterday: A most respectable looking female arrived at the Mackworth Arms inn on Wednesday night by the Cambrian Coach from Bristol. Much agitation was created in the house by her non-appearance Friday morning and, in forcing her chamber door, she was found a corpse, with the remains of a bottle of laudanum on the table and the following note:

MARY   *[Taking the paper from CLAIRE]* "'I have long determined that the best thing I could do was to put an end to the existence of a being whose birth was so unfortunate. Perhaps to hear of my death will give you pain, but you will soon have the blessing of forgetting that such a creature ever existed as. . . .'" There's no name. It isn't her. I'm sure it isn't.

CREATURE *[From memory of the clipping]* "The name appears to be torn off and burnt, but her stockings are marked with the letter 'G.'. . ."

MARY   *[Fearfully]* Godwin.

CREATURE ". . . and on her stays the letters 'M.W.' are visible.[10] She had long brown hair and a fair complexion and seemed to be about 24 years of age. Her reticule contained a red silk handkerchief, a brown berry necklace and eight shillings and sixpence.

MARY picks up William and holds him tightly. The two women exit.

CREATURE "We hope our description of this unhappy catastrophe will lead to the discovery of the wretched object who has thus prematurely closed her existence."

          "Wretched object"—a pleasant turn of phrase. The family never claimed the body. Her suicide was considered a scandal and kept a secret.

The CREATURE closes the drawer of the desk with a sharp crack and exits.
Lights dim as FANNY exits. There is transitional music—gentle Chopinesque piano—as the lights rise again.

Act Two

Several years have passed. MARY, *in her mid-twenties now, is lost in reverie.*

The Sibyl's Cave[11]

MARY removes a sheaf of manuscript pages from the desk drawer. Clutching them to her in pleasure she sits on the desk. As she dreams, much of the paper escapes her and is scattered on the floor about the desk.
As she speaks, a ghostly FANNY *plays with three little bundles.*

MARY
: The descent. . . . I think of it as sacred, yes, a sacred task. It's dangerous, frightening, a plunge into loneliness and yet the downward spin, the intricate spiral of mind, soul, memory weaving down into purifying depths. . . .
  If you were to descend. If you were to take this dark journey down with me, you would come suddenly upon a cabinet of wonders. Memories spread out like engravings clipped from books, thoughts iridescent and shimmering like butterflies, hopes like infants dreaming in glass jars, dressed in beads and old lace, life and death in their little dried-out faces.

FANNY
: Babies in glass jars! Where does she get those thoughts?

MARY
: If you were to come down with me, skeletal beings would beckon you, craniums polished white by time, eye sockets raised in adoration, they would show you such marvels, such antiquities, you would be lost in wonder—curios draped in dust and cobwebs, leaves with old script on them, indecipherable fragments in forgotten languages, to be toiled over, the streams of the mind gathering them up, pondering over them, piecing them together in monstrous and wonderful fabrications that would bring you to the brink of the world.

FANNY
: It's Italy that's doing it to her.

MARY
: Oh my Italy. The mountains of Italy and the caves and mossy ruins and fireflies in the gloom. Naples, Leghorn, Milano, Lucca . . .

FANNY
: It's turning her into something strange. She pretends it's adventure but it's really death. A funeral procession.

MARY   *[Trying not to hear]* Florence, Pisa, Venice, Rome. The
           cities of Italy bask like princes in the evening light while the
           Madonnas in the dark churches keep their thoughts to them-
           selves.[12]

FANNY   *[Indicates the bundles]* This is what Italy has done for her.

MARY   Yes, Italy takes away. Italy is the graveyard of all my hopes.
           Why do you torment me, Fanny, in the one place I seek free-
           dom from torment?

FANNY   Because I can't understand. You seem to be the perfect
           mother.

MARY   I do my best.

FANNY   And in all your letters you contrive to show that perfection,
           how domestic everything is, how idyllic. *[Picks up a paper]*
           Listen to this. "I am surrounded by babes." And this.
           "William is cutting his teeth and is fretful." Here's another.
           "Send flannel for petticoats and a quantity of White Chapel
           needles, balls of cotton of all sizes."

MARY   I was forever running out of those things. *[Taking up a leaf
           FANNY has dropped]* "I am just now surrounded by babes." I
           wrote that. What happy days those were. Surrounded by babes.

FANNY   And you let them all slip away. That was so careless of you,
           Mary.

MARY   Careless! How can you say that?

FANNY   *[Sets a bundle on one of the chairs]* The first baby, that
           could happen to anyone. She was born too soon. But that
           beautiful little Clara—you just let her die. *[Places a bundle
           on a second chair]*

MARY   No! There was nothing I could do. I tried to get her to the
           doctor in Venice. I sat in the carriage with her fevered little
           body in my arms, feeling her life ebbing away.

FANNY   And William.

MARY   I thought he was safe. He was so blooming, so healthy, and
           then . . .

FANNY   *[Picking up the third bundle]* . . . so dead.

MARY   You don't know what it's like.

FANNY   Shelley must be desolated.

MARY   Shelley! We came to Italy for Shelley's health and yet that's
           what destroyed my children.[13]

FANNY   You're surely not blaming Shelley!

MARY   If we didn't move about so much. If we could stay in one
           place for more than ten minutes. If he would consider his
           own family instead of every other living soul in the world!

FANNY   You just don't know when you're well off. You have a won-
           derful husband, another dear little baby,

MARY   Yes, if it wasn't for my little Percy I don't know how I'd
           keep going.

FANNY   You're famous, you have brilliant friends, and you're still
           not happy. Poor Shelley. *[Lays her little bundle down on the
           desk]* He deserves so much better.

MARY   What are you doing?

FANNY   Three. You've lost three. *[Moves off]*

MARY   Fanny! Where are you going?

FANNY   Beware for the fourth.

MARY   No, Percy is fine! He's as healthy as a little horse.

FANNY   *[Drifting off]* Not Percy.

La Mer de Glace

CLAIRE   *[Enters from the front]* The getting and losing of children.
           It's a common theme in the Shelley household.

*Mary gathers up the little bundles and moves to the trunk, where
she sadly packs them away.*

MARY   When I look back on all I've suffered, I sicken with horror.

CLAIRE   Mary thinks some evil fate is pursuing her.

MARY   Well isn't it? I dip my pen into the creative ooze and never
           know what evil spirit will get loose. My mother unleashed
           ideas upon the world. I unleashed something monstrous. I
           knew from the very beginning, from that very first vision at
           Lake Leman. I felt such a premonition of evil.

CLAIRE   Shelley's the same. He sees everything as an ill omen. Or a
           conspiracy. He's convinced that his father is trying to kidnap
           him and have him put away.

MARY   Remember those strange visions he had at Lake Leman?
           And that dog that attacked him. And then in Chamounix I
           was bitten by a squirrel.

CLAIRE   The phantasmagoria of life with the Shelleys.

MARY   And Shelley fell on one of our hikes—remember?—and had
           to be carried back to the hotel. *[Sits disconsolately on the
           desk]*

CLAIRE   I remember. And I remember the man at the post office who
           attacked him with his cane. *Are you that damned atheist?* No

wonder Shelley thinks calamity is pursuing him. It would be laughable, except. . . .

MARY   *[Stretches out on the desk like a corpse]* It was the ice. All that ice.

CLAIRE   *La Mer de Glace.*

MARY   Trapped in caves of ice.

CLAIRE   Shelley says a new ice age is coming.

MARY   Irrevocable ice.

CLAIRE   I, on the other hand, say it will all be melted by a great surge of love.

MARY   That ice got into my deepest soul.

CLAIRE   *[Gesturing comically at* MARY's *heart]* Even now there's a sliver of it, unmelted, in her heart. *[Moves to the chaise longue, where she stretches out and dreams]*

CREATURE   *[Jumps through the clothes rack, snaps down the lid of the trunk and leaps on top of it]* I have to step in here and say a word about Shelley. He does have this, how would you put it, *volatile* side to his character, an almost hysterical fear of conspiracy and doom. And, aided by certain hallucinatory substances, he has pulled off some pretty spectacular visions. But, the fact is, he is a man of exquisite reason and considerable science.

Engravings appear on the overhead canopy. The CREATURE *leaves the trunk and, crossing the room, leaps up on the desk where* MARY *is lying.*

CREATURE   Look at this: A balloon that can move by heated air. Shelley and his first wife, Harriet, filled one of these with pamphlets arguing his atheistic theories and sent them off to spill their contents on his neighbours' estates.

And then there's steam locomotion: Shelley and a friend are currently building a steamship that will run a passenger line between Leghorn and Pisa. They expect to make their fortunes doing this.

Shelley's microscope.

A shaft of sunlight feeds into the scope and is projected into a darkened room. All manner of things can be placed within and be magnified a hundred-fold. There are charlatans who exploit these mechanics and create ghost shows, projecting images of people placed in another room into a cloud of smoke—so that the dead seemed to be revived.

The revival of the dead. I of course have some special insights into that. *[Removes something from his pocket and strokes it gently]* One of my little resurrections. My own design. Nice streamlining of the skeletal structure, I think. I've done a rather good job on the teeth. *[It bites him.]* Ah! Bastard! *[Crushes it in his fist]* Disposition erratic. Haven't yet worked out the psychology. *[Drops it on the floor, steps on it]* Just a little improv, a little practice piece, you might say. *[Dismounts and circles MARY]* You see eventually I want to . . . once I've improved my skills and my knowledge, I want to . . . but that's in the future. It's a task that at present is beyond my capabilities. *[Leaves MARY and considers CLAIRE]* Well think of it, all the intricacies of fibre, muscle, and vein. The materials alone. Bones from charnel houses. Gory little samplings from the dissecting room and the slaughter house.

CLAIRE   Mrs Mason, you're missing everything!

CREATURE   But I'm not giving up. Oh no. I have as much right as you do to companionship. No one will stop me.

CLAIRE   Mrs Mason!

CREATURE   Coming! *[Wraps himself in a skirt and shawl to audience.]* Mrs Mason? Yes I'm Mrs Mason now. You're finding these transformations of mine confusing, no doubt. But if you think I'm going to interpret this shape-shifting habit of mine you're out of luck. It's for Mary's benefit and Claire's, not yours. And besides, you weren't invited here to put your feet up and let me do all the work. I will give you a hint about Mrs Mason though. She's the daughter of Lord and Lady Kingsborough of Ireland and she's run away from her wealthy husband to live an expatriate's life in Italy. And long ago, in her formative years, her governess was Mary Wollstonecraft.

Gabinetto di Fisica[14]

CLAIRE   This is the most *incredible* place.

CREATURE   A museum of physical parts.

CLAIRE   The *Gabinetto di Fisica*. I never thought plaster and wax could be so instructive.

CREATURE   There was a woman in Paris in the last century who reproduced every part of the body in wax. Her masterpiece was an entire human being that could be opened up and the parts removed.

CLAIRE   But what was her reference for building the parts?

CREATURE   Cadavers. She kept them at the bottom of the garden in glass cases.

CLAIRE   A lady Frankenstein, Mary! In a place like this you can see how close you could actually come to building a body.

MARY   Resurrection almost at our fingertips. Look, here's a torso of a man. If I could only look in here and see what causes Shelley's aches and pains.

The CREATURE explores.

CREATURE   Look. Here's an entire room devoted to women.

CLAIRE   Come, Mary.

MARY   *[Lingering before the torso]* I'll just be a minute. His worst pain is here in his side—the kidney—if we could just remove it and smooth it out and get it all in working order. And his heart. *[Strokes it tenderly]* How I would love to wash away all those palpitations and disappointments.

CREATURE   Yes. Here we are. "Ladies Only."

CLAIRE   This is wonderful! It's like a chapel. No, a cathedral. What a place for contemplation, among the organs and mysteries of women. The womb, the breasts, all the gentle, rounded, soothing, and creative forms. I imagine all my dreams here would be natural and kind.

CREATURE   Do you have unkind dreams, my dear?

CLAIRE   Frequently. I'm not a magnanimous person.

CREATURE   That will change when you fashion a life for yourself.

CLAIRE   There is no fabric for the life I would fashion.

CREATURE   Now you must be sensible. You can save yourself years of pain if you accept that Lord Byron is out of reach.

CLAIRE   I don't care a prune for *Byron*. It's Allegra. It's nearly two years since I gave her up to that felon. He never lets me see her. He never writes. And now, my worst fears have come to pass. He's putting her in a convent.

CREATURE   A convent! My dear! I didn't know this.

CLAIRE   At Bagnacavallo. Miles from anywhere.

CREATURE   But this is too bad of him. A four-year-old in a convent. Those places are rife with fever and damp. She'd be much better off with you.

CLAIRE   Or at least somewhere of my choosing, where I could be sure she's cared for and happy. I could support her with my teaching, keep her with a family where I'd be free to visit.

CREATURE   If he puts her in a convent I'll help you get her out.

CLAIRE   But how?

CREATURE   There are lots of ways. I could pose as Byron, and you could
            be what's her name—his mistress.

CLAIRE   The *Guicciola*.

CREATURE   We'd roll up in the latest in carriages; he's famous for his car-
            riages. Perhaps I could even borrow one from him. Wouldn't
            that be a lark? We'd say I'd come to visit my daughter for the
            day, take her for a picnic, and off we'd go all the way over
            the border into Switzerland. We would need money for this,
            though. I don't suppose we could ask Shelley?

MARY enters.

CREATURE   Mary. I was just proposing that I pose as Lord Byron. What
            do you think? An open-necked shirt, my hair in short curls?

MARY   You're much too tall to be Byron. And, my dear Mrs Mason,
            who would ever believe you were a man?

CREATURE   I once posed as a man for over a year.

MARY   When?

CREATURE   Studying medicine at Jena. I slipped on a pair of trousers
            and cut my hair, and no one was any the wiser. Especially
            since I held forth in my usual opinionated way. Now, would-
            n't this have been a great thing when I was a student, to have
            the anatomy of the body displayed in this way.

CLAIRE   Here's a whole woman assembled. You can see right into the
            womb. Look how perfect it is, a perfect little cave. *[Looks
            in]* No one home.

MARY   I've heard that women spend so much time in this room that
            their men get quite worried, as if it were a clandestine act.

CLAIRE   Well I know how it makes *me* feel. It makes me want to rip
            off all my clothes and make comparisons—have a good look
            at everything!

MARY   Claire! This *is* a dangerous place.

CLAIRE   Well, think of it. All our lives we've been scolded if we look
            too closely at the outside of the body, let alone consider its
            internal landscapes.

CREATURE   Such is the stuff of revolution. We overthrow kings, give
            commoners their freedom, and let women know what their
            bodies are like.

CLAIRE   Liberation!

CREATURE   It was your mother, Mary, who unleashed my revolutionary
            heart. She took me out of the nursery and set me galloping,

mane and tail to the wind, across the far-flung fields of politics, science, philosophy. Everything in my heart that's poetic, everything strong, every small bit of wisdom I modestly claim, was first discovered and set free by her.

MARY   And what did *your* mother say to this?

CREATURE   She said that I loved my governess more than I loved her. Which was true. But what she really meant was my being tall, having ideas and feelings and sexuality and muscle and demonstrating and writing pamphlets and running off with Mr Mason and leaving eight children behind. That's what my mother feared, and it was all your mother's doing. She fanned the flames of my calamitous soul, and I must say I've been very, very happy.

CLAIRE   How strong you are. When Allegra was inside me, growing here, I felt strong. No one could take care of her but me. I poured love into this little cave and imagined her into existence.

It was so amazing that I, always totally useless with my hands, could form a perfect little being—down to the last little toenail, a perfect piece of work.

But now. How can I tell if she's getting what she needs? I see your little Percy doing this, discovering that, and I think, did Allegra do this? Did she learn how to count? Does she know all her colours? Does she know she's loved?

I want her back so badly. I want to pour love into her. I want to tell her every day, every *minute*, how beautiful she is, and I can't.

MARY   Oh Claire. *[Puts her arm about her]* You will.

CLAIRE   I'm never going to see her again! *[Pulls away and runs off]*

MARY   That's not so! *[Follows her]*

CLAIRE   She will slip from my grasp! *[They exit]*

Allegra

FANNY enters with a fourth little bundle, rocking it and talking to it.

FANNY   The Italians have such beautiful names for winds: *Tramontano, Libeccio, Sirocco, Mistral*. But the winds themselves are not beautiful.

Mistral, the master wind, comes from the north and is violent and cold. *Sirocco* is an oppressively hot and blighting wind from the north coast of Africa. *Tramontano* is rough and barbarous, and, because it originates across the Alps and not in Italy, the Italians call it *the stranger*.

Your uncle Shelley told me all about these winds and their names. But he didn't tell me what wind it is that creeps about old convents, breathing typhoid and malaria and stealing away innocent little souls. You would never leave a child in the path of that wind. *[Runs off]*

CLAIRE enters, full of cheer and bustle. MARY follows, holding a letter. She looks depressed and despairing.

CLAIRE   Oh that Percy. What a delicious child. Allegra will kill him with love. She'll be a perfect little mother to him. Now Mary, before you start, I'm not going to let you sway me on this. A duel! It's the stupidest thing I ever heard. Byron is not going to challenge Shelley to a duel just because I take my child, my own child. He'd be the laughingstock of Italy.

MARY   Claire . . .

CLAIRE   No! I know what you're going to say. "It's springtime and spring has never been lucky for us." But I'm past waiting for the best time. I have waited and waited and meanwhile Allegra gets older and sadder. And what if she gets ill? No, don't tell me about the healthy weather in Bagnacavallo. I don't want to hear that the sea's only a mile away. What good is the sea to convent dwellers if you never get outside the walls? And the sweetness of the air—in a cold dungeon what does the air matter? It probably never reaches her.

Why are you so quiet? *[Suddenly wary, suspicious]* You're conspiring with him. With Albé. He's hidden her away, hasn't he? You said he might if I annoyed him . . . Mary?

MARY   No, it's not that. Listen, Claire, I . . .

CLAIRE   No! I don't want to listen to you. All your blessed obstacles. Obstacles, obstacles! You will never have done casting them in front of me. "Wait till we have money." "Wait till we have a better place to stay." "Think of the convent she's enclosed in—high walls and bolted doors." What are high walls and bolted doors to me? I could scale those walls in an instant, tear open doors with my bare hands. . . . Mary?

MARY is unable to speak. CLAIRE looks at her for a long time.

CLAIRE   It's bad news, isn't it.

MARY is silent.

CLAIRE   Tell me she's not dead.

MARY   It was typhus. I wanted Shelley to tell you.

CLAIRE   *[A long silence]* We could have all been so happy. For the briefest time we were, weren't we? Our heads in the stars and yet so *au courant*, so up on everything. Bathing in mountain pools. Riding horses. Fascinating ourselves to death with opera and the latest books. Ruling our lives with philosophy and science. And she was going to be like that, a child of all that boldness and daring and intelligence, moving fearlessly through the world.

MARY   Claire

CLAIRE   And *you*. Yes. It comes flooding back. I will never forget that time.

MARY   What time?

CLAIRE   It makes me ill to look at you. The instant I see you, I feel as if I had not blood in my veins but the sickening crawling motion of the death worm.

MARY   Claire! What are you talking about?

CLAIRE   What can one say of a woman who could gaze upon the spectacle of a child led to the scaffold and, after all was over, could claim acquaintance with the executioner and shake hands with him.

MARY   That's a hideous thing to say. I know the way you are sometimes. You make up things as a metaphor for what you're feeling. But all the same . . .

CLAIRE keeps a stony silence.

MARY   . . . that I would ever condone the death of a child. And shaking hands with the executioner? What a fantasy. It makes anything I've ever written seem like a bedtime story.

CLAIRE   Are you telling me that if Albé came into this room right now that you would cut him? That you would order him out of your house?

MARY   Well, that's entirely different.

CLAIRE   I thought not. No, you'll go on cozying up to him, treating him like the "great man," fluttering about him like a little golden butterfly. You won't say one word amiss to him.

MARY   Claire, you must see that . . .

CLAIRE   Don't! Leave me be.

CLAIRE moves out and away from MARY.

MARY	This is your way of expressing pain. Nothing like that ever happened, nothing remotely like it.
CLAIRE	It just happened.
MARY	Allegra meant so much to me.
CLAIRE	You have a very cold way about you, Mary.

Fraught with grief, CLAIRE *moves to the trunk.*

CLAIRE	The death of a child is like an interrupted revel. You prepare yourself a long pleasure, reaching out for years ahead, but the cup of enjoyment is dashed from your lips.

She sinks down in despair, arms and head resting on the trunk, withdrawing into her grief.

Death by Tempest

MARY	*[Moves to the chaise and remembers her own sorrows]* "Surrounded by children." How difficult. How impossible. We just can't seem to keep them. Even this last one ripped from my womb. Washed away in a torrent of blood. I'm not afraid of pain, or even death. But losing. . . . Fanny? What are you doing there?

She turns to see FANNY *moving into view.* FANNY *looks at her blindly.*

MARY	Fanny?
FANNY	It's Shelley.
MARY	No. Not Shelley. Shelley is . . . I just . . .
FANNY	Dead.
MARY	No. Please!
FANNY	He died at sea with his friend Edward . . . don't you remember?

MARY *clutches her stomach with remembered pain.*

FANNY	Death by tempest. Byron and Trelawny gave them a poet's funeral, casting oil and wine and frankincense on the fire. Hunt was there too. It was a high-flying day — the water and sky were baby blue, and white birds drifted like poemless pages overhead. Shelley's heart, his everlasting heart, would not burn. Trelawny snatched it from the fire. And Hunt took it as a keepsake of his dear lost friend. *[Moves to the chair*

at the makeup desk and sits facing back into the dark, lost in her own dreams]

MARY   *[Goes to her desk and picks up a pen; after a moment's reverie puts it down again]* My heart is too full to write tonight. Oh Shelley. My dearest Elf. Sometimes I seem to be in a place where life weighs itself and hosts of memories and imaginations thrust into one scale make the other kick the beam. You remember what you have felt—what you have dreamt—yet shadows and lost hopes cover everything with a funeral pall. The time that was, is, will be, presses upon you and, standing in the centre of a moving circle, you slide giddily as the world reels. *[Rises and looks out]*

The lanes are filled with fireflies. They dart between the trunks of the trees and people the land with Earth stars. I walked among them tonight and, descending toward the sea, I passed through the churchyard and stood on the platform that overlooks the beach. The black rocks were stretched out before me, and beyond them I saw the dark boats with their white sails, and I stood for a long time looking for your boat. Looking for you.

The CREATURE *bursts in on* MARY, *who retreats to her desk. He is clutching a small linen-wrapped object that he is very aware of.*

MARY   My dear Hunt!

CREATURE I can't believe you bothered Lord Byron about this.

MARY   Someone had to take my part in the matter. I'm sorry if your pride was hurt.

CREATURE It is not my pride. My self-love is nothing to me. This is about my love for Shelley, and to give it up for the claims of any other love, man's or woman's, I must have great reasons indeed brought me.

MARY   And you think I have no reason?

CREATURE I'm not saying it's impossible for such reasons to be brought, but, when it comes to Shelley, no ordinary appearance of rights, even yours, can affect me. . . . *[Waving her quiet]* I begged it at the funeral pile; I had it; and his *lordship*, who happened to be at a distance at the moment, knew nothing of the matter till it was in my possession.

MARY   It belongs to me.

CREATURE You didn't earn it.

MARY   Earn it!

CREATURE You weren't there. You didn't see how it was.

MARY Trelawny begged me not to come. Jane as well. He made us both stay here.

CREATURE We found Edward first, in that hasty pit where they'd flung him. Seven days in the water had done its work. He was dreadfully mangled; his hands and one foot had been entirely eaten away by fish. And his face. . . . It was impossible to recognize him.[15]

MARY Beautiful Edward.

CREATURE When we attempted to remove him, his legs separated from his body. We gathered round him, tried to make a poet's funeral of it, casting incense and salt and wine on the flames. It took hours and hours.

We found Shelley the next day. Shelley was . . .

MARY *Shelley . . . [Not wanting to hear]* will suffer a sea change into something rich and strange!

CREATURE I'm sorry.

MARY How can you deny me what is rightfully mine?

CREATURE It should be with someone who truly loved him.

MARY I didn't love him?

CREATURE He told me, you know, the day before he died, how cold you'd been to him.

MARY We were very troubled. We'd been through so much the past few years. Fanny. Three children lost, a fourth miscarried. How can you with your six healthy little animals possibly understand what that's like? And then Allegra. . . . But I loved him passionately.

CREATURE I don't think it's in your nature to love passionately. I mean look at you now. You're supposed to be a woman in mourning, yet you write every day as though nothing was amiss, churning out your sixpenny fantasies.

MARY How can you grudge me my writing! Do you think I want to go on living without Shelley? If it weren't for my boy. . . . It is not true that I was cold! Did I not in the deepest solitude of thought repeat to myself my good fortune in possessing him? I could unveil myself to him. He understood me. I was united to a glorious being. I was the mother of beautiful children.[16] And now, I am reduced to these white pages, which I am to blot with dark imagery.

The CREATURE, relenting at last, places the bundle on the desk beside her.

MARY   *[Lost in her mood]* Am I cold? God knows. At least the tears
        are hot.

*The CREATURE leaves. MARY turns to the parcel and picks it up,
cradling it against her shoulder.*

MARY   How dark, how very dark the future seems. I shrink in fear
        from the mere imagination of coming time. Is any evil about
        to approach me. . . . ? Have I not suffered enough?

*Gentle piano music. The lights fade on the three women, CLAIRE
still mourning at the trunk, FANNY lost in her reverie, and MARY
clasping her sad memento of Shelley.*

Intermission

Act Three

Pestilence

Abstract music and shadows. MARY *lies, feverish and ill, on the slab-like desk. Two faceless figures—one in white (played by* CLAIRE*), one in black (played by* FANNY*)—move slowly into view. As they speak, they stalk each other warily.*

CLAIRE	Keep away.
FANNY	She's dying.
CLAIRE	No! She'll pull through.
FANNY	It's smallpox, though. She's been in a fever for days.
CLAIRE	She was up this morning.
FANNY	For ten minutes.
CLAIRE	She's strong.
FANNY	Pestilence—
CLAIRE	Purity—
FANNY	Darkness—
CLAIRE	Clarity—
FANNY	Death—
CLAIRE	Resurrection.

The dark-cloaked figure moves off and the white-cloaked figure follows. With great difficulty MARY *rises and we see that she is pockmarked and her hair is straggly and thin. There is a small bandage on her finger.*

MARY   I broke a glass this morning. *[Pulls herself to a standing position]* A small red bubble formed on my finger tip, and then ballooned out till time seemed arrested—a moment transfixed in blood.

CREATURE *[Lurking in the background]* Let's see now. This is how it goes. Glass breaks. Then the room shatters too, a kaleidoscope of glassy fragments clicking into bright, delirious patterns.

Faint sounds off—merry voices and dance music.

MARY   A cave of spinning light—bits of my life thrown on the walls—shifting, breaking, shifting again . . .

CREATURE A million little glistening resurrections—mother, sister, babies . . .

MARY   My beloved Shelley.

CREATURE   Fragments of all her dead and of all her lost desires. All those youthful ambitions that twisted and soured and came to nothing.

MARY   We were all so young. We travelled post-haste into our lives without a thought of how we would make do—no money, no skills, nothing at all but our teeming imagination. Imagination was everything to us. But I soon found its gifts are double-edged. I wrote of death, and death stole my loved ones. I wrote of plague, and pestilence struck. I wrote of monsters, and from my mirror an exquisitely ugly woman, pockmarked and scabbed, peers out at me, eyes bleary, hair patchy and falling out, as if I were already dead and deteriorating.

Prospero

The CREATURE *dons a dark coat and top hat and moves forward.*

CREATURE   Are you deteriorating Madame?

MARY   Monsieur Mérimée! Was I speaking aloud? I came in here for a little solitude. Ridiculous isn't it? Solitude is the one thing I have in excess.

CREATURE   It's not fair to deprive us of your company. To hide yourself away like this.

MARY   I'm doing everyone a favour. Look at me. Poverty-stricken, deformed, squinting, lame, bald.

CREATURE   Is that all? Your face is not your fortune, Madame.

MARY   And what is my fortune?

CREATURE   *[Bends over her hand]* It's a certain delectable odour of self-sufficiency. A whiff of such perfume is enough to excite all the men of Paris.

MARY   Hardly.

CREATURE   Monsieur Payne is mad about you.

MARY   John is a good friend.

CREATURE   I think he would not be happy to hear this description of himself: "a good friend." I think he fancies himself as something more. General Lafayette was also fascinated with you, judging from the way he lingered over your hand.

MARY   *[Pulls her hand away, but he retains his hold]* I didn't notice.

CREATURE   I think you noticed very well. I think you like to flirt. *[She pulls away successfully]* In fact, I think you *love* to flirt.

Didn't I hear you telling Madame Douglas that a gathering is not worth a *centime* if there aren't several good men to flirt with?

She smiles but says nothing.

CREATURE I hope you see me as one of the several good men.

MARY You are much too young, and besides you're wrong about me. I am not a flirt. Quite the contrary. I am a gloomy soul. My moods are subterranean at best.

CREATURE Then I am just the fellow for you! Doesn't my name dictate it? I will be the Prospero to your cavernous moods.

MARY The name fits, Prosper Mérimée, but you would find me a rather aging Miranda.

CREATURE Ah, the ancient crone of thirty-one shrinks from the dashing young blade of twenty-five. But I assure you, Madame, I may be a greenhorn on the outside, but inside I am a very old man. If you could turn me inside out, you'd find hopeless decay. You will find this out for yourself as our friendship deepens.

MARY It won't get a chance to deepen, I'm afraid. I'm returning to England the day after tomorrow.

CREATURE You shatter me! How can you think of abandoning me?

MARY You know I'm just here on holiday. I must return to my child and my work.

CREATURE And what about us?

MARY Us? We've known each other, how long? Two or three days?

CREATURE Four. How can you think of leaving me when there is such potential between us, such possibility? I am *desolated*. I hope you weren't hoping for marriage.

MARY Hardly.

CREATURE I myself don't believe in the institution. But from your success in Paris alone I should think you could have a whole lineup of prospective husbands with one little snap of your finger.

MARY I am definitely not looking for a husband. I like the name Mary Shelley too much. I've always found it very pretty and I mean to have it engraved on my tombstone.

CREATURE Well now. You don't want a Prospero. You don't want a husband. That leaves only one role that I can see, and I'm not rich enough for that. But if I had 6000 francs salary and if I were strong and handsome, I would be a professional Don

Juan. It is an interesting career and doesn't have all the disagreeable side effects of honest love.

MARY　　　I can't believe there are no other women in your life.

CREATURE　There are a few.

MARY　　　A *few*.

CREATURE　Well, of course it would be wonderful to find one woman who encompassed all the virtues, but it's impossible. So the practical solution is to have lots of women.

MARY　　　And did you never come across that one woman?

CREATURE　I have indeed met such a woman. *[Lingers over his words to give the impression that it might be her]* And let me say she would be satisfaction enough for any man. Unfortunately she is the mistress of my best friend. And unfortunately I promised I would have nothing to do with her and, unfortunately, I am a man of my word.

MARY　　　I'm glad to hear it.

CREATURE　Thank God, I didn't promise not to think about her. The things I do to that woman in my mind.

MARY　　　For shame.

CREATURE　But now we are talking about us and how I am to survive this trauma of separation.

MARY　　　There's nothing to stop us from writing to each other.

CREATURE　That's true, and what an embarrassment of letters I will send you. You will have to get a bigger house to accommodate them all. But no, writing is not enough. I must have a keepsake, a lock of your hair.

MARY　　　No, *no*. I can't spare any hair!

CREATURE　Then what?

MARY　　　I don't know. Wait. *[Pulls a purse from her pocket]* I made it myself.

CREATURE　A little purse. *[Pokes an exploring finger inside it]* I am delighted you have the art of embroidery under such control. Such fine stitching, such delicate work. Such ghastly colours.

MARY　　　You are cruel.

CREATURE　Lovers should be cruel to each other. So much more invigorating than the usual sentimental trip trap. I have an unending store of cruelty.

MARY　　　You are *mad*.

CREATURE　Lovers should be mad. Is there nothing I can do to persuade you to stay?

MARY　　　Even if wanted to, I cannot afford to stay.

CREATURE I am *bastilled* by despair.

MARY   I am bastilled by poverty. It seems indelicate to mention it.

CREATURE I adore indelicacy. Was Shelley a pauper then?

MARY   No, but his father is still alive.

CREATURE Ah! So you must wait till his death to inherit.

MARY   Something like that. My step-sister and I both have legacies. But as long as Sir Timothy is alive *[shrugs]*, we remain poor.

CLAIRE   *[Sweeping on]* And Sir Timothy absolutely and with malice aforethought refuses outright to die.

MARY   *[Turns her attention unwillingly to CLAIRE]* Claire?

The CREATURE drifts off to his table where he applies blue makeup to his face.

London Drizzle

MARY   Claire! I don't believe it!

CLAIRE   Here I am, ready to bask in the drizzle and fogs of good old London. You *were* expecting me?

MARY   It's wonderful to see you again Claire.

CLAIRE   And you. You can't know what a treat it is to see you all dishevelled and spotty.

MARY   That's very unkind.

CLAIRE   I know. But I can't help myself. This image of you will warm up my Russian winter nights. I can't believe you actually went into society like that.

MARY   I was worse than this, too. And the crazy thing is I feel so cheerful. I seem to have passed through some long shadowy eclipse and come out again into sunshine. I feel my powers again. But what about you? Your letters from Russia were so wonderful.

CLAIRE   Russia!

MARY   Riding by troika through the moonlit snow.

CLAIRE   Yes!

MARY   Sunlight bouncing off the spires and minarets of Moscow.

CLAIRE   A glorious city, with one caveat: Never be a governess in Moscow.

MARY   But I thought you were thriving there.

CLAIRE   In Moscow, a governess is given about as much respect as a beetle. In fact if you listen to the ladies of Moscow, you would think governesses were a swarm of locusts that had arrived and settled upon that unhappy territory and destroyed every vestige of fertility. Governesses are capricious, impertinent, they eat and drink up all that is in the house, they corrupt the children, they ride the horses to death, they break all the furniture, and cost more in doctors' bills than all the other inhabitants of Moscow put together.

MARY   A formidable reputation.

CLAIRE   But that's not all. Governesses are above all lecherous and lustful.

MARY   Can that be true?

CLAIRE   According to the ladies of Moscow. They never give less than a thousand lovers to each governess. If some man speaks to you, or he lends you a book, or he praises you when he quits the room — then that's the proof. He, and every other man within your reach, is your lover.

MARY   Tell me about your German.

CLAIRE   Tell me about your Frenchman.

MARY   I've told you all there is to tell. But yours. Is there any chance of . . . marriage.

CLAIRE   Marriage! You know how I feel about marriage. Besides he's much too poor to marry. Like yours, a poet.

MARY   You should have married Peacock all those years ago. Or Trelawny. He's been desperate to marry you for years now. Really, Claire. You'd be settled and happy and not dependent on the bread of strangers.

CLAIRE   It's not *that* bad, you know. I do have a useful and productive life.

MARY   I know. I didn't mean to hurt you.

CREATURE There are battles to be fought, Mary, in Russia as much as anywhere. All those little girls in a perpetual state of *etiquette*. . . . Boys may jump and play, but girls are made to sit still and be docile little. . . . *[Suddenly caught in a memory]* Allegra. . . . Remember what a little tomboy she was?

MARY   Yes. Imperious and wild. Full of spirit.

CLAIRE   And they knocked that out of her, all right, at that convent.

MARY   Oh now, Claire.

CLAIRE   They did. You remember the time that Shelley went to see her? He said she sat like a little owl for a full twenty minutes — a little owl in a black frock and white pinafore and no expression on her face — and then all of a sudden it sank in that Shelley was there to see *her*. She jumped up and grabbed his hand and pulled him all about the place, like a boisterous little puppy, demanding that he play with her. A whole hour of play . . . and then he was gone, her lovely uncle gone, dooming her again to cadaverous silence.

MARY   It's unbearable to think about.

CLAIRE   Yes. Well. In the education of girls I may safely say the Russians and I are always at cross-purposes. They educate a child by making the external work upon the internal, which is in fact nothing but an education fit for monkeys. I want the internal to work upon the external, that is to say that the pupil should be left at liberty as much as possible and that her own reason should be the prompter of her actions.

MARY   I think I hear my mother in those sentiments.

CLAIRE   Most definitely. Oh your mother! Your mother made me love the word "woman."

MARY   And every day with those young pupils of yours you plant those little Wollstonecraft seeds.

CLAIRE   I think I can with certainty affirm that all the pupils I ever had will be violent defenders of the rights of woman.

On the Boards[17]

The CREATURE throws down his makeup brush impatiently.

CREATURE Well yes, they do go on, don't they? As if their lives mattered a whit. But the truth is, it's my life that's important here. Long after those two are forgotten, I will live on in the literary gene pool, that emanation of darkness that is in every soul. . . .

The ghost of FANNY comes on, looking lost.

CREATURE Who let you in here? This is strictly off limits. If you want an autograph you must see my dresser.

FANNY   I just wanted to . . .

CREATURE You can't come barging in like this. The preparation time for the stage is very important, not just for makeup but a few moments of meditation, of emotional and mental recharging.

FANNY   Don't you know me, Mother? It's Fanny.

CREATURE Dear girl, I'm not your mother.

FANNY   I know. All the same, you could help me. I want to be alive again. I know you know how to do it. I've seen you.

CREATURE   Seen what?

FANNY   Those little things you bring to life.

CREATURE   Well they are very little. Nothing of substance.

FANNY   But why should that matter? Big or little, the spark of life is the same. And you have the secret in that notebook of yours.

CREATURE   The accursed notebook. Do you know what it's like to be always alone with no companion to assuage your suffering?

FANNY   Yes I do. I thought it would be different here. Especially when Shelley died. I thought we would be together. But he never came.

CREATURE   I'm not indiscriminate in my . . . experiments. I consider what I do an art.

FANNY   Well, it is.

CREATURE   There is a purpose to what I do. And I find myself constantly questioned.

FANNY   What do you mean?

CREATURE   You see? *[Walks around her, considering her, unnerving her]* The problem is you want to come back as you were.

FANNY   Well, yes. I know now that I didn't make the most of things. Now I can see I would have done at least as well as Mary and Claire, perhaps even better.

CREATURE   Just as I said, you want to come back as you were.

FANNY   How else would I come back?

CREATURE   *[Looking at her speculatively]* It wouldn't be as you were.

FANNY   What would I be?

CREATURE   *[Coming very close]* Something rich and strange.

He kisses her; she backs away. He is upset. He was taken with her.

CREATURE   But you would be free.

FANNY resists his embrace.

CREATURE   You would be *alive*.

She wrenches away and runs off. He clutches at his heart, upset by her rejection.

CREATURE   I am not well made!

     If a little more care had been taken, a little more thought. . . . I was conceived as a beautiful creature, but somehow along the way I accumulated ugliness. I was meant to be an exemplary man. But the skin just couldn't be

managed, and the eyes. *[He averts his eyes]* I filled my
maker with horror. I must calm myself.

*He puts on a ragged coat, unlooses his hair. There is thunder and
lightning off as he exits in a limping, erratic fashion.*

The Sortes Virgilianae[18]

CLAIRE	It's strange to think of you ending up in England. I always thought it would be Italy.
MARY	I stay in England to please Sir Tim, not myself.
CLAIRE	Ah, the everlasting Sir Tim. My Adonis.
MARY	He's more like a Volpone, I assure you, skinny and bent and scrofulous.
CLAIRE	But he does give you support.
MARY	He gives me nothing. He merely allows me to borrow on the future inheritance. Even that's a mere pittance. It pays for Percy's school. But it's never quite enough and it's always late. As it is, I'm going to have to move to Harrow.
CREATURE	Leave London?
MARY	I can't afford to board Percy at school, but if I move there he can be a day student. It will be much more affordable.
CLAIRE	But you will *die* in Harrow. You have no friends there. And what will you do with yourself?
MARY	There's always my writing. I've begun another novel.
CLAIRE	Why don't you write the book that everyone wants, the definitive work on Shelley?
MARY	Sir Tim would cut me off in an instant.
CLAIRE	He's not that much of a demon, is he?
MARY	When I published the *Posthumous Poems* he stopped the allowance for months. And again when *The Last Man* came out, Percy's school money was delayed for ages.
CLAIRE	Do it anyway. It will make your fortune.
MARY	My writing earns enough to supplement Sir Tim's allowance, not to replace it. I hate to wish death on the fellow, but I will be truly glad to be in charge of my own destiny.
CLAIRE	He's not going to die.
MARY	He has to die eventually. He's nearly eighty, after all. And his father died at eighty-two. We won't have that long to wait. Another three years or so.
CLAIRE	Oh you poor, trusting, optimistic fool. His father died at ninety-two, not eighty-two.

MARY	Ninety-two! No, you can't be right! Another thirteen years? Another thirteen years of dependency! I don't think I can bear it.
CLAIRE	Oh, the everlasting Sir Tim. His jumps toward the grave and then his quick returns to life are too comical. He has ruined you and he has ruined me, but he has entertained us well and I give him permission to live to all Eternity!
MARY	It's not funny. I don't know how you can joke about that miser. And don't tell me how you're ruled by the comic muse. I suppose I should get your bed ready.
CLAIRE	It's much too early. Besides I can make my own bed. You *weren't* expecting me, were you. I know I get on your nerves, don't deny it, but you're all the family I have.
MARY	You have your brother, your nieces and nephews.
CLAIRE	I know. But you represent my real life. The one beyond duty and resignation. You are my one hope in an ocean of destruction.
MARY	I was swept away by that same ocean.
CLAIRE	Yes. But you have wreckage to cling to: your child, your books, and powerful ghosts standing guard.
MARY	You always think it's easier for me.
CLAIRE	I don't think it's easier. I think you have the same pain, more perhaps. But if people snub you for asserting your freedom, they still buy your books. I'm economically bound by my reputation. My mother gossips in London, a week or two later there are reproving frowns in Moscow, and all my chances for advancement vanish.
MARY	Fanny, too. She used to say I had all the advantages.
CLAIRE	Well, what advantages did poor Fanny have?
MARY	Three years with my mother. I had four days. She was too ill to nurse me so they took me away and put puppies at her breast to draw off the milk. Seven days later she died. You could almost say I killed her. . . . When I was little, I lived in terror that my father would sell me or give me away.[19] Fanny never had those doubts.
CLAIRE	She had a great many other doubts, though.
MARY	I'm not saying she didn't. It's just that we always think life is a progression from good to better or from bad to worse. I think it's a jumble. We can never say if it will get better or worse. We just have to keep hold of the bright moments and keep on as though there may be more. Fanny was unhappy. But was she doomed to a whole life of unhappiness?

FANNY, who has been listening, opens a little trunk where she finds books, stays, a bundle or two, the red military jacket worn by the CREATURE at the beginning of the play. She casts the stays aside and picks up the jacket. She listens again.

CLAIRE   Maybe she did give up too soon. Yes, you're right. Life is only chronological while you're living it. You, for instance, will keep on writing books as though each one will be more of a masterpiece than the last, and yet Posterity may see your life as a little heap of obscure moments with one great book resting on the top.

MARY   So, I've made no progress in my work since I was eighteen. That's comforting to hear.

CLAIRE   I didn't mean that and you know it. Come let's not spoil our visit. Let's dwell on happy things.

MARY   What happy things? I'm made to live in this wretched country. I can barely afford to feed and clothe my child. My work is trivial. And I'm doomed to love only the dead.

CLAIRE   Oh Lord. When I arrived you were saying how cheerful you felt, as thought your life had come from an eclipse into the sunshine.

MARY   Well, that was . . .

CLAIRE   I know, before I arrived. It was a mistake to come, wasn't it.

MARY   No. That's not what I meant at all. You're right. You've come all this way, and I'm pouring misery on you. I really am glad to see you.

CLAIRE   I know. It's poverty that's depressing us. If only we knew when that bastard was going to die. I know! Why don't we cast our fortunes? Where's your Virgil?

MARY   The *Sortes Virgilianae.* I haven't done that in years. Virgil. I hope I can find it.

FANNY has loosened her hair. She studies the jacket in her hands.

FANNY   My mother was a born warrior. She leapt into battle, never thinking of the consequences. Then she went to Paris and for the first time she started to doubt herself. Her friends were being imprisoned and tortured and executed. For the first time in her life she was afraid to be alone in the house. Afraid of the dark. Afraid to put out her candle.

          And yet . . . *[Slips on jacket]* And yet it was in that time of despair and fear that she pushed through to something different. She was broken down and remade. She took a

lover. She had a child. Her ideas shifted into new patterns. *[Pulls the jacket about her and buttons it up]*
  And seen through a glass coloured with love and passion and motherhood, those ideas, salvaged from the lips of her dying friends, had real blood in them.

FANNY picks up a book from the trunk and, going to the desk, sits holding it open in her hands.
Tumultuous applause off. The CREATURE comes rushing in, bedraggled and perspiring and euphoric.

CREATURE They love me. I'm brilliant on stage. A natural!

Laughter from the two women. He looks round, irritated. MARY has found the book sitting in FANNY's hands. While they cast their fortunes, the CREATURE removes his makeup and puts on a leather-patched sports jacket.

MARY   Here it is.
CLAIRE   The Virgil?
MARY   With this portrait of Mother. How young she looks.
CLAIRE   *[Takes the book]* So question number one: *When is Sir Tim going to kick the bucket?*
MARY   No! Leave Sir Tim out of this. Who knows what misfortune we could unleash. No, we'll do it for us. We find three lines. One for you, one for me, and one for us both. So, let's see, we start with a question. What messages, images, or inspirations do you have for Claire Clairmont? Here. I'll flip and you point.
CLAIRE   No wait! You first.
MARY   Me? You're usually anxious to put yourself first.
CLAIRE   Don't pout.
MARY   All right.
CLAIRE   What messages, images, or inspirations does the oracle have for the talented and impressive Mary Shelley?

CLAIRE riffles the book in FANNY's hands, and Mary thrusts her finger into the pages.

CLAIRE   Hold the place steady.
FANNY   *[Reads the line where MARY's finger has fallen]* "Having said this she was silent, while pallor spread across her face."
MARY   I don't know if I like that. What does it mean?
CLAIRE   It's your *muse*, Mary. I feel it so strongly.

MARY	My muse?
CLAIRE	"Pallor spread across her face." The pale lady. Remember in Switzerland how Shelley looked at you and had that vision? The ghost-like woman with eyes where her nipples should be.
MARY	You still go on about him, don't you. You're still in love with him.
CLAIRE	Shelley loved *you* Mary. We both know that.
MARY	No thanks to you. Do you know how much I hated you? Always there, always on the spot, colourful, impulsive, passionate, with a voice that inspired poems. I always felt pale beside you.
CLAIRE	You see? She *is* your muse—the pale lady.
MARY	You're evading the question.
CLAIRE	I'm not sure what the question is. Of course I loved him. I loved Shelley as you would love a violent storm or a rainbow.
MARY	Shelley was mine. My husband, my lover. You could never accept that.
CLAIRE	He was very kind to me. Don't take that away from me. I have little enough in my life to cling to. Let me cling to those few kind words and deeds.
MARY	Oh don't turn all pathetic. You just don't understand it, do you. The harm you've done to me. The evil you've caused.
CLAIRE	I was never evil, Mary.
MARY	It was always *you*. You, you, you. So many of our decisions were made because of you. Well, think of it. We took that villa at Lerici to keep you away from Byron.
CLAIRE	Ridiculous.
MARY	It was such a hole of a place, ugly, cramped, uncomfortable. My last weeks with Shelley were hell, and all because of you. If we'd been at Leghorn or Pisa it would have been so much better. My miscarriage might not have happened and . . . Shelley . . . could have met with Byron without . . . without having to . . . to sail across the water. He might still be here today.
CLAIRE	You're saying I killed Shelley now? He would have drowned sooner or later in that rickety boat. Everyone said it was an eggshell of a thing. You can't impute it to some evil act on my part. I won't have it!
MARY	What about Clara?
CLAIRE	Clara?
MARY	She might still be living if you hadn't dragged Shelley off to Venice.

CLAIRE   Mary, how can you say this?

MARY   Once you got an idea in your head, when you wanted some-
           thing, you couldn't wait one day, not an hour.

CLAIRE   I wanted to see Allegra.

MARY   Not a minute. You dragged Shelley off to Venice to intercede
           with Byron. It was such a simple plan. You were to stay in
           Venice at the hotel while he drove out to Byron's villa to ask
           for Allegra. But you couldn't stay with the plan. As always
           you followed your own whim.

CLAIRE   It was not a whim. I hadn't seen my child in months!

MARY   When you turned up together, of course Byron thought the
           obvious, everyone thought the obvious: you and Shelley
           were travelling *alone* together. And Shelley, not wanting a
           scandal said, "Oh no, Mary is with us. She stayed in Venice
           with the children." And to back up the lie, I had to travel to
           Venice, post-haste, with my sick baby.

CLAIRE   You didn't have to come.

MARY   I was as anxious as Shelley to avoid scandal. We were
           always poised on the brink of ruin with you. You just fol-
           lowed your passions at every turn and we all had to pay the
           consequences. I had to travel with her burning up in my
           arms. Dying in my arms.

CLAIRE   That's the difference between us. I would never have let rep-
           utation stand in the way of *my* child's welfare. You were
           always too worried about your honour, your important
           name. *That's* why Clara died. And that's why Allegra died,
           too. You were afraid of what people would think. You were
           so afraid that everyone would think she was Shelley's child,
           you made her stay in that convent and die.

MARY   That's monstrous! I loved Allegra.

CLAIRE   Oh, spare me.

MARY   I loved having children about me. There were never enough
           children. It was you I couldn't stand.

CLAIRE   Oh Mary. Let's not do this. We're much too close. We're
           sisters and friends.

MARY   You were never my friend. Always pulling at Shelley—
           come with me, do this, save me from that. Always the jolly
           companion, the alluring woman, the passionate, irresistible
           woman in need.

CLAIRE   I was a silly young girl.

MARY   Answer the question.

CLAIRE   *[Silence]* I never slept with him.

MARY   But you let everyone think it.

CLAIRE   They would have thought it anyway. I was a foolish girl, flaunting my passions and postures. I allowed rumours to flourish because they made me seem romantic.

MARY   No matter who you hurt.

CLAIRE   I hurt myself.

MARY   And you never . . .

CLAIRE   I told you. I never slept with Shelley. He was my dear, dear friend and the only man I've ever really loved. You can't fault me for loving him.

MARY   And when you lived apart from us. He wrote letters to you all the time. When you were in Florence, your first position. . . .

CLAIRE   God! How miserable I was. Holed up with that stupid family.

MARY   He wrote letters to you.

CLAIRE   He wrote letters to everyone.

MARY   He . . . asked you to go away with him . . . on a boat voyage.

CLAIRE   It never happened. Well, you know that.

MARY   I saw the letter. It said, "Don't tell Mary."

CLAIRE   He was flirting. There was nothing to it. He would have died if I'd accepted.

MARY   It broke my heart reading that letter.

CLAIRE   Shelley was promiscuous only on paper. That was his favourite way to flirt. Poems. Letters. He seduced only with words. A paper Don Juan.

MARY   Yes. That's true, isn't it. Paper.

CLAIRE   Do you feel better? Now that you've taken my one last little scrap of mystery, plucked its feathers and torn out its little heart.

MARY   I don't understand you. You cling to posthumous dreams of Shelley when you could have any number of men.

CLAIRE   Any number. Yes. *[Silence]* I did finally accept Trelawny's offer, you know.

MARY   You did? When? This is good news.

CLAIRE   I was too late. He'd already taken up with someone else.

MARY   Oh Claire. I'm so sorry.

CLAIRE   My own fault.

MARY   I always thought Trelawny was for you.

CLAIRE   After Shelley died, before I went off to Vienna, Trelawny and I. . . .

MARY   Yes, I really did think something would happen then.

CLAIRE   We had a week of purest joy. It was incredible. So incredible I took fright. Ran off to Vienna to join my brother. It was the right thing to do, I'm sure of that. Our destinies were different. His was to adventure, mine was to eat the bread of strangers.

MARY   Don't say that. You make me feel rotten.

CLAIRE   Do you ever think of that first year with Shelley?

MARY   Of course.

CLAIRE   Our first trip to Europe. France. Italy. Totally bumbling innocents. And yet how powerful we were. How enormously strong and daring. Did you feel that way?

MARY   As though a great door had suddenly opened.

CLAIRE   You with your bag of notebooks, me with my lofty ideas. What a pair we were. The door opened and we leapt into the future.

MARY   Yes . . . and ever since we've been trying to get back home.

CLAIRE   No. No! No retreat for me. I still mean to go on. The future is ahead of us and we will conquer it.

MARY   And this oracle of mine is supposed to help?

FANNY   "Having said this she was silent, while pallor spread across her face."

MARY   It arouses nothing but terror in me.

CLAIRE   Your muse is Terror. You make the world tremble with your tales.

MARY   But this bit, "Having said this." Having said what?

CLAIRE   It's your task to find out. Just another little fragment to decipher.

MARY   All right. Let's do yours. What treasures lie in store for Claire? What omens for the future?

FANNY riffles the pages. CLAIRE stabs.

MARY   Claire.

CLAIRE   Yes.

MARY   I watch out for you. You may not think it, but I do.

CLAIRE   It's all right, Mary.

MARY   And I know it's harder for you. And I know what the gossip does to you. You're much more vulnerable.

CLAIRE   Oh it's something in my nature. Something abrasive that arouses the devil in people. You've always been the sympathetic one. The good daughter.

MARY	No, really. . . .
CLAIRE	Pearls and flowers always dropped from your mouth. Whereas I dribbled out toads and frogs.
MARY	Claire!
CLAIRE	I know you do your best to edit all the memoirs that are springing up. Trelawny told me.
MARY	Memoirs of Shelley. Everyone who ever met him on the street is dashing them off. I do what I can to keep you out of them. When they have the grace to show them to me.
CLAIRE	I'm tougher than you think.
MARY	Yes I know.

They embrace.

FANNY	"While all the land lies still, the flocks of painted birds."
MARY	Your fortune.
CLAIRE	"While all the land lies still." It's very lonely, isn't it? I suppose that's my destiny, the lonely traveller.
MARY	Lonely perhaps, but destined also to report back to the rest of us. Long witty letters.
CLAIRE	I do write a good letter.
MARY	You write the most amusing and clever letters in the world.
CLAIRE	Hmm. Your letters, on the other hand, are very curious.
MARY	Oh?
CLAIRE	They always seem written as if mine to you had never been received.
FANNY	"While all the land lies still, the flocks of painted birds."
CLAIRE	This curious prophecy. What can it mean?
MARY	Regeneration. A serene land with regenerative birds.
CLAIRE	Yes! Those beautiful birds in Russian embroidery, orderly, but vivid and imaginative.
MARY	A creative release.
CLAIRE	Oh, I like that! Don't you love doing this? It's the gap between the meaning of the words and the meaning you try to settle on it. Neither meaning is as important as the leap between the two!
MARY	The third is for both of us.
CLAIRE	We must be very careful in our wording.
MARY	What are two young women . . .
CLAIRE	. . . in their prime of life . . .
MARY	. . . miserably poor . . .
CLAIRE	. . . but armed with wit and intelligence and just plain stubbornness . . .

MARY   . . . what do two such women do in the face of unconquerable odds?

>   *FANNY flips, and they stab together.*

FANNY   "They advance and expose their lives to obvious danger."
MARY   That's a bit scary.
CLAIRE   But positive. "They advance."
MARY   "Obvious danger," though.
CLAIRE   Take on the world! You have nothing to lose. It sounds like your mother to me.
FANNY   "They advance and expose their lives to obvious danger."
MARY   Yes it does, doesn't it?
CREATURE   *[Moving into view]* I know you want to know how it all turns out, but let's leave them here on the cusp of hope and terror. I mean, what does it matter after all? As Claire said, Mary's life will be seen by posterity as a little heap of obscure moments with one great book resting on the top.
Some of you will try to reach round me and haul her into the future. But I will be there, standing between you, the extraordinary creation of a young mind at the beginning of an otherwise dreary life.

I am, after all, unique. There never was anyone like me before or since. There have been imitators, Dickens, Poe, and countless others, who have attempted to capture and use my particular essence in their stories. I believe there's a young writer in America who has some kind of aquatic version of me in mind.

And interpretations. I have been and will be interpreted from every possible point of view — Political, Social, Moral, Poetic. I am a virtual Frankenstein's monster of interpretation, and I imagine there are a number among you tonight guilty of adding to the patchwork.

But you don't need a doctorate in psychology to understand what I'm all about. Do you? I am Mary's monster. A million little glistening resurrections of all her dead and all her lost desires. But I could be yours. Couldn't I?

Nothing really specific — an accumulation, a pastiche of little sins, little weaknesses, things that hardly matter. And yet there might be consequences to deal with. If I have my way.

Sinks onto the chaise. Laughter from the two women interrupts him.

CREATURE   Look at them. Doomed to disappointment and mediocrity. You think I'm unkind? Would Iago have sympathy for Shakespeare? Would Satan revere Milton? And look at you, still wanting to pull them forward, to reclaim their pain and their despair and their trivial solutions. I'm telling you there's nothing there to be learned and yet you persist in thinking there might be something. Ah, the human heart is a strange jungle.

MARY   *[Moves over to the* CREATURE*]* Take on the world and hang the consequences. I like that. I like it very much.

She strokes the CREATURE*'s face and runs back to join her sisters. The lights fade to black, then glaring lights flash, then loud raucous music from the canon of songs based on* Frankenstein, *for example, "Feed My Frankenstein," blares out as they all joyfully take their bows.*

Notes

1   Scollard's title conflates "The Cave of Fancy," the title of an incomplete prose tale by Mary Wollstonecraft, included in her *Posthumous Works* (1798), and "Fields of Fancy," Mary Shelley's original title for what eventually became her novella "Mathilda" (1819). (Rather than annotating every one of Scollard's many references to works by members of the Shelley circle, we note important passages and episodes cited or discussed by other contributors to this volume and a few other references that may be obscure to non-specialist readers.—The editors)

2   Cf. Vargo 181.

3   See Robinson 132 and n.8.

4   The London churchyard where Mary Wollstonecraft was buried and where Percy Shelley and Mary Godwin courted.

5   Matthews (91) refers to Fanny Imlay's presence on the journey to Sweden, citing *CLMW* 291. See also Conger 47 and Vargo 183-84, who discuss Wollstonecraft's worries about her infant daughter as expressed in *A Short Residence*.

6   Moskal (216 n.25) mentions the death of Shelley's first child (1 March 1815). See also *JMS* 68-70, especially the entry for 19 March.

7   Robinson (134) discusses the creature's acquisition of language.

8   The passage from *Frankenstein* paraphrased here is quoted in
    McWhir 162.

9   Buss 115-17, 119 pays particular attention to the scene of
    Wollstonecraft's death, as recounted by Godwin (*MAV* 266-71).

10 When Fanny Imlay committed suicide on 9 October 1816, she
    was wearing stays marked with Wollstonecraft's initials. For
    more on her death and on Shelley's attitude toward suicide, see
    Moskal 195-99, 206.

11 This is partly the cave in the Author's Introduction to *The Last
    Man*, partly an actual place near Naples (thought to be an ancient
    site sacred to Apollo and described in Virgil's *Aeneid* 6), and
    partly a return to the imaginative, prophetic space of the play's
    opening scene. See also McWhir 172-73.

12 Moskal's essay explores Shelley's responses, later in life, to the
    Madonnas of Italy.

13 Many contributors to this volume refer to Clara's and William's
    deaths: see, for one example, Moskal 206-07. For this reference
    to Percy Shelley's health, see especially Moskal 215 n. 21 and
    LMWS 1: 101.

14 See McWhir 174 n. 10 and *JMS* 306n.

15 Cf. McWhir 164 and *JMS* 423, July-October 1822. Scollard par-
    aphrases Edward Trelawny's account of the recovery of the bod-
    ies and the funeral, as transcribed by Mary Shelley in her jour-
    nal. Barbour (142) discusses the funeral, referring to Trelawny's
    role of "psychopomp."

16 See *JMS* 438 and cf. Moskal 207.

17 *Frankenstein* was adapted for the stage by Richard Brinsley
    Peake and successfully produced at the English Opera House in
    1823. Shelley enjoyed Thomas Cooke's performance as the
    creature (*LMWS* 1: 378).

18 This is a method of telling one's fortune by selecting lines of
    Virgil at random and then interpreting them. For the passages
    that Mary and Claire choose in the play, see *JMS* 500.

19 Cf. Mellor 234, and see also *LMWS* 1: 4 (3 Nov. 1814).

Works Cited

[Allestree, Richard]. *The Ladies Calling*. 2 vols. Oxford: n.p., 1673.

Althusser, Louis. "Ideology and Ideological State Apparatuses." *Lenin and Philosophy and Other Essays*. Trans. Ben Brewster. London: Monthly Review P, 1971. 127-86.

Andrews, William L. "The Representation of Slavery and the Rise of Afro-American Literary Realism, 1965˜1920." *Slavery and the Literary Imagination*. Ed. Deborah E. McDowell and Arnold Rampersad. Baltimore: Johns Hopkins UP, 1989. 62-80.

Arendt, Hannah. *The Origins of Totalitarianism*. New ed. San Diego: Harcourt Brace, 1975.

Barbour, Judith. "Among the Dead Men: Mary Wollstonecraft Shelley's Biographical Writings." *Proceedings of the 1988 Macquarie Conference of the Australian Victorian Studies Association*. Ed. Catherine Waters and Helen Yardley. Sydney: ˜Macquarie UP, 1989. 10-28.

Barker-Benfield, G. J. *The Culture of Sensibility: Sex and Society in Eighteenth-Century Britain*. Chicago: U of Chicago P, 1992.

Barrell, John. "The Birth of Pandora and the Origin of Painting." *The Birth of Pandora and the Division of Knowledge*. London: Macmillan, 1996. 145-220.

Barry, Jonathan, ed. *The Middling Sort of People: Culture, Society and Politics in England, 1550-1800*. London: Macmillan, 1994.

Barthes, Roland. *Mythologies*. Trans. Annette Lavers. New York: Hill and Wang, 1972.

___. "On Reading." *The Rustle of Language* 1986. 33-43.

___. *The Rustle of Language*. Trans. Richard Howard. Berkeley: U of California P, 1989.

___. "To Write: An Intransitive Verb?" *The Rustle of Language* 11-21.

Belsey, Catherine. *Critical Practice*. London: Routledge, 1988.

___. *Desire: Love Stories in Western Culture*. Oxford: Blackwell, 1994.

Bennett, Betty T. "Finding Mary Shelley in Her Letters." *Romantic Revisions*. Eds. Robert Brinley and Keith Hanley. Cambridge: Cambridge UP, 1992. 291-306.

___. *Mary Diana Dods: A Gentleman and a Scholar*. New York: Morrow, 1991.

___. "Newly Uncovered Letters and Poems by Mary Wollstonecraft Shelley: ('It was my birthday and it pleased me to tell the people so—')." *Keats-Shelley Journal* 46 (1997): 51-74.

Bennett, Betty T., and Stuart Curran. *Mary Shelley in Her Times*. Baltimore: Johns Hopkins UP, 2000.

Bennett, Betty T,. and William T. Little. "Seven Letters from Prosper Mérimée to Mary Shelley." *Comparative Literature* 31 (1979): 134-53.

Benstock, Shari. "Authorizing the Autobiographical." *Feminisms: An Anthology of Literary Theory and Criticism*. 2nd ed. Ed. Robyn R. Warhol and Diane Price Herndl. New Brunswick, NJ: Rutgers UP, 1997. 1138-54.

Benveniste, Emile. *Problems in General Linguistics*. Trans. Mary Elizabeth Meek. Coral Gables: U of Miami P, 1971.

Bernheimer, Charles, and Claire Kahane, eds. *In Dora's Case: Freud—Hysteria—Feminism*. 2nd ed. New York: Columbia UP, 1990.

Berry, Margaret. *An Introduction to Systemic Linguistics*. 2 vols. London: Batsford, 1975.

Beverley, John. "The Margin at the Center: On Testimonio (Testimonial Narrative)." Smith and Watson 91-114.

Billson, Marcus. "The Memoir: New Perspectives on a Forgotten Genre." *Genre* 10.2 (Summer 1977): 259-82.

Blair, Hugh. *Lectures on Rhetoric and Belles Lettres*. Vol. 3. 1785. New York: Garland, 1970.

Blumberg, Jane. *Mary Shelley's Early Novels*. London: Macmillan, 1993.

Bohls, Elizabeth. *Women Travel Writers and the Language of Aesthetics, 1716-1818*. Cambridge: Cambridge UP, 1995.

Brewer, John, and Susan Staves, eds. *Early Modern Conceptions of Property*. New York: Routledge, 1995.

Brewer, John, ed. *Consumption and the World of Goods*. London: Routledge, 1993.

___. *The Consumption of Culture*. London: Routledge, 1995.

Brodzki, Bella. "Mothers, Displacement, and Language." Smith and Watson.

Brooks, Peter. *Body Work: Objects of Desire in Modern Narrative*. Cambridge: Harvard UP, 1993.

Bruss, Elizabeth W. *Autobiographical Acts: The Changing Situation of a Literary Genre*. Baltimore: Johns Hopkins UP, 1976.

Buck, Claire, ed. *Bloomsbury Guide to Women's Literature*. London: Bloomsbury, 1992.

Burton, Deirdre D. "Through Glass Darkly; Through Dark Glasses: On Stylistics and Political Commitment—via a Study of a Passage from

Sylvia Plath's *The Bell Jar.*" *Language and Literature: An Introductory Reader in Stylistics.* Ed. Ronald Carter. London: Allen and Unwin, 1982. 195-214.

Buss, Helen M. "Anna Jameson's *Winter Studies and Summer Rambles in Canada* as Epistolatory Dijournal." Kadar, *Essays* 42-60.

___. *Mapping Our Selves: Canadian Women's Autobiography in English.* Montreal: McGill-Queen's UP, 1993.

___. "Memoir with an Attitude: One Reader Reads *The Woman Warrior: Memoirs of a Girlhood among Ghosts.*" *A/B Autobiography Studies* 12.2 (Fall 1997): 203-24.

Byrd, Max. *Visits to Bedlam: Madness and Literature in the Eighteenth Century.* Columbia: South Carolina UP, 1974.

Byron, George Gordon. *His Very Self and Voice: Collected Conversations of Lord Byron.* Ed. Ernest J. Lovell Jr. New York: Macmillan, 1954.

Calderón de la Barca. *La Estatua de Prometeo.* Ed. Margaret Rich Greer. Kassel, Germany: Reichenberger, 1986.

Cameron, Kenneth Neill. "The Planet-Tempest Passage in *Epipsychidion.*" Rpt. in *Shelley's Poetry and Prose.* Ed. Donald H. Reiman and Sharon B. Powers. New York: Norton, 1977. 637-58.

Campbell, Colin. *The Romantic Ethic and the Spirit of Consumerism.* Oxford: Blackwell, 1987.

Campbell Orr, Clarissa. "Mary Shelley's *Rambles in Germany and Italy,* the Celebrity Author, and the Undiscovered Country of the Human Heart." *Romanticism on the Net* 11 (1998) http://users.ox.ac.uk/~scat0385/rambles.html (8 June 2000).

Carby, Hazel V. *Reconstructing Womanhood: The Emergence of the Afro-American Woman Novelist.* Oxford: Oxford UP, 1987.

Carroll, Michael P. *The Cult of the Virgin Mary: Psychological Origins.* Princeton: Princeton UP, 1986.

Chodorow, Nancy. *The Reproduction of Mothering: Psychoanalysis and the Sociology of Gender.* Berkeley: U of California P, 1978.

Clairmont, Claire. *The Journals of Claire Clairmont.* Ed. Marion Kingston Stocking, with the assistance of David Mackensie Stocking. Cambridge: Harvard UP, 1968. [*JCC.*]

Clairmont, Claire, et al. *The Clairmont Correspondence: Letters of Claire Clairmont, Charles Clairmont, and Fanny Imlay Godwin.* Ed. Marion Kingston Stocking. 2 vols. Baltimore: Johns Hopkins UP, 1995. [*CC.*]

Clemit, Pamela. *The Godwinian Novel: The Rational Fictions of Godwin, Brockden Brown, Mary Shelley.* Oxford: Clarendon, 1993.

Coleman, Linda S., ed. *Women's Life-Writing: Finding Voice/Building Community.* Bowling Green, OH: Bowling Green State U Popular P, 1997.

Coleridge, Samuel Taylor. *Biographia Literaria.* Ed. James Engell and W. Jackson Bate. 2 vols. Princeton: Princeton UP, 1983.

Colley, Linda. *Britons: Forging the Nation, 1707-1837.* New Haven: Yale UP, 1992.

Conger, Syndy McMillen. *Mary Wollstonecraft and the Language of Sensibility*. Totowa, NJ: Fairleigh Dickinson UP, 1994.

___. "Prophecy and Sensibility: Mary Wollstonecraft in *Frankenstein*." *1650-1850: Ideas, Aesthetics, and Inquiries in the Early Modern Era*. Vol. 3. Ed. Kevin L. Cope. New York: AMS, 1997. 301-28.

___. "The Sentimental Logic of Wollstonecraft's Prose." *Prose Studies* 10 (1987): 143-58.

Corbett, Mary Jean. "Literary Domesticity and Women Writers' Subjectivities." *Representing Femininity: Middle Class Subjectivity in Victorian and Edwardian Women's Autobiographies*. New York: Oxford UP, 1992. 83-106.

Crowe, J. A., and G. B. Cavalcaselle. *The Life and Times of Titian*. 2nd ed. 2 vols. London: Murray, 1881.

Dante Alighieri. *The Divine Comedy*. Trans. with a commentary by Charles S. Singleton. 3 vols. in 6 parts. Bollingen Series 80. Princeton: Princeton UP, 1970-75.

Davidoff, Leonore, and Catherine Hall. *Family Fortunes: Men and Women of the English Middle Class, 1780-1850*. Chicago: U of Chicago P, 1987.

"Deaths in and near London." *Monthly Magazine* 4 (1797): 232-33.

Di Scala, Spencer M. *Italy: From Revolution to Republic, 1700 to the Present*. Boulder, CO: Westview, 1995.

Disraeli, Benjamin. *Tancred; or, The New Crusade*. Introd. Philip Guedalla. London: Davies, 1927.

Doherty, Terence. *The Anatomical Works of George Stubbs*. Boston: Godine, 1975.

Dolan Kautz, Beth. "Mary Shelley's *Rambles in Germany and Italy*: A Journey of Aesthetic Healing." *Romantic Geographies*. Ed. Amanda Gilroy. Manchester: U of Manchester P, forthcoming.

Dowden, Edward. *The Life of Percy Bysshe Shelley*. 2 vols. London: Kegan Paul, 1886.

Dryden, John. *The Poems of John Dryden*. Ed. James Kinsley. Vol. 4. Oxford: Clarendon, 1958.

Ducrot, Oswald, and Tzvetan Todorov, eds. *Encyclopedic Dictionary of the Sciences of Language*. Trans. Catherine Porter. 1979. Baltimore: Johns Hopkins UP, 1983.

Duggan, Christopher. *A Concise History of Italy*. Cambridge: Cambridge UP, 1994.

Ehrsam, Theodore G. *Major Byron: The Incredible Career of a Literary Forger*. New York: Boesen, 1951.

Ellis, Markman. *The Politics of Sensibility: Race, Commerce, and Gender in the Sentimental Novel*. Cambridge: Cambridge UP, 1996.

Ellis, Sarah Stickney. *The Women of England: Their Social Duties, and Domestic Habits*. 9th ed. London: Fisher, 1839.

Epstein, William H. "(Post)Modern Lives: Abducting the Biographical Subject." *Contesting the Subject: Essays in the Postmodern Theory and*

Practice of Biography and Biographical Criticism. Ed. William H. Epstein. West Lafayette, IN: Purdue UP, 1991. 217-36.

___. *Recognizing Biography*. Philadelphia: U of Pennsylvania P, 1987.

Favret, Mary. *Romantic Correspondence: Women, Politics and the Fiction of Letters*. Cambridge: Cambridge UP, 1993.

Feldman, Paula. "Mary Shelley and the Genesis of Moore's Life of Byron." *SEL* 20 (1980): 611-20.

Felman, Shoshana. *What Does a Woman Want? Reading and Sexual Difference*. Baltimore: Johns Hopkins UP, 1993.

Ferguson, Moira. *Colonialism and Gender Relations from Mary Wollstonecraft to Jamaica Kincaid: East Caribbean Connections*. New York: Columbia UP, 1996.

___. *Subject to Others: British Women Writers and Colonial Slavery, 1670-1834*. New York: Routledge, 1992.

Figes, Eva. *Sex and Subterfuge: Women Novelists to 1850*. London: Macmillan, 1982.

Fillmore, Charles. *Santa Cruz Lectures on Deixis 1971*. Reproduced by the Indiana University Linguistics Club, Nov. 1975.

Fleishman, Avrom. *Figures of Autobiography: The Language of Self-Writing in Victorian and Modern England*. Berkeley: U of California P, 1983.

Foucault, Michel. *Madness and Civilization: A History of Insanity in the Age of Reason*. Trans. Richard Howard. New York: Vintage, 1988.

Fraistat, Neil. "Illegitimate Shelley: Radical Piracy and the Textual Edition as Cultural Performance." *PMLA* 109 (1994): 409-23.

Franklin, V. P. *Living Our Stories, Telling Our Truths: Autobiography and the Making of the African-American Intellectual Tradition*. New York: Scribner, 1995.

Freud, Sigmund. "Fragment of an Analysis of a Case of Hysteria ('Dora')." Rpt. in *The Freud Reader*. Ed. Peter Gay. New York: Norton, 1989. 172-239.

Frye, Northrop. "Towards Defining an Age of Sensibility." *English Literary History* 23 (1956): 144-52.

Fukuyama, Francis. *The End of History and the Last Man*. New York: Free, 1992.

Gaya Nuño, Juan Antonio. *La obra pictória completa de Murillo*. Barcelona, 1978.

Geertz, Clifford. *The Interpretation of Cultures*. New York: Basic Books, 1973.

Godwin, William. *Collected Novels and Memoirs*. Vol. 1. Ed. Mark Philp. London: Pickering [?], 1992.

___. *An Enquiry concerning Political Justice*. 1793. Ed. Jonathan Wordsworth. 2 vols. New York: Woodstock, 1992.

___. *Essays by the Late William Godwin: Never Before Published*. Ed. Charles Kegan Paul. London: King, 1873.

___. *Memoirs of the Author of* A Vindication of the Rights of Woman. 1798. Holmes 201-77.

___. *Memoirs of the Author of* A Vindication of the Rights of Woman *and Posthumous Works*. 6 vols. London: Johnson, 1798.

___. *The Enquirer. Reflections on Education, Manners, and Literature. In a Series of Essays*. 1797. New York: Garland, 1971.

___. *The Pantheon, or Ancient History of the Gods of Greece and Rome*. 1806. Introd. Burton Feldman. New York: Garland, 1984.

___. *Political and Philosophical Writings of William Godwin*. 7 vols. Ed. Mark Philp with the assistance of Austin Gee. London: Pickering, 1993.

___. *St. Leon*. Ed. with introd. by Pamela Clemit. Oxford: Oxford UP, 1994.

___. *Things as They Are, or The Adventures of Caleb Williams*. 4th ed. London: Colburn and Bentley, 1831.

___. *Thoughts on Man, His Nature, Productions, and Discoveries: Interspersed with some particulars respecting the Author*. London: Effingham Wilson, 1831.

Godwin, William, and Mary Wollstonecraft. *Godwin and Mary: Letters of William Godwin and Mary Wollstonecraft*. Ed. Ralph M. Wardle. Lawrence: U of Kansas P, 1966.

Gombrich, E. H. "Freud's Aesthetics." *Encounter* 26.1 (Jan. 1966): 30-40.

Gregory, John. *A Father's Legacy to His Daughters*. 1774. Introd. Gina Luria. New York: Garland, 1974.

Griffin, Cindy L. "Rhetoricizing Alienation: Mary Wollstonecraft and the Rhetorical Construction of Women's Oppression." *Quarterly Journal of Speech* 80 (1994): 293-312.

Grosz, Elizabeth. *Jacques Lacan: A Feminist Introduction*. New York: Routledge, 1990.

Gubar, Susan. "Feminist Misogyny: Mary Wollstonecraft and the Paradox of 'It Takes One to Know One.'" *Feminist Studies* 20.3 (Fall 1994): 453-73.

Gwin, Minrose C. "Green-eyed Monsters of the Slavocracy: Jealous Mistresses in Two Slave Narratives." *Conjuring: Black Women, Fiction, and Literary Tradition*. Ed. Marjorie Pryse and Hortense J. Spillers. Bloomington: Indiana UP, 1985. 39-52.

Hall, Catherine. *White, Male and Middle Class: Explorations in Feminism and History*. London: Routledge, 1988.

Halliday, M. A. K. "Linguistic Function and Literary Style: An Inquiry into the Language of William Golding's *The Inheritors*." *Literary Style: A Symposium*. Ed. and trans. Seymour Chatman. London: Oxford UP, 1971. 330-65.

Harding, Sandra. "Rethinking Standpoint Epistemology: 'What Is Strong Objectivity?'" *Feminist Epistemologies*. Ed. Linda Alcoff and Elizabeth Potter. New York: Routledge, 1993. 49-82.

Harris, Cheryl I. "Whiteness as Property." *Harvard Law Review* 106.8 (June 1993): 1707-91.

Hart, Francis Russell. "History Talking to Itself: Public Personality in Recent Memoir." *New Literary History* 11.1 (Autumn 1979): 193-210.

Hartley, David. *Observations on Man, His Frame, His Duty, and His Expectations*. Ed. Theodore L. Huguelet. Gainsville, FL: Scholars Facsimiles and Reprints, 1966.

Hartsock, Nancy C. M. *Money, Sex, and Power: Toward a Feminist Historical Materialism*. Boston: Northeastern UP, 1985.

Hawkesworth, Mary E. "Knowers, Knowing, Known: Feminist Theory and Claims of Truth." *Signs* 14 (1989): 533-57.

Hays, Mary. "Memoirs of Mary Wollstonecraft." *Annual Necrology, 1797-1798*. London: Phillips, 1800. 411-60.

Heffernan, James A. W. *Museum of Words: The Poetics of Ekphrasis from Homer to Ashbury*. Chicago: U of Chicago P, 1993.

Heilbrun, Carolyn G. "What She Was Silent About." Rev. of *Virginia Woolf: A Writer's Life*, by Lyndall Gordon. *New York Times Book Review* 10 Feb. 1985: 12.

___. *Writing a Woman's Life*. New York: Ballantine, 1988.

Henley, Nancy M., Michelle Miller, and Jo Anne Beazley. "Syntax, Semantics, and Sexual Violence: Agency and the Passive Voice." *Journal of Language and Social Psychology* 14 (1995): 60-84.

Hesiod. *Remains of Hesiod*. Trans. Charles Abraham Elton. 2nd ed. London: n.p., 1815.

Hesiod and Theognis. *Theogony, Works and Days; Elegies*. Trans. with introd. Dorothea Wender. Harmondsworth: Penguin, 1973.

Hibbard, Christopher. Introduction. *The Life of Samuel Johnson*. By James Boswell. London: Penguin, 1986.

Hill-Miller, Katherine. *My Hideous Progeny: Mary Shelley, William Godwin, and the Father-Daughter Relationship*. Newark: U of Delaware P, 1995.

Hogan, J. F. "Maynooth in the British Parliament." *Irish Ecclesiastical Record*. 1909.

Holmes, Richard, ed. *A Short Residence in Sweden, Norway and Denmark and Memoirs of the Author of "The Rights of Woman."* By William Godwin and Mary Wollstonecraft. London: Penguin, 1987.

Homans, Margaret. *Bearing the Word: Language and Female Experience in Nineteenth-Century Women's Writing*. Chicago: Chicago UP, 1986.

Hunter, William. *Anatomia Uteri Humani Gravidi Tabulis Illustrata [The Anatomy of the Human Gravid Uterus Exhibited in Figures]*. Birmingham: Baskerville, 1774.

Irigaray, Luce. "The Eternal Irony of the Community." *Speculum of the Other Woman*. Trans. Gillian Gill. Ithaca: Cornell UP, 1985. 214-26.

___. "Women, the Sacred, Money." *Sexes and Genealogies*. Trans. Gillian Gill. New York: Columbia UP, 1993. 73-88.

Irwin, David. *John Flaxman, 1755-1826: Sculptor, Illustrator, Designer*. London: Cassell, 1979.

Jacobs, Harriet A. *Incidents in the Life of a Slave Girl*. Ed. Jean Fagan Yellin. Cambridge: Harvard UP, 1987.

Jacobus, Mary. "The Difference of View." *Women Writing and Writing about Women*. Ed. Mary Jacobus. Baltimore: Johns Hopkins UP, 1977. 27-40.

Jakobson, Roman. "Linguistics and Poetics." *Selected Works*. Vol. 3. New York: Mouton, 1981. 18-51.

Jameson, Anna. *Legends of the Madonna*. 1852. Vol. 5 of *The Writings on Art of Anna Jameson*. Ed. Estelle M. Hurll. Boston: Houghton Mifflin, 1892.

___. *Sketches of Art, Literature, and Character*. 1834. Vol. 8 of *Mrs. Jameson's Works*. Rpt. Boston: Tickner and Fields, 1866.

Jardine, Alice A. *Gynesis: Configurations of Women and Modernity*. Ithaca and London: Cornell UP, 1985.

Jay, Paul. *Being in the Text: Self-Representation from Wordsworth to Roland Barthes*. Ithaca: Cornell UP, 1984.

Johnson, Claudia. *Equivocal Beings: Politics, Gender, and Sentimentality in the 1790s. Wollstonecraft, Radcliffe, Burney, Austen*. Chicago: U of Chicago P, 1995.

Johnson, Samuel. *The History of Rasselas, Prince of Abyssinia*. Ed. D. J. Enright. Harmondsworth: Penguin, 1976.

Johnston, Judith. *Anna Jameson: Victorian, Feminist, Woman of Letters*. Leicester: Scolar, 1997.

Jowell, Sharon. "Mary Shelley's Mothers: The Weak, the Absent, and the Silent in *Lodore* and *Falkner*." *European Romantic Review* 8 (1997): 298-322.

Kadar, Marlene. "Coming to Terms: Life Writing—from Genre to Critical Practice." Kadar, *Essays* 3-16.

___, ed. *Essays on Life Writing: From Genre to Critical Practice*. Toronto: U of Toronto P, 1992.

Kaplan, Caren. "Resisting Autobiography: Out-Law Genres and Transnational Feminist Subjects." Smith and Watson 115-38.

Kaplan, Carla. "Narrative Contracts and Emancipatory Readers: *Incidents in the Life of a Slave Girl*." *Yale Journal of Criticism* 6 (1993): 93-120.

Kawash, Samira. *Dislocating the Color Line: Identity, Hybridity, and Singularity in African-American Literature*. Stanford: Stanford UP, 1997.

Keller, Evelyn Fox. *Reflections on Gender and Science*. New Haven: Yale UP, 1985.

Kelly, Gary. Introduction. *Mary and The Wrongs of Woman*. By Mary Wollstonecraft. Oxford: Oxford UP, 1980. vii-xxi.

___. "Mary Wollstonecraft as *Vir Bonus*." *English Studies in Canada* 5 (1979): 275-91.

___. *Revolutionary Feminism: The Mind and Career of Mary Wollstonecraft*. London: Macmillan, 1992.

Kendall, Kathryn. "Catherine Trotter Cockburn and Me: A Duography." *The Intimate Critique: Autobiographical Literary Criticism*. Ed. Diane P. Freedman, Olivia Frey, and Frances Murphy Zauhar. Durham: Duke UP, 1993. 273-82.

Klein, Melanie. "Mourning and Its Relation to Manic-Depressive States." 1940. Rpt. in *The Selected Melanie Klein*. Ed. Juliet Mitchell. New York: Free, 1986. 146-74.

Lacan, Jacques. *Ecrits: A Selection*. Trans. Alan Sheridan. New York: Norton, 1977.

___. "Intervention on Transference." Bernheimer and Kahane 92-104.

"Lady Travellers in Italy and Germany." Rev. of *Rambles in Germany and Italy*, by Mary Wollstonecraft Shelley. *New Monthly Magazine* (1844): 284-86.

Langland, Elizabeth. *Nobody's Angels: Middle-Class Women and Domestic Ideology in Victorian Culture*. Ithaca: Cornell UP, 1995.

LaPlanche, J., and J.-B. Pontalis. *The Language of Psychoanalysis*. Trans. Donald Nicholson-Smith. New York: Norton, 1973.

Lejeune, Philippe. *On Autobiography*. Ed. with a foreword by Paul John Eakin. Trans. Katherine Leary. Minneapolis: U of Minnesota P, 1989.

Lerner, Gerda. *The Creation of Patriarchy*. Oxford: Oxford UP, 1986.

Lloyd, Genevieve. *The Man of Reason*. Minneapolis: U of Minnesota P, 1984.

Lyons, John. "Subjecthood and Subjectivity." *Subjecthood and Subjectivity: The Status of the Subject in Linguistic Theory*. Ed. Marina Yaguello. Paris: Ophrys/Institut français du Royaume-Uni, 1994. 9-17.

Mackenzie, Henry. *The Man of Feeling*. 1771. New York: Norton, 1958.

Marcus, Laura. *Auto/biographical Discourses: Theory, Criticism, Practice*. Manchester: Manchester UP, 1994.

Marcus, Steven. "Freud and Dora: Story, History, Case History." Bernheimer and Kahane 56-91.

Marshall, Mrs Julian (Florence). *The Life and Letters of Mary Wollstonecraft Shelley*. 2 vols. London: Richard Bentley and Son, 1889.

Mascuch, Michael. *Origins of the Individualist Self: Autobiography and Self-Identity in England, 1591-1791*. Cambridge: Polity, 1997.

McGlynn, Paul D. "Sterne's Maria: Madness and Sentimentality." *Eighteenth-Century Life* 3.2 (Dec. 1976): 39-43.

Mellor, Anne K. *Mary Shelley: Her Life, Her Fiction, Her Monsters*. New York: Routledge, 1988.

___. *Romanticism and Gender*. New York: Routledge, 1993.

Rev. of *Memoirs of the Author of* A Vindication of the Rights of Woman, by William Godwin. *European Magazine* 33 (April 1798): 246-51.

Metcalf, Robert. *The Shelley Legend*. New York: Scribner, 1945.

Micheletti, Emma. *Domenico Ghirlandaio*. Florence: Scala Istituto Fotografico, 1990.

Miller, Nancy K. "Changing the Subject: Authorship, Writing and the Reader." *Feminist Studies/Critical Studies*. Ed. Teresa de Lauretis. Bloomington: Indiana UP, 1986. 102-20.

Moore, Jane. "Sex, Slavery and Rights in Mary Wollstonecraft's *Vindications*." *The Discourse of Slavery: Aphra Behn to Toni Morrison*. Ed. Carl Plasa and Betty J. Ring. London: Routledge, 1994. 18-39.

Moskal, Jeanne. "Cervantes and the Politics of Mary Shelley's *History of a Six Weeks' Tour*." *Mary Shelley in Her Times*. Ed. Stuart Curran and Betty T. Bennett. Baltimore: Johns Hopkins UP, 1999. 18-37.

___. "Gender, Italian Nationalism, and British Imperialism in Mary Shelley's *Rambles in Germany and Italy*." *Romanticism* 5.1 (1999): forthcoming.

___. "Gender, Nationality, and Textual Authority in Lady Morgan's Travel Books." *Romantic Women Writers: Voice and Countervoices*. Ed. Paula R. Feldman and Theresa M. Kelley. Hanover, NH: UP of New England, 1995. 171-93, 298-302.

___. Introductory Note. *Rambles in Germany and Italy*. In *Travel Writing*. Vol. 8 of *The Novels and Selected Works of Mary Shelley*. Ed. Nora Crook with Pamela Clemit. London: Pickering, 1996. 49-57.

___. "The Picturesque and the Affectionate in Wollstonecraft's *Letters from Norway*." *Modern Language Quarterly* 52.3 (1991): 263-94.

___. "William Godwin, Wilhelm Tell, and Swiss National Identity in Mary Shelley's *History of a Six Weeks' Tour*." Forthcoming.

Mullan, John. *Sentiment and Sociability: The Language of Feeling in the Eighteenth Century*. Oxford: Clarendon, 1988.

Mullen, Harryette. "Runaway Tongue: Resistant Orality in *Uncle Tom's Cabin*, *Our Nig*, *Incidents in the Life of a Slave Girl*, and *Beloved*." *The Culture of Sentiment: Race, Gender, and Sentimentality in Nineteenth-Century America*. Ed. Shirley Samuels. New York: Oxford UP, 1992. 244-64.

Mulvey, Laura. "The Myth of Pandora: A Psychoanalytical Approach." *Feminisms in the Cinema*. Ed. Laura Pietropaolo and Ada Testaferri. Bloomington: Indiana UP, 1995. 3-19.

Myers, Mitzi. "Godwin's *Memoirs* of Wollstonecraft: The Shaping of Self and Subject." *Studies in Romanticism* 20.3 (Fall 1981): 299-316.

___. "Mary Wollstonecraft's *Letters Written . . . in Sweden*: Toward Romantic Autobiography." *Studies in Eighteenth-Century Culture* 8 (1979): 165-85.

___. "Pedagogy as Self-Expression in Mary Wollstonecraft: Exorcising the Past, Finding a Voice." *The Private Self: Theory and Practice of Women's Autobiographical Writings*. Ed. Shari Benstock. Chapel Hill: North Carolina UP, 1988. 192-210.

Newman, Gerald. *The Rise of English Nationalism: A Cultural History, 1740-1830*. London: Weidenfeld and Nicholson, 1987.

Norman, E. R. *Anti-Catholicism in Victorian England*. London: George Allen and Unwin, 1968.

Nussbaum, Felicity A. *The Autobiographical Subject: Gender and Ideology in Eighteenth-Century England*. Baltimore: Johns Hopkins UP, 1989.

___. "Eighteenth-Century Women's Autobiographical Commonplaces." *The Private Self: Theory and Practice of Women's Autobiographical Writings*. Ed. Shari Benstock. Chapel Hill: North Carolina UP, 1988. 147-71.

Nyström, Per. *Mary Wollstonecraft's Scandinavian Journey*. Trans. George R. Otter. Göteborg, Sweden: Kungl. Vetenskaps-och Vitterhets-Samhället, 1980.

O'Brien, Sharon. "Feminist Theory and Literary Biography." *Contesting the Subject: Essays in the Postmodern Theory and Practice of Biography and Biographical Criticism*. Ed. William H. Epstein. West Lafayette, IN: Purdue UP, 1991. 123-33.

Rev. of *Observations on Madness and Melancholy* by John Haslam, *Pinel's Treatise on Insanity* by Dr. Davis, *Cox's Practical Observations on Insanity*, and *Arnold on the Management of the Insane*. *Quarterly Review* 1 (Aug. 1809): 155-80.

Oxford English Dictionary. 2nd ed. Prep. by J. A. Simpson and E. S. C. Weiner. 20 vols. Oxford: Clarendon, 1989.

Pachter, Marc. "The Biographer Himself: An Introduction." *Telling Lives: The Biographer's Art.* Ed. Marc Pachter. Washington, DC: New Republic Books/National Portrait Gallery, 1979. 1-18.

Palacio, Jean de. *Mary Shelley dans son oeuvre.* Paris: Editions Klincksieck, 1969.

Panofsky, Dora, and Erwin Panofsky. *Pandora's Box: The Changing Aspects of a Mythical Symbol.* 2nd ed. rev. New York: Pantheon, 1962.

Parke, Catherine N. "What Kind of Heroine Is Mary Wollstonecraft?" *Sensibility in Transformation: Creative Resistance to Sentiment from the Augustans to the Romantics. Essays in Honor of Jean H. Hagstrum.* Ed. Syndy M. Conger. Totowa, NJ: Fairleigh Dickinson UP, 1990. 103-19.

Paul, C. Kegan. *William Godwin: His Friends and Contemporaries.* 2 vols. London: Henry S. King, 1876. Rpt. 1 vol. New York: AMS, 1970.

Paz, D. G. *Popular Anti-Catholicism in Mid-Victorian England.* Stanford: Stanford UP, 1992.

Peacock, Thomas Love. *Peacock's Memoirs of Percy Bysshe Shelley.* Introd. Humbert Wolfe. 2 vols. London: Dent, 1933.

Perkin, Joan. *Women and Marriage in Nineteenth-Century England.* Chicago: Lyceum, 1989.

Perreault, Jeanne. *Writing Selves: Contemporary Feminist Autography.* Minneapolis: U of Minnesota P, 1995.

Perry, Ruth. "Colonizing the Breast: Sexuality and Maternity in Eighteenth-Century England." *Eighteenth-Century Life* ns 16.1 (Feb. 1992): 185-213.

Personal Narratives Group, eds. *Interpreting Women's Lives: Feminist Theory and Personal Narratives.* Bloomington: Indiana UP, 1989.

Pollin, Burton R. *Godwin Criticism: A Synoptic Bibliography.* Toronto: U of Toronto P, 1967.

Poovey, Mary. *The Proper Lady and the Woman Writer: Ideology as Style in the Works of Mary Wollstonecraft, Mary Shelley, and Jane Austen.* Chicago: U of Chicago P, 1984.

Pope-Hennessey, John. *Raphael: The Wrightsman Lectures.* [New York]: New York UP, 1970.

Porter, Roy. *Mind-Forg'd Manacles: A History of Madness in England from the Restoration to the Regency.* London: Athlone, 1987.

Rev. of *Posthumous Works of the Author of* A Vindication of the Rights of Woman, by Mary Wollstonecraft. *Monthly Review* 1 (Nov. 1798): 325-27.

Poston, Carol H. Introduction. *Letters Written during a Short Residence in Sweden, Norway, and Denmark.* By Mary Wollstonecraft. Lincoln: U of Nebraska P, 1976. vii-xxi.

Poynton, Cate. *Language and Gender: Making the Difference.* Oxford: Oxford UP, 1989.

Pratt, Mary Louise. *Imperial Eyes: Travel Writing and Transculturation.* London: Routledge, 1992.

Quinby, Leigh. "The Subject of Memoirs: The Woman Warrior's Technology of Ideographic Selfhood." Smith and Watson 297-320.

Rabinowitz, Peter J. *Before Reading: Narrative Conventions and the Politics of Interpretation.* Ithaca: Cornell UP, 1987.

Rajan, Tilottama. "Autonarration and Genotext in Mary Hays' *Memoirs of Emma Courtney.*" *Studies in Romanticism* 32.2 (Summer 1993): 149-76.

___. Introduction and Notes. *Valperga.* By Mary Shelley. Peterborough, ON: Broadview, 1998.

Ramas, Maria. "Freud's Dora, Dora's Hysteria." Bernheimer and Kahane 149-80.

Rev. of *Rambles in Germany and Italy*, by Mary Wollstonecraft Shelley. *Atlas* 17 Aug. 1844: 556-57.

Rev. of *Rambles in Germany and Italy.* *Critic* 2 Sept. 1844: 36-37.

Rev. of *Rambles in Germany and Italy.* *Eclectic Review* ns 16 (1844): 693-706.

Rev. of *Rambles in Germany and Italy.* *Examiner* 1904 (27 July 1844): 467-68.

Rev. of *Rambles in Germany and Italy.* *Globe* 15 Aug. 1844: 14.

Rev. of *Rambles in Germany and Italy.* *Observer* 11 Aug. 1844: 3.

Rev. of *Rambles in Germany and Italy.* *Spectator* 842 (17 Aug. 1844): 782-83.

Rev. of *Rambles in Germany and Italy.* *Sunday Times* 25 Aug. 1844: 2.

Reeve, Clara. *The Progress of Romance.* 1785. 2 vols. New York: Facsimile Text Society, 1930.

Reiss, Timothy J. "Revolution in Bounds: Wollstonecraft, Women, and Reason." *Gender and Theory: Dialogues on Feminist Criticism.* Ed. Linda Kauffman. New York: Blackwell, 1989. 11-50.

Richardson, Ruth. *Death, Dissection and the Destitute.* Harmondsworth: Penguin, 1989.

Roberts, Diane. *The Myth of Aunt Jemima: Representations of Race and Region.* London: Routledge, 1994.

Robinson, Charles E. *The* Frankenstein *Notebooks: A Facsimile of Mary Shelley's Manuscript Novel, 1816-17 (with alterations in the hand of Percy Bysshe Shelley) as it survives in Draft and Fair Copy deposited by Lord Abinger in the Bodleian Library, Oxford (Dep. c. 477/1 and Dep. c. 534/1-2).* Parts One and Two. (Manuscripts of the Younger Romantics, Volume 9.) New York: Garland, 1996.

___. "Mathilda as a Dramatic Actress." *Mary Shelley in Her Times.* Ed. Betty T. Bennett and Stuart Curran. Baltimore: Johns Hopkins UP, 2000. 76-87.

Ross, Val. "Poison Pens." *Globe and Mail* 10 May 1997: C1, C4.

Rousseau, Jean-Jacques. *The Reveries of the Solitary Walker.* 1776. Trans. Charles E. Butterworth. New York: New York UP, 1979.

Rowton, Frederic. *The Female Poets of Great Britain, Chronologically Arranged: With Copious Selections and Critical Remarks.* 1853. Rpt. with critical introd. and bibliographical appendices by Marilyn L. Williamson. Detroit: Wayne State UP, 1981.

St Clair, William. *The Godwins and the Shelleys: The Biography of a Family*. London: Faber, 1989.

Sánchez-Eppler, Karen. "Bodily Bonds: The Intersecting Rhetorics of Feminism and Abolition." *The Culture of Sentiment: Race, Gender, and Sentimentality in Nineteenth-Century America*. Ed. Shirley Samuels. New York: Oxford UP, 1992. 92-114.

Scholes, Robert, and Robert Kellogg. *The Nature of Narrative*. New York: Oxford UP, 1971.

Schor, Esther H. "Mary Shelley in Transit." *The Other Mary Shelley: Beyond Frankenstein*. Ed. Audrey A. Fisch, Anne K. Mellor, and Esther H. Schor. New York: Oxford UP, 1993. 235-57.

Schweickart, Patrocinio P. *A Feminist Theory of Reading*. Baltimore: Johns Hopkins UP, 1980.

Segal, Hannah. *Introduction to the Work of Melanie Klein*. London: Hogarth Press and the Institute of Psychoanalysis, 1973.

Shelley and His Circle, 1773-1822. 8 vols. to date: 1-4, ed. Kenneth Neill Cameron; 5-6, ed. Donald H. Reiman; 7-8, ed. Donald H. Reiman and Doucet Devin Fischer. Cambridge: Harvard UP, 1961-.

Shelley, Lady Jane, ed. *Shelley and Mary*. 4 vols. London: privately published, 1882.

Shelley, Mary Wollstonecraft. *Collected Tales and Stories*. Ed. Charles E. Robinson. Baltimore: Johns Hopkins UP, 1976.

___. "The Dream." *Collected Tales and Stories*. 153-65.

___. *Frankenstein*. 1818. Ed. Nora Crook. *The Novels and Selected Works of Mary Shelley*. Vol. 1. London: Pickering, 1996.

___. *Frankenstein; or, The Modern Prometheus*. 3rd ed. London: Colburn and Bentley, 1831.

___. "Giovanni Villani." *Matilda, Dramas, Reviews and Essays, Prefaces and Notes*. Ed. Pamela Clemit. *The Novels and Selected Works of Mary Shelley*. Vol. 2. London: Pickering, 1996. 128-39.

___. *The Journals of Mary Shelley*. Ed. Paula R. Feldman and Diana Scott-Kilvert. 1987. 2 vols. Rpt. 1 vol. Baltimore: Johns Hopkins UP, 1995.

___. *The Last Man*. 1826. Ed. Jane Blumberg with Nora Crook. *The Novels and Selected Works of Mary Shelley*. Vol. 4. London: Pickering, 1996.

___. *The Letters of Mary Wollstonecraft Shelley*. Ed. Betty T. Bennett. 3 vols. Baltimore: Johns Hopkins UP, 1980-88.

___. *Lives of the Most Eminent French Writers*. 2 vols. Philadelphia: Lea and Blanchard, 1840.

[—-.] *Lives of the Most Eminent Literary and Scientific Men of France*. 2 vols. (Vols. 102-03 of *The Cabinet Cyclopaedia*, ed. Dionysius Lardner.) London: Longman, Orme, Brown, Green, & Longmans, 1838-39.

[—-.] *Lives of the Most Eminent Literary and Scientific Men of Italy, Spain and Portugal*. [Some essays by James Montgomery and Sir David Brewster.] 3 vols. (Vols. 86-88 of *The Cabinet Cyclopaedia*, ed. Dionysius Lardner.) London: Longman, Rees, Orme, Brown, Green, & Longman, 1835-37.

___. *Lodore*. 1835. Ed. Fiona Stafford. *The Novels and Selected Works of Mary Shelley*. Vol. 6. London: Pickering, 1996.

[—-.] "Memoirs of William Godwin." *Caleb Williams*. By William Godwin. London: Henry Colburn and Richard Bentley, 1831. iii-xiii.

___. *The Novels and Selected Works of Mary Shelley*. Ed. Nora Crook with Pamela Clemit, introd. Betty T. Bennett. 8 vols. London: Pickering, 1996. (1: [*FMP*] *Frankenstein; or, The Modern Prometheus*; 2: *Matilda*, Dramas, Reviews & Essays, Prefaces & Notes; 3: *Valperga*; 4: [*LM*] *The Last Man*; 5: *The Fortunes of Perkin Warbeck*; 6: [*L*] *Lodore*; 7: *Falkner*; 8: Travel Writing [including *History of a Six Weeks' Tour* and *Rambles in German and Italy*].) [*NSW*.]

___. *Rambles in Germany and Italy*. 1844. Ed. Jeanne Moskal. In *Travel Writing. The Novels and Selected Works of Mary Shelley*. Volume 8. London: Pickering, 1996.

___. "A Tale of the Passions." 1823. *Collected Tales and Stories* 1-23.

___. *Tales and Stories*. Ed. Richard Garnett. London: W. Paterson, 1891.

Shelley, Percy Bysshe. *The Complete Works of Percy Bysshe Shelley*. Ed. Roger Ingpen and Walter E. Peck. 10 vols. New York: Gordian, 1965.

___. *Essays, Letters from Abroad, Translations and Fragments by Percy Bysshe Shelley*. Ed. Mary W. Shelley. 2 vols. London: Edward Moxon, 1840.

___. *The Letters of Percy Bysshe Shelley*. Ed. Frederick L. Jones. 2 vols. Oxford: Clarendon P, 1964.

___. "Notes on Sculptures in Rome and Florence." *Complete Works* 6: 307-32.

___. "On the Punishment of Death." *Complete Works* 6: 185-90.

___. *Poetical Works*. Ed. Mary Wollstonecraft Shelley. 4 vols. London: Moxon, 1839.

___. *The Prose Works of Percy Bysshe Shelley*. Ed. E. B. Murray. 1 vol. to date. Oxford: Clarendon P, 1993-.

___. *Shelley's Poetry and Prose*. Ed. Donald H. Reiman and Sharon B. Powers. New York: Norton, 1977.

___. *Shelley's Prose, or The Trumpet of a Prophecy*. Ed. David Lee Clark. Albuquerque: U of New Mexico P, 1954.

Sherman, Claire Richter with Adele M. Holcomb. "Precursors and Pioneers (1820-1890)." *Women as Interpreters of the Visual Arts, 1820-1979*. Ed. Claire Richter, Sherman with Adele M. Holcomb. Westport, CT: Greenwood P, 1981. 3-26.

Shipley, Joseph T. *The Origins of English Words: A Discursive Dictionary of Indo-European Roots*. Baltimore: Johns Hopkins UP, 1984.

Simpson, David. "Speaking Personally: The Culture of Autobiographical Criticism." Veeser 2-94.

"Sir Anthony Carlisle." *Gentleman's Magazine* ns 14 (Dec. 1840): 660-61.

Smith, Amy Elizabeth. "Roles for Readers in Mary Wollstonecraft's *A Vindication of the Rights of Woman*." *Studies in English Literature* 32 (1992): 555-70.

Smith, Robert Metcalf, with Martha Mary Schlegel et al. *The Shelley Legend*. New York: Scribner, 1945.

Smith, Sidonie. *A Poetics of Women's Autobiography: Marginality and the Fictions of Self-Representation*. Bloomington: Indiana UP, 1987.

Smith, Sidonie, and Julia Watson, eds. *De/Colonizing the Subject: The Politics of Gender in Women's Autobiography*. Minneapolis: U of Minnesota P, 1992.

Sommer, Doris. "'Not Just a Personal Story': Women's Testimonios and the Plural Self." *Life/Lines: Theorizing Women's Autobiography*. Ed. Bella Brodzki and Celeste Brée. Ithaca: Cornell UP, 1988.

Spitz, Ellen Handler. *Image and Insight: Essays in Psychoanalysis and the Arts*. New York: Columbia UP, 1991.

Stanton, Domna C. "Autogynography: Is the Subject Different?" *The Female Autograph: Theory and Practice of Autobiography from the Tenth to the Twentieth Century*. Ed. Domna C. Stanton. Chicago: Chicago UP, 1987. 3-20.

___. "Difference on Trial: A Critique of the Maternal Metaphor in Cixous, Irigaray, and Kristeva." *The Poetics of Gender*. Ed. Nancy K. Miller. New York: Columbia UP, 1986. 157-82.

Sterne, Laurence. *The Life and Opinions of Tristram Shandy, Gentleman*. 1759-67. Ed. Graham Petrie. Harmondsworth: Penguin, 1974.

___. *A Sentimental Journey and Other Writings*. Ed. Tom Keymer. London: Dent, 1994.

Steussy, Fredric S. *Eighteenth-Century German Autobiography: The Emergence of Individuality*. New York: Lang, 1996.

Stevens, Wallace. *Opus Posthumous*. Ed. and introd. Samuel French Morse. New York: Knopf, 1957.

Sunstein, Emily W. *A Different Face: The Life of Mary Wollstonecraft*. New York: Harper and Row, 1975.

___. *Mary Shelley: Romance and Reality*. Boston: Little Brown, 1989.

Thurman, William Richard, Jr. *Letters about Shelley from the Richard Garnett Papers*. Austin: U of Texas P, 1972.

Todd, Janet. "The Language of Sex in *A Vindication of the Rights of Woman*." *Mary Wollstonecraft Newsletter* 1.2 (1973): 10-17.

___. *Mary Wollstonecraft: An Annotated Bibliography*. New York: Garland, 1976.

___. *Sensibility: An Introduction*. London: Methuen, 1986.

Todd, Janet, and Marilyn Butler, eds. *The Works of Mary Wollstonecraft*. 7 vols. London: Pickering, 1989.

Tomalin, Claire. *The Life and Death of Mary Wollstonecraft*. London: Weidenfeld and Nicolson, 1974.

Tompkins, Jane. "Sentimental Power: *Uncle Tom's Cabin* and the Politics of Literary History." 1981. *Feminisms: An Anthology of Literary Theory and Criticism*. Ed. Robyn R. Warhol and Diane Price Herndl. New Brunswick, NJ: Rutgers UP, 1991. 20-39.

Tooke, Andrew. *The Pantheon*. 1713. Rpt. New York: Garland, 1976.

Toolan, Michael J. *The Stylistics of Fiction: A Literary-Linguistic Approach.* London: Routledge, 1990.

Treichler, Paula A. "The Construction of Ambiguity in *The Awakening*: A Linguistic Analysis." *Women and Language in Literature and Society.* Ed. Sally McConnell-Ginet, Ruth Borker, and Nelly Furman. New York: Praeger, 1980. 239-57.

Tuite, Clara. "William and Mary: Muse, Editor, Executrix in the Shelley Circle." *The Textual Condition.* Ed. M. Blackman, F. Muecke, and M. Sankey. Sydney: U of Sydney P, 1995. 102-03.

Ty, Eleanor. *Unsex'd Revolutionaries: Five Women Novelists of the 1790s.* Toronto: U of Toronto P, 1993.

___. "Writing as a Daughter: Autobiography in Wollstonecraft's Travelogue." Kadar 61-77.

Underkuffler, Laura S. "On Property: An Essay." *Yale Law Journal* 100 (1990-91): 127-48.

Veeser, H. Aram, ed. and introd. *Confessions of the Critics.* New York: Routledge, 1996.

Voltaire. *Pandore, Opéra en cinq actes. Oeuvres Complètes.* Paris: Furne, 1846. 1: 426-34.

Wake, Ann M. Frank. "Women in the Active Voice: Recovering Female History in Mary Shelley's *Valperga* and *Perkin Warbeck*." *Iconoclastic Departures: Mary Shelley after* Frankenstein. Ed. Syndy M. Conger, Frederick S. Frank, and Gregory O'Dea. Madison and Teaneck: Fairleigh Dickinson UP, 1997. 235-59.

Walker, Constance. "Kindertotenlieder: Mary Shelley and the Art of Losing." *Mary Shelley in Her Times.* Ed. Stuart Curran and Betty T. Bennett. Baltimore: Johns Hopkins UP, 2000. 134-46.

Walling, William A. *Mary Shelley.* New York: Twayne, 1972.

Wardle, Ralph. *Mary Wollstonecraft: A Critical Biography.* Lincoln: U of Nebraska P, 1951.

Warner, Marina. *Alone of All Her Sex: The Myth and Cult of the Virgin Mary.* 1976. New York: Random House, 1983.

Weir, Allison. *Sacrificial Logics: Feminist Theory and the Critique of Identity.* New York: Routledge, 1996.

Wethey, Harold E. *The Paintings of Titian.* 3 vols. London: Phaidon, 1969.

White, Hayden. *Metahistory: The Historical Imagination in Nineteenth-Century Europe.* Baltimore: Johns Hopkins UP, 1973.

White, Newman Ivey. *Shelley.* 2 vols. London: Secker & Warburg, 1947.

White, Newman Ivey, Frederick L. Jones, and Kenneth N. Cameron. *An Examination of the Shelley Legend.* Philadelphia: U of Pennsylvania P, 1951.

Williams, Patricia. *The Alchemy of Race and Rights: Diary of a Law Professor.* Cambridge: Harvard UP, 1991.

Wolf, Naomi. *The Beauty Myth.* Toronto: Vintage, 1997.

Wolfson, Susan J. "Editorial Privilege: Mary Shelley and Percy Shelley's Audiences." *The Other Mary Shelley: Beyond* Frankenstein. Ed. Audrey A.

Fisch, Anne K. Mellor, and Esther H. Schor. New York: Oxford UP, 1993. 39-72.

Wollstonecraft, Mary. *Collected Letters of Mary Wollstonecraft*. Ed. Ralph M. Wardle. Ithaca: Cornell UP, 1979.

___. *Letters Written during a Short Residence in Sweden, Norway, and Denmark*. 1796. Holmes 57-200.

___. *Mary and The Wrongs of Woman*. 1798. Ed. Gary Kelly. Oxford: Oxford UP, 1980.

___. "On Poetry, and Our Relish for the Beauties of Nature." 1797. Todd and Butler 7: 7-11.

___. *Thoughts on the Education of Daughters*. 1787. Introd. Gina Luria. New York: Garland, 1974.

___. *The Vindications: A Vindication of the Rights of Men, in a Letter to the Right Honourable Edmund Burke; Occasioned by his Reflections on the Revolution in France and A Vindication of the Rights of Woman: With Strictures on Political and Moral Subjects*. 1790, 1792, Ed. D.L. Macdonald and Kathleen Scherf. Peterborough, ON: Broadview, 1997.

___. *The Works of Mary Wollstonecraft*. Ed. Janet Todd and Marilyn Butler, with the assistance of Emma Rees-Mogg. 7 vols. New York: New York UP, 1989.

Wordsworth, William. *Wordsworth's Preface to* Lyrical Ballads. 1800. Ed. W. J. B. Owen. Westport, CT: Greenwood, 1979.

Yeazell, Ruth Bernard. *Fictions of Modesty: Woman and Courtship in the English Novel*. Chicago: U of Chicago P, 1991.

Zonana, Joyce. "'They Will Prove the Truth of My Tale': Safie's Letters as the Feminist Core of Mary Shelley's *Frankenstein*." *Journal of Narrative Technique* 21.2 (Spring 1991): 170-84.

Contributors

Judith Barbour is an honorary associate in the School of English at the University of Sydney. She is the author of articles on Mary Shelley and John William Polidori, and is editor of the University of Sydney electronic edition of "Mary Shelley's Life of William Godwin," from the Shelley-Godwin Manuscripts of the Abinger Collection deposited at the Bodleian Library, Oxford. The internet address for this edition at the Scholarly Electronic Text and Imaging Service (SETIS) of the University of Sydney's Fisher Library is: http://setis.library.usyd.edu.au/arts/godwin

Betty T. Bennett teaches literature at the American University, Washington, DC. She is the author of *Mary Diana Dods: A Gentleman and a Scholar* (1991) and *Mary Wollstonecraft Shelley: An Introduction* (1998), the editor of *The Letters of Mary Wollstonecraft Shelley* (1980-88), and the co-editor (with Charles E. Robinson) of *The Mary Shelley Reader* (1990) and (with Stuart Curran) of *Mary Shelley in Her Times* (2000).

Helen M. Buss (aka Margaret Clarke) is a professor in the English Department at the University of Calgary. She is the author of novels, plays, and poetry, as well as books and articles on Canadian literature and life writing. In 1983, she won a best first novel prize in Manitoba for *The Cutting Season*, and in 1983 won the Gabrielle Roy Prize for her study of Canadian women's autobiography, *Mapping Our Selves (1993)*. Her current writing and research centre on the memoir form. She has recently published *Memoirs from Away: A New Found Land Girlhood* (1999), and has completed a book on women's uses of the memoir form, with the working title *Repossessing the World: Reading and Writing Contemporary Women's Memoirs*.

Syndy McMillen Conger teaches English at Western Illinois University. She is the author of *Mary Wollstonecraft and the Language of Sensibility* (1994) and co-editor of *Iconoclastic Departures: Mary Shelley after* Frankenstein (1997).

Gary Kelly teaches English at the University of Alberta. He is the author of *Revolutionary Feminism: The Mind and Career of Mary Wollstonecraft* (1992) and *Women, Writing, and Revolution, 1790-1827* (1993), and the editor of *Mary and The Wrongs of Woman*, by Mary Wollstonecraft (1980).

Lawrence R. Kennard is a doctoral student in English at the University of Calgary. He has published articles on Coleridge.

D. L. Macdonald teaches English at the University of Calgary. He is the author of *Poor Polidori: A Critical Biography of the Author of "The Vampyre"* (1991) and *Monk Lewis: A Critical Biography* (2000), and the co-editor of *Frankenstein*, by Mary Shelley (1994; 2nd ed. 1999), and *The Vindications*, by Mary Wollstonecraft (1997).

S. Leigh Matthews is a doctoral student in English at the University of Calgary, where she specializes in nineteenth- and twentieth-century Canadian literature and theories of life writing. She is currently researching and writing her dissertation, "Self(s) Surveyed: Intersections of Identity in Canadian Women's Prairie Memoirs," and has forthcoming a number of articles on other Canadian life-writing texts.

Anne McWhir teaches English at the University of Calgary. She is the author of articles on Burke, Wordsworth, Mary Shelley, and Percy Shelley, and the editor of *The Last Man*, by Mary Shelley (1996).

Anne K. Mellor teaches English at the University of California, Los Angeles. She is the author of *Blake's Human Form Divine* (1974), *English Romantic Irony* (1980), *Mary Shelley: Her Life, Her Fiction, Her Monsters* (1988), *Romanticism and Gender* (1993), and *Mothers of the Nation: Women's Political Writing in England, 1780-1830* (2000), editor of *Romanticism and Feminism* (1988), and co-editor of *The Other Mary Shelley: Beyond* Frankenstein (1993) and *British Literature, 1780-1830* (1996).

Jeanne Moskal is a professor of English at the University of North Carolina at Chapel Hill. She is the author of *Blake, Ethics, and Forgiveness* (1994) and of articles on the travel writings of Ann Radcliffe, Mariana Starke, Lady Morgan, Mary Shelley, and Mary

Wollstonecraft. She is editor of *Travel Writing*, by Mary Shelley (1996; volume 8 in *The Novels and Selected Works of Mary Shelley*), and of *Letters from Norway*, by Mary Wollstonecraft (forthcoming), and co-editor of *Reading and Teaching Eighteenth- and Nineteenth-Century British Women Writers* (forthcoming).

Jeanne Perreault teaches English at the University of Calgary. She is the author of *Writing Selves: Contemporary Feminist Autography* (1995).

Charles E. Robinson teaches English at the University of Delaware. He is the author of *Shelley and Byron: The Snake and Eagle Wreathed in Fight* (1976), editor of Mary Shelley's *Tales and Stories* (1976), of her *Mythological Dramas: Proserpine and Midas* (1992), and of *The* Frankenstein *Notebooks: A Facsimile of Mary Shelley's Manuscript Novel, 1816-1817* (1996), and co-editor (with Betty T. Bennett) of *The Mary Shelley Reader* (1990).

Rose Scollard is a Calgary playwright. She is the author of *Bête Blanche/Tango Noir* (1988), *Uneasy Listening: Three Plays for Radio* (1995), and *Shea of the White Hands* (1995), and co-author of *Aphra* (1997).

Eleanor Ty teaches English and women's studies at Wilfrid Laurier University, in Waterloo, Ontario. She is the author of *Unsex'd Revolutionaries: Five Women Novelists of the 1790s* (1993) and *Empowering the Feminine: The Narratives of Mary Robinson, Jane West, and Amelia Opie, 1796-1812* (1998), and editor of *The Victim of Prejudice* (1994) and of *Memoirs of Emma Courtney* (1996) by Mary Hays.

Lisa Vargo teaches English at the University of Saskatchewan. She is the author of articles on Anna Barbauld, Anna Jameson, and Mary Shelley, and is editor of *Lodore*, by Mary Shelley (1997).

Index

[Note: *Caves of Fancy* is indexed only for Scollard's quotations from/allusions to primary texts. Since playtexts do not usually include parenthetical citations, these references take the form "x (y)," where "x" is the page number of the play and "y" is the page number of the primary text. Thus "250 (1: 9-10)" means that on p. 250 of Scollard's play there is a quotation from vol. 1, pp. 9-10 of a primary text—in this case, *The Clairmont Correspondence* (*see* Clairmont, Claire).]

317